NOTE-BANDI

T0364690

NOTE-BANDI

Demonetisation
and
India's Elusive Chase for Black Money

Edited and Introduced by
R. Ramakumar

With writings from the archives of the
Economic & Political Weekly

OXFORD
UNIVERSITY PRESS

OXFORD
UNIVERSITY PRESS

Oxford University Press is a department of the University of Oxford.
It furthers the University's objective of excellence in research, scholarship,
and education by publishing worldwide. Oxford is a registered trademark of
Oxford University Press in the UK and in certain other countries.

Published in India by Oxford University Press
2/11 Ground Floor, Ansari Road, Daryaganj, New Delhi 110 002, India

Cover photograph: The demonetisation effect: Long queues at ATMs to withdraw cash
© Ravi Choudhary/Hindustan Times via Getty Images

The moral rights of the authors have been asserted.

First Edition published in 2018

ISBN-13 (print edition): 978-0-19-948679-3
ISBN-10 (print edition): 0-19-948679-4

ISBN-13 (eBook): 978-0-19-909272-7
ISBN-10 (eBook): 0-19-909272-9

Typeset in Adobe Garamond Pro 10.5/12.5
by The Graphics Solution, New Delhi 110 092
Printed in India by Replika Press Pvt. Ltd

**Disclaimer: The views expressed in this volume are those of the volume
editor and authors and do not, in any way, reflect the publisher's viewpoint.**

Every effort has been made by the editor to contact the copyright holders, some
of whom could not be identified or located. The publisher hereby states that any
information brought to notice regarding these copyright holders will be acknowledged
in future reprints of the book.

Dedicated to the memory of Indian citizens who lost
their lives due to demonetisation

Contents

Tables and Figures

Tables

Figures

Preface

'Demonetisation'—the withdrawal of legal tender status of notes of denomination Rs 500 and Rs 1,000—announced by India's Prime Minister Narendra Modi over a televised address on 8 November 2016 will go down in history as one of the most reactionary and illogical economic policies ever attempted in independent India. It crippled an economy that ran on cash and was plagued by a slowdown; it destroyed the livelihoods of millions of farmers, workers, traders, women and the elderly; and it violated the dignity and liberty of law-abiding citizens.

Yet, in a post-truth world, demonetisation also left public opinion in India deeply polarised. The language of the state had a deceptive appeal. In a society marked by abject poverty and inequality, and where everyday lives of citizens are marred by myriad forms of corruption, it came as no surprise that Modi's misadventure was received as a decisive measure. Economists like me knew of the earlier demonetisation of 1978. But we also knew that it had failed to unearth any significant amount of black money. We were also aware of quack ideologues of the right-wing who demanded measures like demonetisation and the substitution of income tax with a blanket transactions tax. But we had also dismissed them as obscurantist drivel. Never did one imagine that one among these irrational ideas would actually find a place in economic policy. Of course,

---

In this book, information stated as taken from the Reserve Bank of India (RBI) is available at the website https://www.rbi.org.in/ (last accessed on 24 October 2017), unless a specific RBI reference work is mentioned.

many aspects of neoliberal economics are intrinsically inverted on logic. But the demonetisation of 2016 beat them all.

At such a juncture, it becomes imperative of those who continue to have trust in reason to say, ever more loudly, that the emperor is naked. But then, one irrationality cannot be fought with another. The struggle against irrationality is also a battle for reason. Facts have to be marshalled; claims have to be broken down and analysed; and inferences have to be fed into an alternative discourse. This volume is an effort towards building up such an alternative, fact-based discourse on demonetisation.

In his address to the nation, the Prime Minister made two major claims in defence of demonetisation: on the one hand, it would stamp out counterfeit currency that was aiding terrorism; on the other, it would help the government unearth 'black money'. Soon after the address, one also heard television commentators waxing eloquent on India's imminent embrace of a cashless economy.

A day into demonetisation, I had an opportunity to write a response to these three claims.[1] First, the claim that demonetisation would hit terror financing was overstretched because the total circulation of counterfeit currency did not exceed 0.002 per cent of the total notes in circulation. Second, no significant mobilisation of black money may be expected, as about 94 per cent of the unaccounted wealth was stored in the form of non-cash assets. Third, a cashless economy can never be created over diktats, as the persistence of cash was a structural feature of the economy. What India needed was a structural transformation of its informal economy into a modern and productive sphere, which would systemically reduce the dependence on cash. A 'war on cash' would thus be ineffective and premature. Sycophants apart, these views were also shared by economists across the left-right spectrum.

As I write this preface almost a year later, I see no reason to revise my position. First, according to the Reserve Bank of India's (RBI) *Annual Report* for 2016–17, the total value of counterfeit notes of denomination Rs 500 and Rs 1,000 detected by banks rose from Rs 27.4 crore in 2015–16 to Rs 40.8 crore in 2016–17: an increase by just about Rs 14 crore. As a share of the value of Rs 500 and Rs 1,000 notes in circulation in November 2016, the value of counterfeit notes detected in 2016-17

---

[1] See R. Ramakumar, 'Demonetisation: Ineffective, Inadequate and Premature,' *Businessworld*, 11 November 2016, available at http://bit.ly/2eW9zPb, last accessed on 31 March 2017.

amounted to just 0.0027 per cent. The critics were right; the extent of circulation of counterfeit notes did not, in any way, justify a drastic action like demonetisation.

Second, the RBI also released estimates of the value of old notes returned to the banks between 10 November 2016 and 30 June 2017. Out of the Rs 15.44 lakh crore worth notes of Rs 500 and Rs 1,000 in circulation as on 8 November 2016, about Rs 15.28 lakh crore had returned to the banks. In other words, 98.96 per cent of the demonetised notes were back in the banks and only 1.04 per cent remained outside. Even this was not a final estimate; just on the previous day, i.e., 29 June 2017, the RBI had provided a one-month window for District Central Co-operative Banks (DCCBs) for remitting their remaining cash stock and exchanging for new notes. These did not form part of the estimate of old notes returned as on 30 June 2017.[2] The return of about 99 per cent of the demonetised notes is the most important indicator of the failure of demonetisation. In December 2016, the Attorney-General of India, Mukul Rohatgi, had informed the Supreme Court that the government did not expect more than Rs 12 lakh crore to be back in the banks. The remaining Rs 3 lakh crore was black money, which would not return to the banks and could be 'extinguished' and passed on by the RBI to the government as dividend. Red-faced, the government tried to contain the damage by claiming that demonetisation was intended to bring back all cash into the formal banking system. But in the public eye, the jury was no more out. There was no black money left to be 'extinguished'.

Third, the Central Statistics Office (CSO) releases quarterly estimates of gross value added (GVA). As chapters in this volume would argue, these estimates typically do not account for changes in the informal sector. Yet, despite methodological infirmities, on a year-to-year basis, the growth rate of GVA showed a decline from 7.6 per cent in the first quarter (Q1) of 2016–17 to 5.6 per cent in the Q1 of 2017–18. This decline was in continuation of a similar decline reported for the fourth quarter (Q4) of 2016–17. The CSO estimates have officially signalled that demonetisation was instrumental in intensifying recessionary tendencies in the Indian economy.

* * *

[2] See RBI circular 'Specified Bank Notes held by DCCBs', dated 29 June 2017, available at http://bit.ly/2ztk33c, last accessed on 7 November 2017.

Stung by the estimates released by the RBI and the CSO, the Modi government tried to initiate a campaign to celebrate the 'success' of demonetisation in August–September 2017. This campaign made three major claims. First, demonetisation resulted in the 'highest ever black money detection'. Black money worth Rs 16,000 crore (i.e., the remaining 1.04 per cent of Rs 15.44 lakh crore) did not return to the banking system. Secondly, there was an 'unprecedented increase in tax compliance' after demonetisation. About 56 lakh taxpayers were newly added and the number of tax returns filed rose by 24.7 per cent in 2017–18 over 2016–17. Third, digital banking grew rapidly after November 2016. The number of digital transactions rose by 56 per cent between October 2016 and May 2017.

All the three claims were false. Chapters in this volume provide a comprehensive coverage in this regard.

First, the claim of detection of Rs 16,000 crore was actually an admission of failure, because the very premise of demonetisation was the existence of at least Rs 3 lakh crore as black money. In fact, the costs of demonetisation hugely outrun its benefits. One, even if we assume, conservatively, that India's GVA shrank by 1 per cent after November 2016, the resulting economic loss would be about Rs 1.5 lakh crore. Two, due to demonetisation, banks were inundated with new deposits worth lakhs of crores while credit outflows largely stagnated. As a result, the RBI had to mop up excess liquidity worth Rs 10.1 lakh crore from banks under the Market Stabilisation Scheme (MSS). The total interest outgo of the RBI on this count alone was Rs 5,700 crore.[3] Three, the RBI's costs incurred for printing new notes rose from Rs 3,420 crore in 2015–16 to Rs 7,965 crore in 2016–17: a rise by Rs 4,545 crore. These costs did not include intangibles, such as the time spent by bank staff on consumer interface and paperwork over many months. Four, due to the higher costs incurred by the RBI under different heads, the total surplus transferred by the RBI to the government fell from Rs 65,876 crore in 2015–16 to Rs 30,659 crore in 2016–17: i.e., a decline of Rs 35,217 crore. In sum, demonetisation was an extraordinarily loss-making proposition for the exchequer.

[3] These figures pertain only to cash management bills (CMB) issued for tenors ranging from 14 to 63 days. Another Rs 1 lakh crore was mopped up using CMBs of tenors ranging from 312 to 329 days, the costs of which are not included here. Also not included here is the interest outgo of the RBI for the deposits made by banks over the reverse repo rate window before and after the MSS scheme.

Second, the claim of rise in tax compliance after demonetisation is simply unimpressive. One, there is nothing remarkable about the rise in the number of tax returns filed in 2017–18 compared to earlier years. Compared to the corresponding previous year, the rise in the number of tax returns filed was 51 per cent in 2013–14; 12.2 per cent in 2014–15; 29.9 per cent in 2015–16; and 24.3 per cent in 2016–17.[4] Two, even among the 56 lakh assessees newly added, about 38.8 lakh assessees (or about 69.4 per cent) reported an annual income of less than Rs 5 lakh.[5] The average annual income of these new taxpayers was only Rs 2.7 lakh. In sum, the increase in tax revenue from the new assessees would be insignificant.

Third, the claims of the government on the extent of spread of digital banking defy basic statistical logic. The analysis in the introduction to this volume shows that, one, the percentage rise in the number of digital transactions were primarily owing to low base effects. Two, the total value of non-cash transactions rose by only 18.8 per cent between November 2016 and August 2017. Despite efforts to popularise mobile banking, the value and volume of mobile-based transactions recorded negative growth rates between November 2016 and August 2017. All available evidence till August 2017 point to the return of cash in everyday transactions. The government's aim of forcing citizens to shun cash had failed.

* * *

As the marketing campaign of August-September 2017 fizzled out, the government came out with two fresh claims in October-November 2017. First, it claimed that demonetisation had been successful in reducing the cash-to-GDP ratio in India from around 12.2 per cent in March 2016 to about 8.8 per cent in March 2017. Such a decline, it claimed, showed increasing formalisation of the economy. Second, it claimed to have identified Rs 17,000 crore worth suspicious transactions undertaken by 35,000 shell companies and 58,000 bank accounts after November 2017.

[4] See Arun Giri (2017), 'Did Demonetisation "Substantially Increase" Number of Tax Returns? A Fact Check,' available at http://bit.ly/2jd6xKY, last accessed on 3 September 2017.

[5] See Khushboo Narayan, 'ITR numbers up 25% this year, but bulk of it is small tax payers,' *Indian Express*, 3 September 2017, available at http://bit.ly/2hWjvtd, last accessed on 3 September 2017.

These two new claims were also specious. First, as arguments in this volume would show, there is no clear relationship between the level of cash-to-GDP ratio and the extent of formalisation in an economy. Further, the reduction in cash-to-GDP ratio was not because people moved into formal, non-cash, forms of payment systems but because the RBI was not printing new notes in adequate quantities. As remonetisation proceeded after March 2017, and as (and if) economic growth picks up, the cash-to-GDP ratio was expected to rise again back to levels close to 12 per cent.

Second, much of the action that the government claimed to have been taking—such as against fake shell companies—could have been undertaken without demonetisation also. Further, the amount of Rs 17,000 crore put out as suspicious transactions of shell companies was a very small amount, constituting only about 1 per cent of the cash in circulation as on 8 November 2016. All of this amount may not be 'black' (hence 'suspicious'), and only a part of this amount proven as unaccounted may be liable to be taxed or penalised. In other words, there was nothing significant about the claim related to the identification of suspicious transactions, as claimed by the government.

* * *

If the conceptual fragility of demonetisation was obvious to economists of all hues, its implementation was appallingly chaotic. The RBI was totally unprepared for an intervention of such proportion. The Central Board of the RBI spent very little time to discuss the feasibility of the initiative. All evidence suggests that it hurriedly signed on the dotted line. As Raghuram Rajan, former Governor of the RBI, noted in an interview, 'I think the view of any monetary economist would be that you first print the money and then do the demonetisation...'.[6] But in reality, new notes were yet to be printed when demonetisation was announced. When printing began, it turned out that the new notes did not fit into the cassettes of the ATMs. This meant that every ATM in the country had to be re-calibrated. As a result, for many months, people waited in long queues to access their hard-earned savings from banks and ATMs.

---

[6] See interview with Raghuram Rajan, 'I left because there was no offer on the table from the govt,' *Times of India*, 3 September 2017, available at http://bit.ly/2AvWQLN.

Meanwhile, the public perception of demonetisation did not necessarily conform to any demand for reason. Modi, thanks to his histrionics and ability to elevate anything cockeyed to the level of a spectacle, had convinced many that the pain of demonetisation was worth going through. According to the hyper-nationalist discourse let loose by his marketing team, citizens were voluntarily contributing to the greatness of the nation through their sufferings. But in reality, economic transactions were crippled. Livelihoods were wrecked. And most unfortunately, about 100 Indian citizens died either while standing in queues or due to the adversities that demonetisation wrought in their lives.

* * *

In February 2017, Paranjoy Guha Thakurta, the then editor of the *Economic & Political Weekly* (*EPW*), asked me if I could put together a collection of articles published in the journal on demonetisation. He also requested me to write an introduction to the collection, which would also be a stand-alone analysis of demonetisation. I started outlining the scope of the project in March 2017. But I soon realised that a collection of articles published after November 2016 would not do justice to the richness of the contributions to which the *EPW* was host to from the time of its inception. Many of these contributions offered top-notch analyses of issues related to the generation and growth of black money in India. I became convinced that only a broader selection of articles would do justice to the topic and the journal's glorious history.

I returned to meet Paranjoy in March 2017 to share the new, expanded, idea. He agreed. By the time I completed the manuscript, Paranjoy had resigned as the editor. But he was keen that the book project should be completed. I thank Paranjoy for his encouragement and perseverance. I also thank the members of the *EPW* editorial team who were part of the initial discussions about the volume.

Of course, a few excellent books on demonetisation have already been published.[7] Most of them were published within a few months after November 2016. This book differs from them on two counts. First, the analysis in this book takes into account data for a longer period i.e., till August-September 2017. Secondly, this book takes on board a larger gamut of issues into consideration. In addition to demonetisation per se,

[7] See Ghosh, Chandrasekhar and Patnaik (2017); Reddy (2017); Kapila (2017); and Kumar (2017).

it also provides a historical review of the issues related to the generation of black money in India. As I have emphasised in the volume, a journey through these selections from the *EPW* constitute a journey through the Indian black money debate itself. I hope that the volume would serve both as a 'collector's edition' for the larger 'EPW community', as well as a useful reference text for the students of Indian economy.

Overall, this book provides the reader with 26 articles in addition to the introductory chapter. Of these 26 articles, 24 articles have already been published in the *EPW*. I thank the authors of these 24 articles for their permission to edit and reprint their contributions. I must emphasise here the need for a clear distinction between my introductory chapter (which forms the first part of this volume) and the selections from the *EPW* archives (which form the rest of this volume). Nothing I state in the first part should be a burden on the other authors; these opinions and views are mine alone. The two remaining articles need special mention and acknowledgement. First, Prabhat Patnaik offered a special contribution titled 'The Legacy of Demonetisation'. Second, Amitava Bandyopadhyay, Ranjan Sett, and Dipak K. Manna—researchers from the Indian Statistical Institute (ISI), Kolkata—offered a special article that summarises the results of a study commissioned by the National Investigation Agency (NIA) on fake Indian currency notes (FICN). The findings of this study, though widely quoted in the media, have never been published anywhere till now. I thank them too for their contributions.

* * *

This book owes much to the support offered by my employer—the Tata Institute of Social Sciences (TISS), Mumbai, India. Vineet Kohli and R. Mohan read the draft manuscript and offered suggestions on improving the core arguments as well as organising the chapters. My students were patient listeners to my lectures on demonetisation as well as critical questioners. K. Smrithilal offered able research assistance while I worked on the volume. Subir Ghosh copy-edited the first draft of the manuscript. It was wonderful to work with the Oxford University Press India team. I thank all of them.

R. Ramakumar

Mumbai, India

8 November 2017

References

Reddy, C. Rammanohar (2017), *Demonetisation and Black Money*, Orient Blackswan, Mumbai.

Ghosh, J., Chandrasekhar, C. P. and Patnaik, P. (2017), *Demonetisation Decoded*, Routledge, New York.

Kumar, Arun (2017), *Understanding the Black Economy and Black Money in India: An Enquiry into Causes, Consequences and Remedies*, Aleph Book Company, New Delhi.

Kapila, Uma (ed.) (2017), *Demonetisation: The Economists Speak*, Academic Foundation, New Delhi.

Credits

The following 24 chapters were previously published in various issues of the *Economic & Political Weekly*:

Shankar Acharya, 'Unaccounted Economy in India: A Critical Review of Some Recent Estimates', *Economic & Political Weekly*, Vol. 18, Issue No. 49, 03 Dec, 1983.

O. P. Chopra, 'Unaccounted Income: Some Estimates', *Economic & Political Weekly*, Vol. 17, Issue No. 17-18, 24 May, 1982.

Poonam Gupta and Sanjeev Gupta, 'Estimates of the Unreported Economy in India', *Economic & Political Weekly*, Vol. 17, Issue No. 3, 16 Jan, 1982.

J. C. Sandesara, 'Estimates of Black Income: A Critique of Gutmann Method', *Economic & Political Weekly*, Vol. 18, Issue No. 14, 02 Apr, 1983.

Sacchidananda Mukherjee and R. Kavita Rao, 'Estimating Unaccounted Income in India: Using Transport as a Universal Input', *Economic & Political Weekly*, Vol. 52, Issue No. 7, 18 Feb, 2017.

Dev Kar, 'An Empirical Study on the Transfer of Black Money from India: 1948-2008', *Economic & Political Weekly*, Vol. 46, Issue No. 15, 09 Apr, 2011.

D. Ravi Kanth, 'On a Wild Goose Chase for Black Money in Switzerland', *Economic & Political Weekly*, Vol. 49, Issue No. 47, 22 Nov, 2014.

S. S. S. Kumar, 'Participatory Note Investments: Do Indian Markets Need Them?', *Economic & Political Weekly*, Vol. 50, Issue No. 44, 31 Oct, 2015.

Paranjoy Guha Thakurta, Shinzani Jain and Advait Rao Palepu, 'Did Adani Group Evade Rs 1,000 Crore Taxes?', *Economic & Political Weekly*, Vol. 52, Issue No. 2, 14 Jan, 2017.

I. S. Gulati, 'HUF Tax Avoidance Revisited', *Economic & Political Weekly*, Vol. 8, No. 7, 17 Feb, 1973.

Gopinath Pradhan and M. Govinda Rao, 'Excise Duty Evasion on Cotton Textile Fabrics', *Economic & Political Weekly*, Vol. 20, Issue No. 44, 02 Nov, 1985.

Jagdeep S. Chhokar, 'Black Money and Politics in India', *Economic & Political Weekly*, Vol. 52, Issue No. 7, 18 Feb, 2017.

J. Dennis Rajakumar and S. L. Shetty, 'Demonetisation: 1978, the Present and the Aftermath', *Economic & Political Weekly*, Vol. 51, Issue No. 48, 26 Nov, 2016.

Vineet Kohli and R. Ramakumar, 'Economic Rationale of Demonetisation: An Analysis of the Claims of the Government', *Economic & Political Weekly*, Vol. 51, Issue No. 53, 31 Dec, 2016, Web Exclusives.

C. P. Chandrasekhar, 'Negative Interest Rates: Symptom of Crisis or Instrument for Recovery', *Economic & Political Weekly*, Vol. 52, Issue No. 12, 25 March, 2017.

Atul Sood and Ashapurna Baruah, 'The New Moral Economy: Demonetisation, Digitalisation and India's Core Economic Problems', *Economic & Political Weekly*, Vol. 52, Issue No. 1, 07 Jan, 2017, Perspectives

Parag Waknis, 'Demonetisation through Segmented Markets: Some Theoretical Perspectives', *Economic & Political Weekly*, Vol. 52, Issue No. 9, 04 Mar, 2017, Web Exclusives

Ashok K. Lahiri, 'Demonetisation and Cash Shortage', *Economic & Political Weekly*, Vol. 51, Issue No. 51, 17 Dec, 2016, Web Exclusives

Ashok K. Nag, 'Lost Due to Demonetisation', *Economic & Political Weekly*, Vol. 51, Issue No. 48, 26 Nov, 2016, Commentary

P. Sainath, 'The Cashless Economy of Chikalthana', Vol. 51, Issue No. 46, 12 Nov, 2016, Web Exclusives.

Rahul M., 'Curry Mixed with Demonetisation and a Pinch of Pesticide', Vol. 51, Issue No. 47, 19 Nov, 2016, Web Exclusives.

R. Mohan, 'Impact of Demonetisation in Kerala', Vol. 52, Issue No. 18, 6 May, 2017.

R. Nagaraj, 'Quarterly GDP Estimation: Can It Pick Up Demonetisation Impact?', *Economic & Political Weekly*, Vol. 52, Issue No. 10, 11 Mar, 2017.

Ritika Mankar and Sumit Shekhar, 'Demonetisation and the Delusion of GDP Growth', *Economic & Political Weekly*, Vol. 52, Issue No. 18, 06 May, 2017.

I

INTRODUCTION

1

A Nation in the Queue

On How Demonetisation Wrecked the Economy and Livelihoods in India

R. Ramakumar

Nothing, in any recent period, has captured public discourse in India more intensely as Prime Minister Narendra Modi's announcement of demonetisation. The step touched literally every pocket and wallet in India. For weeks after 8 November 2016, no news coverage was complete without the mention of an impact of demonetisation. No discussion between friends or relatives was devoid of a sharp exchange of views on whether demonetisation was good or bad. No visit to a market or a restaurant was divorced from a thought on whether one had enough cash in hand. No visit to a bank or an automated teller machine (ATM) was planned without an assessment of the time to be spent in the queue. Indeed, the image of the queue was not just a metaphor for what demonetisation had left behind, but also an experiential takeaway for every citizen.

This book is about India's disastrous demonetisation experiment in 2016. It has two parts. The first, where we are now, is a long discussion on the initiative itself. Here, I will first attempt to discuss the conception of the policy of demonetisation and its implementation. Second, I will review the impact of demonetisation on different spheres of the economy and different sections of the people. Third, I will lay down the major claims of the government vis-à-vis demonetisation and critically examine each one of them. Can demonetisation reduce the circulation of fake currency? Can demonetisation check the origin and growth of black money? Fourth, I will try to place the so-called 'war on cash' within the analytical framework of neoliberal economics and discuss if the dream of a 'cashless' economy is of any worth in the Indian context.

The second part of the book is a tribute to India's premier academic journal—the *Economic & Political Weekly* or the *EPW*. Right since its inception, the *EPW*, as the journal is fondly known across the globe, was home to a large number of research articles and notes on questions related to black money, tax evasion and the two demonetisations of 1978 and 2016. A careful selection of such writings, among others, forms the second part of this volume. In fact, a journey through these writings in the journal constitutes a journey through the Indian black money debate itself. This book, then, is not just a book on demonetisation, but one that places questions on demonetisation within the broader debates on black money and tax evasion in India over the last six decades.

I: Demonetisation: Announcement and Implementation

> For a traveler from what will soon be Donald Trump's America, the most striking part of *notebandi*, however, involves its political aesthetics. On Friday, when Trump is inaugurated as President, he will join Modi as the latest figure in the world's swelling ranks of populist-nationalist leaders, a gallery of strongmen in countries rich and poor, some more democratic and some less so, who govern partly through intimidation and a certain curated arbitrariness, a methodology of deliberate surprise. (Coll 2017)

At 8 pm on 8 November 2016, when most Indian families were preparing for dinner, Prime Minister Narendra Modi came on television to deliver an address to the nation. It has not yet been officially confirmed if the address was live or prerecorded.[1] However, the contents of the address had all the elements of a self-styled shock-and-awe strategy. The address began by appealing to the national pride of the *sava sau karod deshwasi* (the 125 crore Indians), a phrase that Modi has used freely in political rallies to great effect. According to him, India had become a 'bright spot' in the global economy under his

---

[1] Anon. (2016, November 30). Why Does It Matter If PM's Demonetisation Address Was Recorded. *News Laundry*. Retrieved March 31, 2017, from http://bit.ly/2xJMGpv

leadership. His government, over two-and-half years of rule, had made rapid strides in reducing poverty and ensuring that the fruits of development reached all citizens. However, his efforts to reduce poverty were being weakened by 'the spectre of corruption and black money.' He stated that 'corruption, black money and terrorism are festering sores, holding us back in the race towards development.' And then came the announcement:

> To break the grip of corruption and black money, we have decided that the Rs 500 and Rs 1,000 currency notes presently in use will no longer be legal tender from midnight tonight, that is, 8 November 2016. This means that these notes will not be acceptable for transactions from midnight onwards. The 500 and 1,000 rupee notes hoarded by anti-national and anti-social elements will become just worthless pieces of paper. (PMO, 2016a)

With some exceptions, the Rs 500 and Rs 1,000 notes had to be exchanged at bank counters for either the existing notes of denominations Rs 100, Rs 50, Rs 20, Rs 10, Rs 5, Rs 2, and Rs 1 or coins of Rs 10, Rs 5, Rs 2 and Re 1. The exchange was to begin on 10 November; banks were to remain closed on the next day. The old notes (termed 'specified bank notes' or SBNs) could be exchanged till 30 December. For those not able to return the SBNs till 30 December, an extended window of time till 31 March 2017 was promised subject to the submission of a declaration form.

In the same address, the Prime Minister also announced that new notes of Rs 500 and Rs 2,000 were being introduced by the Reserve Bank of India (RBI). Given that the supply of these new notes was in short supply, there were to be restrictions on cash withdrawal from banks and from the ATMs. For exchange from bank branches, the per day withdrawal limit was set at Rs 4,000 till 24 November 2016. For withdrawals from ATMs, the per day withdrawal limit was set at Rs 2,000, which was later raised to Rs 4,000.

It was an address to the nation laced with an invocation to the glory of nationalism. To ensure the great march of the 'nation,' the country had to be 'cleansed.' The people of the nation had to make a 'contribution' to this march of the nation by ignoring 'temporary hardships' and being ready to make 'grand sacrifices.' The address ended with a call to the *sava sau karod deshwasi* to join the 'festival of integrity and credibility' and a cry of *Bharat Mata Ki Jai* (Hail Mother India).

Public reaction to the address was mixed. A large section was actually appreciative of the announcement, which purportedly aimed to eliminate black money and corruption, which were persistent and everyday problems faced by millions of Indians. A common refrain among this section was that finally, after years of passivity, a decisive measure was being undertaken by the government. The invocation of nationalism and terrorism in the address also appeared to have tilted the balance of public opinion. Another section of the public, among them Left activists, trade-unionists, liberals as well as economists of varying hues, pointed to the flaws of the strategy and expressed doubts on whether demonetisation can effectively address the problems of black money, corruption and terror.

The Role of the RBI

Soon after the Prime Minister's address, Urjit Patel, the governor of the RBI, and Shaktikanta Das, the then economic affairs secretary, addressed a joint press conference in New Delhi. As per the Reserve Bank of India Act of 1934, 'any series of bank notes of any denomination shall cease to be legal tender' only 'on recommendation of the central board' of directors of the RBI. Logically, journalists raised questions on the RBI's role in the design and implementation of the initiative. But Das was evasive and stated that there was 'no need to go into the process which led to this decision.'

A few days after the announcement, Piyush Goyal, the union power minister, stated in Parliament that the decision to withdraw the legal tender status of SBNs was not of the government, but of the RBI. What Goyal did not reveal was that the government had made a request to the RBI to consider such a recommendation. Patel himself admitted to a parliamentary standing committee in January 2017 that the government and the RBI were in talks regarding demonetisation from January 2016 itself. According to his written response to the committee:[2]

> It occurred to Government of India and the Reserve Bank that the introduction of new series of notes could provide a very rare and profound opportunity to tackle all the three problems of counterfeiting, terrorist

---

[2] Mishra, Anand (2017, January 10). Demonetisation: On Nov 7, It Was Govt Which 'Advised' RBI to 'Consider' Note Ban, Got RBI Nod Next Day. *The Indian Express.* Retrieved March 31, 2017, from http://bit.ly/2vFMhXZ

financing and black money by demonetising the banknotes in high-denominations of Rs 500 and Rs 1,000 or by withdrawing legal tender status of such banknotes…Though no firm decision was taken initially, whether to demonetise or not, preparations still went on for introduction of new series notes, as that was needed in any case.

But the RBI was always well-known for its scepticism towards demonetisation. According to K.C. Chakrabarty, a former deputy governor of the RBI, whenever the RBI's opinion was sought on demonetisation in the past, it had advised in the negative.[3] Raghuram Rajan, Patel's predecessor, had also publicly offered views against demonetisation.[4] In September 2017, Rajan revealed that the RBI under his governorship had warned the government of the 'costs' of demonetisation as well as 'alternatives' that could achieve the same aims. In clear terms, he signaled that the government had overruled his recommendation:

> I was asked by the government in February 2016 for my views on demonetisation, which I gave orally. Although there might be long-term benefits, I felt the likely short-term economic costs would outweigh them, and felt there were potentially better alternatives to achieve the main goals. I made these views known in no uncertain terms. I was then asked to prepare a note, which the RBI put together and handed to the government. It outlined the potential costs and benefits of demonetisation, as well as alternatives that could achieve similar aims. If the government, on weighing the pros and cons, still decided to go ahead with demonetisation, the note outlined the preparation that would be needed, and the time that preparation would take. The RBI flagged what would happen if preparation was inadequate. (Rajan, 2017, p. 10)

Nevertheless, as documents show, on 7 November, the Modi government officially advised the RBI to consider the withdrawal of legal

---

[3] Anon. (2016, November 18). UPA Government Also Proposed It, We Said No. *The Hindu*. Retrieved March 31, 2017, from http://bit.ly/2xK74qM

[4] In his 20th Lalit Doshi Memorial Lecture, delivered on 11 August 2014, Rajan had stated that while demonetisation was often talked of as a solution, the 'clever find ways around it'. He further stated: 'I think there are ways around demonetisation. It is not that easy to flush out the black money' (*see* Dutt, Rimin. 2016, November 9). Here's What Raghuram Rajan Thinks of Currency Demonetisation. *HuffPost*. Retrieved March 31, 2017, from http://bit.ly/2eVQb4n).

tender status of SBNs. According to Patel's written response to the standing committee:[5]

> Government, on 7 November, 2016, advised the Reserve Bank that to mitigate the triple problems of counterfeiting, terrorist financing and black money, the central board of the Reserve Bank may consider withdrawal of the legal tender status of the notes in high-denominations of Rs 500 and Rs 1,000 … It was advised in that letter that cash has been a facilitator of black money … [and the] elimination of black money will eliminate the long shadow of the ghost economy and will be positive for India's growth outlook. They also observed that in the last five years, there has been an increase in circulation of Rs 500 and Rs 1,000 notes with an increasing incidence of counterfeiting of these notes … There have been widespread reports of the usage of fake Indian currency notes (FICN) for financing of terrorism and drug financing. The FICN have their origin in [a] neighbouring country and pose a grievous threat to the security and integrity of the country. Hence, the government has recommended that the withdrawal of the legal tender character of these notes is apposite. The Government of India advised the Bank to place these matters of immediacy before the Directors of the Central Board of the Reserve Bank of India for consideration …

Accordingly, on 8 November 2016, an emergency meeting of the RBI's central board of directors was called in New Delhi. The meeting, which began at around 5.30 pm, recommended to the government that the legal tender status of Rs 500 and Rs 1,000 notes be withdrawn. This recommendation was sent to the government immediately. A cabinet meeting that had already begun was informed of the RBI's recommendation. The cabinet approved the recommendation and the Prime Minister's address to the nation was telecast at 8 pm.

The chronology of events show that the government had actively sought the RBI's recommendation on demonetisation and the RBI's central board had obliged. The board also did not spend adequate time discussing the merits of the government's proposal, or the level of preparedness of the banking system. To begin with, Rajan has revealed that 'at no point during my term [which ended in early-September 2016] was the RBI asked to make a decision on demonetisation' (*see* Rajan 2017, p. 10). Responses to right to information (RTI) queries have further

---

[5] Mishra, Anand (2017, January 10). Demonetisation: On Nov 7, It Was Govt Which 'Advised' RBI to 'Consider' Note Ban, Got RBI Nod Next Day. *The Indian Express*. Retrieved March 31, 2017, from http://bit.ly/2vFMhXZ

showed that the board had not discussed proposals for demonetisation at any of its meetings before 8 November 2016.[6] Instead, the recommendation appears to have been hurriedly forwarded to the government. Since then, the RBI has also staunchly refused to share the minutes of the board meeting in response to multiple RTI queries.

How much currency was in circulation in the denominations of Rs 500 and Rs 1,000 on 8 November? For many weeks, neither the government nor the RBI provided any information in this regard. The annual reports of the RBI provide information on bank notes in circulation in the chapter titled 'Currency Management'. According to the *Annual Report 2015–16* of the RBI, as in end-March 2016, the total bank notes in circulation amounted to Rs 16.42 lakh crore. Within these, notes of denomination Rs 500 and Rs 1,000 constituted Rs 14.2 lakh crore, or 86.4 per cent of the total value of bank notes in circulation. It was thus assumed that the government had withdrawn 86.4 per cent of the total currency from circulation on 8 November 2016. However, it was later revealed that more notes of Rs 500 and Rs 1,000 were printed and circulated between March 2016 and November 2016. According to RBI (2017a), the total value of SBNs in circulation as on 8 November 2016 was actually Rs 15.4 lakh crore, which constituted 86.9 per cent of the bank notes in circulation.

The morning of 9 November opened with screaming newspaper headlines, such as 'The Great Cash Clean-up'; 'Cash Wash'; 'The Black Buck Stops Here'; 'Surgical Strike on Terrorism'; 'Surgical Strike on Black Money'; 'Modi's Attack on Money Pollution'; and 'Black Money in the Gutter'.[7] Editorials called the step 'bold' and 'stunning'. While such one-sided press coverage helped tilt the public mood in favour of the announcement, few could guess what was in store for the next day.

The Mayhem at Banks and ATMs

The enormity of the step—i.e., the withdrawal of 87 per cent of the currency in circulation—had not quite sunk in even on 9 November. India

---

[6] Nag, Anirban, Chaudhary, Archana, & Roy Choudhary, Abhijit. (2017, January 12). Central Bank Cites Security Threat in India Cash Mystery. *Bloomberg Quint*. Retrieved March 31, 2017, from http://bit.ly/2x5AoLa

[7] Anon. (2016, November 9). Front-page Headlines: How Indian Papers Reported Modi's Currency-Note Move. *Scroll*. Retrieved March 31, 2017, from http://bit.ly/2gG7Lx1

is a heavily cash-intensive economy. As some estimates indicate, about 78 per cent of all consumer payments in India are in cash (MoF 2016). The persistence of agriculture as a major economic activity in the rural areas, a large informal sector in the rural and urban areas (where traders fall back on cash balances to meet their needs of working capital) and the poor penetration of banking infrastructure are some of the reasons why cash transactions continue to be predominant. Cultural factors too play a major role in the preference for cash payments rather than cashless payments. In such an economy, a sudden withdrawal of 87 per cent of the currency was certain to not just cripple regular economic transactions but also create a great rush for fresh cash in the notes of new denominations.

Not surprisingly, the morning of 10 November witnessed mayhem across the country. There was chaos and long queues in front of every bank branch and ATM. About 10 crore exchange transactions were reported across the country on that single day.[8] Bank branches ran out of cash in a few hours, and shut their doors. The ATMs were also closed as they ran out of cash. The lack of preparedness was everywhere to be seen. There simply were not enough notes![9]

The RBI and the government did not anticipate such chaos. On 11 November, the RBI released a press note that stated: 'There is enough cash available with banks.'[10] However, the same day, Arundhati Bhattacharya, chairperson of the State Bank of India (SBI), appeared to disagree; she said that it would take at least 10 days for ATM operations to return to normal (as events progressed, this proved to be a huge underestimate).[11] On 12

---

[8] Reserve Bank of India. (2016, November 12). Withdrawal of Legal Tender Character of Rs 500 and Rs 1,000: RBI Statement [Press release]. Retrieved March 31, 2017, from http://bit.ly/2wB2Ml3

[9] Kumar (2016) argues that while the announcement of demonetisation may have been on legally sound grounds, the mayhem at banks and atms could well be interpreted as 'a fundamental breakdown in the rule of law'. It adversely affected the citizen's faith in the currency as well as the ability of the government in governing by the rule of law.

[10] Reserve Bank of India. (2016, November 11). Enough Cash Is Available, RBI Reassures; Urges Public to Exercise Patience and Exchange Notes at Convenience [Press release]. Retrieved March 31, 2017, from http://bit. ly/2xJEiXd

[11] Chauhan, Subhang. (2016, November 11). Currency Notes Scrapped Day 2: ATMs Open to Long Queues after Banks; Chaotic Scenes Continue across Country. *India.com*. Retrieved March 31, 2017, from http://bit.ly/2vFHc1V

November, the RBI released another statement, which blamed the people for crowding the banks; it said: 'as there is ample time, people need not rush to exchange putting avoidable strain on the banking branch network.'[12] The RBI also urged people 'to switch over to alternative modes of payment, such as pre-paid cards, RuPay/credit/debit cards, mobile banking, Internet banking,' which would 'alleviate the pressure on the physical currency and also enhance the experience of living in the digital world.' On 13 November, the RBI modified its 11 November statement to state that there was 'enough cash *in small denominations* … available at the Reserve Bank and banks' (emphasis added).

Urging people to shift to digital payments was a clear afterthought. The claims of attacking counterfeit currency, terror financing and black money had fallen apart in just a few days after 8 November. An alternative narrative was necessary to maintain the momentum and induce some logic into the demonetisation policy. Thus, it was argued that demonetisation would help transform India into a 'cashless' economy, or at least a 'less-cash' economy. A number of incentives to use digital payment systems, *albeit* insignificant, were announced by the government and the RBI over the following weeks (*see* RBI 2017a, for summary).

There were two major reasons for the chaos at banks after 10 November. First, as on 8 November, the total stock of notes of Rs 2,000, with the RBI and different currency chests, was only 473.3 million pieces, worth Rs 94,660 crore (or, just about 6 per cent of the total value of SBNs withdrawn from legal tender status).[13] In other words, the RBI's central board of directors had not checked its own stock of notes before hurriedly agreeing to the government's proposal on 8 November. Second, the RBI had printed the new notes of denomination Rs 2,000 in a new size and design. Normally, each ATM contained four cassettes; two of them held notes of denomination Rs 500 and the other two held notes of denomination Rs 1,000 and Rs 100.[14] The new note

[12] Reserve Bank of India. (2016, November 12). Withdrawal of Legal Tender Character of Rs 500 and Rs 1,000: RBI Statement [Press release]. Retrieved March 31, 2017, from http://bit.ly/2wB2Ml3

[13] Zarabi, Siddharth, & Ray, Raj Kumar. (2016, December 22). Month after Demonetisation, Rs 15,150 cr of New Rs 500 Notes Printed. *Business Television India*. Retrieved March 31, 2017, from http://bit.ly/2eyMml5

[14] Venkatesh, Mahua. (2016, November 13). Non-compliant Currency: ATMs May Take 2-3 Weeks to Become Fully Functional. *Hindustan Times*. Retrieved March 31, 2017, from http://bit.ly/2eEnRXo

of Rs 2,000 would not fit into any of these four cassettes. As a result, each one of the 2.2 lakh ATMs in India had to be 'reconfigured' or 'recalibrated' so that the ATMs could accurately count and dispense the new notes. The RBI officially admitted to this problem only on 14 November.[15] It stated that recalibration was a massive and complex exercise necessitating coordination among multiple agencies: banks, ATM manufacturers, the National Payment Corporation of India (NPCI), and switch operators. Engineers had to personally visit each ATM and spend 2–4 hours per ATM to complete the recalibration. Arun Jaitley, the finance minister, justified the delay in recalibration; he said: 'Secrecy could not have been maintained if we had recalibrated the ATMs earlier.'[16]

As the ATMs were not calibrated to store the new notes, banks began to pack all cassettes in the ATMs with notes of Rs 100. When banks approached the RBI for more notes of denomination Rs 100, the RBI ended up giving them soiled notes that the banks had earlier returned to the RBI. Use of soiled notes led to the frequent jamming of ATMs, which only added to the chaos. According to Thomas Franco, senior vice-president of the All India Bank Officers' Confederation (AIBOC):

> Recalibration started only a week after Modi's announcement ... Most ATMs can accommodate currency worth Rs 2.1 lakh if they are dispensing only Rs 100 notes. This means that an ATM can cater to only 105 persons if each draws the maximum allowed value of Rs 2,000 [per day]. But there were at least 300–400 people at most ATMs.[17]

A major argument of the government in favour of demonetisation was that most illegal transactions and stocks of cash were in notes of higher denomination. Given this logic, it was surprising that the RBI released new notes of denomination Rs 2,000. It turns out that the RBI had actually suggested to the government on 7 October 2014 that new

---

[15] Reserve Bank of India. (2016, November 14). Constitution of Task Force for Enabling Dispensation of Mahatma Gandhi (New) Series Banknotes - Recalibration and Reactivation of ATMs [Press release]. Retrieved March 31, 2017, from http://bit.ly/2gzWHOp

[16] Venkatesh, Mahua (2016, November 13). Non-compliant Currency: ATMs May Take 2–3 Weeks to Become Fully Functional. *Hindustan Times*. Retrieved March 31, 2017, from http://bit.ly/2eEnRXo

[17] Sridhar, V. (2016, December 9). Banks Have Suspended All Normal Operations. *Frontline*. Retrieved March 31, 2017, from http://bit.ly/2xKdaHw

notes of denomination Rs 5,000 and Rs 10,000 be introduced in view of rising inflation and problems of managing currency logistics.[18] However, the government declined this proposal on 18 May 2016 and advised the RBI to introduce new notes of Rs 2,000. No explanation has been provided on how the notes of Rs 2,000 would help reduce hoarding that used to happen in notes of Rs 500 and Rs 1,000. According to the government, notes of Rs 2,000 were released 'primarily to ensure faster remonetisation'.[19] However, a week into demonetisation, the fallacy of this reasoning was visible; those who possessed notes of Rs 2,000 were unable to spend it, as no one would offer change or a balance payment over a transaction. In effect, the problem of short supply of notes was exacerbated by the release of Rs 2,000 notes.

The chaos at the banks and ATMs continued through November and into December. As a study of 214 households in a Mumbai slum showed, the average waiting time at a bank or ATM was 1–3 hours for 63 per cent of the households (Krishnan and Siegel 2016). For one-fourth of the households, the waiting time was more than 4 hours. Sadly, a number of people died while standing in queues. By 18 November, according to news reports, 55 persons, most of them elderly persons, had died.[20] By 31 December, news reports put the total number of deaths owing to demonetisation at 105.[21] All these 105 deaths were not due to long waits at the queue; there were many who embraced death in disappointment. As Rahul M. has documented in this volume, Varda Balayya, a 42-year-old farmer from Siddipet in Telangana, 'killed himself and tried to poison his entire family by mixing pesticide in their chicken curry'. Balayya had wanted to sell his land to pay off debts and organise his daughter's wedding, but realised that 'no one would be able to buy his land for a while' due to the cash crunch. In New Delhi, 25-year-old

---

[18] Mishra, Anand. (2017, January 10). Demonetisation: On Nov 7, It Was Govt Which 'Advised' RBI to 'Consider' Note Ban, Got RBI Nod Next Day. *The Indian Express*. Retrieved March 31, 2017, from http://bit.ly/2vFMhXZ

[19] Anon. (2017, March 21). Focus on Supply of Rs 500 and Lower Denomination Notes: Das. Press Trust of India. Retrieved March 31, 2017, from http://bit.ly/2x5eXd4

[20] Vij, Shivam. (2016, November 18). Day 9: Demonetisation Death Toll Rises to 55. *HuffPost*. Retrieved March 31, 2017, from http://bit.ly/2eEc1ga

[21] Shaji, Shilpa (2016, December 22). Here Are the 105 People Who Died in 45 Days of Demonetisation. Narada News. Retrieved March 31, 2017, from http://bit.ly/2wBOOiT

Virendar Basoya hanged himself to a ceiling fan, as he was reportedly depressed due to his failure to exchange Rs 12 lakh worth of SBNs.[22] An infant child died at a hospital in Mumbai after being denied admission and treatment by a doctor who refused to accept payment in old notes of Rs 500. In an interview with *Mumbai Mirror*, the doctor asked: 'She could not pay for the treatment with valid currency; so, how could I forcibly admit her?'[23]

Even bank employees were affected by the stress at work; according to bank trade unions, more than 11 bank staff died due to stress at work.[24] To cite an instance, Tukaram Tanpure, a bank peon in Pune, Maharashtra died of a massive heart attack while handling large crowds; working hours at his bank branch had been extended to 12 hours after 10 November.[25]

Narendra Modi, who asked for great sacrifices from the people for the great march of the nation, appeared unaffected by the miseries of people. Speaking to Indian diaspora in Japan, he laughed, made fun of people's difficulties and quipped: '*Ghar mein shaadi hai! Paise nahin hai!*' ('There is a wedding in the house, but there is no money!').[26] In another speech in Goa, he mocked people waiting in long queues and said: 'Those involved in scams, now have to stand in a queue to exchange Rs 4,000.' Leaders of his party—the Bharatiya Janata Party (BJP)—joined in. Manoj Tiwari, the president of the BJP in Delhi, was caught on video

[22] Anon. (2016, November 18). Delhi: Unable to Exchange Notes, Man Commits Suicide. *The Indian Express*. Retrieved March 31, 2017, from http://bit.ly/2eyElgd

[23] Dhupkar, Alka (2016, November 12). Doc Says No to Deposit in Rs 500 Notes, Baby Dies Awaiting Help. *Mumbai Mirror*. Retrieved March 31, 2017, from http://bit.ly/2eyyEyL

[24] Bose, Adrija (2016, November 21). 11 Bankers Died Due To Stress': Leader of Bank Officers' Union Wants RBI Governor to Resign for Demonetisation 'Havoc'. *HuffPost*. Retrieved March 31, 2017, from http://bit.ly/2wyTOqg

[25] Joshi, Satyajit (2016, November 16). Demonetisation: 'Stressed' Bank Employee, 'Tired' Customer Die in Maharashtra. *Hindustan Times*. Retrieved March 31, 2017, from http://bit.ly/2x5ZGsI

[26] Anon. (2016, November 13). Watch: Prime Minister Modi Laugh And Cry While Talking About Currency Demonetisation. *HuffPost*. Retrieved March 31, 2017, from http://bit.ly/2gHvIUJ

making fun of people in queues.[27] Tiwari was explaining, shaking with laughter, how he invoked patriotism and escaped from a crowd that was angry over cashless ATMs:

> I went to stand in the [ATM] line in my area … I saw that a crowd had started running towards me. In order to defend myself from the crowd, I sang a patriotic song … (and sings …) … 'The patriots are standing in queues, there is a huge crowd, India's destiny is getting decorated with hardships … '[28]

As the chapter by Atul Sood and Ashapurna Baruah in this volume points out, standing in the queue to withdraw one's hard-earned money was enlisted as a way to honour the nation. A new 'moral political project' was being unleashed, which sought to redefine the relationship between the citizen and the state. Here, every citizen was either 'a patriot or a criminal' while the state epitomised virtue and stood above everyone else.

The last date for submitting SBNs to the RBI offices was 31 March 2017. It was telling that even on the last day, the police had to be called in to control crowds that had come from long distances. A journalist from New Delhi reported that 'tears and expletives, scuffles and rants marked the day as crowds occupied half of the Sansad Marg [where the regional office of the RBI is located], slowing down traffic till 4 pm'.[29] Many were turned away citing changed rules that allowed only non-resident Indians (NRIs) to exchange SBNs after 30 December. In the line were wives who had discovered that their husbands, who died after 30 December but were critically ill when demonetisation was announced, had kept cash worth Rs 40,000 or Rs 50,000 under their beds. These notes, the hard-earned savings of working people, had turned into pieces of waste paper when they were found by family members. Narain Saini,

27 Anon. (2017, January 4). Caught on Camera: Delhi BJP Chief Manoj Tiwari Mocks People in ATM Queues. *The Indian Express*. Retrieved March 31, 2017, from http://bit.ly/2x5tA0d

28 Rakshit, Pratik. (2017, January 6). Delhi BJP Chief Manoj Tiwari in Spot over ATM Queue Clip. *Mail Today*. Retrieved March 31, 2017, from http://bit.ly/2eyBh3B

29 Hafeez, Sarah (2017, April 1). Last Day to Get Old Notes Exchanged: On Deadline Day, Chaos and Desperation Outside RBI Office. *The Indian Express*. Retrieved April 1, 2017, from http://bit.ly/2wBXXYM

a 40-year-old hearing-and-speech impaired man, had reached the RBI office with a hand-written letter that said:

> Respected governor sir, I humbly submit that I am a physically challenged man. I have Rs 3,000 in old notes which are out of circulation now. Signed, an Indian citizen of yours.

Little did Saini realise that his rights associated with 'citizenship' stood seriously circumscribed after 8 November.

On whose door did the blame lie? On the one hand, the government had forced the hands of the RBI to recommend demonetisation without adequate planning or thought. On the other hand, the RBI had allowed itself to be forced by the government, surrendered much of its autonomy and ended up losing much of its credibility and legitimacy. Y.V. Reddy, former governor of the RBI, was rather scathing in his remarks that 'the institutional identity of the RBI has been damaged'.[30] Usha Thorat, a former deputy governor of the RBI, was equally harsh:

> It is indeed a sad day to see one of the most respected public institutions in India becoming an object of ridicule and scorn. There have been times when the Old Lady of Mint Street was criticised for being too conservative and cautious—for not being able to keep up with innovation and markets—but never has she been accused of not knowing her job. Never has she been the butt of as many jokes as in the last few days.[31]

The Status of Remonetisation

Though more than ten months have passed since November 2016, remonetisation of the economy—the extent to which new notes are introduced into circulation—has remained painfully incomplete. Between 10 November and 18 November, Rs 5.44 lakh crore worth SBNs were deposited/exchanged with banks by the public.[32] However,

[30] Nag, Anirban, Chaudhary, Archana, & Roy Choudhary, Abhijit. (2017, January 12). Central Bank Cites Security Threat in India Cash Mystery. *Bloomberg Quint*. Retrieved March 31, 2017, from http://bit.ly/2x5AoLa

[31] Thorat, Usha. (2016, December 28). A Note to RBI. *The Indian Express*. Retrieved March 31, 2017, from http://bit.ly/2iWCtTn

[32] Reserve Bank of India. (2016, November 21). Activity at Banks during November 10 to November 18, 2016 [Press release]. Retrieved March 31, 2017, from http://bit.ly/2gA1DTr

during the same period, only 1.03 lakh crore (or just 18.9 per cent) was withdrawn by the public due to shortage of new notes. Between 10 November and 27 November, Rs 8.45 lakh crore worth SBNs were deposited/exchanged with banks by the public.[33] During the same period, the public was able to withdraw only Rs 2.17 lakh crore (or 25.7 per cent) from the banks. Between 10 November and 10 December, Rs 12.44 lakh crore worth SBNs were deposited/exchanged with banks by the public. During the same period, only 4.61 lakh crore (or 37.1 per cent) worth of new notes were supplied to the public.[34]

The total currency in circulation (in all denominations) as on 20 October 2017 (as we take the book to print) was Rs 16.21 lakh crore. Given that about Rs 17.7 lakh crore of currency was in circulation on 8 November 2016, the extent of remonetisation in the economy between 10 November 2016 and 20 October 2017 would have been only 91.6 per cent (*see* Figure 1.1). The RBI's *Weekly Statistical Supplements* provide data on 'currency with public' on a weekly basis, which is defined as currency in circulation minus cash held by banks. Currency with public (in all denominations) amounted to Rs 17.01 lakh crore as on 28 October 2016, the last data point available prior to 8 November 2016. As on 13 October 2017, currency with public was only Rs 15.34 lakh crore, or only 90.2 per cent of that as on 28 October 2016.

The extent of reduction in currency with the public is an indicator of how much money moved out of people's pockets as deposits in banks. If we compare 28 October 2016 and 13 October 2017, an approximate amount of Rs 1.7 lakh crore stood appropriated by the state from its citizens. Ashok K. Lahiri had argued in his article in the *EPW*, included in this volume, that even if currency presses were to operate at full capacity to print the new notes of Rs 2,000 and Rs 500, 'the cash shortage would disappear only by mid–June or the first week of July 2017.' The plot in Figure 1.1 attests to the soundness of Lahiri's projection.

[33] Reserve Bank of India. (2016, November 28). Withdrawal of Legal Tender Status of Banknotes of Rs 500 and Rs 1000: Activity at Banks during November 10-27, 2016 [Press release]. Retrieved March 31, 2017, from http://bit.ly/2wzn9Rw

[34] Reserve Bank of India. (2016, December 13). Shri R Gandhi and Shri SS Mundra, RBI Deputy Governors Brief Agencies on Currency Issues: Edited Transcript [Press release]. Retrieved March 31, 2017, from http://bit.ly/2eWUv3D

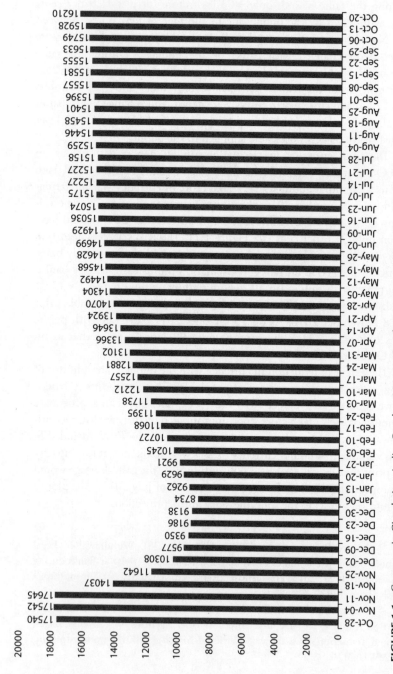

FIGURE 1.1 Currency in Circulation, India, October 2016 to October 2017, Weekly, in Rs Billion

Source: Reserve Bank of India

SBNs Returned: Failing the Litmus Test

The litmus test for the success of any demonetisation is the amount of cash that does not return to the banking system. For long, economists and observers were intrigued by the refusal of the RBI to share data on SBNs returned to banks after 10 December 2016. Information on SBNs returned was important because any amount not returned to the banking system was supposed to be 'black money', which could be 'extinguished' by the RBI. It was also expected that the amount not returning to the banking system could be 'extinguished'. Consequently, the RBI could pass over an equivalent amount to the government, which in turn could spend it for welfare purposes. The government's expectations were shared by the Attorney-General of India, Mukul Rohatgi, with the Supreme Court. According to Rohatgi, the government did not expect more than Rs 12 lakh crore to be returned to the banks, which implied that about Rs 3 lakh crore worth of 'black money' was to be 'extinguished' and passed over to the government.

As demonetisation proceeded, these hopes stood belied. To begin with, Patel was forced to clarify on 7 December 2016 that 'the withdrawal of legal tender characteristic status does not extinguish any of the RBI balance sheets ... They are still the liability of the RBI.' On 8 December, revenue secretary Hasmukh Adhia told journalists that 'the expectation is that the entire money which is in circulation has to come to the banking channel'.[35] In other words, the pace at which SBNs were being returned to the banking system had convinced the government that there would be no currency left to extinguish. By 10 December, Rs 12.44 lakh crore worth SBNs had already returned to the banking system.

The government staunchly refused to share any figure on SBNs returned after 10 December. Instead, it attempted to obfuscate facts and confuse the public with convoluted stories of 'double counting.' On 15 December, Das told the media that data on SBNs returned were being withheld because the RBI suspected 'double counting' of currency notes. Das' statement was soon shown to be wrong. There were two ways in which returned SBNs could be counted. One, through the simple addition of the cash position of individual banks with respect to the SBNs returned. There could be double-counting here, as banks without

[35] Narayan, Khushboo. (2016, December 8). Expect All Demonetised Money to Come Back to System: Revenue Secretary Hasmukh Adhia. *The Indian Express*. Retrieved March 31, 2017, from http://bit.ly/2w0egNa

currency chests may have deposited cash with banks that had currency chests. Two, directly from the currency chests, in which case there was no scope for double-counting. Usha Thorat, in an interview, pointed out that 'there is no question of double counting ... RBI only looks at the currency chest data.' In an interview with the *Economic Times*, Rajnish Kumar, the then managing director of the SBI, further clarified this in no uncertain terms:

> ... currency chest position is the correct position, there cannot be any flaw in that ... double counting can only happen if the individual banks and post offices are reporting the deposit position ... but [in] currency chest reporting which is done every day and which is an automated process, the possibility of any discrepancy does not exist ... If Reserve Bank has given the number based on the currency chest position, then there should not be discrepancy. But if the data is given on the basis of daily reports of deposits being given by the bank, then there is a possibility of some double counting.[36]

In its regular media briefings, the RBI was indeed providing SBN data from currency chests and not by adding the cash positions of individual banks. The RBI's deputy governor R. Gandhi told the media on 13 December 2016 that 'specified bank notes (SBNs) of Rs 500 and Rs 1,000 returned to the RBI and *currency chests* amounted to Rs 12.44 lakh crore as on 10 December 2016 (emphasis added).'[37] Yet, the RBI was to state on 5 January 2017 that 'figures [on SBN] would need to be reconciled with the physical cash balances to eliminate accounting errors/possible double counts.'[38] The effort, clearly, was to hide.

It was only in August 2017 that the RBI, ultimately, released the updated figures for the SBNs returned. According to the RBI's *Annual Report for 2016–17*, out of the Rs 15.4 lakh crore worth currency in circulation as on 8 November 2016, Rs 15.3 lakh crore had returned to the

---

[36] Anon. (2017, December 8). Now We Are Flush With Funds: Rajnish Kumar, SBI . *ET Now*. Retrieved March 31, 2017, from http://bit.ly/2eWrg0B

[37] Reserve Bank of India. (2016, December 13). Shri R Gandhi and Shri SS Mundra, RBI Deputy Governors Brief Agencies on Currency Issues: Edited Transcript [Press release]. Retrieved March 31, 2017, from http://bit.ly/2eWUv3D

[38] Reserve Bank of India. (2017, January 5). Clarification Regarding Specified Bank Notes (SBNs) [Press release]. Retrieved March 31, 2017, from http://bit.ly/2gzVWoC

banking system as on 30 June 2017. In other words, 98.96 per cent of the SBNs was back in the banking system and only 1.04 per cent of the SBNs remained outside. The verdict was finally out: as most critics predicted, demonetisation had failed to extinguish any amount of money that could be alleged as 'black.'

II: Economic Impacts of Demonetisation

> Some economists predicted that demonetisation would dampen economic activity over the next two quarters. But I believe that the decision to scrap high-value banknotes would push GDP growth up by 2 per cent.
>
> — Arjun Ram Meghwal, union minister of state for finance, Government of India, 4 December 2016[39]

Organised Sector

The impact of demonetisation was sharply felt in many segments of the organised sector for at least 10 months after November 2016 (*see* Table 1.1). Historically, the organised sector in India has had strong downward linkages with the unorganised and the informal sectors, and any adverse trend in the organised sector was also quickly transmitted to the unorganised and informal sectors.

- First, though with fluctuations, there was a fall of the year-on-year (Y-O-Y) growth rates in the Nikkei Manufacturing purchasing manager's index (PMI) between October 2016 and December 2016, and then again after April 2017. Twice in the period examined, the index fell below 50, which indicated contraction.
- Second, the index of industrial production (IIP) that grew at an average rate of 5.6 per cent between April 2016 and October 2016, did not fall in November 2016, but fell sharply over many months after December 2016. Manufacturing production growth rates followed suit. No revival of industrial and manufacturing production was visible even by August 2017.

---

[39] Anon. (2016, December 4). Demonetisation Will Push GDP Growth to 10%: Arjun Ram Meghwal. Press Trust of India. Retrieved March 31, 2017, from http://bit.ly/2wCuApk

- Third, the growth rate of gross bank credit to industry, which averaged 0.5 per cent between April and November 2016, did fall to negative levels in October 2016 itself, but began to shrink rapidly from November 2016. In fact, August 2017 was the 10th consecutive month after November 2016 that recorded negative growth rates for gross bank credit to industry.
- Fourth, the growth rates in the mining and electricity sectors were largely unaffected.
- Fifth, there was a slowdown of growth across the services sector from November 2016. The Nikkei Services PMI remained below 50 for all the three months of November 2016, December 2016 and January 2017, and then again for July and August 2017. Automobile sales— i.e., of commercial vehicles, motor cycles, two wheelers and three wheelers—sharply declined into negative levels for many months after November 2016. Three-wheeler sales recorded significantly negative growth rates for every month between November 2016 and July 2017. While some revival was visible in August 2017, the automobile industry was clearly struggling to survive the long period of shrinking sales after November 2016.
- Sixth, indicating a slowdown in the real estate and construction sector, growth rates of cement production fell from 6.7 per cent in October 2016 to 0.7 per cent in November 2016. For eight out of the ten months between November 2016 and August 2017, the growth rates for cement production were in the negative territory.
- Seventh, the growth rate of gross bank credit to services for all months between November 2016 and August 2017 was lower than the corresponding average for April–October 2016.
- Finally, the growth rate of gross bank credit began to fall from November 2016. In fact, the growth rates of bank credit after November 2016 were the lowest rates recorded for any month after 2011–12.

In other words, except in mining and electricity, growth slowdown was clearly visible in most industrial and services sectors of the economy from November 2016. Within these sectors, the fast-moving consumer goods (FMCG) companies, consumer durables companies, apparel and textiles industries and automobile companies were the most severely affected. The growth of volumes and value in the segments of microwaves, refrigerators, air conditioners, washing machines and flat panel televisions shrank by 30–50 per cent between October and November

TABLE 1.1 Growth Rates of Select Indicators of Economic Activity India, April 2016 to August 2017, in Per Cent

Indicator	Year-on-year growth rate (in per cent)																
	Apr–Oct 2016*	Oct 2016	Nov 2016	Dec 2016	Jan 2017	Feb 2017	Mar 2017	Apr 2017	May 2017	Jun 2017	Jul 2017	Aug 2017
Nikkei Manufacturing PMI index	52.0	54.4	52.3	49.6	50.4	50.7	52.5	52.5	51.6	50.9	47.9	51.2
Nikkei Services PMI	52.6	54.5	46.7	46.8	48.7	50.3	51.5	50.2	52.2	53.1	45.9	47.5
Index of Industrial Production (IIP)	5.6	4.2	5.1	2.4	3.5	1.2	4.4	3.2	2.8	−0.2	0.9	4.3
Manufacturing production	5.9	4.8	4.0	0.6	2.5	0.7	3.3	2.9	2.6	−0.5	−0.3	3.1
Mining, production	2.7	1.0	8.1	10.8	8.6	4.6	10.1	3.0	0.2	0.4	4.5	9.4
Electricity production	6.1	3.0	9.5	6.4	5.1	1.2	6.2	5.4	8.3	2.1	6.5	8.3
Cement production	5.0	6.7	0.7	−7.9	−13.1	−15.9	−6.0	−3.7	2.0	−5.7	−2.7	−1.4
Commercial vehicles production	7.3	9.8	15.6	−19.3	−0.3	−4.8	2.8	−28.8	−26.5	−8.4	12.4	7.8

(Cont'd)

TABLE 1.1 (*Cont'd*)

Indicator	Year-on-year growth rate (in per cent)											
	Apr–Oct 2016*	Oct 2016	Nov 2016	Dec 2016	Jan 2017	Feb 2017	Mar 2017	Apr 2017	May 2017	Jun 2017	Jul 2017	Aug 2017
Gross bank credit to industry	0.5	-1.7	-3.4	-4.3	-5.1	-5.2	-1.9	-1.4	-2.1	-1.1	-0.3	-0.3
Gross bank credit to services	11.8	9.3	7.1	8.3	8.1	7.7	9.1	4.1	4.0	4.7	4.9	5.0
Gross bank credit	8.4	6.4	4.0	3.3	3.3	3.0	7.4	3.8	3.5	4.4	4.7	5.0
Motorcycle sales	7.1	5.5	-9.3	-20.0	-6.9	0.5	-0.1	5.7	7.7	2.4	15.0	13.6
Passenger car sales	5.1	3.5	3.9	-0.4	12.5	6.3	11.1	15.4	8.9	-5.9	8.5	3.8
Commercial vehicle sales	8.0	13.5	-7.1	-5.7	-2.4	5.7	6.7	-25.0	-9.3	-4.2	5.7	14.9
Two-wheeler sales	12.4	7.5	-5.2	-19.7	-7.7	2.1	2.3	10.5	11.0	4.0	12.7	15.2
Three-wheeler sales	-10.9	-2.1	-22.0	-37.4	-26.9	-22.2	-23.1	-6.3	-6.8	-13.1	-6.6	7.8

Sources: RBI; Ministry of Finance; Market Economics; SIAM.

Notes: i) NA: not (yet) available.

ii) * denotes simple average of monthly Y-O-Y growth rates in the period.

iii) A PMI value of more than 50 indicates expansion.

2016 (RBI 2017a). Vyas (2017a) has a useful collation of assessments from the representatives of FMCG and consumer durable companies for the months November and December 2016:

- Varun Berry, MD, Britannia Industries: retailers are reporting sales of 30–70 per cent of what they were doing earlier; production has been reduced by 15–20 per cent.
- B. Krishna Rao, deputy marketing manager, Parle Products: production has been cut and inventories have piled up. Sales in November were 10–12 per cent lower than in November last year.
- Sunil Duggal, CEO, Dabur: sales are down 20 per cent over earlier week, supply chain is down-stocking and production is being calibrated.
- Harsh V. Agarwal, director, Emami: production will be cut across categories since consumers are postponing purchases.
- Manish Aggarwal, director, Bikano: production reduced by 10–15 per cent.
- Pradeep Bakshi, Voltas: impact of demonetisation higher in December; demand in tier-III and tier-IV towns down 50 per cent; in bigger towns demand is down 25–30 per cent.
- Manish Sharma, CEO, Panasonic: business down 40 per cent in November and December.
- Kamal Nandi, business head, Godrej Appliances: business down 40 per cent in November, lost two months but some recovery signs in top towns. Production cut 15 per cent.

The All India Manufacturers' Organisation (AIMO) released the results of its two-stage study on the impact of demonetisation in December 2016 and January 2017 (AIMO 2017). The first stage of the AIMO study analysed the changes across small, medium, and large-scale industries over the first month after 8 November 2016. According to the results, the extent of job cuts in most industries in November 2016 was in the range of 30–35 per cent. The extent of revenue lost in November 2016 was in the range of 20–50 per cent. The second stage of the AIMO study was conducted between 1 January and 15 January 2017. The extent of job losses and revenue losses between 8 November and 31 December 2016 was highest in establishments with less number of employees; for instance, in establishments with 1–5 staff, the job losses were 45 per cent and revenue losses were 55 per cent (*see* Figure 1.2). Traders, shops, micro-industries and small-scale industries had higher job losses (32–60 per cent) and revenue losses (35–47 per cent) than

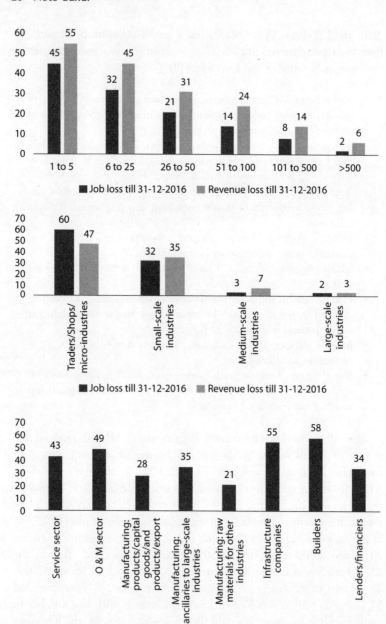

FIGURE 1.2   Job Loss and Revenue Loss in Establishments and Sectors Due to Demonetisation as Astimated by AIMO, November and December 2016, in Per Cent

Source: AIMO (2017).

medium and large-scale industries. Most persons who lost jobs were in the age group of 45–55 years. The reasons for these losses were identified as: inadequate cash withdrawal limit; lack of currency in banks and ATMs for withdrawal; fall of demand due to fears of market collapse; piling up of receivables; shrinking of margins; and loss of business from purchasers who used cash.

In sum, the impact of demonetisation on the organised corporate sector was uneven. A few segments remained resilient, but most other segments faced a sharp downturn. While large firms stayed afloat, small and medium-sized firms entered a period of prolonged contraction, if not shut down.

Unorganised and Informal Sectors

The unorganised sector accounts for 45 per cent of the gross value added (GVA) in the economy (RBI 2017a). Sectoral data show that the unorganised sector accounts for about 95 per cent of the GVA in agriculture and about 42 per cent of the GVA in services. The unorganised sector also accounts for 82.4 per cent of the total employment in the economy, of which 48.7 per cent is in agriculture, 8.5 per cent in industry and 25.2 per cent in services.

The direct impact of demonetisation on the unorganised and informal sectors was severe due to the high dependence on cash for everyday transactions. Reports suggest that most unorganised sector activities came to a grinding halt after 8 November 2016 (*see*, especially, the excellent field reports in *Frontline*, 10–23 December 2016). Trucks and lorries stopped transport services for many days. Incomes of taxi drivers were reported to have reduced to half. Vegetable and flower sellers in local markets reported significant fall in sales. Market clusters in major cities reported less sales of textiles and grocery. Vendors of pan and snacks on busy street sides reported less sales. As weddings were either postponed or made more austere, suppliers of equipment and decoration items reported less business. Restaurants and hotels reported fall in business; most hotels also reported low occupancy rates over Christmas and New Year as parties and get-togethers were cancelled. Movie shoots were scaled down or cancelled leading to the loss of jobs for workers. Construction sites halted work for weeks, leading to contractors dumping large numbers of workers from work. Weavers, masons, beedi workers, coir workers, carpenters, blacksmiths and workers in most traditional occupations, too, reported large losses of work. Major destinations of migrant labour reported a huge exodus of workers heading back home for want of work. Workers demanding jobs at the work sites of Mahatma Gandhi National Rural Employment Guarantee Scheme (MGNREGS) increased considerably in November and December 2016 due to loss of work at other sites.[40]

GDP Growth Rates

In the weeks after 8 November 2016, government spokespersons appeared extremely nervous about the adverse macroeconomic consequences of demonetisation. Arun Jaitley stated that people may suffer hardships for one or two quarters. According to Arvind Panagariya, vice-chairman of the NITI Aayog, there was to be an adverse impact on GDP growth in the third and fourth quarters of 2016–17. Arvind Subramanian, the chief economic adviser, said he expected 'uncertainty' in the third quarter of 2016–17. These admissions from the inner echelons of the government were based on ground reports of severe cash crunch and demand compression.

The defensive stance of government spokespersons lasted only till the data for the third quarter (Q3) of 2016–17 (October–December) were released by the Central Statistics Office (CSO). Though it was widely expected that the compression of demand, disruption of production activities and loss of employment will lead to a fall in growth rates, CSO data released in February 2017 showed that growth rates of gross value added, on a Y-O-Y basis, were 6.8 per cent for Q2 and 6.7 per cent for Q3 (see Table 1.2).

The government and BJP immediately began to cite these numbers to argue that demonetisation had no adverse impact on the economy as critics had forecast. Politics quickly overtook reason in the public discourse. Rebutting the earlier claims of Oxford-educated former Prime Minister Manmohan Singh and Amartya Sen of Harvard University that India's GDP growth was likely to fall post-demonetisation, Modi quipped: 'Hard work is much more powerful than Harvard.'[41] He said:

[40] Roche, Elizabeth, & Kapoor, Prerna. (2017, January 27). MGNREGS to See Record Spending as Demonetisation Drives Demand for Work. *Mint*. Retrieved March 31, 2017, from http://bit.ly/2x5o4dM

[41] Rodrigues, Jeanette, & Pradhan, Bibhudatta. (2017, March 2). Harvard Economists Face PM Modi's Censure after GDP Surprise. *Bloomberg*. Retrieved March 31, 2017, from http://bit.ly/2gGDe2n

TABLE 1.2 Growth Rates of Gross Domestic Product (GDP), Gross Value Added (GVA) at Basic Prices and Its Components over the Previous Year, at 2011–12 Prices, in Per Cent

Industry	2015–16				2016–17				2017–18
	Q1	Q2	Q3	Q4	Q1	Q2	Q3	Q4	Q1
Agriculture, forestry and fishing	2.4	2.3	−2.1	1.5	2.5	4.1	6.9	5.2	2.3
Mining and quarrying	8.3	12.2	11.7	10.5	−0.9	−1.3	1.9	6.4	−0.7
Manufacturing	8.2	9.3	13.2	12.7	10.7	7.7	8.2	5.3	1.2
Electricity, gas, water supply and other utility services	2.8	5.7	4.0	7.6	10.3	5.1	7.4	6.1	7.0
Construction	6.2	1.6	6.0	6.0	3.1	4.3	3.4	−3.7	2.0
Trade, hotels transport and communications and services related to broadcasting	10.3	8.3	10.1	12.8	8.9	7.7	8.3	6.5	11.1
Financial, real estate and professional services	10.1	13.0	10.5	9.0	9.4	7.0	3.3	2.2	6.4
Public administration, defence and other services	6.2	7.2	7.5	6.7	8.6	9.5	10.3	17.0	9.5
GVA at basic prices	7.6	8.2	7.3	8.7	7.6	6.8	6.7	5.6	5.6
GDP	7.6	8.0	7.2	9.1	7.9	7.5	7.0	6.1	5.7

Source: CSO.

'On the one hand, there are these intellectuals who talk about Harvard, and on the other, there is this son of a poor mother, who is trying to change the economy of the country through hard work.' The current vice-chairman of the NITI Ayog, Rajiv Kumar, went to the extent of asking Manmohan Singh and Amartya Sen to 'publicly recant and apologise' for their forecasts. The effort, clearly, was to drive home the point that it was the just the elite who thought that demonetisation was a bad idea; the poor were with him in believing that demonetisation would eliminate black money, cleanse the economy, and raise growth. The elite versus poor contrast, and the Q3 results, were underlined by the BJP during the election campaigns in Uttar Pradesh and Uttarakhand, in which it won with remarkable margins in March 2017.

The euphoria of Q3 was, however, short-lived. As Ashok K. Lahiri's article in this volume, published in *EPW* in December 2016, argued, almost half of Q3 had already passed by the time the cash shortage had set in and the fuller impacts of demonetisation were likely to be reflected in official figures only in Q4. That was exactly what happened. CSO data for Q4 released in May 2017 showed that growth rates of gross value added had fallen sharply from 6.7 per cent in Q3 to 5.6 per cent in Q4 (*see* Table 1.2). The GDP growth rates fell from 7.0 per cent in Q3 to 6.1 per cent in Q4. Growth rates in manufacturing fell from 8.2 per cent in Q3 to 5.3 per cent in Q4. The construction sector shrank in absolute terms between Q3 and Q4: from 3.4 per cent to –3.7 per cent. Sectors like trade, financial services and real estate also witnessed a decline of growth rates between the two quarters.

The decline of manufacturing growth rates in Q4 broadly endorsed an explanation offered by many for the resilient Y-O-Y growth rates of IIP and industrial production in November 2016 (*see* Table 1.2). According to Vyas (2017b), the impact of demonetisation was not felt over industrial production in November 2016 due to many reasons. First, SBNs continued to be accepted in railways, petrol pumps, electricity payments and government payments in November, which led to growth in petroleum consumption and railway freight. Second, while retail sales and consumption of consumer goods may fall immediately after an economic shock like demonetisation, production was likely to follow only with a lag. For instance, even as automobile sales fell in November, automobile production had increased. He argued:

> The fall in consumption initially leads to inventory pile-up, then cancellation of orders and then a cut in production lines. Individual companies

are loathe to cut back production and risk loss of market shares or report fall in sales unless it becomes necessary to do so. There are also legal, operational and logistics reasons that would slow down the process of a production cut. (Vyas 2017b)

But the real shock for the government was to arrive in August 2017, when the CSO released the growth estimates for Q1 of 2017–18. In a clear indication that the adverse impacts of demonetisation would persist, the growth rate of GDP fell from 6.1 per cent in the Q4 of 2016–17 to 5.7 per cent in the Q1 of 2017–18. For a second consecutive quarter, the growth rate of gross value added stayed below 6 per cent: at 5.6 per cent. With Q1 figures out, India had also lost the tag of the fastest growing large economy in the world to China for a second consecutive quarter. The government's claims had finally been put to rest. It was now officially revealed that demonetisation had a sharp deflationary impact on the Indian economy. The figures of GDP growth for Q2 of 2017–18 were not expected to be encouraging, particularly because of another shock that the Modi government had inflicted on the economy from July 2017: the implementation of the goods and services tax (GST).

What is also important is to note that the official growth figures for GVA and GDP released by the CSO are actually overestimates. Though official figures showed that GVA and GDP growth rates were resilient in the Q3 of 2016–17, a sharp deflationary trend had set in during Q3 itself. If the official figures for Q3 did not show a decline of growth rates, it was because of the shortcomings in the CSO's methodology of computing GVA.

From 2015 onwards, the CSO has been releasing data on GDP based on a new methodology (with base year 2011–12).[42] As per the earlier methodology (with base year 2004–05), the CSO used to release estimates for GDP at factor cost. The GDP at factor cost included all payments for the factors of production (rent, wages, interest, profits, dividends and other costs). A major change in the method of estimation after 2015 was the introduction of the concept of GVA at basic prices. The GVA at basic prices was taken as the indicator of economic activity from the supply side. It was arrived at by adding the net indirect production taxes (i.e., indirect taxes—subsidies on production) to the earlier concept of GDP at factor cost. From the supply side indicator of GVA at basic prices, the GDP

---

[42] Government of India. (2015). *Economic Survey 2014–15*. Ministry of Finance. Retrieved March 31, 2017, from http://bit.ly/2gzL4XE

at market prices, the indicator of economic activity from the demand side, was arrived at by adding to it the net indirect product taxes (i.e., indirect taxes—subsidies on products). The growth in GDP at market prices was regarded as the headline indicator of economic growth.[43]

There are two important problems with the existing methodology of estimating the GVA. First, data from the unorganised sector are either unavailable or available only with major lags. Such data are collected only once in 3–4 years and are largely extrapolated for the period in between based on a few assumptions. In fact, even data from the organised sector are available only with a lag. Second, quarterly estimates for the unorganised sector are regularly extracted from quarterly estimates for the organised sector. In other words, quarterly data on GVA do not capture short-term trends in the unorganised sector at all. Soon after the release of Q3 estimates, India's chief statistician TCA Anant was to admit that the CSO's estimation was based mainly on information collected prior to 8 November 2016.[44] The RBI report on demonetisation, which incidentally argued that effects of demonetisation were 'transient,' was also to admit the serious limits of the CSO's methodology:

> Hard data on the unorganised sector are collected only infrequently and then used for fixing the base period benchmark by the CSO (i.e., 2011–12 for the new GVA/GDP series). For subsequent years, estimates are extrapolated from the base year benchmarks *using suitable proxy indicators from the organised sector or by applying past trends.* Following the standard 'labour input (LI)' methodology, the number of workers (from the 68th round of Employment and Unemployment Survey, NSSO) and the value added per worker (from the 67th round of Enterprises Survey of NSSO) in the industry are used for fixing the base year estimates. For example, for estimating the unorganised manufacturing GVA, labour input (LI) and GVA per effective worker (GVAPEW) *are fixed for the base year 2011–12,* and *subsequent quarterly/annual estimates are generated by applying the* IIP *growth,* until data from the Annual Survey of Industries (ASI) become available…. (RBI 2017: 7–8; emphasis added)

[43] Further, in the earlier method, data from the Annual Survey of Industries (ASI) for about 2 lakh factories, was used to estimate figures for the industrial sector. In the new methodology, data from the annual company accounts (enterprise-level), filed with the ministry of corporate affairs (MCA), was used to estimate figures for the industrial sector.

[44] Sharma, Shantanu Nandan. (2017, January 8). Not Enough Data to Figure Put Demonetisation Impact on GDP: T.C.A. Anant, Chief Statistician. *The Economic Times.* Retrieved March 31, 2017, from http://bit.ly/2eAGJTI

Even the quarterly data on the IIP, as R. Nagaraj argues in his chapter in this volume, are partial. As IIP data are based on data for relatively large factories, it may not provide reliable estimates for smaller and quasi-corporate enterprises not registered under the Companies Act. As a result, according to Nagaraj, 'the methodology underlying the estimation of quarterly data is seriously flawed and may not pick up the underlying reality of production and consumption.'

There were other discrepancies too. For example, as the article by Ritika Mankar and Sumit Shekhar in this volume shows, there was a major divergence between nominal GDP growth and bank credit in the Q3 of 2016–17, and the gap between the two was actually at its all-time high during this quarter. Mankar and Shekhar also employ a simple monetarist assumption that nominal GDP would equal 'currency in circulation' multiplied by 'velocity of money,' and argue that the velocity of money should have risen four times after demonetisation to catch up with the growth in nominal GDP. Ashok K. Nag's chapter in this volume also uses a monetarist framework to construct different scenarios of decline in GDP growth given different levels of fall in the velocity of money after demonetisation.

Prabhat Patnaik, in his invited contribution to this volume, makes another key conceptual point. According to him, an economic indicator like the GDP at market prices is incapable of capturing the conditions of distress of working people. This would be true even if there were no shifts of factor shares from wages to profits and even if the economy was demand-constrained. Using a simple Kaleckian model with two sectors—investment goods and consumption goods—Patnaik shows how demonetisation may cause a fall of output, GVA and worker's consumption, but may lead to a rise in advance tax payments (as people get rid of SBNs), which, if not spent immediately, can still lead to a rise of the GDP at market prices. His argument is that the GDP at market prices is 'simply the wrong thing to look at' if we are interested in understanding the conditions of working people.[45]

---

[45] One State that commissioned a study of the impact of demonetisation was Kerala (*see* GoK, 2017 and Mohan, in this volume). The report argued that Kerala's economy was likely to be acutely affected by demonetisation due to (a) high levels of cash dependence in transactions in the economy; (b) the presence of a large informal or unorganized sector, especially in traditional industries like coir, cashew, handloom and fisheries; (c) the predominant presence of a cooperative structure; (d) importance of tourism in driving the state's economic growth; and (e) the role that remittances played in sustaining household incomes.

Agriculture and the Rural Economy

The initial stance of the government on the impact of demonetisation in agriculture was in the dismissive. According to the union minister for agriculture Radhamohan Singh, '75 per cent [of rural] people have not been affected by [demonetisation]. In a village economy, 80 per cent of the people take Rs 50 and Rs 100 notes to local mandis and do trading, with hardly 2–3 people using the bigger currency notes of Rs 500 or Rs 1,000.'[46] Singh was clearly out of tune with the realities of rural India, which was thrown into a deep crisis after demonetisation. Available information suggests that multiple spheres were affected: agricultural production and prices; agricultural incomes; rural demand; and rural credit.

Agricultural Production

India's agriculture has hardly grown after 2011. If we consider the GVA in agriculture, annual growth rates over the previous year were 1.5 per cent in 2012–13, 4.2 per cent in 2013–14, –0.2 per cent in 2014–15 and 0.7 per cent in 2015–16. That is, except over 2013–14, the GVA in agriculture did not grow at more than 1.5 per cent a year. But 2016–17 was to be different. According to a pre-demonetisation analysis by CRISIL, Indian agriculture was projected to grow at 4 per cent in 2016–17 over 2015–16; it also expected 'the favourable monsoon to revive rural incomes' (CRISIL 2016). In 2016, the rainfall received was higher than in previous years. If 46–49 per cent of the 629 districts in India (for which data was available) received less than normal rainfall in 2014 and 2015, the corresponding share in 2016 had declined to 33 per cent. Consequently, much hope was placed on agricultural growth rates in 2016–17.

An expected impact of demonetisation was on crop production in the rabi season of 2016–17. The ministry of agriculture has claimed that sowing in the rabi season was not just unaffected, but also represented a rise over the previous year.[47] According to the ministry, 315.55 lakh hectares (ha) of rabi wheat was sown till 27 January 2017, which was higher than

[46] Sally, Madhvi, & Watts, Himangshu. (2016, November 20). Demonetisation Is Not Affecting 70% of rural India: Radha Mohan Singh. *The Economic Times.* Retrieved March 31, 2017, from http://bit.ly/2w1h6RZ

[47] Government of India. (2017, January 27). Rabi Crops Sowing Crosess 637 Lakh Hactare [Press release]. Press Information Bureau, Ministry of Agriculture. Retrieved March 31, 2017, from http://bit.ly/2gABu6W

the 292.52 lakh ha sown till end–January 2016. CSO estimates show that GVA in agriculture grew at 4.9 per cent in 2016–17 as compared to 0.7 per cent in 2015–16. However, these figures give no room for satisfaction. First, the area sown with rabi wheat in 2016–17, as claimed, was indeed higher than the normal. Nevertheless, given the previous record of the government in data collection, there are reasons to doubt the veracity of these estimates. Official data on progress in sowing are largely 'eye estimates' provided by the states and not based on actual field surveys.[48] Basing policy on such data have, often in the past, resulted in blunders. For instance, in 2015–16, the government had projected wheat production at 94.04 million tonnes (MT). However, more recent assessments put the actual production for 2015–16 at less than 85 MT. Given the difference between the expected and the actual production, the government ended up with just enough wheat for its buffer stock, and additional wheat had to be imported at higher prices to ensure stocks for open market sales. In other words, only a final estimate of the actual rabi wheat production for 2016–17 would show the nature of impact that demonetisation had on rabi sowing.

Second, even if rabi sowing was on track, it was at a cost to the peasantry. The cash crunch limited the ability of farmers to purchase seeds and other inputs on time and at reasonable prices. Farmers largely purchase seeds and fertilisers from private traders and cooperatives, and not government outlets. To sow wheat in one acre, a farmer would require approximately Rs 2,500 to buy seeds, about Rs 700 to buy fertilisers and about Rs 1,000 to meet labour costs: a total of about Rs 4,200 per acre. Thus, a five-acre wheat farmer would require at least Rs 20,000 to complete sowing, which was extremely difficult to mobilise given the limits on cash withdrawal after 8 November 2016. Reports suggest that traditional village networks between farmers and traders were revived to meet the emergency and most transactions were running on credit. Farmers also borrowed from money-lenders at high interest rates to pay for inputs. Surely, costs of sowing had risen (see P. Sainath's chapter in this volume).

Agricultural Incomes

Demonetisation disrupted agricultural supply chains and hit at even the meagre incomes agricultural households earned. November was the

---

[48] Bera, Sayantan. (2017, January 30). How Reliable Are India's Agriculture Statistics? *Mint.* Retrieved March 31, 2017, from http://bit.ly/2xKKRsp

month when kharif harvests arrived in the mandis. But cash shortages prevented the smooth sale of harvest. In some regions, traders did not pick up farmers' harvests from fields and yards. In other regions, farmers were forced to sell at a lower-than-market price to traders or sell in exchange of older notes of Rs 500 and Rs 1,000. Those producing perishable commodities—fruits and vegetables—and who did not have access to storage facilities were among the worst affected by the decline of prices. According to RBI (2017a), on a month-on-month basis, vegetable prices declined by 6.2 per cent in November 2016, 11.7 per cent in December 2016 and 4.7 per cent in January 2017. The decline in prices was recorded for a wide range of vegetable products: potato, onion, tomato, cabbage, cauliflower, leafy vegetables, brinjal, gourd, beans and beans. The RBI's own assessment of demonetisation noted:

> As the transactions in fruits and vegetables have always been cash-intensive, following demonetisation, as cash ran dry, there was some compression in demand for fruits and vegetables. Anecdotal evidence also pointed to some distress sales by farmers, given the perishable nature of green vegetables and fruits. On the whole, demonetisation-induced supply chain disruptions, which could have pushed up prices, seemed to have been more than counteracted by demand compression and distress sales of vegetables. (RBI 2017a: 13)[49]

A striking indicator of supply-chain disruption was the sharp decline of arrivals in agricultural markets in November 2016. Researchers showed that in the first week after demonetisation, market arrivals in select major states fell by 87 per cent for soybean, 55 per cent for paddy, 61 per cent for guar, 51 per cent for maize, 38 per cent for tur and 23 per cent for cotton.[50] If we take the second week after demonetisation, the fall in arrivals over the week preceding demonetisation was to the extent of 61 per cent for paddy, 77 per cent for soybean and 29 per cent for maize.

The decline of agricultural prices and incomes after demonetisation was a proximate rallying factor in the spate of farmer's protests that

[49] As Kohli and Ramakumar note in this volume, demonetisation achieved a decline of inflation by squeezing the consumption budgets of the middle class and the poor.

[50] Aggrawal, Nidi, & Narayanan, Sudha. (2016, November 25). Demonetisation Alone Can't Turn Agricultural Markets Cashless. *The Wire*. Retrieved March 31, 2017, from http://bit.ly/2eFm5Fu

swept the Indian countryside in the months of May and June of 2017.[51] Maharashtra, Madhya Pradesh, Haryana, Rajasthan and Punjab were the states that witnessed intense protests. Faced with a serious crunch of incomes and profitability, farmers blocked highways and cut off food supplies to the cities; they demanded a waiver of outstanding farm loans as well as the fixation of minimum support prices at 150 per cent of the cost of production. Among them, the governments of Maharashtra and Rajasthan were forced to announce loan waiver packages in July and September 2017. Punjab, Uttar Pradesh and Tamil Nadu also announced loan waiver packages of varying sizes in 2017.

Rural Demand

About 68 per cent of India's population lives in rural areas; 54 per cent of the total consumption expenditure comes from rural households; about 35–40 per cent of the GDP comes from the rural areas; and about a third of the total savings comes from rural areas. Though agriculture contributes only about 15 per cent to India's GDP, there continues to be a fairly high correlation between GVA in agriculture and total value added in the economy.

As higher rural incomes would lead to higher consumer spending, the CRISIL report of October 2016 was optimistic. It projected that 'the upturn in rural incomes should push private consumption [growth rate] above 8 per cent in fiscal 2017, compared with 7.4 per cent in fiscal 2016.' Higher rural income growth was expected to lead to higher rural sales of television sets, electric fans, motorcycles, tractors and multi-purpose vans. For most of these goods, there was 'de-growth' in 2014–15 and 2015–16. However, for 2016–17, the report pointed to 'green shoots,' and projected that 'the recovery [of rural demand] is likely to gain strength in the coming months.'

As most of the rural wholesale channels were cash-based, demonetisation shrank rural demand.[52] According to an assessment by AC Nielsen, the Indian rural market was down by 60 per cent over November and

[51] Damodaran, Harish. (2017, June 12). The Crops of Wrath. *The Indian Express*. Retrieved June 30, 2017, from http://bit.ly/2gACTKz

[52] The worst assessment was from Ambit Capital, which projected the possibility of negative GDP growth in the third quarter of 2016–17 and an overall agricultural growth rate in 2016-17 of just 0.8 per cent (*see* http://bit. ly/2gGFiar).

December 2016.[53] According to another report, 'rural demand was the worst affected at the height of the liquidity crunch in November 2016,' and continued to be a concern even in March 2017 in large parts of northern and eastern India.[54] According to an analyst, 'rural demand was the worst hit; so, we will see an impact on rural demand-based companies like Dabur and Colgate;' the reason: 'not all villages have ATMs and not all ATMs have cash.'

Rural Credit

Cash crunch in rural areas turned more acute due to the near-shutting out of the cooperative bank network from the purview of cash exchange. In rural India, cooperatives accounted for about 15 per cent of the total debt outstanding of agricultural households in 2012–13. In states like Kerala and Maharashtra, cooperatives accounted for more than 40 per cent of total debt outstanding of agricultural households.

Yet, after 14 November 2016, primary cooperative societies were not allowed to either exchange SBNs for new notes, or provide fresh crop loans with new notes, or even accept repayments of outstanding debt in SBNs. The primary societies were also not allowed to exchange their existing stock of Rs 500 and Rs 1,000 notes, collected between 10–14 November 2016, with either the RBI or the banks. As a result, most cooperative institutions became totally dysfunctional through November and December of 2016. In the absence of cooperative credit, moneylenders emerged as new sources of finance for many rural households.

In sum, first, the government created a major credibility crisis for the century-old cooperative banking network. There were reports that customers were eager to withdraw deposits from cooperative banks triggering fears of a run on these banks in many areas.

Second, with the shutdown of the cooperative credit network, rural households were forced to turn to commercial banks to exchange their SBNs. But commercial banks did not have the spread of branch network like the cooperatives. As on 31 December 2015, there were about 5.55

[53] Malviya, Sagar, & Tyagi, Neha. (2017, February 6). Here's Why Indian Consumer-Goods Companies' Revival May Take Time. *ET Brand Equity.* Retrieved March 31, 2017, from http://bit.ly/2eFKn2f

[54] Gupta, Soumya, & Agarwal, Sapna (2017, March 6). Consumer Goods Firms on Recovery Path after Demonetisation Downturn. *Mint.* Retrieved March 31, 2017, from http://bit.ly/2vGhBWx

lakh unbanked centres—defined as centres without a brick and-mortar bank branch—in India. Of these, about 5.54 lakh unbanked centres were in the rural areas. The total population that resided in the unbanked centres in rural areas amounted to 62.9 crore. In other words, about 81 per cent of the rural population did not have access to a bank branch within their centres.

The response of the RBI was to allow business correspondents (BCs) of banks to undertake exchange of SBNs in rural areas. On 14 November 2016, the government also raised the cash holding limit of BCs to Rs 50,000 per day to allow for the smooth exchange of SBNs.[55] However, the BC model proved totally incapable in dealing with the huge pressure of cash demand in the villages. As adequate numbers of new notes were not printed, most BCs never obtained the increased cash holdings from banks. Even when they did, assuming a withdrawal limit of Rs 4,000 per person, one BC could serve only about 12 persons a day. Consequently, rural households were largely left in the lurch, forced to depend on traders and informal money-changers at a discount.

Banking

Commercial Banks

An immediate fallout of demonetisation was that banks were flush with liquidity worth lakhs of crores. The cumulative amount of SBNs deposited with the banks after 8 November 2016 amounted to Rs 5.44 lakh crore by 18 November, Rs 8.45 lakh crore by 27 November and Rs 12.44 lakh crore by 10 December. At the same time, only Rs 4.61 lakh crore had been supplied back to the depositors till 10 December. Such a situation created a crisis of sorts for the banks. To begin with, banks were already reeling under the stress of rising non-performing assets (NPAs); between March 2016 and September 2016, the gross NPA of the banking system, as a percentage of total advances, had risen from 7.8 per cent to 9.1 per cent.[56, 57] The growth rate of credit flow

---

[55] Reserve Bank of India. (2016, November 8). RBI Instructions to Banks [Notification]. Retrieved March 31, 2017, from http://bit.ly/2eYiQ93

[56] Care Ratings. (2016, December 30). *NPA Analysis and Conjectures for Q3 and Q4*. Retrieved March 31, 2017, from http://bit.ly/2ezUUbo

[57] This was primarily owing to a rise in NPAs on loans to industry from 11.9 per cent to 15.8 per cent between March and September 2016.

from the banking system had also declined sharply between 2014 and 2016 due to a severe lack of aggregate demand in the economy. The outcome: banks, already burdened with NPAs, were able to neither get rid of the higher deposits by giving out more loans, nor shoulder the costs of interest payments on the new deposits that were continuing to flow in.

In the normal course, when banks are flush with liquidity, they park the surplus funds with the RBI for which they receive a fixed interest rate, which is called the reverse repo rate. Using this *fixed* reverse repo rate window, then at 5.75 per cent, banks began to deposit Rs 30,000 crore to Rs 50,000 crore per day with the RBI from 11 November 2016.[58] However, the RBI was not ready to accept such large deposits of surplus funds from the banks at fixed reverse repo rates, as it would have significantly drained its profits. As a result, the RBI shifted to a *variable* reverse repo rate window, where the rates were not fixed but determined through auctions. At the variable rates, banks began to deposit Rs 60,000 crore to Rs 150,000 crore per day with the RBI. Given that deposit rates were about 3–4 per cent, banks were only too happy to use the reverse repo window and earn a spread on deposits of about 2–3 per cent.

Realising that the reverse repo window would be a drain on its profits, the RBI took a second step that flummoxed many. On 26 November 2016, it announced that all banks should maintain an incremental cash reserve ratio (CRR) of 100 per cent on the increase in the net demand and time liabilities between 16 September 2016 and 11 November 2016.[59] Though it was notified as a temporary measure, the decision brought worry to the banks. Deposits under CRR did not earn any interest, and the banks would be making losses if they earned zero interest on investments but paid 3–4 per cent on deposits.

A more stable solution to the liquidity glut was designed only in December 2016. On 2 December 2016, the RBI recommended to the government that the ceiling for the issue of securities under the market stabilisation scheme (MSS) be revised from Rs 30,000 crore to Rs 6 lakh

[58] Merwin, Radhika (2016, November 25). Flush with Deposits, Banks Lend to RBI under Reverse Repo, Invest in G-Secs. *The Hindu Business Line*. Retrieved March 31, 2017, from http://bit.ly/2eXyFNh

[59] Reserve Bank of India. (2016, November 26). Reserve Bank of India Act, 1934 – Section 42(1A) Requirement for maintaining additional CRR [Notification]. Retrieved March 31, 2017, from http://bit.ly/2xKXiEH

crore.[60] Consequently, on 7 December, the requirement of incremental CRR of 100 per cent was withdrawn.[61]

The MSS was a scheme first initiated in February 2004, when the then government was faced with a situation of a surge in foreign capital inflows.[62] When foreign capital surged in beyond expectations, the government was forced to purchase larger amounts of foreign exchange to ensure that the rupee did not appreciate. As a result, rupee liquidity in the system increased. At this point, the RBI could sell treasury bills and dated securities to mop up—or 'sterilise'—the excess liquidity. However, the intensive use of bills and securities would increase borrowings under the consolidated fund of India (CFI), and raise the fiscal deficit. So, another method had to be found to mop up the excess liquidity without raising the fiscal deficit. The MSS performed that role. Bills and securities under the MSS were to have all the attributes of the normal bills and securities except one. When the MSS bills and securities were issued, the government ensured that an equivalent cash balance was held in the public account (instead of the CFI) with the RBI, which was not used for any expenditure of the government. As these cash balances were kept outside the CFI, they did not lead to a rise in the fiscal deficit. The only cost item that the government bore, and which contributed to a rise in the fiscal deficit, was the interest payments on the MSS bills and securities.

The use of MSS securities to sterilise liquidity after demonetisation, then, posed a major cost to the exchequer. The government had to reimburse the RBI the interest rate paid on MSS securities that the banks purchased. Kohli and Ramakumar, in their article in this volume, had estimated that if Rs 12.44 lakh crore was assumed to be mopped up under the MSS at 6 per cent annual interest, the total interest outgo of the government would be at least Rs 6,000 crore. The actual costs, as revealed by the RBI's Annual Report of 2016–17, were about the same.

---

[60] Reserve Bank of India. (2016, December 2). Market Stabilisation Scheme (MSS)—Revision of Ceiling for 2016–17 [Press release]. Retrieved March 31, 2017, from http://bit.ly/2x6Gef9

[61] Reserve Bank of India. (2016, December 7). Reserve Bank of India Act, 1934 – Section 42(1A) Withdrawal of the Incremental CRR [Notification]. Retrieved March 31, 2017, from http://bit.ly/2eYgZRR

[62] Reserve Bank of India. (2004, February 23). Launching of Market Stabilisation Scheme [Press release]. Retrieved March 31, 2017, from http://bit.ly/2xLkwKW

After November 2016, the RBI mopped up Rs 10.2 lakh crore by issuing cash management bills (CMB) under MSS for tenors ranging from 14 to 63 days. The total interest outgo on these CMBs was Rs 5,700 crore (see RBI 2017b). An additional amount of Rs 1 lakh crore was mopped up by issuing T-bills under MSS for tenors ranging from 312 to 329 days. The interest outgo on these T-bills are yet unknown. In other words, the government incurred at least Rs 5,700 crore as interest costs under the MSS scheme, which was in addition to the interest outgo over the reverse repo window.

Regardless of these costs, the government went on to claim that the flush of liquidity with banks would lead to a fall of interest rates.[63] Modi was also to claim that because the 'excess of [black] cash' in the economy was sucked into banks as deposits by demonetisation, inflation rates also fell.

Kohli and Ramakumar offer a critique of both these claims. First, the fact that more than Rs 12 lakh crore of SBNs were deposited with banks till 10 December 2016 was no reason for interest rates to fall. This was because these deposits could be withdrawn by depositors, almost fully, as soon as enough currency was available with the banks. The excess of liquidity was, thus, just a transient phenomenon and any fall in interest rates was also to be transient.

Second, it is often wrongly presumed that interest rates are determined in the market once banks have fixed the amount of credit to be lent. Kohli and Ramakumar argue that, in reality, 'the quantity of bank credit is demand-determined whereas its price is cost-determined.' In other words, if commercial banks are short of liquidity, they can always enlarge their liquidity levels by borrowing from the RBI through the repo rate window. This window exhausts itself only when the RBI is exhausted of its full stock of securities. The repo rate then becomes the minimum interest rate that the banks charge their borrowers. In sum, if the RBI wants to reduce interest rates, they simply have to reduce the repo rates and there is no justification for a step like demonetisation even if banks were facing a liquidity crunch (which is not true, because banks were facing no liquidity crunch prior to demonetisation).

Finally, the relationship that Modi was attempting to establish between demonetisation and inflation was nothing but spurious.

---

[63] Anon. (2016, May 18). Demonetisation Will Redefine New Normal for Indian Economy: Arun Jaitley. *The Economic Times*. Retrieved March 31, 2017, from http://bit.ly/2x7c7EB

Inflation had declined from 4.2 per cent in October 2016 to 3.6 per cent in November 2016, 3.4 per cent in December 2016 and 3.2 per cent in January 2017.[64] Modi's argument was that the stock of black cash in the economy was feeding into inflation, and because this cash was transformed into bank deposits after demonetisation, inflation had declined. Such a diagnosis was faulty. Inflation may result from either a cost escalation or an excessive rise in demand. This excess demand may originate either from cash or from deposits. Conversion of cash into deposits does not, in any way, deprive economic agents of their capability to demand goods and services.

What had actually happened after demonetisation was that banks had literally confiscated cash from working people in the form of SBN deposits, and did not exchange them for new notes. As a result, within a cash-intensive economic system, working people were deprived of their capability to demand goods and services. Shrinkage of demand also resulted from loss of jobs for workers and fall of prices for farmers. Furthermore, as remonetisation progressed, inflation had begun to rise again from February 2017. In other words, the fall of inflation after October 2016 was primarily because demonetisation squeezed the purchasing power of the working people and not because black cash was transformed into bank deposits.

Cooperative Banks

Cooperative banks across India were completely sidelined during the implementation of demonetisation. In this section, I shall discuss the case of Kerala, which has the best functioning and most widespread cooperative credit network in the country, as illustrative of the crisis in cooperative banking that demonetisation engendered (*see* GoK 2017 and Mohan, in this volume for details).

In 2016, Kerala had more than 1,600 primary agricultural credit societies (PACs), and such a network matched, if not overtook, the branch network of commercial banks. About 62 per cent of Kerala's population was registered as members of PACs, while in India the corresponding share was just 10 per cent. About 70 per cent of the deposits in all PACs in India was in Kerala. About 60 per cent of all deposits in Kerala were in cooperatives, while in India just 20 per cent of all deposits were in

[64] Ferreira, Joana. (2017, August 14). India Inflation Rate. *Trading Economics*. Retrieved August 15, 2017, from http://bit.ly/2eA2jHT

cooperatives. For every 100 credit accounts in the banks, the number of borrowers in the PACs was 35 in India, but 184 in Kerala.

The All India Debt and Investment Survey (AIDIS), conducted by the National Sample Survey Office (NSSO), provides data on the share of debt outstanding of rural households from different sources. In India as a whole in 2012, 56 per cent of the total debt outstanding of rural households came from the formal sector. In Kerala, the corresponding share was 78 per cent. If moneylenders supplied 33.2 per cent of the debt outstanding of rural households in India, they supplied only 14.1 per cent in Kerala. These achievements of Kerala were, without doubt, owing to its widespread cooperative credit network. Cooperatives accounted for 47.4 per cent of the debt outstanding of rural households in Kerala, while in India they accounted for only 24.8 per cent. Such a phenomenal presence of the cooperative network helped Kerala weaken usurer's capital in its early stages of development itself (Ramakumar 2005). Cooperatives were, thus, a critical component of Kerala's history of 'public action' and social transformation in the second half of the 20th century.

Despite such a glorious history, Kerala's cooperatives were disallowed to participate in the exchange of SBNs after 14 November 2016. They were also not allowed to exchange with the RBI the SBNs that they had legally accepted from the public between 10–14 November 2016. The PACs were disallowed to accept SBNs based on the argument that they were non-banking entities under the Banking Regulation Act of 1949. But even the district central cooperative banks (DCCBs) were disallowed to accept SBNs even though they were licensed under the 1949 Act and had KYC (know your customer)-compliant deposits. Only urban cooperative banks were allowed to accept SBNs. More intriguingly, each PACs in the state—which had an average outstanding deposit base of Rs 19.9 crore per branch—was treated as an individual and a bizarre withdrawal limit of Rs 24,000 per week was applied to them. Such gross discrimination against the cooperatives brought economic activities in Kerala to a standstill and even fed into fears of a crisis in cooperative banking and a run on the banks.

Leaders of the BJP in the state, however, were on the aggressive. Given that most cooperatives in Kerala were under the control of the Left and Congress, the state BJP led a major misinformation campaign against cooperatives. They argued that Kerala's cooperatives were storehouses of black money. One BJP leader asked: 'What will happen if the cooperatives of Kerala perish? Nothing will happen.' Little did he appear to realise, given the short-run political gains in sight, that any weakening of the cooperative network would reopen the state's rural credit market to traders and money-lenders.

III: Demonetisation and Counterfeit Currency

… have you ever thought about how these terrorists get their money? Enemies from across the border run their operations using fake currency notes. This has been going on for years. Many times, those using fake five hundred and thousand rupee notes have been caught and many such notes have been seized. (Narendra Modi, in PMO, 2016)

Modi's speech on 8 November 2016 was a classic invocation of an external threat to justify a domestic financial emergency. Across the world, it has been a time-tested method within right-wing political groups to manufacture external enemies and then ideologically externalise antagonisms in their attempts to unify and mobilise societies. In the context of the BJP and the Rashtriya Swayamsevak Sangh (RSS) in India, the phrase 'enemies from across the border' has always had a built-in communal angle too. The resulting war-like scenario provided these groups with justifications for a series of fascist actions: violation of civil liberties; clampdown on freedoms; and surveillance of groups. Even the mildest of dissents or scepticisms are dismissed away as 'anti-national.'

Immediately after 8 November, right-wing commentators flooded the media with the argument that Islamic terror, funded by Pakistan, was badly hit by demonetisation. Demonetisation was an 'existential war of India's future' to ensure that 'Pakistan was checkmated,' said the website of a Hindutva group.[65] According to GD Bakshi, a former army general and a panelist on television, Pakistan's strategy was equivalent to an 'economic Pearl Harbour.' Detailed stories appeared in the media on how Dawood Ibrahim, a criminal on the Interpol wanted list, was a ring-leader in the printing and distribution of Indian counterfeit notes in Pakistan. A retired police chief from Uttar Pradesh said that 'by demonetising big currency notes, all anti-India forces lose.'[66] Even

[65] Anon. (2016, November 28). Demonetisation: Detailed Drama of How Modi Checkmated Pakistan's Devastating Assault. *Internet Hindu*. Retrieved March 31, 2017, from http://bit.ly/2wD6b2M

[66] Sawant, Gaurav C. (2016, November 9). Black Money Surgical Strike Destroys Pakistan's Fake Currency Network. *India Today*. Retrieved March 31, 2017, from http://bit.ly/2eYqH6B

a short respite in the stone-throwing protests in Jammu and Kashmir was attributed to the 'daring' step of demonetisation by none other than defence minister Manohar Parrikar.[67] But the BJP's political ally and the chief minister of Jammu and Kashmir, Mehbooba Mufti, dismissed Parrikar's claim on the floor of the state's legislative assembly. In January 2017, she stated that 'no case has been received about fake currency being used for generating violence during the unrest,' and that her 'government has not received any report so far on effects of demonetisation on the recent unrest in the [Kashmir] Valley.'[68] But Parrikar's much-publicised claim had a major impact on public opinion, however baseless or irresponsible it might have been.

Truth was indeed a casualty in the overflow of fear and jingoism after 8 November 2016. As Kohli and Ramakumar argue in this volume, while the flow of FICN from other countries was a reality, there was no accurate measure of its quantum so as to justify a drastic measure like demonetisation. Data on FICN are available from two sources: (i) from the banks, when notes are intercepted over the counter, published in the RBI annual reports; and (ii) from the police and the security forces, when they seize notes, published in the reports of the National Crime Records Bureau (NCRB). Data put together by Kohli and Ramakumar show that the share of FICN detected by banks was only 0.000016 per cent of all the Rs 500 notes and only 0.00002 per cent of all the Rs 1,000 notes in 2015–16. Similarly, the share of FICN intercepted by the police was 0.0019 per cent of all Rs 500 notes and 0.0028 per cent of all Rs 1,000 notes.

India's National Investigation Agency (NIA) has an in-house terror funding and fake currency cell.[69] In 2014, this cell decided to contact the Indian Statistical Institute (ISI) in Kolkata for a study on FICN. The decision had the backing of the Economic Intelligence Council, an apex body on financial crimes. Within ISI, statisticians at the Statistical Quality Control & Operations Research (SQCOR) Unit were in charge

[67] Anthony, Hepzi (2016, November 15). Stone Throwing in Kashmir Stopped. *The Hindu*. Retrieved March 31, 2017, from http://bit.ly/2vHjJgD

[68] Anon. (2017, January 17). No Impact of Demonetisation on Stone Pelting in the Valley, Says Mehbooba Mufti. *HuffPost*. Retrieved March 31, 2017, from http://bit.ly/2gBayEg

[69] Anon. (2014, August 17). NIA, Indian Statistical Institute to Conduct Study on Fake Currency Notes. Press Trust of India. Retrieved March 31, 2017, from http://bit.ly/2gHBkOQ

of the study. An article that summarises the methodology and results from the ISI study—authored by Amitava Bandyopadhyay, Ranjan Sett and Dipak K. Manna—is published in this volume. They identified a few problems with the data on FICN: some banks did not regularly report FICN to the RBI and non-banking financial companies (NBFCs) were not under the ambit of FICN detection and reportage. While acknowledging such drawbacks in the quality of data, the group developed a method of estimation using data between 2010–11 and 2014–15. This method of estimation was validated using data from April–September 2015. The authors were convinced through validation that 'the method developed is sufficiently robust and may be implemented in general.'

According to Bandyopadhyay, Sett and Manna, the value of FICN in circulation in India was Rs 414.94 crore in 2014–15. Every year, attempts were made to infuse Rs 70 crore worth FICN into India. They thus argue that 'both the value of FICN in circulation and that being infused are minuscule compared to the size of the Indian economy'. Their original study had further argued that 'the existing systems of seizure and detection are enough to flush out the quantum of FICN being infused'. First, about one-third of the Rs 70 crore being infused every year was being seized. Second, the overall occurrence of FICN was estimated to be about 235 notes per million in 2014–15, while the corresponding figure for United States (US) and Canada was about 200 notes per million. 'So', according to Bandyopadhyay *et al*, the Indian numbers were 'not probably that bad'.[70] Third, the detection rate for FICN of denomination Rs 1,000 was about 80 per cent in 2014–15. The study estimated that if the detection rate could be raised from 80 per cent to 90 per cent, the amount of FICN could be reduced by 50 per cent over 3–5 years. The study concluded:

> Implementation of the recommendations may require development of [a] system for financial institutions and may require providing hardware for detection of counterfeit currency notes. However, once these steps are taken, the value of FICN in circulation is expected to reduce by at least 20 per cent per year ... An improvement of detection [of Rs 1,000 notes] coupled with improvement of seizure from 1/3rd to may be about 40 per cent and extending the detection net to other financial institutions would lead to a minimum improvement of 20 per cent.

[70] Abrams, Corinne. (2016, May 20). Are Your Indian Rupees Real? *The Wall Street Journal*. Retrieved March 31, 2017, from http://on.wsj.com/2gDXCgB

Clearly, the quantum of FICN in circulation in India did not provide any logic for the implementation of demonetisation. The problem of FICN could be addressed more effectively by strengthening the existing measures of detection and seizure.

Data on the extent of counterfeit notes seized by banks after demonetisation, as revealed by the *Annual Report* of the RBI for 2016–17, was a vindication of the findings of the ISI study. The total value of counterfeit notes of denomination Rs 500 and Rs 1,000 detected by banks rose from 27.4 crore in 2015–16 to just Rs 40.8 crore in 2016–17. As a share of the value of Rs 500 and Rs 1,000 notes in circulation in November 2016, the value of counterfeit notes detected in 2016–17 amounted to just 0.0027 per cent.

As demonetisation unfolded after 8 November 2016, the quality of the new series of notes of denomination Rs 2,000 and Rs 500 came into question. Many notes in the new series were poorly printed:[71] some had a shadow of Mahatma Gandhi's face in addition to the photograph; others had uneven borders; and some still were of varying colour, shades and size. In many places, farmers were duped by criminals by being paid in fake Rs 2,000 notes, which were just high-resolution photocopies of the original note.[72]

But a more serious problem related to FICN was at the exchange counters of banks. Due to the rush at the counters and the need to speed up work, many bank staff were not adequately checking for FICN when they exchanged SBNs.[73,74] As a result, many FICN may have

---

[71] Parmar, Beena. (2016, November 25). After Complaints of Printing Variations, RBI Says Rs 500, Rs 2000 Notes Legal. *Hindustan Times*. Retrieved March 31, 2017, from http://bit.ly/2vZMNLI

[72] Girish, M.B. (2016, November 13). Conman Dupes Karnataka Farmer With 'Photocopied' Rs 2000 Note. *Deccan Chronicle*. Retrieved September 5, 2017, from http://bit.ly/2eWnLqY

[73] Pramod Kumar, G. (2016, November 21). Why Does It Matter If PM's Demonetisation Address Was Recorded. *HuffPost*. Retrieved September 5, 2017, from http://bit.ly/2xJB2uM

[74] *HuffPost* reported: 'Since 8 November, banks have been literally invaded by irate people and in their hurry to mitigate the pressure, the staff could have made mistakes. The riotous situation that the bank counters experienced so far is not normal, but extraordinary and possibly it conduces the bad note creeping back in' (see Pramod Kumar, G. (2016, November 21). Why Does It Matter If PM's Demonetisation Address Was Recorded. *HuffPost*. Retrieved September 5, 2017, from http://bit.ly/2xJB2uM).

found their way into the banking system as valid claims. The RBI has not published data on the FICN detected at the bank counters after 8 November 2016. But, ironically, a scheme that was introduced to fight FICN may have actually ended up rendering at least a part of these notes legal.

IV: The Great Black Money Chase

> Which honest citizen would not be pained by reports of crores worth of currency notes stashed under the beds of government officers? Or by reports of cash found in gunny bags? (Narendra Modi, in PMO 2016a)

A crucial failure of demonetisation in India was the absence of conceptual clarity on what constituted 'unaccounted money.' This absence of conceptual clarity meant that the search for 'black money,' as the government called it, ended up being a wild goose chase.

For countries across the world, tracking 'unaccounted money' has been a major hassle over the years. The idea of 'unaccounted money' is also called by different names in different contexts, though, wrongly so, often interchangeably too: black money, black income, black wealth, dirty money, parallel economy, shadow economy, underground economy, or unofficial economy (GoI 2012a). There is neither a uniform understanding of the definition of unaccounted money nor a consensus understanding of its size relative to the economy. The case is most complex in developing economies like India, which are marked by large informal and unorganised sectors in both the rural and urban areas as well as poor banking penetration. In such economies, a significant proportion of economic activities escape the attention of the tax authorities and the government; neither are taxes paid nor are they adequately accounted for in the estimation of national income.

The nature of the economy that allows a large number of economic activities to go unaccounted is primarily a structural feature. Only deep-going structural transformations can help reduce the extent of unaccounted activities. As such transformations were largely bypassed in many developing countries including India, unaccounted activities have become entrenched within the traditional structures of these economies. In many commentaries, all such unaccounted activities are bundled together as 'black.' However, what is unknown is not necessarily illegal; a good proportion of economic activities that are unaccounted for may be perfectly legal.

So, to begin with, some clarity on terminologies may be in order. The chapter by Kohli and Ramakumar deals with this question. Specifically, in the context of demonetisation, they call for a distinction between 'black economy', 'black money' and 'black cash'. According to them:

> The term 'black economy' may simply refer to a broad set of economic activities that generate production and income flows that are under-reported or unreported or result from economic illegality. A portion of incomes generated in the black economy, when saved, adds to the stock of black wealth or, what we may call, 'black money' ... A part of the black money is held as 'black cash'.

The need for such conceptual clarity across terms was always reiterated in the articles on 'unaccounted income' and 'unaccounted money' that appeared in the *Economic Weekly (EW)* and the *EPW* in the 1960s and 1970s. Interestingly, these discussions were also in the context of the demands for demonetisation (implemented finally in 1978) raised by different groups in the 1960s. An article in November 1964, titled 'Unaccounted Income or Money?' referred to finance minister TT Krishnamachari's assurance to the Rajya Sabha that 'the government had no intention of demonetising the currency to unearth unaccounted money.' The article went on to point to a conflation in the minister's statement between 'unaccounted money' and 'unaccounted income:'

> There is a distinction between what is described as *unaccounted* money and *unaccounted* income. The former is only a part of unaccounted income, which is held in the form of currency at any point of time, while unaccounted income itself is a wider category and refers to the flow of income generated over a period of time, which has evaded fiscal levies. What evades the authorities is income, only a part of which is held in currency ... The currency hauls yielded by raids do not give even a measure of undetected incomes.

Another article in the *EW* published in May 1965, titled 'Black Money Stays Black' criticised the 'failed' voluntary disclosure scheme of Krishnamachari. It called the scheme 'amateurish in its conception' and reiterated and elaborated on the view stated in the 1964 article:

> Unaccounted income is not generally held in liquid form. It has a circulation of its own and it continuously changes form. The volume of black money (in cash form) is likely to be small. On the other hand, the

amount of evaded income must be many times larger. But this income is likely to have been put to various uses.

In May 1967, a short report titled 'Demonetisation and 'Black' Money' was published in the *EPW* on the 'vague reports of a possible demonetisation.' This report argued that as '1,000-rupee notes are no longer used as a store of value,' any effective demonetisation would have to include notes of denomination Rs 100 also. The report argued:

> Only a small proportion of hidden wealth at any point of time is likely to be held in the form of currency notes. Currency is the medium for continuously financing illegal transactions and converting illegal income into various assets such as real estate or gold ...

The arguments were clear. First, unaccounted income is not a *stock* like unaccounted money; it is a *flow* over a period of time. Consider an amount of money that may have been generated either illegally, or generated legally but hidden from tax authorities. This money may be invested in a perfectly legal enterprise. The wages paid in these enterprises are *illegal at the source, but legal at the point of use*. For the worker who receives these wages, it is legal income and he/she may file returns on the income as well as pay taxes. Conversely, an amount of income generated legally, and even accounted for, may be invested in an enterprise that is illegal, or is legal but whose proceeds are hidden from the tax authorities. Here, the money is *legal at the source, but illegal at the point of use*. Such investments are commonplace in many economies, and reveal the extreme difficulties in conceptually distinguishing between accounted and unaccounted money, as well as estimating their respective sizes.

Second, only a small part of the unaccounted income is held as unaccounted money, or currency. The rest enters the process of circulation in the economy. Karl Marx wrote in *Capital* about the difference between 'idle money' and 'capital' in capitalist economies. Idle money is the money of the idle, where cash is just stored without being invested. But capitalists are not idle; they try to multiply profits by investing money in productive activities. *Money* is thus transformed into *capital*. As soon as money enters the process of circulation, it also loses its identity of being 'unaccounted' or 'black.' The *EW* article published in 1964 had referred to the 'various uses' to which the unaccounted money may have been employed by the evaders; it said, 'Wild speculations in urban property, the smuggling of gold and other smuggleables, the scramble for ownership of flats and the foreign exchange leaks are all of one piece in this context.'

In 1984, the Central Board of Direct Taxes (CBDT) commissioned the National Institute of Public Finance and Policy (NIPFP) a study on India's black economy (NIPFP 1985). The NIPFP report arrived at a number of tentative conclusions based on interviews and informal discussions. First, about half to two-thirds of 'black income' earned was spent on the consumption of goods and services. In other words, this part of black income earned had become a part of the flow of money circulation in the economy. Second, the significant forms in which black income was held were (a) undervalued commercial real estate; (b) undervalued residential real estate; (c) undervalued stocks in business; (d) gold, silver and other precious metals; (e) benami financial investment; (f) undisclosed holdings of foreign assets; and (g) diamonds and other gems. Cash was a very significant form of holding black income for only 7 per cent of the respondents. Further, professionals and salary earners were more represented than businessmen among those who held black income as cash because businessmen had access to alternatives like stocks and investments to hold black income. The report noted:

> … less than 7 per cent of the respondents considered cash to be a 'very significant' form for holding black wealth; indeed, two-thirds of respondents put it in the category 'minor.' This is consonant with both our interview information and common sense. Unlike all the other asset forms, cash yields no return. Furthermore, large quantities of cash are vulnerable to detection in the raids by tax authorities, whereas in the case of most of the other assets, problems of establishing ownership and of valuation serve as effective lines of defence. (NIPFP 1985: 302)

Media analysis of data from tax raids by the income tax department from 2012–13 onwards show that only 6 per cent of the undisclosed income was kept in the form of cash by tax evaders.[75] Between 1 April 2016 and 31 October 2016, out of a total of Rs 7,700 crore of assets seized from black money holders, only Rs 408 crore (or 5 per cent) was in the form of cash. It has also been argued that the share of cash in the total store of black money might be even lower than the above-cited

[75] Suresh, Appu Esthose. (2017, February 16). Why Govt's Demonetisation Move May Fail to Win the War against Black Money. *Hindustan Times*. Retrieved March 31, 2017, from http://bit.ly/2eIJeqF

shares, as the income tax department classifies currency and ornaments as one single unit.

The upshot is that measures like demonetisation would affect only a small section of persons who hold black incomes. This conclusion was as true for the 1960s and 1970s as it was for 2016.

Demonetisation, 1978 and 2016

Regardless of the available evidence that black money is not a stock but a flow, and that it is rarely held as cash, the RSS, BJP and its political predecessors like the Bharatiya Jana Sangh have historically held a contrarian view. According to them, the long-standing problems of corruption and nepotism in India can be traced to the pollution that black money has engendered in the economy. The scourge of black money in India, accordingly, represented a crisis of morality in the social and public sphere, which necessitated 'cleansing.' For instance, the Jana Sangh's economic resolution at its Ujjain session of 1974 stated that the Indian economy was 'diseased' with 'incurable cancer' due to the problems of 'privileges, licences, black money, and quotas.' The document went on to argue that 'currency should be demonetised to unearth present hordes of black money.'

The Jana Sangh's call for demonetisation followed a recommendation to this effect by the Direct Taxes Enquiry Committee, headed by Justice KN Wanchoo, in 1971. An article titled 'Is the Government Serious?', published in the *EPW* in 1972, had offered a strong criticism of this suggestion in the Wanchoo report. It had argued that as most black income is not held in cash and as black marketers think ahead of honest citizens, demonetisation 'would cause more inconvenience and earn more unpopularity than revenue for the government.'

Yet, an attempt at demonetisation was made in 1978 a year after the Janata Party headed by Morarji Desai came to power. The Jana Sangh was an ally of the Janata Party in the government. On 16 January 1978, the Desai government demonetised notes of denomination Rs 1,000, Rs 5,000 and Rs 10,000 as per the High Denomination Bank Notes (Demonetisation) Ordinance, 1978. The objectives of demonetisation in 1978 were somewhat similar to the demonetisation in 2016 (though there were differences too). For example, the ordinance stated in its preamble:

> The availability of high-denomination bank notes facilitates the illicit transfer of money for financing transactions which are harmful to the

national economy or which are for illegal purposes and it is therefore necessary in the public interest to demonetise high-denomination notes. (RBI 2005: 451)

According to a report in the *Times of India* on 17 January 1978, demonetistion was expected to 'hit black money hard:'

A press note issued tonight said that the ordinance had been promulgated because there was reason to think that high-denomination notes were facilitating the illegal transfer of money for financing transactions which are harmful to the national economy or which are for illegal purposes. There has been concern in recent months over the behaviour of agricultural prices particularly of edible oils. In spite of a bumper harvest, agricultural prices are ruling much higher than after the poor harvest of 1976–77. Massive imports of edible oil have failed to bring down prices and the mustard oil price control order has failed miserably to give the consumer his requirements at the specified rate. There has been a feeling that a considerable amount of black money has gone to finance hoarding and speculation. The demonetisation of high-denomination currency notes will hit black money hard.[76]

Secrecy was sought to be ensured in the announcement. According to the official history of the RBI, the governor IG Patel was not in favour of demonetisation (RBI 2005). Yet, R Janakiraman, a senior official of the RBI, was telephoned on 14 January 1978 to reach Delhi from Mumbai for an 'urgent work' related to 'exchange control.' Janakiraman asked another official M Subramanian to accompany him. Once in Delhi, they were confidentially told of the decision of the government to demonetise high-denomination notes. The mandate given to the two RBI officials— who were denied communication with their Mumbai office—was the drafting of the ordinance 'within twenty-four hours.' The ordinance they drafted was sent for the signature of the President in the morning of 16 January 1978 and the news was announced on All India Radio in their 9 am bulletin.

As in 2016, all banks and government treasuries remained closed the following day, 17 January. People were given three days to surrender the demonetised notes for exchange. At the exchange counter, people

[76] Shankaran, Sanjiv. (2016, November 15). Demonetization in 1946 and 1978: Stories from the Past. *The Times of India*. Retrieved March 31, 2017, from http://bit.ly/2eIbxpi

were also asked to fill up an application form, which included questions pertaining to the source of the notes and the reasons for storing them. People thronged banks from 18 January. The RBI's official history notes:

> Long-winding queues started forming in front of the Reserve Bank office right from the morning as also at the main office of the State Bank of India, to collect declaration forms. According to press reports on 18 January 1978, the day started with utter confusion over the issue of declaration forms at the Reserve Bank headquarters at Bombay and the working hours stretched to 6.30 pm. Enterprising city printers are said to have made quick money selling forms in sets of three for Rs 3. As expected, there were frayed tempers and a considerable hue and cry from the public as well as foreign tourists, especially those who did not have, or did not care to preserve, documentary proof to support the exchange of notes. (RBI 2005: 453)

If the above quote was left undated, it would fit as well for 10 November 2016.

As two articles in the *EPW* published after the demonetisation—titled 'Demonetisation: Limited Objective' (January 1978) and 'Demonetisation: The Ones That Got Away' (March 1978)—pointed out, the success or failure of demonetisation should be judged by the amount of currency that did not return to the banking system. On 16 January 1978, the total currency in circulation as notes of Rs 1,000, Rs 5,000 and Rs 10,000 was Rs 145 crore. The total amount that was returned to the banking system was Rs 125 crore, leaving only Rs 20 crore as not exchanged (*see* Rajakumar and Shetty, in this volume).

According to the NIPFP report, there were three reasons why demonetisation of 1978 was ineffective as a tool to address black income generation (NIPFP 1985). First, cash was not an important form in which black income was held. Second, even when black income was held as cash, the holders found multiple means to convert the notes into lower denominations through intermediaries at a discount. The *Times of India*'s Jay Dubashi had reported that old notes were exchanged with new notes at a discount rate of 70 per cent in Mumbai's Zaveri Bazar.[77,] Shyamaprasanna Bhattacharyya, a CPI(M) MP from West Bengal, spoke in Parliament on how black marketeers in Calcutta 'took sufficient precautions to go to various areas and asked the panwallas and other poor

---

[77] Dubashi, Jay. (1978, February 15). Demonetization: No-Value Notes. *India Today*. Retrieved March 31, 2017, from http://bit.ly/2gDWFoH

persons to go to the banks and get [the notes] changed.'[78] Vayalar Ravi, a Congress MP from Kerala, spoke of how a few errant bank managers were helping in the launder; he said: 'In Calcutta and Bombay, many bank managers used to convert and change the high-denomination notes through backdoor methods.'[79] Third, demonetisation was a one-time measure or penalty, and did not address the underlying causes of black income generation. Once demonetisation was completed, everyone was on guard and more cautious, but incentives to generate black income continued to exist. Patel, in his memoirs, had a sharp assessment on the demonetisation of 1978:

> ... such an exercise seldom produces striking results. Most people who accept illegal gratification or are otherwise the recipients of black money do not keep their ill-gotten earnings in the form of currency for long. The idea that black money or wealth is held in the form of notes tucked away in suitcases or pillow cases is naïve. And in any case, even those who are caught napping—or waiting—will have the chance to convert the notes through paid agents as some provision has to be made to convert at par notes tendered in small amounts for which explanations cannot be reasonably sought. But the gesture had to be made, and produced much work and little gain. (Patel 2002: 159)

Thus, by all means, demonetisation of 1978 was a failure. A comparative analysis of the demonetisations of 1978 and 2016 by J. Dennis Rajakumar and SL Shetty is included in this volume. They note that alongside similarities, there were also three differences between the two demonetisations. First, the demonetisation of 1978 did not affect the daily lives of people as much as in 2016, as the demonetised notes represented only 0.6 per cent of the total currency in circulation. In contrast, 86 per cent of the currency was demonetised in 2016. Second, in 1978, 45 per cent of the high-denomination notes that were demonetised were not with the public, but with banks and government treasuries. However, in 2016, about 95 per cent of the high-denomination notes that were demonetised were with the public.

---

[78] Dam, Shubhankar. (2016, December 19). Demonetisation: If Only the Modi Government and the Indian Parliament Had Looked Back at 1978. *Quartz India*. Retrieved March 31, 2017, from http://bit.ly/2gEaqUy

[79] Dam, Shubhankar (2016, December 19). Demonetisation: If Only the Modi Government and the Indian Parliament Had Looked Back at 1978. Quartz India. Retrieved March 31, 2017, from http://bit.ly/2gEaqUy

Third, an objective of demonetisation notified in 2016, but absent as an objective in 1978, was the presence of FICN in circulation, which were used by terrorists.

Despite these differences, the lessons from the failure of demonetisation in 1978 should have remained good for 2016 too. But remarkably, in spite of the failure of demonetisation in 1978, ideologues of the RSS and BJP came forward and offered rationales for the demonetisation of 2016, which were nothing but rehashed versions of the Jana Sangh's economic resolution of 1974. According to one ideologue of the RSS, Rakesh Sharma, 'black money took off with the neoliberal turn to the Indian economy in 1991.'[80] Neoliberalism, the argument went, transformed the State into 'an executive of big business and capital', while the common people were faced with 'inequality and black money.' In such a context, demonetisation was intended to 'humanise the market and legalise hidden assets;' it would reverse 'surrendering the state's role in economics'; its 'ideological premise' was 'of minimising the gap between rich and poor;' and it would revive 'political morality and culture.'

On the one hand, Sharma's counter-posing of demonetisation against neoliberalism was a bit rich given that Modi rode to power in 2014 promising 'minimum government, maximum governance.' Though Sharma spoke of reviving the State's role in economic policy, he had conveniently forgotten Modi's note on his own website in 2014 where he argued that 'for decades, we have had extraordinarily large governments' and what was required was 'a small and less intrusive government'.[81] Modi had also declared: 'I believe government has no business to do business.'

But on the other hand, Sharma was also attempting to revive the RSS and Jana Sangh's spiritual thrust on the question of black money. In this framework, the problem of black money was a moral problem and could be resolved only by enforcing a new moral order.[82] The intent of demonetisation was *shudheekaran* (purification) to break free from

---

[80] Sinha, Rakesh. (2016, December 20). First Economic Satyagraha. *The Indian Express*. Retrieved March 31, 2017, from http://bit.ly/2x8prIX

[81] Narendra Modi (2016, May 14). Minimum Government, Maximum Governance. Retrieved March 31, 2017, from http://bit.ly/2x8tTqZ

[82] Jayaraman, T. (2016, December 18). Demonetisation: Hindutva's Obscurantism in the Economic Sphere. *Peoples Democracy*. Retrieved March 31, 2017, from http://bit.ly/2j2v7xw

'evils brought in over time,' as Modi argued in a speech on 31 December 2016.[83] Given the noble intent, any error in the very conceptualisation of the problem of black money was asked to be excused. In his speeches, Modi regularly invoked patriotism and nationalism to justify the pains people went through; just as Indians displayed patriotism in the wars of 1962 and 1965, demonetisation was an occasion where the government and the people 'fought shoulder to shoulder' against 'evils' and for 'a bright future.' It was a war, for the *sava sau karod deshwasi* for *'sachchai'* (truth) and *'achchai'* (goodness). The results of the Uttar Pradesh assembly elections of 2017, where the BJP scored a thumping win, were witness to the sheer power of the rhetoric of patriotism in camouflaging policy blunders.

The Size of the Black Economy

Estimation of the size of the black economy is, by nature, a difficult exercise. Nevertheless, a large number of researchers have attempted to estimate the size of India's black economy from different theoretical perspectives. In his article in this volume, originally published in 1983, Shankar Acharya reviews the different approaches followed to estimate the size of the black economy, all of which yield widely differing estimates. Interestingly, most of these approaches were represented in the papers published by the *EPW*, and are republished in this volume. Here, we focus on three major approaches: the fiscal approach, the monetary approach and the physical input approach.

The Fiscal Approach

Here, estimates are arrived at for the *total assessable income* and the *total assessed income*. The difference between the two represents the *total unaccounted income*. The estimates for the assessable income are often drawn from the national income accounts. Such a method was used in India for the first time by Nicholas Kaldor; he estimated that the loss of income tax due to evasion was between Rs 200 crore and Rs 300 crore in 1953–54. A similar method was also used by the Wanchoo Committee in 1972. For 1960–61, it estimated the assessable non-salary income at

[83] Biswas, Indroneil. (2016, December 31). PM Narendra Modi's Speech on Demonetisation on New Year's Eve: Highlights. *NDTV*.com. Retrieved March 31, 2017, from http://bit.ly/2gG3hTB

Rs 2,686 crore and the assessed non-salary income at Rs 1,875 crore. Thus, the income that evaded taxation was Rs 811 crore for 1960–61, which after adjusting for exemptions and deductions was estimated at Rs 700 crore for 1961–62, Rs 1,000 crore for 1965–66 and Rs 1,800 crore for 1968–69. O.P. Chopra, in his article published in 1982 and reprinted in this volume, used the Wanchoo methodology with some revisions to estimate unaccounted incomes for 1960–61 and 1976–77. Chopra's estimates for unaccounted income were Rs 916 crore (6.9 per cent of the GDP) in 1960–61 and Rs 8,000 crore (12.06 per cent of the GDP) in 1976–77.

Acharya's article discusses the limitations of the fiscal approach. First, national income accounts may not provide accurate estimates of the total assessable income. They may be underestimates, especially in trade, manufacturing, ownership of dwellings and other services where there is wide prevalence of tax evasion. Second, all salary incomes may not be reported for taxation, particularly when people undertake a secondary occupation to 'moonlight' their primary source of income. Third, studies using the fiscal approach, as Chopra's, assume a number of constant ratios in order to generate estimates across time: between evaded income and assessable income; between non-salary income and total income in a sector; and between non-salary income above the exemption limit and total income in a sector. Acharya argues that these assumptions are not supported by either evidence or argument.[84]

The Monetary Approach

To follow the monetary approach, one needs estimates of a base year and of another later year. At the base year, the unaccounted income is assumed to be insignificant. Estimates are then derived for the ratio between currency and demand deposits at the base year and the later year. As Peter Gutmann argued, the difference between these two ratios 'may be taken as a measure of the amount of currency held for illegal purposes' (Gutmann 1977: 27). Thus, one can obtain separate estimates for currency held legally and illegally. Using a conversion ratio between legally held currency and the official gross national product (GNP) estimates, and applying the same for illegally held currency, one can estimate the unaccounted GNP. The key here is in two assumptions: one, all money is used for transaction purposes and no money is held for

---

[84] For another recent study using the fiscal approach, see Kumar (2016).

speculative or precautionary purposes; two, whoever is holding currency more than at the base year is holding it for illegal purposes.

Thanks to the intriguing assumptions that Gutmann used, his methodology came in for severe criticism. J.C. Sandesara, in his article published in 1983 and carried in this volume, used the Gutmann method to estimate the share of unaccounted income in India. He found that the Gutmann method yielded negative estimates for black income in India for a prolonged period between 1953–54 and 1979–80. These were 'absurd' estimates and pointed to the 'irrelevance of the method in the Indian context,' Sandesara argued.

A variant of the Gutmann method was offered by Edgar Fiege. He followed an idea first offered by Irving Fisher according to which 'if one simply added all transactions paid for by cash and all transactions paid for by cheque, the resulting magnitude would represent a good measure of total macroeconomic activity (Fiege 1979: 7).[85] Following this basic tenet of monetarist economics, Fiege further assumed that the ratio of total transactions to total income would be stable over time in normal circumstances. Given that total transactions would include legal and illegal transactions, but total income or GDP includes only legal economic activity, any significant rise in the ratio of transactions to income must be due to illegal economic activity. In their paper published in 1982 and published in this volume, Poonam Gupta and Sanjeev Gupta tried to estimate the size of India's unofficial economy between 1967 and 1978. They argued that the total size of the black economy in India was 9.5 per cent of the GDP in 1967–68, which rose to 48.8 per cent in 1978–79.

The estimates of Gupta and Gupta were questioned by Sandesara (1982). According to Sandesara, if Gupta and Gupta's estimates were real, the Indian economy must have been booming in the 1970s and not in a period of 'stagnation' or 'retrogression' as usually argued. For him, their estimates of black economy were hugely overstated.[86] Acharya argued that the crucial issue with the Fiege method followed by Gupta and Gupta was the assumption of a constant ratio of transactions to

---

[85] According to the quantity theory of money, the total money supply multiplied by the velocity of money (the rate at which money changes hands) provides us with the total nominal expenditure in the economy (quantity of goods and services sold multiplied by price).

[86] Gupta and Gupta, of course, replied and argued that Sandesara's critique was not based on sound methodology and their estimates were not unrealistic.

income. Changes in this ratio may well be due to reasons other than growth of the black economy, such as advances in technology, increase in inter-industry transactions, expansion of vertically-integrated industries and the diversification of financial transactions. Acharya also took exception to the use of a constant figure for the turnover rate for a currency note used by Gupta and Gupta, which in turn was borrowed from studies on Canada.

Physical Input Approach

Here, one starts with an intermediate input widely used in the production process, such as electric power or transport, for which the data on total output and consumption are reliably available. Then, a relationship is worked out between the input and the output after allowing for temporal changes in technology and the output mix. The assumption is that there should be a stable relationship between input use and output. That part of the input use not represented in the output is considered as a measure of the unaccounted economy.

Sacchidananda Mukherjee and R. Kavita Rao, in their paper published in 2017 and carried in this volume, use the physical input approach using transport as a universal intermediate input. They first estimated the annual demand for road freight services from the national accounts statistics. Then, they estimated the annual supply of road freight transport using data on diesel sales, stock of goods carriages, average freight transport capacity per vehicle, average annual distance travel and average fuel efficiency per vehicle. The mismatch between the demand and supply estimates represented the unaccounted portion of the GDP. Their estimates of unaccounted income amounted to 29–35 per cent of the GDP for 2009–10 and 2011–12.

Summing Up

It is very difficult to assess the reliability of any estimate of the black economy referred to above. Due to the very nature of the problem at hand, any estimate of the black economy will have to be approached with extreme caution and scepticism. The nature and size of the informal sector in India, as opposed to the developed economies, makes these exercises even more complex. As Kohli and Ramakumar remark in this volume, 'we are not sure if there could be any realistic estimate of black money in India.' In any case, differences over the exact size of the black economy should not distract from efforts to address its prevalence and growth. Acharya's reasoned assessment is worth quoting in this context:

> ... an excessive preoccupation with the estimation of the size and trends of the unaccounted economy has its dangers. It can detract from serious exploration of its causal origins, its functioning characteristics, as well as the economic and social consequences of the phenomenon. True, such enquiries will be bedeviled by some of the doubts that plague the estimation efforts. But such doubts should not preclude the deduction of qualitative conclusions backed by piecemeal empirical evidence ... Put simply, the attempts to estimate the dimensions of the black economy should complement, and not substitute for, analyses of its causes, nature and consequences.

The Real Sources of Black Income

One of the most definitive statements on the question of black money in India was released in 2012. This statement was a report titled *Measures to Tackle Black Money in India and Abroad* authored by a team headed by the chairman, CBDT and submitted to the ministry of finance (GoI 2012a). Inputs from this report were incorporated and released as a white paper on black money by the ministry (*see* GoI 2012b).

The white paper began with a definition of black money: 'assets or resources that have neither been reported to the public authorities at the time of their generation nor disclosed at any point of time during their possession.' The CBDT report listed out three major sources of black money in India: crime, corruption and business. The realm of crime in the generation of black money included the proceeds from activities, such as 'racketeering, trafficking in counterfeit and contraband goods, forgery, securities fraud, embezzlement, sexual exploitation and prostitution, drug money, bank frauds and illegal trade in arms' (GoI 2012a: 5). Corruption generated black money through 'bribery and theft by those holding public office' (GoI 2012a: 5). Business contributed to black money through 'tax evasion.' Here, we shall discuss the second and third sources in some detail.

Corruption

Corruption, as a phenomenon, is deep-rooted in India. It begins from the lower levels of bureaucracy and government offices, where ordinary people are forced to pay bribes for getting licenses or access to public services that otherwise are their entitlement. At the higher levels, there are cases of corruption at larger scales, which may include bribes or commissions to grant different permissions/permits, register property, alter land use, regularise unauthorised constructions, save criminals from police cases, settle other corruption cases, circumvent obstructive clauses in the law, speed up action on a rather slow process of engagement, and so on.

The opportunities for corruption at public offices has, over the years, been enlarged by the neoliberal economic reforms (Chandrasekhar 2010).[87] Over the 1990s and 2000s, India was rocked by a number of corruption scandals, in most of which the collusion of politics and big business was evident. Many of these instances could be linked to the withdrawal of the State from economic activities and its marginalisation as a facilitator of private investment. In such a period of transition and change, contrary to beliefs that the scope for the State's arbitrariness declines, there was actually an enlargement of the scope for private accumulation through unfair means as well as an opening up of new arenas of private profits whose proceeds could be shared between big business and willing/acquiescing political parties. Cronyism has, thus, been an important by-product of neoliberalism in India, leading many to use the term 'crony capitalism' to denote the phenomenon of the corrupt relationship between the political leadership and a select set of business groups. As the CBDT report argued:

> With increased economic activity, bribes in public private partnership of large projects and large civil works have been detected. Allocation of natural resources is allegedly discretionary and non-transparent. Corruption has also been alleged in defence procurement, foreign consultancy, aircraft purchases, petroleum and gas sectors, purchases abroad, etc. It is reported that despite prohibition on kickbacks in the developed world, ways are found to make such payments through spurious agreements and shady entities, which in turn are alleged to be secreted away in bank accounts in tax havens. (GoI 2012a: 10)

Crony capitalism and other related forms of corruption also feed into the election process in India and have contributed to its decay. The article by Jagdeep S. Chhokar in this volume covers the relationship between black money and elections and describes the long struggle by the civil society—in particular, the Association for Democratic Reforms (ADR)—to

---

[87] For a contra view, see http://on.ft.com/2f2dGZO.

democratise the election process in India. Over the years, any meaningful attempt at contesting elections has come to require extraordinarily large funds. The limits of expenditure set by the Election Commission of India (ECI) are regularly fulfilled in the breach, and most of the funding over and above the limits is financed through black incomes.[88]

Chhokar also deals with more recent efforts by major political parties to sabotage efforts to increase transparency in elections. For instance, there have been attempts by the BJP and Congress to circumvent a provision in the Foreign Contribution (Regulation) Act (FCRA), 1976. The FCRA prohibits political parties from receiving foreign contributions. Yet, there were electoral trusts set up by three companies registered in the UK, which were regularly donating money to the BJP and Congress. An editorial of the EPW, dated 17 December 2016, named these as 'companies associated with the Vedanta/Sterlite/Sesa Goa mining and metals conglomerate headed by Anil Agarwal.' The defence of the BJP and Congress was that Agarwal was of Indian origin, and hence the contributions would not fall under the ambit of the FCRA. Chhokar's article details the legal battle waged by the ADR to contest the argument in the Delhi High Court. When the court found such donations violative of the FCRA, the Modi government stealthily attempted an amendment in the Finance Bill of 2016, according to which an 'Indian' company could also include a corporate firm with less than a specified share of foreign shareholding. This amendment, however, did not cut ice with the court, which ruled that the 2016 amendment could not be considered as having retrospective value. Yet, no penal action has been initiated by the ministry of home affairs against the two political parties.

Business

Business is the largest source of black income in India. The major means by which businesses generate black income is through tax evasion, which is evasion of tax/taxes to be paid on the net profit/income of firms. Evasion also happens when, for instance, firms understate the number of workers employed in order to not pay statutory obligations over social security.

---

[88] The value of assets owned and declared in the affidavits by the members of Parliament (MPs) and members of the legislative assemblies (MLA) have shown sharp increases over short periods: between 2009 and 2014, the value of assets of four MPs rose by more than 1,000 per cent, and of 22 MPs rose in the range of 500–999 per cent.

As tax is charged on the difference between expenditure and receipts, tax evasion is generally practiced through the understating of revenues and/or the overstating of expenditures.[89] To begin with, firms need to pay excise duties charged by the central government (except on items like alcohol, where states are in charge). Firms attempt evasion of excise duties through underreporting[90] (by declaring less than actual output or by overstating wastage), misclassification (by declaring higher than actual production of goods with less tax burden) and undervaluation (by declaring a lower than actual sale price or by declaring higher than actual post-manufacturing expenses or by falsely claiming losses in transit). Excise duties were also evaded by declaring higher production in 'ghost' units of the firm located in states that offer tax exemptions (with the introduction of GST, there are no area-based exemptions). A paper by Gopinath Pradhan and M. Govinda Rao, published in the *EPW* in 1985 and republished in this volume, discusses in great detail the nature of excise duty evasion in one industry: cotton textiles. They note two major methods of evasion: '(i) inter-sectoral misclassification of the output, and (ii) intra-sectoral misclassification, which also involves understatement of production and undervaluation.'

If excise and customs duties are charged by the central government, sales tax and value added tax (VAT) were charged by the states before the GST was introduced. The VAT was evaded through multiple means, such as claiming refunds using fake invoices, forming fictitious companies that sell receipts, claiming tax credits on items purchased for personal use, and over-reporting sales of zero-rated products. (As developed country experiences tell us, the GST does not in any way preclude evasion through the operation of an entirely parallel chain.)

The second method used in tax evasion is the inflation of expenditures or costs. Firms show higher costs by submitting bogus and inflated invoices obtained from 'bill masters' at a small commission. These bill

---

[89] Data released from the finance ministry show that between 2013 and 2016, the tax evasions detected amounted to Rs 13,952 crore in excise duties and Rs 11,405 crore in customs duties. Actual evasions may be expected to be in multiples of the amounts detected (*see* 'Tax Evasion: Rs 1.37 lakh cr Detected in Last 3 Years, Says Finance Ministry', *The Hindu Business Line*. Retrieved April 10, 2017).

[90] A widely reported case is of jewelers in India, who sell gold and silver without bills to customers at a discount.

masters are often impossible to track down because they leave the business and the city concerned at regular intervals.

Trade-based money laundering is also an important source of generation of black incomes. Customs duties, payable on imports and exports of goods, are widely evaded by misclassifying invoices, manipulating documents and suppressing the quantities of goods imported. Evasion of customs duties also happens when firms misuse the advance authorisation scheme, where 100 per cent duty-free imports of raw materials are allowed if they are to be used for export production. Paranjoy Guha Thakurta, Shinzani Jain and Advait Rao Palepu, in their article in this volume, deal with one alleged case of customs duty evasion in detail. They report on an investigation by the directorate of revenue intelligence (DRI) about how the Adani Group allegedly evaded taxes of up to Rs 1,000 crore and laundered money while trading in cut and polished diamonds and polished jewellery. The Adani Group allegedly misused export incentive schemes by trading through a complex web of front shell companies in different parts of the world and indulging in 'high-velocity circular trading.' The DRI's allegation, as the authors report, was that freight-on-board (FOB) prices of diamonds and gold jewellery were mis-declared to inflate exports and obtain undue benefits from the export-incentive schemes.

Tax havens, also called offshore financial centres, are also widely used by business groups to evade taxes. Globally, there are tax havens with no taxes at all, with low rates of taxation, and with tax systems that favour specific activities or entities. Typically, conduit companies are set up in these havens and multinational transactions between two high-tax jurisdictions are routed through these companies. As a result, a major share of the profits get reported in the tax haven and not in the origin or destination. In his article in this volume, Dev Kar estimates that a total of $213.2 billion was the illicit flow of wealth out of India in the 61 years between 1948 and 2008. These flows, in nominal terms, were also growing at a rate of 11.5 per cent per annum during this period.

With the growth of international trade, transfer-pricing has emerged as a preferred method of evasion within large multinational firms. Here, the attempt is to shift the taxable income from a jurisdiction/country of higher tax rates to another jurisdiction/country of lower tax rates. For this purpose, a company in a high-tax jurisdiction overstates the value of goods or services exported to its own affiliate in another low-tax jurisdiction using internal 'transfer prices,' and vice versa.

With the growth and liberalisation of the financial sector, participatory notes (P-Notes) are also used to evade tax. Typically, a P-Note is a derivative instrument issued to overseas investors by registered foreign institutional investors (FIIs) against underlying Indian securities. The FIIs would act as the investment managers of their clients, who would hold sub-accounts with the FIIs. Investments would be made by the FIIs on behalf of the clients. As a result, the clients need not register with the market regulator in India, i.e., the Securities and Exchange Board of India (SEBI) and their identity remains anonymous. Tax authorities have claimed that P-Notes offer a route for black incomes generated and stored abroad by Indians to legally return to India.

S.S.S. Kumar's article in this volume is a statistical analysis to understand the factors that guided the flow of P-Note investments into India over two time periods: 2006–07 and 2007–09. Kumar arrives at three important conclusions. First, Indian stock market indices were influenced by inflows of P-Note investment. Second, inflows of P-Note investment were not statistically related to either fundamental indicators like the price-earnings ratio (PER) or sentiment-related indicators like the put-call ratio (PCR). Third, the chief determinant of P-Note investment inflows into India was the rupee–dollar exchange rate. In other words, P-Notes were vehicles of speculative short-term financial flows into India in addition to being instruments to invest unaccounted money. In 2016, the SEBI tightened norms for P-Notes by bringing them under the ambit of KYC rules and anti-money laundering laws. However, P-Notes themselves have not been phased out yet.

Much public discussion in India about black incomes have been about deposits in banks in Switzerland. D. Ravi Kanth, in his article in this volume, addresses the relationship between tax havens and black incomes in India. Kanth contests the view that the bulk of black incomes from India are parked in Swiss banks. He argues that Switzerland is no longer a safe or trusted destination for black income holders, as the secrecy provisions in Swiss banks have been significantly whittled down. India has also entered into an agreement with Switzerland for automatic exchange of information on transactions and assets of Indian citizens (though after 2019). As a result, according to Kanth, black incomes from India have been increasingly moving into new financial centres like Dubai, Singapore, the British Virgin Islands and Luxembourg. In these centres, black incomes are not held as deposits but as funds managed through structured companies or trusts.

The Hindu Undivided Family (HUF) Act has for years been an important tool of tax evasion and a generator of black incomes within trading communities. The HUF is typically understood as a family, which lives jointly and belongs to the Hindu, Jain, Sikh or Buddhist religion.[91] The HUF, under the Income Tax Act of 1961, is like a firm headed by the head of the HUF or the *karta*. The *karta* has a dual role: one, as an individual who pays his/her personal income tax; and two, as the head of the HUF. The income tax laws in India allow a maximum tax deduction of only up to Rs 2,50,000 per year for an individual. However, as a *karta*, the same individual can both avail the deduction of Rs 2,50,000 as well as enjoy additional tax deductions and other tax exemptions on behalf of the HUF. Dividend incomes and long-term capital gains are exempted from tax for the HUF. Income from short-term capital gains are subjected to lower tax rates of 15 per cent for the HUF. Any gift received by the HUF from a member of the same HUF is exempted from tax. The HUF can obtain life insurance and health insurance for its members and claim tax deductions on the premiums paid. Tax deductions are allowed for the treatment of dependent members of the HUF with disability. Finally, tax deductions on the interest on self-occupied house property is also allowed for an HUF.

The role of HUFs in evading taxes and generating black incomes was a topic for I.S. Gulati's paper published in 1973 and carried in this volume. Gulati discusses the desirability of continuing with the HUF in the Income Tax Act. Gulati argues that while the K.N. Raj Committee in 1972 on the taxation of agricultural income and wealth had recommended the scrapping of HUF as a unit of assessment, the Wanchoo Committee had recommended higher rates of taxation on the HUF. However, no significant action was forthcoming from any government in this regard. Compared to 1973, the use of HUFs has, partly, given way to the use of charitable trusts, but the historical relevance of Gulati's argument remains intact.[92]

Land and real estate transactions form another major business-related source of black income generation. Manipulation of valuations in real

---

[91] Till 2005, when a woman married into an HUF, she became a part of that HUF and moved out of the HUF of her parents. However, after 2005, she was treated as a co-parcenor like a son.

[92] Gulati concluded that 'the withdrawal of recognition from the HUF for tax purposes ... would amount to terminating an important, and well-entrenched, privilege of the rich and wealthy—a privilege whose continuation cannot be justified on any score, sentimental, social or economic.'

estate units, which allow for evasions of stamp duty on the buyer side and recording of lower incomes on the seller side, is one method adopted to generate black income; such proceeds are laundered elsewhere soon after. For instance, the proceeds may be used to buy land in rural areas where the selling farmer may not be traceable post-transaction. High-net-worth individuals (HNWIs) also invest in residential property to sell them later on; these proceeds are shown as capital gains, which enjoys tax benefits. Gold—treated globally as a hard-to-tax good—too is a major site for tax evasion in business. On the one hand, as long as wealth tax existed in India, the stock of gold, bullion and jewellery was regularly understated. On the other hand, schemes for importing gold to design and re-export ornaments are also abused, and a large quantity of gold is diverted for domestic use. Land, gold and bullion are, thus, major sources of black income generation, and, due to their intrinsic high value, also strongly preferred as asset-forms in which black income is stored.

The Misplaced Focus on Cash

The foregoing discussion on the sources of black income and the modes of their storage show that the fight against black incomes is not equivalent to a fight against cash. The fight against black incomes is a serious and complex exercise that requires addressing crime through better policing, reducing corruption through clean governance, and tightening the tax administration to reduce evasion. Moreover, it has major international ramifications in a globalised financial regime. Thus, in addition to regulating speculative financial investments that are by-products of financial liberalisation, the government would also have to enter into bilateral and multinational negotiations to ensure that new avenues of laundering are regularly plugged. To put cash at the centre of all action against black incomes would not just be poor policy; it would also end up serving as a smokescreen to divert attention from the real problem at hand. The CBDT has been more than aware of this reality than anyone else. In its report to the government in 2012, it had suggested a strategy based on four pillars: preventing the generation of black money; discouraging the use of black money; effective detection of black money; and effective investigation and adjudication (GoI 2012a: 29). It said:

> There are two dimensions of the issue of black money—first, its generation and, second, its consumption and use, including laundering of

black money back to mainstream economy ... So far as generation of black money from crime or corruption is concerned, its remedy does not lie merely in legislative or enforcement domains but also in finding much deeper socio-economic solutions ... Further, consumption and laundering of black money, if effectively tracked and controlled, may have the 'squeeze effect' on the overall activities resulting in creation and sustenance of black economy. While there may not be any need to have new laws to especially deal with black money and black economy, various existing laws need to be comprehensively reviewed by the concerned administrative ministries on a regular basis keeping in view the changing economic scenario, and provisions dealing with violations need to be strengthened accordingly. (GoI 2012a: 29)

The CBDT report had also comprehensively rejected the use of demonetisation as an instrument to address the black money problem; it noted:

One common demand from the public is that high-denomination currency notes, particularly Rs 1,000 and Rs 500, should be demonetised. In this connection, it is observed that demonetisation may not be a solution for tackling black money or economy, which is largely held in the form of benami properties, bullion and jewellery, etc. Further, demonetisation will only increase the cost, as more currency notes may have to be printed for disbursing the same amount. It may also have an adverse impact on the banking system, mainly logistic issues, i.e., handling and cash transportation may become difficult and may also cause inconvenience to the general public as the disbursal or payments of wages/salaries to the workers will become difficult. Besides, it may also adversely impact the environment as more natural resources would be depleted for printing more currency notes. Demonetisation undertaken twice in the past (1946 and 1978) miserably failed, with less than 15 per cent of high currency notes being exchanged while more than 85 per cent of the currency notes never surfaced as the owners suspected penal action by the government agencies. (GoI 2012a: 14)

Black Cash Laundered

A question could still be asked: even if only 6 per cent of black incomes existed as cash, would not demonetisation be worth it? A part of the answer to this question may be had from the experience of demonetisation of 1978, when most black cash was easily laundered, or turned white. IG Patel's memoirs, parliamentary debates and press reports speak eloquently about the widespread nature of money laundering soon after 16 January 1978. Demonetisation of 2016 was no different. Multiple methods were used to launder whatever stock of cash existed with hoarders.

For instance, one report spoke about the 'old trick' of a Mumbai-Kolkata route in money laundering.[93] Due to the very nature of their business and cash turnover rates, a number of firms based in Mumbai were cash-rich, while a number of firms based in Kolkata were cash-deficit. Cash-deficit firms refer to those whose books of account show 'cash on hand,' but cash actually held is negligible. Cash-rich firms in Mumbai transferred cash to the Kolkata firms, who 'legally' deposited them in their bank accounts. In return, the Mumbai firms were provided cheques by the Kolkata firms, which were shown as loans in their books of account. After a few months, the Mumbai firms would provide the Kolkata firms with cheques repaying the 'loans' with a commission passed off as interest payments. At this stage, the Kolkata firms would, again 'legally,' withdraw cash from the banks in the form of the new Rs 2,000 notes and return them to the Mumbai firms. The cycle was thus completed.

Other reports spoke of how the Nagaland route of money laundering worked. As per the Indian constitution, residents of Nagaland and the Sixth Schedule areas of the Northeast are exempted from income tax; there is also no limit on the amount of money they could keep in their bank accounts. Businessmen from across India were routing black incomes to agents in the Northeast after demonetisation. According to one report, a businessman from Bihar had arranged a chartered flight from Hisar in Haryana to Dimapur in Nagaland with Rs 3.5 crore worth SBNs.[94] The agent was intercepted at the Dimapur airport and the cash was confiscated. However, soon after, a local businessman reached the airport, claimed the cash and walked away with all of it. The argument, in many such cases, was that a Nagaland resident had made a large advance payment to a Haryana resident for a farm land deal prior to

[93] Ghosh, Sugata. (2016, November 9). 'Cash on Hand' Firms Emerge as Laundering Vehicles to Sidestep Ban on 500/1000 Notes. *The Economic Times*. Retrieved March 31, 2017, from http://bit.ly/2f1Lt5d

[94] Srivastava, J.V. Shivendra (2016, November 24). Banned Notes Worth Rs 3.5 crore Flown from Hisar to Nagas in Dimapur to Make Them White. *India Today*. Retrieved March 31, 2017, from http://bit.ly/2eDXahQ

demonetisation.[95] As the land deal did not materialise, the cash was being returned to the Nagaland resident.

There were numerous other methods too. Friends, relatives and office staff were given SBNs and were asked to make deposits in their personal bank accounts—sometimes with a commission. Large amounts of gold were purchased with pre-dated bills.[96] The government had allowed the purchase of petrol and diesel, as well as air tickets, with the SBNs till 15 December 2016. Taking cue, fuel was purchased in bulk and stored. Refundable international tickets were purchased in advance to be cancelled later and encashed in new denomination notes. Moneylenders were reportedly giving interest-free loans to farmers and the poor to be encashed at a discount later. In many agricultural markets, traders insisted that if farmers needed cash payments, it could be made only in SBNs.

The government's own Jan Dhan bank account scheme was used in money laundering, though the allegation that the poor were used widely as money-mules was a gross overstatement. Between 9 November 2016 and 1 March 2017, 2.3 crore additional Jan Dhan accounts were opened across India (RBI 2017). As on 9 November, Jan Dhan accounts had a total deposit of Rs 45,640 crore, which rose to Rs 74,000 crore by end–November and then fell to Rs 64,290 crore as on 1 March 2017. In other words, between 9 November 2016 and 1 March 2017, the net addition to Jan Dhan accounts was Rs 18,650 crore. On a per account basis, considering only the 2.3 crore newly opened accounts, the additional deposits would average at a paltry amount of Rs 8,108. If we consider that additional deposits may have gone into all Jan Dhan accounts, old and new, the average deposit figure declines to just Rs 670. Further, it may be noted that between November 2016 and March 2017, the total withdrawal from Jan Dhan accounts was only about Rs 10,000 crore, which, over 27.8 crore bank accounts was nothing more than a trickle.

The Myth of 'Secrecy'

But apart from laundering *after* demonetisation, doubts have emerged if black cash was laundered *before* demonetisation itself. According to the

[95] Shekhar, Praveen. (2016, November 24). How Black Money hoarders Are Using Northeast to Outsmart the Government. *DailyO*. Retrieved March 31, 2017, from http://bit.ly/2xNJSYz

[96] Alok, Rohit. (2016, November 10). Demonetisation Effect: At Zaveri Bazaar, Civilians Rush to Convert Cash into Gold. *The Indian Express*. Retrieved March 31, 2017, from http://bit.ly/2vK8AvD

RBI, discussions with the government on demonetisation had begun in January 2016. Evidence shows that businessmen and currency dealers across India knew of the plan in great detail, expected the measure to be announced any time and took precautionary measures soon after January 2016. For instance, the monthly research brief of the SBI, *State Bank Ecowatch*, asked a question in the March 2016 issue: why was currency with the public surging on a year-to-year basis in January 2016 at a rapid rate 12.3 per cent? This was puzzling because, on the one hand, inflation was falling, credit card transactions were rising and the IIP was shrinking. On the other hand, there was a huge production surge in the gems and jewellery segment. The brief went on to offer a reason: 'As per unconfirmed available reports, higher currency denomination notes may be discontinued in the near future so as to tackle the menace of unaccounted money (SBI 2016a).'

In the April 2016 issue of *Ecowrap*, also from the SBI stable, the news of possible demonetisation was further explored. This issue rejected the view held by a few that currency with the public was growing because 2017 was an election year. In no earlier election year had currency with the public grown as in 2016. *Ecowrap* then went on to offer a reason:

> We believe election may be only a small reason, but the bigger reason could be the trend in demonetisation … The news of the demonetisation of currencies of denomination [Rs] 500 and [Rs] 1,000 has been doing the rounds for a while, and this may be a plausible reason for increase in currency with public. The rationale for this is that people are taking out cash and buying other assets such as gold so that when the currency is demonetised they do not face a problem … [P]eople may be using more of high value currency to purchase safe haven assets. (SBI 2016b)

It was shocking that an announcement, which according to the government was a top secret till the last minute, was so widely discussed in the public domain for at least eight months before November 2016.[97]

There was more. In an open letter to the Prime Minister, Yatin Oza, a former BJP legislator from Gujarat, alleged that big industrialists in Gujarat 'were intimated well in advance about demonetisation' and they

---

[97] Srinivas, Anuj. (2016, November 21). Were Rs 1000 Notes Moving Towards Safe Haven Assets in Early 2016? *The Wire*. Retrieved March 31, 2017, from http://bit.ly/2eDQW1F

had moved cash into safe assets before 8 November 2016.[98] A sitting BJP legislator from Kota in Rajasthan, Bhawani Singh, told reporters that industrialists like [Mukesh] Ambani and [Gautam] Adani were 'given hints of demonetisation' after which they had laundered old notes.[99] Regardless of the actual veracity of these statements, the view was widespread that, unlike the poor, the rich had got away rather easily from the aftermaths of demonetisation.

V: The 'War on Cash' in Context

The Indian story [of demonetisation] is a particularly recent and extreme example of the firepower behind the War on Cash.[100]

Globally, a 'war on cash' is being waged, as part of which, governments of many countries have been initiating proactive policies to phase out the use of physical cash, and promote alternative non-cash forms of payments. As an initial step, notes of higher denomination have been withdrawn in some countries (while, unlike in India, existing notes in circulation may be used freely in transactions). In fact, in 2016, Lawrence Summers had called for 'a global agreement to stop issuing high-denomination notes (Summers 2016).' Singapore stopped issuing its $10,000 bank note in 2014; the European Central Bank (ECB) has announced the discontinuation of printing the €500 banknote from 2018; there are calls in the US to not print new $100 notes; there are similar calls in UK to stop printing the GBP50 note; and in Australia, there were discussions in 2016 to stop printing the AUS$100 note.[101] Sweden has begun to remove ATMs from rural areas (its urban areas are largely cashless). South Korea has a plan to eliminate paper currency by 2020.

---

[98] Maanvi. (2016, November 21). Gujarati Bizmen Knew of Note Ban in Advance: Ex-BJP MLA Yatin Oza. *The Quint*. Retrieved March 31, 2017, from http://bit.ly/2w5tiRO

[99] Quazi, Aabshar H. (2016, November 17). Watch: Adani, Ambani Had Prior Info on Demonetisation, Says BJP MLA Rajawat. *Hindustan Times*. Retrieved March 31, 2017, from http://bit.ly/2vKVaQ5

[100] Desjardins, J. (2017, January 19). Governments Have Declared a War on Cash. *Business Insider*. Retrieved March 31, 2017, from http://read.bi/2w5CcPh

[101] Durden, Tyler. (2016, December 14). War on Cash Escalates: Australia Proposes Ban on $100 Bill; No Cash Within 10 Years? *Zero Hedge*. Retrieved March 31, 2017, from http://bit.ly/2eJaQfs

Rationales Cited for Abolishing Cash

The 'war on cash' has multiple rationales, as argued by its proponents. The first rationale is, as Summers (2016) argues, the so-called 'linkage between high-denomination notes and crime.' According to Kenneth Rogoff, 'paper currency has always facilitated tax evasion and crime' (2016: 114) and 'shifting away from cash will … help reduce crime-related expenditures' (2016: 58). For both Summers and Rogoff, the focus is on the elimination of high-denomination notes. At the same time, others like Willem Buiter, the chief economist with the Citigroup, argue for 'abolishing currency' (Buiter 2010). According to him, if a government 'does away with currency completely,' it has the 'benefit of inconveniencing the main users of currency—operators in the grey, black and outright criminal economies.' Governments, like in France, have begun to act on such suggestions. In the aftermath of the terrorist attacks on *Charlie Hebdo* and the Jewish supermarket in January 2015, France's finance minister Michel Sapin argued for the need to 'fight against the use of cash and anonymity in the French economy.' France has, since, prohibited cash payments of size more than €1,000 (the limit till then was €3,000) and set a new limit for currency conversion from euro to other currencies at €1,000 (the limit till then was €8,000). As a 2016 report of the European Union Commission states:

> Cash has the important feature of offering anonymity to transactions. But, such anonymity can also be misused for money laundering and terrorist financing purposes. The possibility to conduct large cash payments facilitates money laundering and terrorist financing activities because of the difficulty to control cash payment transactions.[102]

The second rationale is that a cashless economy improves the effectiveness of monetary policy via removing the 'zero lower bound' (ZLB) problem and pull economic growth rates out of the post–2008 recession levels. For Rogoff, this might be a major 'collateral benefit' of phasing out paper currency (2016: 115). The argument is as follows. The primary instrument of monetary policy to deal with inflation is the interest rate. Monetarist economists, as is well known, believe that money supply is the chief determinant of inflation, and income; as Milton Friedman

---

[102] European Commission. (2017, January 23). Proposal for an EU Initiative on Restrictions on Payments in Cash. Retrieved March 31, 2017, from http://bit.ly/2vKgDbP

said, 'inflation is always and everywhere a monetary phenomenon.' In countries where 'inflation targeting' (say, at 2 per cent) is a policy goal, monetarists advocate the use of high interest rates to control the amount of money in the economy and reduce inflation.[103] This reasoning was the basis of the sharp rise in interest rates in the US and UK during the Reagan-Thatcher years. The result, however, was a sharp fall in the economic growth rate. Even as inflation targeting remained a rigid goal, interest rates were reduced in the 1990s and 2000s, to levels close to zero, so as to raise economic growth rates. Thus, both interest rates and inflation rates hovered close to zero levels. Such a phenomenon was a crisis for monetarist theory itself; contrary to their predictions, the relationship between money supply and economic growth rate had broken down.

In the new situation, policymakers faced a new dilemma. If the primary instrument of monetary policy was the interest rate, to what extent can interest rates fall? Here arose a problem that John Maynard Keynes pointed to in 1936, called the 'liquidity trap.' Interest rates cannot fall below zero; if interest rates turn negative, savers will withdraw money from banks and shift to cash-based savings, which are immune from negative interest rates. As a result, at the ZLB, monetary policy becomes totally ineffective. As Keynes noted:

> There is the possibility ... that, after the rate of interest has fallen to a certain level, liquidity-preference may become virtually absolute in the sense that almost everyone prefers cash to holding a debt, which yields so low a rate of interest. In this event, the monetary authority would have lost effective control over the rate of interest. (Keynes: 1936).

After 2008, wherever central banks have begun to charge negative interest rates, banks, on their part, have tried to pass on these negative rates to big corporations, pension funds and insurance companies. These big entities, in turn, have been attempting to hoard cash worth billions of dollars, and, according to Rogoff, would intensify efforts to hoard more if the interest rate fell below −0.75 per cent. Thus, if monetary policy needs to be more effective, savers should be prevented from shifting to cash when interest rates fall beyond the ZLB. *The best way to achieve it might be to abolish cash itself, or at least reduce the extent of cash with the public to a bare minimum.* Two benefits from banning cash are

---

[103] Of course, assuming stable velocity of money.

cited. First, if cash is abolished, negative interest rates can be imposed when banks deposit excess cash with the central banks. As a result, banks will be forced to expand credit supply to borrowers, which will boost economic activity. In Sweden, Denmark, Switzerland and Japan, central banks have already begun to charge negative rates for holding excess bank funds.[104] Second, in the absence of cash, big entities like corporations, pension funds and insurance companies will be disincentivised from hoarding, forcing them to either save with banks (thus expanding bank liquidity) or move cash into investments (thus driving growth).

Last, individual/household savers, who might shift to cash if interest rates turn negative on retail/savings deposits (not a reality yet, but not to be ruled out in the future given that banks will pass on a part of their cost to depositors too), can be forced not to shift out of bank deposits. Even if they do, the cash is likely to be diverted to consumption spending. The intent of banning cash, thus, is also to move people from *saving* to *spending*; as borrowers have higher propensity to consume than savers, economic activity is expected to be boosted.

According to Buiter (2010), who was previously with the Bank of England, there are three ways in which the 'war on cash' can be played out. First, one may abolish currency completely. Instead of currency, 'adequate substitutes' may be identified for general use. Andrew Haldane of the Bank of England and economist Miles Kimball have argued that physical currency can actually be fully substituted by electronic cash; this will allow interest rates to become as negative as possible or necessary.[105,106] According to Haldane:

> One interesting solution, then, would be to maintain the principle of a government-backed currency, but have it issued in an electronic rather

---

[104] As Peter Praet of the European Central Bank (ECB) noted in a March 2017 speech: 'More than half of the new deposits held by corporations and close to 40 per cent of those held by households are de facto no longer remunerated. Slightly more than 40 per cent of the stock of corporate deposits and 35 per cent of household deposits have virtually zero return' (*see* http://bit.ly/2eEfRSK).

[105] Kimball, Miles. (2012, November 5). How Paper Currency Is Holding the US Recovery Back. *Quartz.* Retrieved March 31, 2017, from http://bit.ly/2wF6aNO

[106] Haldane, Andrew. (2015, September 18). How Low Can You Go? Speech Presented at Portadown Chamber of Commerce, Northern Ireland. Retrieved March 31, 2017, from http://bit.ly/2xNJNnA

than paper form. This would preserve the social convention of a State-issued unit of account and medium of exchange, albeit with currency now held in digital rather than physical wallets. But it would allow negative interest rates to be levied on currency easily and speedily, so relaxing the ZLB constraint.

Narayana Kocherlakota, a former president of the Federal Reserve Bank of Minneapolis, argues that abolition of cash may disappoint some savers, but the idea should nevertheless be pursued.[107] For him, every potential loss in social security that follows from negative interest rates should be compensated using the new entrant into social policy—direct cash transfers. He says:

> Some groups of people, particularly retirees and soon-to-be-retirees, might react with horror to such an idea. That is to be expected. After all, consumers in poorer countries respond similarly to removing distortionary price ceilings from bread and milk. That doesn't make price controls desirable. If a government wants to redistribute resources to the elderly or the poor, it's much better off just giving them money.

The second alternative suggested by Buiter is similar to an old idea suggested by Silvio Gessel in 1916: 'tax currency by making it subject to an expiration date.' Currency will have to be periodically stamped by central banks to keep them valid, and at that point a positive or negative interest is paid to the holder. The third alternative of Buiter is to end the fixed exchange rate between currency and bank reserves with the central bank. Here again, the holder of the currency would go to the central bank periodically to re-validate them, and at that point the currency would be bestowed a new value, higher or lower (depending on whether interest rates would be positive or negative).

As I shall try to argue below, both the proposed rationales for banning cash or reducing its use are flawed. One, will a ban on cash plug the sources of finance for terrorists, and also reduce crime rates? Two, can we just ban cash and ensure that negative interest rates become a reality? Three, will negative interest rates serve their intended purpose of raising economic growth rates? There is no affirmative answer to any of these questions.

[107] Kocherlakota, Narayana. (2016, September 1). Want a Free Market? Abolish Cash. *Bloomberg*. Retrieved March 31, 2017, from https://bloom.bg/2j11a18

Crime, Terror and Cash

Money laundering contributes centrally to terror financing and crime. In money laundering, the purchase or possession of an asset is made to look as if it were obtained through perfectly legal means or source of funds. In many cases, the identity of the purchaser itself may be a deception to hide the true user of the asset. What is not clear, however, is the extent of cash involved in money laundering activities, and how much of that cash is used for activities like terrorism. It is also unclear if terror financing and crime would significantly decline with the onset of a cashless society, or they would become more difficult to identify and control.

Cash centrally contributed to terrorism in the early years. Typically, illicit cash or counterfeit currency was moved stealthily across borders either hidden in vehicles amongst other goods or through 'cash couriers', who are persons moving illicit funds through borders, sometimes even by disclosing a part of the funds that may be legally reportable. For security forces, the control of such cash flow has been difficult because of the impossibility of distinguishing between legitimate and illegitimate cash. As a result, it has been argued that large cash payments need to be stopped to begin with, and cash may be phased out over a period of time.

The problem, however, is that physical cash may no more be an important vehicle of terror funding. To begin with, terrorist attacks are not as expensive to execute as they are assumed to be. Mai (2016) cites a study of 40 jihadist attacks in Europe over the last twenty years to argue that most of the attacks were self-funded, and the amount of money involved in about 75 per cent of the attacks was less than $10,000. While self-funding is almost impossible to detect, amounts as low as $10,000 may be legally exchanged or withdrawn through multiple wire or card transfers without either raising suspicion or crossing the legal limits for transfers. Small remittance transfers of workers constitute an excellent example of fund transfer in the above category. A 2016 report of the Commonwealth of Australia on terrorist financing in Southeast Asia and Australia notes:

> Most countries assess *self-funding from legitimate sources to be the most commonly used method of raising terrorism funds* across the region, particularly for foreign terrorist fighters traveling to conflict zones. *It generally occurs in small volumes, and transactions are most often conducted in cash or through legitimate financial channels.* In observed cases, funds are mainly derived from income, sale of personal items, credit cards,

loans, welfare payments and pension funds or superannuation. (emphasis added)[108]

Second, the old idea that exclusive channels exist for terror financing may not be true any longer. Terror, crime and business are increasingly and closely inter-twined, and most transactions in this realm are *not* anymore in cash. New and general forms of money laundering are used to finance terror and legitimise criminal proceeds (*see* Schneider and Linsbauer 2016, for a list). Long-winding wire transfers, in collusion with businessmen, and passing through many countries, banks and jurisdictions, is one such method, where the illicit origin of the funds as well as actual users of the funds are concealed. Terrorists also create fake shell companies with no legitimate business activity as a cover for moving funds. Further, securities are used to facilitate the transfer of funds where the security itself provides a neat cover.

Third, proceeds from major international crimes, such as drug trafficking, counterfeiting and weapon sales, are laundered using multiple channels to make them perfectly legal. Most of these methods involve no cash at all, or involve very little use of cash. As Schneider and Linsbauer (2016) have documented, one method is to purchase a long-term single-premium insurance using dirty money, redeem it early by paying the stipulated penalty and receive a clean cheque to deposit in banks. Another method is gambling in casinos, horse races and lotteries; criminals buy winning tickets or casino chips, redeem the ticket or chip and obtain a clean bank cheque in return. Yet another method is the purchase and sale of art works in auction houses and precious stones. Real estate transactions and ownership of hotels and restaurants are other common means used where the use of physical cash is minimum. More recently, cybercrimes, transactions in virtual currencies like bitcoin and use of pre-paid credit/debit cards are also widely used methods of laundering money.

This is not to argue that an abolition or shrinkage of cash will not harm terror or crime at all. The argument here is that cash might be the instrument of crime or terror only at the 'retail' level and in sectors where the participants lack the finesse of handling technology, accounting and law. But at this 'retail' level, the transactions involved are small enough

---

[108] Commonwealth of Australia. (2016). *Regional Risk Assessment on Terrorism Financing 2016: South-East Asia & Australia.* Retrieved March 31, 2017, from http://bit.ly/2eDEyyD

to pass off as perfectly legitimate transactions and may be impossible to track. Large and major transfers related to crime and terror are, probably, already in the non-cash format. As Mai (2016: 10) argues:

> Any decision to limit the use of cash would have to be justified by the reduction in crime that could reasonably be expected. As crime reduction looks likely, but limited in scale, less controversial and radical law enforcement measures should be considered first. And conventional law enforcement methods can still be improved, for example via better coordination and information sharing between different agencies (police, customs) and countries—measures which will help to detect and deter criminals.

Cash and Negative Interest Rates

When cash is abolished or shrunk in quantity, the immediate outcome is a breakdown of trust in the currency and a shift out of long-standing patterns and incentives in savings and investment. Those economists who argue for a ban on cash refuse to see the complexity of these decision-making processes across banks, financial agents and households. The proponents of cash ban also miss the fact that decisions of agents in the financial sector are ultimately dependent on the structural strengths and weaknesses of the real economy itself. Not surprisingly, evidence shows that when interest rates have become negative, neither have banks expanded credit availability nor have savers increased spending.

First, how would households react if interest rates turn negative? Frankly, we do not know. If households withdrew cash in large numbers, as they did during the Lehman crisis of 2008, there may be a run on the banks (Krueger 2016). At that instance, if cash is abolished, savers may resort to online credit transfers across banks or countries in search of higher interest rates. Such transfers were a reality during the 2008 crisis too, when savers transferred funds from unsafe banks to safe banks on a large scale (Mai 2016). Savers may also move from holding cash to holding other official currencies or fixed investments like in gold, precious metals and assets like land, houses and buildings. In the former case, the monetary authority would be left with much less monetary power, and in the latter case, there would be inflation of asset prices.[109]

---

[109] Financial analysts also strongly advise their customers to pay down their debts if interest rates turn negative. Paying back higher amounts of one's student loan, car loan or home loan is considered a better use of cash than paying the banks for storing it. *See* Jenkin, Ted. (2016, June 4). Where to Put Your Money

Second, there is no evidence yet that negative interest rates have increased growth in bank credit in either Europe or Japan. According to Peter Praet of the ECB, growth of bank lending in Europe between 2014 and 2017 had an 'upward trend', but 'remained relatively weak'.[110] Negative interest rates may have increased liquidity with banks, but lack of liquidity was never the reason why bank lending was weak.[111] The real reason was the lack of demand for credit. After 2008, corporate houses and banks in Europe were allowed to reduce their debts and clean up their books through counter-cyclical fiscal policies of governments. However, household debts were not cleaned up using similar fiscal policy interventions; fiscal policy was not used to raise employment or expand social security.[112] With no active growth of aggregate demand in sight, negative interest rates have had little impact on credit off-take.

Third, in the face of negative interest rates, banks in Europe and Japan have moved away from parking funds with central banks to hold risk-free bonds, mainly sovereign bonds. The adoption of quantitative easing (QE) policies by European countries and Japan, much after the US initiated it in 2008, lent strength to this phenomenon after 2014. But evidence shows that the vigour in the bond markets too may be dying down. C.P. Chandrasekhar, in his article this volume, discusses the curious case of bond purchases. As Europe and Japan escalated bond purchases, bond prices rose and yields on bonds fell. In fact, the yields of a large share of bonds have become negative. According to Chandrasekhar, the total value of negative-yielding bonds rose from $476 billion in August 2014 to $12.2 trillion in June 2016. A course correction would be inevitable,

---

If Interest Rates Turn Negative. *The Wall Street Journal*. Retrieved March 31, 2017, from http://on.wsj.com/2xNqjQ2.

[110] Praet, Peter. (2017, March 16). The ECB's Monetary Policy: Past and Present. Speech presented at Febelfin Connect, Brussels/Londerzeel. Retrieved March 31, 2017, from http://bit.ly/2eEfRSK

[111] Shaffer, Leslie. (2016, June 10). Negative Interest Rates By ECB, BOJ Can't Boost Growth, Allianz Says. CNBC. Retrieved March 31, 2017, from http://cnb.cx/2j2EGwG

[112] As C.P. Chandrasekhar explains in this volume, finance capital had actively mobilised against running government deficits to finance employment growth or social security even though all post–2008 stimulus packages to rescue banks were financed by government deficits. Thus, fiscal policy was sidelined and the burden of revival fell solely on monetary policy.

and QE in Europe and Japan may have reached its limits in terms of driving economic revival.

Fourth, a major outcome of negative interest rates is that inter-bank competition would rise and the net interest margin between deposit and lending rates shrink.[113,114] To remain competitive, banks may adopt riskier and speculative investment choices. Financial institutions like pension funds and insurance companies, which service long-term liabilities, would find it difficult to remain viable. Financial fragility would rise.

In sum, the attempt to move interest rates negative to improve the effectiveness of monetary policy is bound to fail. Such intensive use of monetary policy measures arises out of a refusal to give primacy to counter-cyclical fiscal policies in expanding aggregate demand. The 'war on cash' is being waged to facilitate the introduction of negative interest rates. *Ipso facto*, it turns out to be a futile war, which can only exacerbate the miseries of people.

VI: Towards a Cashless Economy

Ask a Swedish customer, 'Do you have cash on you?' 'I never have cash on me.' 'We are thinking of taking away cash.' 'No, you cannot take away cash!' 'But you don't have any cash.' 'Yeah, but if I want to have cash you should have cash.' 'But you never have cash!' He leaned back and smiled. 'You get into a kind of cash twenty-two situation.'[115]

The push towards a cashless, or a less-cash, economy was not a feature of the Prime Minister's speech on 8 November 2016. It appeared in a statement of the RBI on 11 November after it became clear that the mayhem in banks and ATMs might drive public opinion against demonetisation.

What is missed in the discussions around demonetisation and cashlessness is that around the world, and in India, the drive to reduce the

---

[113] See https://pnccapitaladvisors.com/default.fs, accessed on 31st March 2017.

[114] According to Praet (2017) of the ECB, 'rising competitive pressures have been a key contributor to margin compressions' between 2014 and 2016 and bank 'profitability is likely to remain vulnerable for some years to come' (*see* Praet, Peter, 2017).

[115] Heller, Nathan. (2016, October 10). Imagining a Cashless World. *The New Yorker*. Retrieved March 31, 2017, from http://bit.ly/2wFsiYf

use of cash has a history of many decades. The terms 'cashless economy' or 'cashless society' emerged for the first time in the 1950s in the US and Europe, when computers and information technology began to be used in banking.[116] The first effort to move people out of cash was by encouraging them to use cheques in transactions, particularly of larger amounts. By the 1960s, the debate was on how to create a cashless and cheque-less society where electronic messages would replace cash and paper cheques (Batiz-Lazo, Haigh, and Stearns 2016). Interestingly, Batiz-Lazo, Haigh and Stearns suggest that once the unreasonable euphoria around a cashless and cheque-less society died down by the late-1960s, these were replaced by more reasonable terms like 'less-cheque and less-cash society.'

A more rational framework to begin a discussion on cashlessness, then, is the policy on 'payment systems' i.e., 'a set of instruments, banking procedures and, typically, interbank funds transfer systems that ensure the circulation of money' (BIS 2003: 38). A review of the debates around modernising payment systems in the developed and developing world would reveal that efforts to reduce the use of cash in the economy have a long history; that policymakers always recognised the complexity of the task at hand; that caution and phased approaches were preferred over top-down diktats; and that it was always recognised that cash would continue to be a reality even in the most technologically advanced scenarios.

Payments Systems Policy in India

In India too, the RBI has always had a carefully crafted policy approach towards ushering in a less-cash economy (Padmanabhan 2011; Mundra 2015). The earliest efforts to reduce the use of cash—in the 1980s—were based on promoting the use of cheques as well as reducing the time taken to encash cheques. In the early 1990s, the RBI pioneered the magnetic ink character recognition (MICR) to process and clear cheques quickly. In the 1990s, it introduced the electronic clearing service (ECS)

---

[116] Indeed, one is aware of the writings of Thomas More in the 16th century, and of Robert Owen, William Morris and Samuel Butler in the 19th century, where any physical expression of money was seen as backward and a sign of greed and corruption associated with capitalism. These were also calls for a cashless society, but fundamentally distinct from the arguments offered in the 20th century (*see* Batiz-Lazo and Efthymiou 2016).

and electronic funds transfer (EFT) to further improve the speed of interbank transfers. In 1996, the Institute for Development and Research in Banking Technology (IDRBT) was established to equip the RBI with upgraded technology and develop a reliable communication framework. Credit cards and debit cards were permitted to be issued by banks in the 1990s itself. When the National Financial Switch was made possible in 2003, ATMs across the country became inter-connected. In 2004, core banking solutions (CBS), real time gross settlement (RTGS) and the national electronic funds transfer (NEFT) were introduced. The cheque truncation system (CTS) was inaugurated in 2008, and an enhanced RTGS was developed in 2013. Another important intervention, in 2009, was the introduction of second factor authentication for card-not-present transactions. RuPay—India's domestic card payment network—was introduced in 2012.

In other words, the efforts in India to modernise payment systems were not based on either banning cash or blindly pushing cashless modes of transactions. Instead, policies were based on realistic assessments of the specifically Indian conditions. S.S. Mundra—a deputy governor of the RBI—had a rather sound assessment of the potentials of technology in Indian banking in 2015:

> India is diverse—in the sense of social customs, culture [and] religious beliefs. The diversity and multitude of population and geographic spread of the country—are some factors which make our task extremely complex. The ease with which people can handle technology also differs across people of different age groups, income levels, literacy levels, etc. Hence, it is difficult to design products which can work seamlessly across all sections of the society. Thus, while it is true that no scheme or model can work seamlessly across all economies, what might indeed be best is to learn from the other successful delivery models and customise the product and service offerings to suit the DNA of the respective economy and society. (Mundra 2015)

Given such a nuanced understanding that prevailed (prior to demonetisation), India's second vision statement on payments systems—titled *Payment Systems in India: Vision 2012–15* and released in 2012—set its goals on moving towards a less-cash economy very cautiously. It said:

> One of the biggest challenges towards a less-cash society is that dependency on cash is a deep rooted habit in India. From a customer's perspective, cash is seen as a better mode of payment vis-à-vis non-cash modes

from several aspects such as acceptance, cost, speed, anonymity, having a control of spending, familiarity, cash rebates, etc. For non-cash payments to have wider acceptance, there are several underlying factors which need to impact the behavioural traits. For non-cash payments to proliferate, they should be easy to use, readily available and accepted, provide the same degree of comfort, should not impose any undue financial burden on the merchant and user, and should offer an appropriate level of security in its repeated and regular usage with a zero-fail rate. Therefore, a marked change in the behavioural patterns of both customers and merchants is required for faster and greater adoption of non-cash payment modes. (RBI 2012: 36)

According to Padmanabhan, another senior RBI official, the idea of cashless India was 'utopian:'

> It would be utopian to assume that we can achieve a cashless India unless we have a well-established infrastructure for acceptance of alternative means of making payments which is accessible, safe and easily operable by each citizen. It is also necessary to remember that in India only 55 per cent of the population has bank accounts and it is hard to imagine a cashless society with the exclusion of a vast population from the formal financial system ... financial inclusion is key to have a major reduction in the use of cash in our society ... *Even if we achieve total financial inclusion, we also have to recognise that habits die hard.* (Padmanabhan 2011; emphasis added)

An example of habits dying hard may be the persistence of cheque-based payments over electronic payments, though both are forms of non-cash payment. One reason why cheques continue to be preferred over electronic transactions is the comfort factor, as cheques have had a stable history of safe use even among illiterate households in addition to offering facilities like being issued post-dated. A second reason is the cost factor, as cheque transactions are free but electronic transactions invite an *ad valorem* charge. A third reason is related to asymmetries in the norms for consumer protection. In a fraudulent transaction over cheque, the bank bears the burden of proving good faith, but the burden is largely on the customer in a fraudulent electronic transaction.

If cheques and electronic transfers were the earliest non-cash modes of payment, a more recent innovation has been in mobile banking. Countries like Kenya (M-Pesa), South Africa and Philippines introduced mobile banking on a large scale in the 2000s. In India, shrill demands have been made to embrace mobile banking as the technology of the future. However, the RBI had kept a studied distance from the euphoria till demonetisation. According to Mundra:

> There are many success stories within different geographies across the globe in the arena of payment systems. To mention a few—the M-Pesa system of Kenya, the 'tap and go' card scheme at Singapore, the union pay card scheme of China. If these models have worked so well and have been so successful in their respective countries, can we not simply replicate the model in our jurisdictions? The answer, I am afraid, is a big NO. (Mundra 2015)

Mundra went on to list the reasons why mobile banking—as an instrument in the delivery of financial and payment services—might not take off in India as is often assumed.

> In the Indian context, an objective analysis would reveal various reasons for slow adoption. There are technical issues like type of handsets, variety of operating systems, encryption requirements, inter-operable platforms or the lack of it, absence of standardised communication structures, difficulty in downloading applications, time lag in activation, etc. These get accentuated by the operational difficulties in on-boarding merchants and customers and customer ownership issues. The interplay of these factors has stymied the deployment and adoption of mobile banking as an effective and widely accepted delivery channel. Issues of coordination and cooperation between banks and telcos, is another aspect which acts as either a driver or a barrier to the adoption of mobile banking. (*ibid*)

Abandoning RBI Policy

In the days after demonetisation was announced, the RBI's reasoned stance that we elaborated above was abandoned. As doubts grew on the official narrative on counterfeit notes and black money, the government and the RBI were forced to shift gears and push for a new agenda: a 'cashless' economy, later revised to a 'less-cash economy.' The results had to be achieved and demonstrated quickly too. This was the context in which caution and grounded vigilance, which marked the earlier efforts, were abandoned and efforts on a war footing were unleashed to go 'cashless'. Thus, the government and the RBI announced a slew of measures to promote non-cash modes of payments, including different forms of electronic and mobile banking. Private FINTECH companies were encouraged to expand business. Impressed by the turn of events, Bill Gates, whose Bill and Melinda Gates Foundation supports the Better Than Cash Alliance of the United Nations (along with e-Bay, MasterCard, and USAID), came out in praise of the government. He declared that demonetisation would give a boost to digital banking and the temporary pain it caused may be worth going through.[117] If the announcement of demonetisation took place at 8PM on 8 November 2016, the next day's newspapers carried front page advertisements, with the Prime Minister's photograph, of a private e-wallet firm called Paytm. The Prime Minister or the government did not appear to object at all.

Yet, the policy measures to promote digital payments after November 2016 were failures. Let us first consider the shares of each mode of payment in the total volume and value of payments (*see* Table 1.3).

Among all the different payment systems, the RTGS represents large-sized transfers.[118] Hence, in Table 1.3, I have provided the shares of volume and value of each payment system in the total volume and value of payments after excluding RTGS. *After excluding* RTGS payments, NEFT was the dominant mode of payment accounting for about 61 per cent of the total value of payments in August 2017. The CTS and the national automated clearing house (NACH) modes followed NEFT in that order. Taken together, NEFT, CTS and NACH modes accounted for about 94 per cent of the total value of payments and 51 per cent of the total volume of payments (both excluding RTGS) in August 2017. Between November 2016 and August 2017, the combined share of NEFT, CTS and NACH in the total value of payments rose from 88.5 per cent to 94 per cent.

But the government's effort after demonetisation was to promote new forms of payment systems, such as debit cards, credit cards and pre-paid instruments (PPI). It also launched the unified payment interface (UPI) and the unstructured supplementary service data (USSD) to boost mobile banking. *Yet, the share of credit cards, debit cards and mobile banking in the total volume and value of payments fell between November–December 2016 and August 2017.* The UPI and the USSD routes accounted for minuscule shares in both the total volume and value of payments. The UPI mode

---

[117] Anon. (2016, November 18). Bill Gates Backs Demonetisation, Says It's Worth the Pain. *The Times of India*. Retrieved March 31, 2017, from http://bit.ly/2xOyD2f

[118] In August 2017, of all the official non-cash modes of payments (including mobile payments), the RTGS route was the most predominant accounting for roughly 82 per cent of the total value of payments.

TABLE 1.3 Shares of Modes of Payment in the Total Volume and Value of Transactions (Excluding RTGS), Non-cash Payment Systems, India, Monthly, November 2016 to August 2017, in Per Cent

Mode of payment	Shares of each mode of payment in total (%)										
	Nov'16	Dec'16	Jan'17	Feb'17	Mar'17	Apr'17	May'17	Jun'17	Jul'17	Aug'17
NEFT, volume	16.7	16.3	17.7	18.3	19.9	17.0	18.4	18.5	17.4	17.3
NEFT, value	52.5	54.1	54.8	55.9	58.9	57.6	59.3	60.7	59.4	60.5
CTS, volume	11.8	12.8	12.8	12.4	12.7	11.3	11.4	11.2	10.8	10.5
CTS, value	32.3	31.9	31.9	30.8	28.9	33.1	32.2	30.6	31.4	30.1
IMPS, volume	4.9	5.2	6.7	7.4	7.2	7.7	7.9	8.0	8.1	8.7
IMPS, value	1.9	2.0	2.4	2.5	2.0	2.7	2.8	2.9	3.0	3.2
NACH, volume	20.7	19.5	17.1	18.6	19.4	25.2	22.9	24.0	24.0	23.5
NACH, value	3.6	2.9	2.6	3.0	3.0	4.3	3.3	3.4	3.8	3.6
UPI, volume	0.04	0.19	0.45	0.51	0.66	0.82	1.08	1.24	1.34	1.90
UPI, value	0.01	0.03	0.08	0.10	0.09	0.10	0.13	0.15	0.17	0.20
USSD, volume	0.001	0.010	0.034	0.028	0.023	0.024	0.024	0.024	0.022	0.022
USSD, value	0.000	0.000	0.002	0.002	0.001	0.001	0.001	0.001	0.001	0.001
Debit/Credit cards at POS, volume	27.9	30.5	28.7	26.2	24.1	27.4	27.5	27.3	27.9	27.8

(Cont'd)

TABLE 1.3 (Cont'd)

| Mode of payment | Shares of each mode of payment in total (%) | | | | | | | | | | |
	Nov'16	Dec'16	Jan'17	Feb'17	Mar'17	Apr'17	May'17	Jun'17	Jul'17	Aug'17
Debit/Credit cards at POS, value	2.1	2.4	2.3	2.0	1.5	2.0	2.2	2.2	2.2	2.2
PPI, volume	8.0	8.6	9.4	9.7	9.6	10.6	10.8	9.7	10.4	10.3
PPI, value	0.1	0.1	0.1	0.1	0.1	0.1	0.1	0.1	0.1	0.1
Mobile banking, volume	9.8	6.9	7.0	6.9	6.4	7.2	7.7	9.1	8.2	8.1
Mobile banking, value	7.4	6.4	5.8	5.6	5.4	6.8	9.3	7.2	5.0	5.0
Total, volume	100.0	100.0	100.0	100.0	100.0	100.0	100.0	100.0	100.0	100.0
Total, value	100.0	100.0	100.0	100.0	100.0	100.0	100.0	100.0	100.0	100.0

Source: RBI.

Notes: Card transactions pertain to only four banks; ppi pertains to eight non-bank issuers for goods and services transactions; mobile banking figures are for five banks.

accounted for just 1.9 per cent of the total volume and 0.2 per cent of the total value of payments. The corresponding shares for the USSD mode were 0.02 per cent and 0.001 per cent respectively.

Let us now consider the growth rates in the volume and value of each mode of payment (*see* Table 1.4). Between November 2016 and August 2017, the total volume of non-cash payments rose by 18.8 per cent and the total value of non-cash payments rose by 15.3 per cent. However, if we exclude the payment modes like RTGS, NEFT, CTS and NACH, the growth rates in volumes was lower at just 13.9 per cent; the growth rate of value was actually negative, at –39.2 per cent. Transactions through debit and credit cards grew rather modestly, at 18.2 per cent (volumes) and 29.7 per cent (value). The UPI and USSD exhibited extraordinary rates of growth between November 2016 and August 2017, but these were mainly due to low base effects. The PPIs also grew in volume and value, but again, the total value of payments through PPIs constituted 0.1 per cent of the total value of payments. Mobile payments grew in terms of volumes by just 8.1 per cent and in terms of value by 5 per cent.

In other words, no striking shift to other non-cash modes, particularly electronic modes, was visible between November 2016 and August 2017. On the contrary, all evidence till August 2017 pointed to the return of cash in everyday transactions as remonetisation proceeded. The government's aim of forcing citizens to shun cash had failed. Equally important, the RBI's seasoned assessments prior to November 2016 had stood the test of time. Soon after his retirement as deputy governor of the RBI in April 2017, R. Gandhi (who, incidentally, piloted demonetisation within the RBI) was to caution the government against rushing with digital payments to reduce the use of cash. According to him, the conveniences of cash cannot be easily replaced by digital banking; 'cash is a reality. It will continue,' he said.[119]

How Much Cash Will Be Printed?

In the context of the revival of cash usage, a proposal of the government to not print all the currency that was in circulation prior to

[119] Dugal, Ira, & Jain, Mayank. (2017, April 11). Rushing on Digital Payments Will Create Security Risks, Says Former RBI Deputy Governor R Gandhi. *Bloomberg Quint.* Retrieved April 18, 2017, from http://bit.ly/2f1GcKT

TABLE 1.4 Volume and Value of Transactions, Non-cash Payment Systems, India, Monthly, November 2016 to August 2017, Volume in Million, Value in Rs Billion, and Growth in Per Cent

Mode of payment	Nov-16	Dec-16	Jan-17	Feb-17	Mar-17	Apr-17	May-17	Jun-17	Jul-17	Aug-17	Growth (%), Nov to Aug
RTGS, volume	7.9	8.8	9.3	9.1	12.5	9.5	10.4	9.8	9.4	9.5	20.1
RTGS, value	78479	84096	77486	74219	123376	88512	90171	92813	87149	89163	13.6
NEFT, volume	123.0	166.3	164.2	148.2	186.7	143.2	155.8	152.3	148.1	151.6	23.2
NEFT, value	8808	11538	11355	10878	16294	12156	12411	12694	12012	12500	41.9
CTS, volume	87.1	130.0	118.5	100.4	119.1	95.3	97.1	91.9	92.2	92.1	5.7
CTS, value	5419	6812	6618	5994	8003	6991	6746	6410	6343	6224	14.9
IMPS, volume	36.2	52.8	62.4	59.7	67.4	65.1	66.7	65.8	69.1	75.7	109.2
IMPS, value	325	432	491	482	565	562	586	597	605	652	100.6
NACH, volume	152.5	198.7	158.7	150.5	182.3	212.6	194.4	197.3	204.3	205.2	34.5
NACH, value	607	627	541	592	831	905	692	709	771	752	24.0
UPI, volume	0.3	2.0	4.2	4.2	6.2	6.9	9.2	10.2	11.4	16.6	5678.8
UPI, value	1	7	17	19	24	22	28	31	34	41	4459.3
USSD, volume	0.0	0.1	0.3	0.2	0.2	0.2	0.2	0.2	0.2	0.2	2598.1
USSD, value	0.0	0.1	0.4	0.4	0.3	0.3	0.3	0.3	0.3	0.3	3871.2

Debit/Credit cards at POS, volume	205.5	311.0	265.5	212.3	225.7	231.1	233.4	224.1	237.6	243.0	18.2
Debit/Credit cards at POS, value	352	522	481	391	411	431	451	455	439	457	29.7
PPI, volume	59.0	87.8	87.3	78.4	90.0	89.2	91.3	80.1	88.7	89.7	52.0
PPI, value	13	21	21	19	21	22	25	23	25	27	106.1
Mobile banking, volume	72.3	70.2	64.9	56.2	60.5	61.0	64.9	74.6	69.5	70.8	-2.2
Mobile banking, value	1245	1366	1207	1080	1499	1444	1941	1498	1019	1033	-17.0
Total, volume	743.8	1027.7	935.3	819.2	950.6	853.1	858.5	831.7	861.1	883.4	18.8
Total, value	95249	105421	98218	93674	151025	109602	111109	113731	107378	109818	15.3

Source: RBI.

Notes: Card transactions pertain to only four banks; PPI pertains to eight non-bank issuers for goods and services transactions; mobile banking figures are for five banks.

demonetisation came in for serious criticism. On 15 December 2016, Shaktikanta Das had stated that remonetisation would only be as per requirement after accounting for the spread of digital banking.[120] On 17 December, Arun Jaitley restated the point and said that only 'a reduced cash currency could remain' in the system, with digital currency constituting the rest.[121] In March 2017, the RBI's new deputy governor Viral Acharya was to note that 'full currency in circulation' would imply 'slightly lower' figures compared to before demonetisation.[122]

First, the government and the RBI appeared ignorant of the point that the decision to use cash or any other mode of payment in a liberal democracy should be the sovereign decision of each citizen. Any effort to override this freedom of choice would hit at the very roots of the liberties and rights that the idea of citizenship bestows. Second, printing less currency than actually demanded would end up prolonging the cash shortage and undoing the efforts to revive growth rates in many key sectors of the economy. Third, any effort to print inadequate amounts of cash in a cash-demanding economy would lead to new underground/black markets for cash. Gandhi's post-retirement statement is worth quoting here:

> If a public service authority, the government or the Reserve Bank, decides to have an artificial control on currency to force the people to go for an alternate [sic] course of payment, which will not work. It is the mindset of the people. That you cannot dictate. People will find their own way around it. Earlier, when there was an actual currency shortage in the 1980s, people found their own method of tokens.[123]

---

[120] Anon. (2016, December 15). No Target of Printing New Notes Worth Entire Rs 15.44 lakh cr: Govt. Indo-Asian News Service. Retrieved March 31, 2017, from http://bit.ly/2wGCuhz

[121] Anon. (2016, December 17). Not All Scrapped Currency Will Be Remonetised, Hints Arun Jaitley. Press Trust of India. Retrieved March 31, 2017, from http://bit.ly/2xNOH49

[122] Srinivas, A. (2017, March 31). Demonetisation Questions: When Will the RBI Stop Printing Notes? *The Wire*. Retrieved March 31, 2017, from http://bit.ly/2gG6B0V

[123] Dugal, Ira, & Jain, Mayank. (2017, April 11). Rushing On Digital Payments Will Create Security Risks, Says Former RBI Deputy Governor R Gandhi. *Bloomberg Quint*. Retrieved April 18, 2017, from http://bit.ly/2f1GcKT

Cash, Informality and Corruption

A claim forwarded in support of demonetisation was that it would hasten India's shift from a predominantly informal economy towards a formal economy. It was argued that as the use of cash declines and more people use cashless/digital modes of payment, informal activities would become integrated with the formal economy. As more informal activities are transformed into formal activities, the scope for corruption would also drastically decline. The assumption here is that cash is the primary driver of informality, which in turn fosters the growth of corruption.

Global cross-country data show that the assumption that cash drives informality and corruption is misplaced (*see* Kohli and Ramakumar; in this volume). In this section, cash-to-GDP ratio is used as an indicator of the extent of currency circulation in an economy (Rogoff 2016). In 2015, India had a cash-to-GDP ratio of 12.5 per cent. Reliable data on the size of the informal sector across countries are not available. Even the definitions of informal sector followed in different countries are not comparable. Hence, to ensure comparability, estimates of the size of the 'shadow economy' are used as an indicator of informality. Schneider, Buehn and Montenegro (2010) adopted a multiple indicators multiple causes (MIMIC) model to estimate the size of the shadow economy in 162 countries of the world. They defined the shadow economy as 'all market-based legal production of goods and services that are deliberately concealed from public authorities' to avoid payment of taxes and social security contributions, to avoid meeting labour market standards and regulations and to avoid complying with administrative requirements of governments, such as filling up of forms (p. 5). In 2006, the size of India's shadow economy was estimated at 21.4 per cent of the GDP. Similarly, data on the extent of corruption is available from the Corruption Perceptions Index of Transparency International, where the perceived level of public sector corruption is scored on a scale of 0 (highly corrupt) to 100 (very clean). For 2015, India's Corruption Perceptions Index was 38.

Table 1.5 provides data for a set of countries on all the three indicators. On the one end of the spectrum are economies with a high cash-to-GDP ratio like Japan, Hong Kong and Switzerland. The preference for cash in economies like Japan is rather famous. According to reports, the ratio of bank notes to GDP in Japan doubled between 1996 and 2016,

TABLE 1.5   Cash-to-GDP Ratio, Size of the Shadow Economy and Corruption Perceptions Index, Selected Countries, in Per Cent

Country	Cash to GDP ratio, 2015, in %	Shadow economy. as % of GDP, 2006	Corruption PerceptionIindex, 2015 (0 to 100)
Japan	18.6	8.8	75
Hong Kong	14.7	15.0	75
India	12.5	21.4	38
Switzerland	11.1	7.6	86
Mexico	5.7	28.5	35
Indonesia	4.1	19.1	36
Chile	3.6	18.5	70
Brazil	3.4	38.5	38
South Africa	3.4	26.8	44
Denmark	3.3	13.8	91
Argentina	2.1	24.2	32
Sweden	1.8	14.7	89

Sources: Rogoff (2016); Schneider, Buehn and Montenegro (2010); Transparency International.*
* Table of Results: Corruption Perceptions Index 2015. (2016, February 1). In Transparency International. Retrieved March 31, 2017, from http://bit.ly/2eFprVx

even as its population declined.[124] Though the first credit card in Japan was issued in 1960 and there were three credit cards per adult on an average in 2016, about 38 per cent of all consumer transactions were still cash-based.[125] Yet, Japan's shadow economy was estimated at just 8.8 per cent of its GDP and its Corruption Perceptions Index was as high as 75. In European countries like Germany and Austria too, cash is widely used

[124] Mayger, James, & Anstey, Chris. (2016, November 8). Cash Is Still King in Japan, and That Could Be a Problem for the BOJ. Bloomberg. Retrieved March 31, 2017, from https://bloom.bg/2wHgWBl

[125] Among the reasons cited are low crime rates and a predominance of small shops and restaurants that cannot afford *ad valorem* charges on cards. *See* Soble, Jonathan. (2014, February 28). Cash Remains King in Japan. *Financial Times.* Retrieved March 31, 2017, from http://on.ft.com/2eKKqtv.

in small-sized as well as large-sized transactions. In 2014, ECB researchers studied payments diaries of 18,500 consumers (amounting to 103,000 transactions) in Australia, Austria, Canada, France, Germany, the Netherlands and the US between 2009 and 2012 (Bagnall *et al* 2014). The results showed that 46–82 per cent of the number of all payments was made in cash. In Germany and Austria, the shares of cash transactions were recorded at 82 per cent (*see* Table 1.6).[126] Yet, the size of the shadow economy in Germany and Austria were just 13.5 per cent and 7.9 per cent respectively.

Switzerland is another country with a large cash-to-GDP ratio but a small-sized shadow economy and low levels of corruption (*see* Table 1.5).[127] At the World Banknote Summit in February 2017, Fritz Zurbrügg, the deputy chairman of the Swiss National Bank (SNB), remarked that 'reports of the death of cash [in Switzerland] have been greatly exaggerated' (Zurbrügg 2017). According to him, there were a number of reasons why cash persisted even in predominantly formal economies like Switzerland:

> Why then is cash still so popular? First, many people use cash on a daily basis for personal reasons: be it simply out of habit, convenience or a lack of technical knowhow. Survey respondents also often cite the more effective budget control that cash allows—cash helps people to more easily keep an eye on their spending and their remaining funds. Moreover, in some situations, it just seems more appropriate to use cash rather than a bank transfer, for example when giving a gift. And there is a strong psychological aspect to the use of cash which should not be underestimated. It's not for nothing that we have the saying 'Cash is King.' Obviously, a 100-franc note has the exact same value as the entry 'balance = CHF 100 francs' on your bank statement. But cash is visible and tangible, and for that reason alone is imbued with a greater value than non-cash.

On the other end of the spectrum are countries like Mexico, Indonesia, Chile, Brazil, South Africa and Argentina—i.e., with low

---

[126] In the Eurozone as a whole, the total currency in circulation by the end of Q3 of 2016 was €1.1 trillion, which was three times the currency in circulation in Q1 of 2003. The ratio of cash-to-GDP rose from 5 per cent to 10 per cent. The rate of growth of cash was higher than the rate of growth of GDP in most stretches of this period (*see* Mai, 2016).

[127] Bosley, Catherine. (2016, April 4). Cash Is Still King in Switzerland. *Bloomberg*. Retrieved March 31, 2017, from https://bloom.bg/2vL428c

TABLE 1.6 Shares of Cash, Debit Cards and Credit Cards in Total Payments, Diary-Based Surveys, 2009 to 2012, in Per Cent

Payment method	Australia	Austria	Canada	France	Germany	Netherlands	United States
By volume (%)							
Cash	65	82	53	56	82	52	46
Debit cards	22	14	25	31	13	41	26
Credit cards	9	2	19	1	2	1	19
All (including others)	100	100	100	100	100	100	100
By value (%)							
Cash	32	65	23	15	53	34	23
Debit cards	32	25	30	43	28	60	27
Credit cards	18	5	41	3	7	4	28
All (including others)	100	100	100	100	100	100	100

Sources: Bagnall *et al.* 2014

cash-to-GDP ratios but relatively large shadow economies and high levels of corruption (Table 1.5). For instance, Mexico had a cash-to-GDP ratio of 5.7 per cent but the size of its shadow economy was 28.5 per cent of the GDP. Similarly, Brazil had a cash-to-GDP ratio of 3.4 per cent but had a shadow economy of size 38.5 per cent of the GDP. All these countries—except Chile—had poor ranks with respect to the Corruption Perceptions Index, i.e., higher levels of perceived corruption.

In sum, the claim that demonetisation—by facilitating cashless transactions—would formalise India's large informal sector stands on very weak grounds. Data from across countries show that there is no clear relationship between the cash-to-GDP ratio and the extent of informality in the economy. The formalisation of the informal sector in developing countries cannot be achieved by forcefully digitalising transactions. The persistence of the informal sector is a structural feature of these economies. Only a structural transformation of the sphere of production, particularly in agriculture and rural areas, can pave the way to create a formal economy, which is modern, technologically-advanced and productive.

The Rise and Promise of FINTECH

Digitalisation of economic transactions also imply the proliferation of a new set of intermediaries between the state and the citizen: the financial technology (or FINTECH) companies. Proponents of digitalistion have often spoken about the power of innovation that FINTECH companies can unleash and the 'creative disruption' it can cause to the existing systems of financial services. The growth of FINTECH firms, thus, is seen as an outcome of demonetisation, which can create growth in India's services sector.

Globally, the growth of FINTECH firms is seen as on the upswing in the recent past (KPMG 2017). Two distinct trends are discernable from the data on investments into FINTECH firms after 2010: FINTECH investments rose between 2010 and 2015 and then fell between 2015 and 2016. The total amount invested in these firms declined from $46.7 billion in 2015 to $24.7 billion in 2016. The only silver lining, globally, was the continuing interest shown by venture capitalists in FINTECH. If we consider India, the total investment in FINTECH firms has been relatively small compared to other economies like China. As a consequence, future growth prospects have been seen as rather bright.[128] Given the potential for growth, a worrying phenomenon for observers has been the plateauing out of investment interest in Indian FINTECH. If 1,181 FINTECH firms were set up in India in 2015, only 546 were set up in 2016. Cumulative FINTECH investments, except for a spike in 2015, were flat afterwards (Nathan Associates 2017). More worryingly, contrary to global trends, venture capital investments in Indian FINTECH fell from $1.6 billion in 2015 to $216 million in 2016. Most successful FINTECH firms are in the spheres of mobile wallets and digital payments; the investment spike in 2015 was mostly due to investments in these two spheres.[129] And even during the 2015 spike, about 40 per cent of the total investment was in just one company: Paytm.[130]

The declining interest of private investment in Indian FINTECH is the outcome of a specific economic reading of the sector. According to analysts, the sector has been unable to position itself within the Indian financial landscape (Nathan Associates 2017). First, the FINTECH firms are not expected to compete with, or capture the existing market shares of, large and powerful banks that house most of the country's financial assets. 'Disruption,' then, may be a wrong word to use, and the function of FIN-TECH firms may be more in the nature of technology-led 'facilitation' of the roles played by banks.[131] Second, in addition to facilitation and outside the traditional clientele of banks, a major section of the market left for FINTECH firms to attract and cover is the income-poor and unbanked population, particularly in the rural areas. A Swissnex report noted that '… the current set of financial products and services do not cater to the vast majority of Indians and are only designed for the top 40 million

---

[128] As a Swissnex report on the Indian FinTech sector noted, 'VC firms have only just begun skimming the Fintech potential in India' (Swissnex 2017: 7).

[129] Two FINTECH firms—Paytm and FINO PayTech—had also received RBI licenses for becoming 'payment banks' in 2015–16.

[130] Baid, Yash. (2016, November 28). $1.77 Bn in 158 Deals: Indian Fintech Market Report 2014-2016. *Inc42*. Retrieved March 31, 2017, from http://bit.ly/2gKDAVD

[131] As Nathan Associates (2017) remarked, 'there are no existing relationships to disrupt' (p. 4). Aditya Puri, the managing director of HDFC Bank, was to warn after demonetisation: 'you [FINTECHs] must keep the level of your importance within bounds.' *See* Shukla, Saloni, & Bhakta, Pratik. (2017, March 22). Fintechs, Banks Understand the Need for Co-operation. *The Economic Times*. Retrieved March 31, 2017, from http://bit.ly/2f2dSYL.

of the population' (Swissnex, 2017, p. 22). However, in addressing the needs of the unbanked, while there is scope for technological innovation, margins are meagre due to the levels of competition and the low levels of income of the clientele. To make matters worse, levels of mortality in the FINTECH sector are very high; about 1,000 FINTECH firms reportedly closed down after 2010. The future of Indian FINTECH, then, is uncertain and new investments have not been forthcoming at the expected pace.

It is in this context that demonetisation was seen as a major stimulus to the FINTECH sector. The reduced use of cash was expected to boost the business of FINTECH firms, particularly in the sphere of mobile wallets and digital payments. Mobile wallet companies like Paytm, PayU India, MobiKwik, and FreeCharge witnessed a rise in business after 8 November 2016. Firms in the field of pre-paid instruments, like Qwikcilver, also saw higher revenue flows.

Yet, the rapid return of cash into circulation, alongside remonetisation, has once again unsettled prospects in the FINTECH space. After December 2016, volumes in mobile banking fell; growth of values in mobile banking slowed down; volumes and values in PPIs rose only modestly; and the newly introduced UPI and USSD systems did not gain more than a 1 per cent share within the non-cash modes of payment (*see* Table 1.3). It is only fair, then, to doubt whether the so-called FINTECH boom was real or just an inflated balloon.

As business dries up in the financial space, the prospects of FIN-TECH companies are now argued to be larger in new areas of operation outside payments, such as big data analytics and distributed ledger technologies. According to Nandan Nilekani, the founding chairman of the Unique Identification Authority of India (UIDAI), big data has enormous potential to drive innovations in India; he said: 'As we go from data-poor to data-rich, we are just getting started in FINTECH' (Swissnex 2017). But as FINTECH branches out into new areas, new concerns have also emerged. These are related to whether digitalisation of finance transactions can lead to heightened surveillance and whether citizen's rights like privacy may be a casualty.

Surveillance in the Cashless Society

In most liberal democracies, citizens have realistic fears if the ban on cash and digitalisation of banking would erode the foundations on which the State-citizen relationship has historically been structured. An important attraction of using cash is that it leaves no trail, and ensures the privacy of transactions. On the other hand, digital transactions leave a trail and can be traced back even after decades. In most modern legal systems, the right to personal liberty subsumes the right to privacy. Thrusting cashless and digital transactions robs citizens of this fundamental right, and this has been a matter of contention even in countries that are the home to cutting-edge innovations in financial technologies, like Switzerland. The SNB's Zurbrügg articulated this deep-rooted concern in his country:

> Are my electronic payment and account data protected against unauthorised access and misuse? In other words, is my financial privacy guaranteed? In contrast to cashless payment methods, cash presents no data security problems. It offers the certainty that one's privacy is protected. Please do not misunderstand me: the suppliers of cashless payment applications invest a great deal of money in ensuring the security of their systems, and the existing systems can generally be considered to be secure. However, the availability of cash means that anyone can decide, at any time, exactly how secure they consider it to be, and how much information they want to share with whom. Or, as my Bundesbank colleague, Carl-Ludwig Thiele, put it recently: 'The right to informational self-determination and respect of privacy is a valuable commodity, which should not be watered down or ceded lightly.' (Zurbrügg 2017)

The distinction between privacy and informational self-determination, which Thiele emphasises in the above quote, is a more recent outcome of the phenomenal growth of computational technology and the Internet. The early view of privacy, as enshrined in the famous Warren and Brandeis essay of 1890, was the 'right to be let alone.'[132] While the fundamental principle enshrined in the 1890 formulation remains powerful, the growth of computing technologies and the Internet over the years have meant that personal information of citizens are collected and stored by multiple agencies, public and private; this is what Nilekani referred to as a 'data-rich' world. What happens to the bits of personal information lying scattered all around? Can anyone access it without the knowledge of the individual? If accessed without the knowledge of the individual, can it be characterised as violating the spirit of 'the right to be let alone?' Consequently, the understanding of privacy has been enriched

---

[132] Warren, Samual D., & Brandeis, Louis D. (1890, Dcember 15). The Right to Privacy. *Harvard Law Review*, IV(5). Retrieved March 31, 2017, from http://bit.ly/2xOqFpO

into the idea of informational self-determination, which underlined the importance of 'consent' of individuals. The right to informational self-determination of an individual was defined by a German constitutional court in 1983 as follows:

> ... in the context of modern data processing, the protection of the individual against unlimited collection, storage, use and disclosure of his/her personal data is encompassed by the general personal rights of the German constitution. This basic right warrants in this respect the capacity of the individual to determine in principle the disclosure and use of his/her personal data. Limitations to this informational self-determination are allowed only in case of overriding public interest.[133]

In sum, inside a cashless and digital world of finance, it is not just the right to privacy that is potentially violated. The right to informational self-determination is also violated. This is the reason why activists demand both a privacy law and a data protection law that go hand-in-hand. A country like India, unfortunately, has neither a privacy law nor a data protection law.

There are two further issues. One, in competitive market societies, can personal information be turned into a commodity for private profiteering? If yes, it may be tantamount to the commodification of the person itself. Two, given that enormous amounts of personal information will be available to the State, can the State misuse it to target dissenting citizens and monitor their everyday activities? If yes, the outcome would be a surveillance state, where the assumed trust between the citizen and the State breaks down. As governments push cashless transactions, the potential for surveillance of the citizens rise. In countries like India with no privacy or data protection legislations, the threat is only more real.

A major threat to privacy and informational self-determination in India comes from Aadhaar, the country's massive unique identity scheme.[134] Here, all Indian residents are provided a unique identification number linked to their demographic particulars and biometrics—photograph, fingerprints and iris scans. On the one hand, the government has been forcing the hands of citizens to compulsorily register for an

---

[133] Informational Self-Determination. In *Wikipedia*. Retrieved March 31, 2017, from http://bit.ly/2gKw3G6

[134] Ramakumar, R. (2016, April 15). Freedom in Peril. *Frontline*. Retrieved March 31, 2017, from http://bit.ly/2f3mWNm

Aadhaar number and 'seed' it into the service providing agencies. On the other hand, it has been trying to 'leverage' Aadhaar to create a cashless economy. The UIDAI has, for years, been working in close coordination with multiple private providers of cashless payment instruments such as credit cards, debit cards, mobile banking and digital wallets. After demonetisation, the government also launched a new mobile application—Bharat Interface for Money (BHIM) based on the UPI—to encourage electronic payments through mobile devices. Such efforts to render Aadhaar ubiquitous in a cashless world has strengthened fears of commodification of personal data as well as the entrenchment of a surveillance State.

In a financial ecosystem driven by Aadhaar, there are also strong and genuine fears of exclusion of the poor. In Aadhaar-based cashless transactions, fingerprints of users are used to authenticate individual identities. However, given that a large share of India's population is involved in manual labour and the share of the elderly in the population structure is rising, the average quality of fingerprints is poor. As a result, as has been documented, there are large error rates in the centralised biometric authentication of beneficiaries in addition to the presence of disruptive factors like lack of electricity and poor Internet connectivity. Even a one per cent error rate in a population of 1.2 billion implies the exclusion of more than 10 million persons. In reality, however, the error rates have been unacceptably large. The Indian government's own *Economic Survey 2016–17* presented a depressing picture in this regard:

> While Aadhaar coverage speed has been exemplary, with over a billion Aadhaar cards being distributed, some states report authentication failures: estimates include 49 per cent failure rates for Jharkhand, 6 per cent for Gujarat, 5 per cent for Krishna district in Andhra Pradesh and 37 per cent for Rajasthan. Failure to identify genuine beneficiaries results in exclusion errors.[135]

Biometrics are also poorly secured as an authentication token. Normally, when a password or PIN (personal identification number) is stolen or lost, the user can change the password; only the user knows the password. In contrast, biometric passwords like fingerprints cannot

---

[135] Government of India (2017). Universal Basic Income: A Conversation with and within the Mahatma. *Economic Survey 2016–17*. Ministry of Finance. Retrieved March 31, 2017, from http://bit.ly/2w79Io9

be changed. Fingerprints are also left behind wherever one goes and on whatever one touches. Once stolen or lost, the security of a user's account is permanently compromised. In other words, when Aadhaar-based biometric authentication becomes pervasive, identity thefts are likely to rise. Such glaring threats to security and freedom have not been appreciated in India before making Aadhaar compulsory for all residents and using it in financial transactions.

Typically, liberal societies need to uphold the freedom of the individual to choose his/her mode of payment. Such a freedom of choice should be the foundational principle that guides currency management policies. For instance, according to Zurbrügg, the SNB had no plans to do away with cash in Switzerland, and:

> … moreover, *it has no preference for one payment method over the other—cash or cashless.* Instead, it ensures both that the demand for cash is satisfied and that cashless payments function smoothly. We are mandated by law to perform both tasks, and they have equal status. *The public is therefore free to choose between cash and cashless payment methods. This is an important point.* The possibility of carrying out payments is a basic prerequisite for participation in economic life, and must be available to all. It should not be attached to conditions such as the need to hold a bank account. (Zurbrügg 2017: 4; emphasis added)

Unfortunately, the Indian liberal response to demonetisation was not distinguished by such an 'enlightened' view. Liberal, and libertarian, articulations on demonetisation, which typically pitch the war on cash as adversarial to free markets and individual liberties, came not from India but from the West. Two examples should suffice. In a January 2017 article, Steve Forbes drew parallels between demonetisation and India's forced-sterilisation programme in the 1970s.[136] For Forbes, a cashless economy should be created not by force but by people's choice, and a free market economy would over time lead to a reduced use of cash. Instead, to create a cashless economy, the Indian government had committed 'a massive theft of people's property without even the pretense of due process.' A *Wall Street Journal* editorial was another sharp indictment calling the imposition of a cashless society as 'antithetical to

---

[136] Forbes, Steve. (2017, January 24). What India Has Done to Its Money Is Sickening and Immoral. *Forbes*. Retrieved March 31, 2017, from http://bit.ly/2f2Q9I6

economic liberty.'[137] It argued that the policy thrust to forcefully create a cashless society was a 'blunder,' and India 'should respect citizens who want to keep at least some cash.' Indian liberals, it would appear, had fallen between two stools: neither able to argue for a free market nor up to the task of protecting individual liberties!

VII: Conclusions

> Populist politics is often constructed from a blend of nativism, bigotry, grandiosity, and coarse speech. Yet its aesthetic has an intimate quality. By banning cash with a symbolic sweep of his hand, Modi reached into the pockets of almost every Indian ... The Prime Minister made himself felt. India is racked by severe poverty and hindered by illiteracy; many citizens in the countryside cannot name a world leader or even their own national leader. After November 8th, many more knew Modi's name. (Coll 2017)

History, as it sits down for stock-taking, would have to judge the Narendra Modi government's demonetisation on many fronts. On the economic front, demonetisation would have to be judged as a policy that was illogical in conception, mismanaged in execution, disruptive to the economy, and acutely burdensome on the working people.

Both experience and analysis available with the government was clear. The earlier demonetisation of 1978 had failed to unearth any black money. Only a part of the black economy was illegal; only a part of the black money so generated was a *stock* and the rest was a *flow*; and only a part of the stock of black money—about 6 per cent—was in cash. The total circulation of FICN in the Indian economy at any given time was not more than Rs 400 crore. But these lessons were completely disregarded by Modi, when he announced the demonetisation of Rs 500 and Rs 1,000 notes on 8 November 2016.

It was no surprise then that only a small section, which stored cash in large amounts either for future use or as revolving cash in business/trade transactions, was adversely affected by demonetisation. Even here, a portion of the cash stock could be legally converted into new notes through official banking channels. Another portion, even if illegally earned, was converted into new notes using myriad innovative methods. About 99 per cent of the SBNs had returned to the official banking system by June

---

[137] Anon. (2016, December 22). India's Bizarre War on Cash. *The Wall Street Journal*. Retrieved March 31, 2017, from http://on.wsj.com/2eFtOzW

2017. Demonetisation, then, cannot be credited with any major detection of black money.

Demonetisation was also supposed to end the circulation of 'counterfeit notes' (FICN) from Pakistan. But only about Rs 14 crore worth FICN was additionally detected in 2016–17 compared to 2015–16. Thus, the claim that demonetisation would hit terror financing was absolutely overstretched.

The execution of demonetisation was thoroughly mismanaged. Available information show no substantive preparatory work in printing new notes and equipping the ATMs. Citizens were left stranded in queues, while the banking system froze into months of helplessness. More than 100 persons died in the aftermath. Former heads of the RBI accused the institution of squandering its credibility and autonomy, earned over many decades.

The Indian economy was hit hard by demonetisation. Official data on GDP growth released for Q3 of 2016–17 showed resilience, but it was largely because the method of estimation employed data for the period prior to 8 November 2016. The methodology of GDP estimation covers the formal sector inadequately and almost totally blacks out the informal and unorganised sectors, which bore the brunt of demonetisation. But yet, GDP growth rates fell sharply in Q4 of 2016–17 and Q1 of 2017–18, showing a strong lagged impact of demonetisation on GDP estimates. In agriculture, the kharif harvest fetched lower value to the farmers as market arrivals, demand and prices fell. The rabi sowing was completed at higher costs and in the midst of uncertainties. In industry, there was a major slowdown in the sectors of consumer goods, textiles and apparel, cement and automobiles. Large parts of the informal and unorganised sector literally shut down for weeks, and millions of workers lost jobs. The clearest indication of economic slowdown was the historic lows to which the offtake of bank credit fell after demonetisation.

The commercial banking system was, at least temporarily, inundated with liquidity. However, the very temporariness of the liquidity rush implied that any fall of interest rates was to be transient. At the same time, the liquidity rush imposed major costs on the government. With no rise in credit demand, the RBI and the government ended up spending a minimum of Rs 6,000 crore as interest costs on the new deposits. The cooperative banking system across the country was thrown into disarray by demonetisation. Excluded from cash exchange in their strongholds, these banks faced a crisis of credibility that might need years to be repaired.

As the official narratives of blocking terror financing and unearthing black money came to be questioned, the government shifted the goalpost. Demonetisation was projected as a step to usher in a cashless economy, or, as modified later, a less-cash economy. Much effort of the government went into promoting digital modes of payment, including card and mobile-based banking and e-wallets. Data analysed in this chapter till August 2017 show that after some initial pickup, the growth of volumes and value transacted through these non-cash platforms slowed down, and even shrank at places. Cash was back. Demonetisation, then, may be judged by history as a Himalayan blunder that badly crash-landed on the economy and the people. It had failed to crack the structural and cultural barriers that fostered the preference for cash in the Indian economy and society.

With the war on cash lost in India, the global movement to ban cash also faces an ambiguous future. Globally, the ban on cash is argued for to weaken terror financing and increase the effectiveness of monetary policies in being able to bypass the liquidity trap. While evidence on the former has been thin, the claims on the latter have been shown as misplaced.

If demonetisation was a sure failure on the economic front, the matter was more complex on the political front. The BJP and its Prime Minister emerged rather unscathed from a blunder, at least in the initial months. There was a seamlessness with which Modi rode through with the illogicality of his announcement. Here was a sure-footed administrator, skilled as a *pracharak* in rhetoric and polemic, who could transform an extraordinarily irrational initiative into a grand spectacle. This spectacle had all the ingredients typical of a right-wing populist offensive. Disguised as anti-elite and pro-poor, the demonisation of an external other, the invocation of terrorism and the pretense of modernity were all built into a hyper-nationalist discourse on black money. A lure of the right-wing everywhere is also the ability to reduce complex problems of politics and economics into simplistic dichotomies. It is under these dichotomies that irrationalities get buried and the power of binary building elevates hearsays into truths. The experience with Modi's demonetisation was no different.

The victory of the BJP in the assembly elections to Uttar Pradesh and Uttarakhand in March 2017 exemplified the success of such a strategy. At the same time, to see the BJP's victory in two states as a people's sanction of demonetisation would also be fallacious. First, the BJP and its allies did not win in three other states for which elections were held alongside. Second, during the election campaign in Uttar Pradesh and Uttarakhand, demonetisation was consciously downplayed by Modi and a deeply polarising communal discourse—the *shamshaan* versus *kabristan* and the Ramzan versus Diwali dichotomies—was let loose in its place. Thus, the victories of the BJP in Uttar Pradesh and Uttarakhand can also be seen as the continuation of the BJP's series of successes in the region that began with the Muzaffarnagar riots of 2013.

But regardless of such scepticisms, Indian politics has entered a new phase under the leadership of Modi. That even the bungling up of demonetisation could not challenge the BJP's rise is both a curtain-raiser to what is in store for the immediate future as well as the sign of a deeply regressive turn in Indian politics. Whether Modi and the BJP can continue their success stories is a hypothetical question, but the message to his opponents is clear. They need to fine-tune an alternative, fact-based, narrative that can challenge Modi's in the public domain.

References

All India Manufacturers' Organisation. (2017, January 16). Press Release on Demonetisation [Press release]. Mumbai.

Bagnall, J., Bounie, D., Huynh, K.P., Kosse, A., Schmidt, T., Schuh S. and Stix, H. (2014) Consumer Cash Usage: A Cross-Country Comparison with Payment Diary Survey Data. *Working Paper 1685*. European Central Bank, Frankfurt.

Batiz-Lazo, Bernardo & Efthymiou, Leonidas (eds). (2016). *The Book of Payments: Historical and Contemporary Views on the Cashless Society.* London: Palgrave Macmillan.

Bátiz-Lazo, Bernardo, Efthymiou, Leonidas and Michael, Sophia. (2016). Milestones for a Global Cashless Economy. In *The Book of Payments: Historical and Contemporary Views on the Cashless Society.* London: Palgrave Macmillan.

BIS. (2003). A Glossary of Terms Used in Payments and Settlement Systems. Basel: Committee on Payments and Settlement System.

Buiter, Willem. (2010, March), Don't Raise the Inflation Target, Remove the Zero Bound on Nominal Interest Rates Instead. *Global Macro View.* London: Citigroup,

Chandrasekhar, C.P. (2010, November 30). Corruption in the neoliberal era. *The Hindu.* Retrieved March 31, 2017, from http://bit.ly/2wNyNZb

Coll, Steve. (2017, January 18). The Strongman Problem, from Modi to Trump. *The New Yorker.* Retrieved March 31, 2017, from http://bit.ly/2xhdVuR

CRISIL. (2016, October) Best-distributed Rains in 3 Years. *Monsoon Granular Review.* Mumbai.

Krishnan, Deepa, & Siegel, Stephan. (2017, January 21). Survey of the Effects of Demonetisation on 28 Slum Neighbourhoods in Mumbai. *Economic & Political Weekly, 52(3).*

Fiege, Edgar L. (1979), 'How Big is the Irregular Economy?', *Challenge,* November-December, pp. 5-13.

GoI (2012a), *Measures to Tackle Black Money in India and Abroad: Report of the Committee Headed by Chairman, CBDT,* Ministry of Finance, Government of India, New Delhi.

————. (2012b), *Black Money: White Paper,* Ministry of Finance, Government of India, New Delhi, May.

Gutmann, Peter M (1977), 'The Subterranean Economy', *Financial Analysts Journal,* Vol. 33, No. 6, pp. 26-34.

Keynes, John Maynard (1936), *The General Theory of Employment, Interest and Money,* Palgrave MacMillan, London.

KPMG (2017), *The Pulse of FinTech Q4 2016,* London.

Krueger, Malte (2016), 'Pros and Cons of Cash: The State of the Debate', in Christian Beer, Ernest Gnan and Urs W. Birchler (eds.) *Cash on Trial,* SUERF – The European Money and Finance Forum, Vienna and Zurich.

KSPB (2017), *Committee to Study the Impact of Demonetisation on the State Economy of Kerala,* Chairman: C. P. Chandrasekhar, Kerala State Planning Board, Government of Kerala, Thiruvananthapuram.

Kumar, Alok Prasanna (2016), 'Demonetisation and the Rule of Law', *Economic & Political Weekly,* Vol. 51, Issue No. 50, 10 December.

Kumar, Arun (2016), 'Estimation of the Size of the Black Economy in India, 1996-2012', *Economic & Political Weekly,* Vol. 51, Issue No. 48, 26 November.

Mai, Heike (2016), 'Crime, Terror and Cash', *EU Monitor,* Deutsche Bank Research, Frankfurt.

Ministry of Finance (2016), 'Medium Term Recommendations to Strengthen Digital Payments Ecosystem', Committee on Digital Payments, Chairman: Ratan Wattal, available at http://finmin.nic.in/reports/watal_report271216. pdf, accessed on 31st March, 2017.

Mohan, R (2017), 'Impact of Demonetisation in Kerala', *Economic & Political Weekly,* Vol. 52, Issue No. 18, 06 May.

Mundra, S. S (2015), 'Indian Payments System Kaleidoscope', *RBI Bulletin,* May.

Nathan Associates (2017), FinTech in India, Prepared for the British High Commission, New Delhi.

NIPFP (1985), *Aspects of the Black Economy in India,* Report submitted to the Ministry of Finance, National Institute of Public Finance and Policy, New Delhi.

Padmanabhan, G. (2011), 'Payment System: Issues and Challenges', *RBI Bulletin,* December.

Patel, I. G. (2002), *Glimpses of Indian Economic Policy: An Insider's View,* Oxford University Press, New Delhi.

PMO (2016a), 'PM's Address to the Nation', dated 08 November 2016, available at http://www.pmindia.gov.in/en/news_updates/prime-ministers-address-to-the-nation/ accessed on 31st March, 2017.

Rajan, Raghuram (2017), *I do what I do*, Harper Collins, New Delhi.

Ramakumar, R. (2005), 'Formal Credit and Rural Worker Households in Kerala: A Case Study of a Malabar Village', in V. K. Ramachandran and Madhura Swaminathan (eds.) *Financial Liberalisation and Rural Banking in India*, Tulika Books, New Delhi.

RBI (2005), *The Reserve Bank of India*, Volume 3, 1967-1981, Reserve Bank of India, Mumbai.

RBI (2016), 'Payment Systems in India Vision 2012–15', Reserve Bank of India, Mumbai.

RBI (2017a), Macroeconomic Assessment of Demonetisation: A Preliminary Assessment', Mumbai, March 10.

RBI (2017b), *Annual Report 2016-17*, Mumbai.

Rogoff, Kenneth S. (2016), *The Curse of Cash*, Princeton University Press, Princeton, New Jersey.

Sandesara, J.C., 'Estimates of Unreported Economy in India', Vol. 17, Issue No. 12, 20 Mar, 1982.

SBI (2016a), *State Bank Ecowatch*, March, State Bank of India, Mumbai.

SBI (2016b), 'Currency Increase and Demonetisation', *Ecowrap*, Issue No. 2, April, State Bank of India, Mumbai.

Schneider, Friedrich and Linsbauer, Katharina (2016), 'The Financial Flows of Transnational Crime and Tax Fraud: How Much Cash Is Used and What Do We (Not) Know?', in Christian Beer, Ernest Gnan and Urs W Birchler (eds.) *Cash on Trial*, SUERF – The European Money and Finance Forum, Vienna and Zurich.

Schneider, Friedrich, Buehn, Andreas and Montenegro, Claudio E. (2010), 'Shadow Economies All over the World: New Estimates for 162 Countries from 1999 to 2007', Policy Research Working Paper 5356, Development Research Group, The World Bank, Washington.

Swissnex (2017), *FinTech in India*, Consulate General of Switzerland, Bangalore.

Vyas, Mahesh (2017a), 'Consumption Demand Hit Severely by Demonetisation', CMIE, available at https://www.cmie.com/kommon/bin/sr.php?kall=warticle&dt=2017-01-12%2017:28:45&msec=270, accessed on 31st March 2017.

Vyas, Mahesh (2017b), 'Why November 2016 IIP Does Not Reflect Demonetisation Impact?', available at https://www.cmie.com/kommon/bin/sr.php?kall=warticle&dt=2017-01-13%2014:04:00&msec=406, accessed on 31st March 2017.

Zurbrügg, Fritz (2017), 'Cash—Tried and Tested, and With a Future', Speech at the World Banknote Summit, Swiss National Bank, Bern.

II

DEBATES ON THE SIZE OF THE BLACK ECONOMY

The articles in this section examine a key question debated in the pages of the *EPW*: what is the size of the black economy in India? The opening article by Shankar Acharya, which the *EPW* published in 1983, was a review of different perspectives from which the question was approached: the fiscal approach, the monetary approach, the physical input approach, the labour market approach, and the national accounts approach. Notably, key papers with regard to the first three approaches were published in the *EPW* itself. O.P. Chopra's paper published in 1982 adopted a fiscal approach; Poonam Gupta and Sanjeev Gupta's paper published in 1982 adopted a monetary approach; and the paper by Sacchidananda Mukherjee and R. Kavita Rao published in 2017 adopted a physical input approach. Edited versions of all the three papers are carried in this section.

This section also has an article by J.C. Sandesara. Sandesara's article, published in 1983, was an empirically rich critique of the monetarist approach offered by Peter Gutmann to measure the size of the unaccounted economy in 1977.

2

Unaccounted Economy in India

A Critical Review of Some Recent Estimates

Shankar Acharya

The principal objective of this chapter is to present a critical survey of the estimates of the unaccounted economy in India. A second objective of this chapter is to outline a taxonomy for the various estimation approaches that have been essayed in India and abroad. This is done in Section II, immediately following a brief Section I, which draws some key conceptual distinctions. Sections III through VI evaluate four studies recently conducted for India, each exemplifying a different approach to the problem. Section VII draws together the estimates produced by the various approaches for ready comparison and comment. The final section offers some concluding remarks.

I: Concepts and Definitions

First of all, it is important to distinguish between the *flow* of *black income* over a period of time (such as a year) and the *stock* of *black wealth* at any given point of time. Unfortunately, the term 'black money' is frequently, and confusingly, used in common parlance to refer to both black income and black wealth when, in fact, its meaning, strictly speaking, should be limited to that portion of black wealth which is held in the form of currency and liquid bank deposits or, in short, money.

Given the possibilities of 'laundering' black wealth into white, the problems of estimating the stock of black wealth are even more formidable than those faced in estimating black income. Not surprisingly, all the estimates reviewed in this chapter confine their scope to the estimation of black or unaccounted income in the economy.

Second, at least two distinct meanings of unaccounted income should be recognised:

The aggregate of incomes that should have been reported to tax authorities but were not (in principle this includes incomes from illegal activities); and

The extent to which estimates of national income and output are biased downwards because of such non-reporting (or under-reporting) of incomes and output.

Each of these two main definitions can be refined and sub-classified in a number of ways. The point that merits emphasis is that the two concepts *are* distinct, and *a* case can be made for the relevance of each.

II: Alternative Methods for Estimating Unaccounted Income: A Taxonomy

Given the proliferation of methods and estimates in the recent years, a modest taxonomic exercise may not be wholly redundant. The following broad approaches may be distinguished:

a) Fiscal approaches,
b) Monetary approaches,
c) Physical input approaches,
d) Labour market approaches,
e) National accounts approaches.

Fiscal Approaches

Most variants of this approach attempt to arrive at independent estimates of incomes subject to tax, compare these with the incomes actually assessed for taxation (typically much lower amounts) and call the discrepancy a measure of unaccounted income. Usually, the 'independent estimate' of the tax base starts from income information contained in the national accounts. Kaldor (1956) was an early exponent of this approach in India. His methodology was used by the Wanchoo Committee to obtain more updated estimates of tax-evaded income in India. A variant of the same method has recently been used by Chopra (1982) to estimate a time series of unaccounted income in India from 1960–61 to 1976–77; his work is reviewed in Section III. Studies based on the same underlying idea have also been conducted in the United States (US) (Kenadjian 1982) and the United Kingdom (UK) (O'Higgins 1982). The fiscal approaches, unlike the others that follow, generally make use of the first of the two definitions of unaccounted income sketched above.

Monetary Approaches

In essence, monetary approaches rest on the assumed stability in the relationship of various money stock aggregates to each other and to the total of income or transactions in the economy, and attribute departures from the 'norm' values to the growth of unaccounted income in the economy.

Two variants of the monetary approach have become quite common. The first, pioneered by Gutmann (1977), for the US in 1976, picks a base year when the size of the unaccounted economy is assumed to be negligible, takes the currency-to-demand-deposits ratio for that year to be a fixed norm, and attributes all subsequent increases in this ratio to the disproportionately growing demand for cash-to-finance-transactions in a growing unaccounted economy. Since the currency-to-deposits ratio has been falling steadily in India since 1950, the application of the Gutmann method for India yields nonsense results, such as a 'negative black economy' in many of the years since 1952–53. A recent and succinct critique of Gutmann's method as applied to India is provided by Sandesara (1983; published in this volume).

Another monetary variant, first deployed by Feige (1979) in the US for 1976, also starts with a base year when the underground economy is assumed to be non-existent, estimates the ratio of total monetised transactions (by cheque and by currency) to total nominal GNP (gross national product) for that year, and attributes any subsequent increase in this ratio to the growth of the unaccounted economy. Gupta and Gupta (1982; published in this volume) have applied this method to India to estimate a time series for the black economy from 1967–68 to 1978–79. Section IV summarises and assesses their work.

Physical Input Approaches

Physical input approaches share a close family resemblance to monetary approaches in that both seek to identify some stable 'norm' linking the use of physical inputs (or monetary stocks) to the national output. Here, one starts with an intermediate input that is widely used throughout the economy, such as electric power, and for which the aggregate output and consumption data are deemed reliable. The next step is to estimate a relationship between national (or sectoral) output and input use, making due allowances for changes in technology and output mix. To the extent that the consumption of the input (electric power, for example) cannot be explained in terms of growth in officially measured GNP and other relevant variables, such as changes in technology and output mix, to that extent the 'residual' consumption is attributed to the unaccounted economy and serves as a measure of its size. Section V reviews the attempt by Gupta and Mehta (1982) to apply this approach to India.

Labour Market Approaches

It has been suggested that the size of the unaccounted economy can be gauged from official labour force participation rates, if these are inexplicably low compared to periods or countries where the black economy is of limited significance. This approach has been used mainly by researchers in Italy (as in, Contini 1981), where the official labour force participation rate has declined drastically since the late 1950s. Unofficial surveys have estimated participation rates much higher than the official ones in recent years, suggesting that growing numbers of Italians are finding gainful employment in activities that are not reported to the authorities. Given an estimate of the 'underground' labour force and one of average value added per worker, it is easy to compute an estimate of the size of the unaccounted economy. The relevance of this approach to India is limited because of the numerous difficulties with the quality of data on employment.

National Accounts Approaches

Several alternative approaches fall into this category. The first relies on the fact that a country's GNP is frequently estimated independently, from both the income and expenditure sides. Typically, the estimate from the income side is somewhat lower than that from the expenditure side. In the UK, it has been hypothesised that the discrepancy constitutes a measure of unaccounted incomes, which escapes national output accounting from the income side but are 'caught' by the expenditure side estimates (see Macafee 1980). This approach hinges crucially on the independence of the national income estimates from the income and expenditure sides. Where such independence is not complete, as in India, the approach cannot be effectively applied.[1] Furthermore, this approach cannot deal with those black economy activities that escape national accounting from both the income and expenditure sides.

An alternative national accounting approach to estimating the unaccounted economy is to scrutinise the national account estimates of value added for each sector and gauge the probable extent to which under-reporting of outputs, prices and values might be imparting a downward bias to these estimates. Some work along these lines has been done by Ghosh *et al.* (1981), which is reviewed in Section VI.

III: Fiscal Approach: Chopra's Estimates

The Method

Chopra's study closely follows the Kaldor/Wanchoo methodology. The key assumptions and steps in this method are as follows:

i) Incomes by sector of origin from the national income accounts form the starting point;

ii) It is assumed that there is no question of tax evasion (and therefore of tax-evaded income) for incomes originating in agriculture, and, that in all other sectors, salary incomes are fully reported for income taxation;

iii) For all non-agricultural sectors, the ratio of non-salary income to total income is estimated;

iv) For each sector, the proportion and amount non-salary income above the income tax exemption limit is estimated;

v) Summation across the sectors yields an estimate of total non-salary income assessable to tax;

vi) Actual non-salary income assessed for income taxation is estimated and subtracted from the above total to obtain the estimate of unaccounted income for the relevant year.

---

[1] The national accounts estimates of private final consumption expenditure rely on estimates of gross output by sector of origin and the latter are intimately linked to the estimates of value added by sector of origin (Government of India 1980).

Chopra deployed this method to obtain a time series of unaccounted income from 1960–61 to 1976–77. In implementing the crucial steps (iii) and (iv), Chopra used the same proportions that had been used by the Wanchoo Committee in its estimate of unaccounted income for 1961–62.

In carrying out step (vi), the Wanchoo report had obtained information on income assessed to tax for 1961–62 (assessment year 1962–63), but had resorted to a simplifying assumption for 1965–66, namely, that the ratio of evaded (or unaccounted) income to non-salary assessable income had remained constant and equal to that observed for 1961–62. This simplifying assumption was invoked to cope with the awkward fact that incomes earned in any given year are actually assessed over the next several years.[2] Chopra presents one set of estimates using the same simplifying assumption as the one used in the Wanchoo report for 1965–66. He also estimates an alternative series for unaccounted income based on 'a relatively less demanding assumption' for step (vi), namely, that 'the ratio of the sum of assessed non-salary income in different years for their given year to the actually assessed non-salary income of the given year remain(s) constant.'

The estimates obtained by Chopra are presented in Table 2.1, both as absolute magnitudes and percentages of net and gross national product. It is interesting to observe that after 1972–73 there is a marked divergence between the two series computed by Chopra. For the final year, 1976–77, the estimate based on Chopra's 'own' methodology is nearly 80 per cent higher than that obtained by a direct application of the Wanchoo report assumptions.

A Critique

Chopra himself points out some of the limitations of the exercise, though, he does not always draw out their full implications. First, and perhaps most important, the sectoral national income data are assumed to provide sound estimates of total income originating in each sector. Yet, there are good reasons to believe that in key sectors like trade, manufacturing, ownership of dwellings and other services, the estimates of income reported in the official national income estimates may be

---

[2] For 1961–62 financial year (1962–63 assessment year), the Wanchoo Committee had obtained the full-time profile of assessments from the revenue authorities.

TABLE 2.1 Chopra's Estimates of Unaccounted Income, 1960–61 to 1976–77, in Rs Crore and Per Cent

Year	Wanchoo method (Rs in crore) (1)	Own method (Rs in crore) (2)	Unaccounted Income			
			Column (1) as % of NNP at current factor cost (3)	Column (2) as % of NNP at current factor cost (4)	Column (1) as % of GNP at current factor cost (5)	Column (2) as % of GNP at current factor cost (6)
1960–61	747	916	5.6	6.9	5.3	6.5
1961–62	801	716	5.7	5.1	5.4	4.8
1962–63	897	837	6.1	5.6	5.7	5.3
1963–64	1008	1452	5.9	8.6	5.6	8.1
1964–65	1132	1564	5.7	7.8	5.4	7.4
1965–66	1231	1539	6.0	7.5	5.6	7.0
1966–67	964	1685	4.0	7.1	3.8	6.4
1967–68	1563	1816	5.6	6.5	3.9	4.6
1968–69	1651	1318	5.8	4.6	5.5	4.4
1969–70	2104	2714	6.7	8.6	6.3	8.1
1970–71	1908	2662	5.6	6.0	5.2	5.7
1971–72	2208	1392	6.0	3.8	5.7	3.6
1972–73	1897	1795	4.7	4.5	4.4	4.2
1973–74	2869	4757	5.7	9.4	5.4	8.9

(Cont'd)

TABLE 2.1 (Cont'd)

Year	Wanchoo method (Rs in crore) (1)	Own method (Rs in crore) (2)	Column (1) as % of NNP at current factor cost (3)	Column (2) as % of NNP at current factor cost (4)	Column (1) as % of GNP at current factor cost (5)	Column (2) as % of GNP at current factor cost (6)
			Unaccounted Income			
1974–75	4110	8611	6.9	14.5	6.5	13.7
1975–76	4107	7292	6.6	11.7	6.2	11.0
1976–77	4551	8098	6.8	12.1	6.4	11.4

Sources: Chopra (1982); Government of India, Economic Survey, 1982–83.

biased downwards by substantial margins for reasons of tax evasion and related motives (*see*, for example, Ghosh *et al.* 1981). Not coincidentally, those are also sectors in which the proportion of non-salary incomes are relatively high. Taken together, these points suggest that the estimates of total assessable non-salary income may be substantially below the true levels, which, in turn, indicates significant under-estimation of tax-evaded income.[3]

Second, the assumption that salary incomes are fully reported for tax may embody some optimism. Aside from various hidden perquisites, there is considerable anecdotal evidence suggesting that payment, by employers, of additional unaccounted emoluments to private sector salary earners may be widespread. Many wage and salary earners also augment their incomes through 'moonlighting' on the side.[4] While the earnings from such moonlighting are unlikely to be reported to tax authorities (or included in national accounts estimates), this does not, strictly speaking, constitute evasion on *salary* incomes; rather, it is a case of evasion with respect to non-salary incomes. A similar remark applies to bribes accepted by wage and salary earners.[5]

Third, Chopra's application of the Wanchoo methodology assumes that the ratio of evaded income to non-salary, assessable income remains constant. As Chopra notes, this is a strong assumption, which he proceeds to relax in his alternative, 'own,' estimate. However, Chopra feels that even his weaker assumption (quoted earlier) is subject to criticism, since, he notes, it implies 'an unchanged efficiency of tax administration.' Actually, it is not at all clear that this implication follows from the assumption underlying his 'own,' modified estimate. What his assumption appears to accomplish is to give him a device to go from

---

[3] This judgment has to be qualified. While the incentives to evade taxes and earn illegal incomes may be powerful in these sectors, the extent to which the associated suppression of incomes and output is reflected in national income data depends crucially on national income estimation methods—a point made earlier.

[4] A school teacher may undertake private tuition; a PWD carpenter may take up remunerative projects on his own account, etc.

[5] In national accounting terms, bribes may be classified as transfers and therefore excluded from the estimates. But from the viewpoint of the tax authorities, non-reporting of bribe incomes constitutes tax evasion. On the other hand, payment of bribes reduces the payer's income without altering his tax liability. Where bribes have to be paid often and regularly, it may be reasonable to assume that the payer makes such payments out of tax-evaded income.

published information on non-salary incomes assessed in a given year (but pertaining to several years) to an estimate of assessed non-salary incomes *attributable* to the given year. But the basis for his assumption is not supported by argument or evidence.

Fourth, the methodology assumes that the ratio of non-salary income to total income of a sector remains constant. Chopra finds some support for this assumption in the observation that the ratios are the same for the two years for which data are presented in the Wanchoo report. This may be rather cold comfort, since the observed constancy is more likely to be the result of extrapolation of the ratios observed in one year to the other. Certainly, over the 17-year-period covered by Chopra's work, there is little reason to believe, *a priori*, that these ratios would stay constant.

Fifth, it is also assumed that the ratio of non-salary income above the exemption limit to total income originating in a sector remains constant. There are several problems with this assumption. To begin with, the empirical basis for the base year (1961–62) values of these ratios is absent from both the Wanchoo report and Chopra's article. It is noteworthy that Kaldor (1956) characterised the corresponding and similar assumptions in his estimates as being 'based on very slender foundations.' Furthermore, even if one could give credence to the base year estimates, there is no reason to believe that these proportions would remain invariant to changes, over time, in the structure and organisation of production within each sector, to inflation, or to changes in tax laws, which have altered the effective exemption limits.[6] Chopra contends that 'on balance there may not be a significant change,' but he does not marshall arguments in support of this claim.

There are other problems with this methodology that do not appear to have been fully appreciated by Chopra. First, the national income estimates, do not, by deliberate convention, include estimates of income earned in illegal occupations, such as smuggling. But for the estimation of tax-evaded income, such income ought to be included, since the tax laws require the declaration of all earnings, including those from illegal activities.

Second, in computing non-salary incomes actually assessed to tax, Chopra relies on the data published in the annual issues of the All India Income Tax Statistics (AIITS). But, owing to the delays in reporting

---

[6] In fact, a significant weakness of the Kalder/Wanchoo/Chopra approach is its failure to distinguish between corporate and non-corporate income earners, when exemption limits, deductions, evasion possibilities and incentives to evade are likely to vary substantially across these categories.

and other reasons, the information contained in the AIITS is far from complete. The main point is that the assessments analysed and tabulated in the AIITS publications do not cover all assessees and there are strong grounds for believing that the extent of underreporting is substantial. Therefore, Chopra's estimates of assessed non-salary income, which are based on the AIITS, are likely to be serious underestimates. This source of error imparts a strong *upward* bias to Chopra's estimates of unaccounted (tax-evaded) income.

To sum up, there are serious problems with the estimates of tax evaded income obtained by Chopra. At best, Chopra's study provides a point of departure for further explorations along the fiscal approach.

IV: Monetary Approach: Estimates by Gupta and Gupta

Method and Results

Feige's method relies on the standard Fisherian identity, $MV = PT$, where M is the stock of money, V is its transactions velocity and PT is the total value of monetised transactions in the economy. Further, the method assumes that there is a constant proportional relationship between the total value of monetised transactions in the economy, PT, and the total nominal income of the economy, Y. Here, PT includes the value of monetised transactions in the black or unreported economy, just as Y includes the value of income originating in the unreported economy. Application of the method involves the following steps:

i) Compute 'the total value of monetised transactions $PT (= MV)$ for a base year when the unreported economy is assumed to be non-existent;

ii) Observe the ratio of PT to officially measured GNP in the year (since, by hypothesis, there is no unreported economy in that year, GNP will be equal to V);

iii) Compute the value of total monetised transactions in the subsequent years, and by applying the ratio computed from (ii) estimate the total nominal income, Y, for the corresponding years;

iv) For each year, the difference between the computed value of Y and officially measured nominal GNP yields estimates of the unreported economy. Looked at in another way, whenever the ratio of PT to measured GNP exceeds the base year value, the presence of a black economy is signalled.

The computational burden of this method rests with calculating the total value of monetised transactions in each year. Following Feige, Gupta and Gupta (henceforth GG) subdivided the task into two parts: estimating the value of transactions supported by cheques and that by currency. They estimated the value of cheque transactions by multiplying the average stock of demand deposits by their turnover rate. Data on deposits were readily available, and information on their turnover rates was available for certain years.

Estimating the value of currency transactions required some bold assumptions. In principle, the value of currency transactions can be obtained by aggregating, for all currency denominations, the product of the value of the currency with the public and its turnover rate (per year) per unit. The value of currency with the public, by different denominations, was readily available. It was in computing their respective turnover rates per unit that assumptions had to be made. Like Feige, GG estimated the turnover rates per unit of currency by recourse to the following identity:

Turnover rate per year = (Lifetime transactions of currency note)
÷ (Average life of currency note)

For lifetime transactions, that is, the total number of times a currency note can change hands before it has to be retired, GG followed Feige in taking Robert Laurent's (1970) estimate of 125 for the United States. For average length of life, they could only obtain indigenous information for the Rs 1 note, and they assumed the same length of life for the Rs 2 note. For denominations Rs 5 through Rs 100, they used estimates pertaining to Canadian dollars of denominations ranging from $1 to $100. For Rs 1,000 and Rs 5,000 notes, they used Feige's estimate of 22 years for the US $100 bill.

Based on these assumptions, GG obtained the time series for currency transactions, demand deposit transactions and the black economy (Table 2.2). In obtaining the last series, they used the average transactions to income ratio for the years 1949–50 to 1951–52 as their base period norm on the assumption that the black economy was of negligible dimensions during these years.

A Critique

A crucial assumption in the Feige/GG method relates to the constancy of the ratio of total monetised transactions to total nominal income, that

TABLE 2.2 Estimates of the Size of the Black Economy in India, in Rs crore

Year	Currency transactions (Rs crore)	Demand deposits transactions (Rs crore)	Total transactions (Rs crore) (1+2)	Ratio of total transactions to official GNP	Size of the black economy	Black economy as % of official GNP	Currency transactions as percent of total transaction, Column (1)/(3)*100
	(1)	(2)	(3)	(4)	(5)	(6)	(7)
1967–68	127974.5	82272.4	210246.9	6.56	3034.4	9.50	60.9
1968–69	133399.3	91582.0	224981.3	6.81	4504.2	13.64	59.3
1969–70	145252.8	106770.0	252022.8	6.89	5458.8	14.92	57.6
1970–71	158738.7	135479.9	294218.6	7.32	8900.3	22.15	54.0
1971–72	171925.9	161520.9	333446.8	7.70	12354.8	28.56	51.6
1972–73	182731.7	194626.6	377358.3	7.90	15195.5	31.82	48.4
1973–74	214030.9	234142.5	448173.5	7.61	15894.9	27.00	47.8
1974–75	230685.7	274531.2	505217.0	7.24	14518.1	20.81	45.7
1975–76	237077.4	309402.7	546480.1	7.52	18458.0	25.39	43.4
1976–77	268784.9	372391.4	641176.3	8.33	30014.8	39.01	41.9
1977–78	284537.1	442028.0	726565.1	8.37	34335.2	39.53	39.2
1978–79	315284.3	541782.2	856966.4	8.92	46866.9	48.78	36.8

Sources: Gupta and Gupta (1982) for Columns (1) through (6); Column (7) is computed as shown.

Notes: Average value of the ratio of total transactions to official GNP for 1949–50 to 1951–52 is 5.995. Divisions of yearly figures in column (3) by 5.995 and then subtraction of measured GNP gives column (5).

is, the ratio of PT to Y. If this ratio changes over time, for reasons other than the growth of a black economy, then the estimates for the black economy are undermined.

In fact, there are some good reasons to expect the ratio of transactions to income to change with economic development. First, with increasing monetisation of the economy, the ratio can be expected to increase, since monetisation will tend to increase the numerator without necessarily affecting the denominator. Second, with development, the density of inter-industry transactions normally increases, or, in other words, the input-output matrix for the economy gradually fills up. Thus, the growth of inter-industry transactions, and hence of total transactions (the numerator) can be expected to be more rapid than the growth of nominal value added (the denominator). So, once again, the ratio of transactions to income can be expected to increase.

Third, as GG themselves note, economic development will normally be associated with disproportionately higher growth in purely financial transactions, reflecting growing diversification and sophistication in financial and capital markets.[7] This too would tend to increase the ratio of transactions to income over time. On the other side of the coin, a growing proportion of economic transactions may be conducted within vertically integrated production units. This would tend to reduce the transactions/income ratio, though its effect is likely to be much less than the three factors noted above, working in the opposite direction. On balance, *a priori* reasoning would suggest that the transactions/income ratio will increase as development proceeds. But if this is the case, then the observed increases in the ratio of transactions to nominal, measured GNP cannot be wholly attributed to the development of an imported economy. It may, at least partly, reflect the effect of the influences cited above.

A second set of doubts regarding the GG estimates relate to their use of proxy values (from the United States and Canada) for their estimates of lifetime transactions of currency notes and the average of different denomination notes. One can sympathise with their need to make some assumptions without suspending doubts about the specific ones they have used.

Quite apart from the issue of the actual values assumed (for lifetime transactions and average length of life), their method freezes the currency

---

[7] Gupta and Gupta suggest some evidence to the contrary in India, but it is not compelling.

turnover rates for the entire period. Thus, on their assumptions, inter-temporal variations in the value of currency transactions are attributable solely to variations in currency stocks (of different denominations) held by the public.

Fourth, the method makes no allowance for possible differences in velocity of transactions in the reported and unreported economies. The same turnover rates for demand deposits and currency are implicitly assumed to be applicable irrespective of the nature of the transactions.

None of the last three considerations allows one to deduce the possible direction of bias in the estimates of the unaccounted economy; they simply undermine the fragility of their basis.

A fifth reason for doubting the GG estimates derive from the time profile of the ratio of currency transactions to total transactions, which is implied by their estimates. Table 2.2, column (7) shows the evolution of this ratio from 1967–68 to 1978–79. There is a marked and steady decline from 61 per cent in 1967–68 to 37 per cent in 1978–79.

This decline occurs during a period, when, according to GG, the unreported economy grew rapidly in relation to officially measured GNP from under 10 per cent of the officially measured GNP in 1967–68 to nearly 50 per cent in 1978–79. In absolute nominal terms, the scale of the black economy is estimated to have increased by more than 1,500 per cent over this period. These opposing trends do not co-exist comfortably. It is one thing to admit that black economy transactions may not be wholly financed through cash. It is quite another to reconcile a rapid growth in the black economy with a declining share of cash transactions in total transactions. This is so because both reasoning and casual empiricism strongly suggest that black economy transactions are likely to be mainly financed through cash.[8]

Finally, what of the results obtained by GG? A careful scrutiny of the national accounts suggests that about half of officially measured GNP in 1978–79 was in sectors such as agriculture, public administration and defence, electricity, gas and water supply, banking and insurance, and railways—sectors in which the incidence of the unreported economy is generally believed to be negligible. It follows that virtually all of the Rs 46,867 crore of unreported income estimated for 1978–79 by GG was in the remaining sectors for which the total of officially measured NDP (net domestic product) was less than Rs 42,000 crore. This, in turn,

---

[8] Tanzi (1982a) levels a similar criticism against Feige's estimates of the underground economy for the United States.

implies that those responsible for constructing India's official national accounts were managing to account for only about a half of total value added in those sectors where the black economy is believed to flourish. While this implication is not impossible, it is certainly implausible.

To sum up, there are serious methodological reasons to doubt the validity of the Feige approach as applied to India by GG. These methodological concerns are compounded by the *prima facie* implausibility of the results obtained through this approach. Furthermore, as in the case of Chopra's estimates, doubts about the methods and results pertaining to any single year are reinforced when it comes to considering the plausibility of the estimated time series, not to mention the regressions advanced to 'explain' the series.

V: Physical Input Approach: Estimates by Gupta and Mehta

Method and Estimates

Gupta and Mehta (henceforth GM) generate estimates of the unreported economy based on trends in the consumption of electric power in the economy. As noted earlier, the basic approach is to identify a stable relationship between the use of electric power and national output (with due allowance for changes in output-mix and technology) and then see if the growth of officially measured GDP can account for the growth of electricity consumption; to the extent it cannot, unreported economic activity is inferred. The main steps and assumptions of their method are summarised below:

i) they start with the assumption that there is a fixed linear relationship between total value added (reported plus unreported) in the economy and the consumption of electric power, which can be represented by the following equation.

$$a = \frac{Total\ value\ added\ in\ economy}{Input\ of\ electricity\ power} = \frac{IN_t}{TY_t}$$

ii) In any year, t, a variable b_t is defined such that,

$$b_t = \frac{Total\ GDP}{Reported\ GDP} = \frac{TY_t}{RY_t}$$

This allows one to write:

$$IN_t = a.b_t \, RY_t = \beta_t RY_t$$

Where $\beta_t = ab_t$

In order to allow for changes in technology and output-mix, GM define the proxy variables IT_t and IP_t to represent these phenomena. The resulting form of the equation to be estimated is:

$$IN_t = \alpha + \beta_1 RY_t + y_1 IT_t + \lambda_2 IP_t$$

iii) Recognising that the value of β_t can change over time (because of underlying changes in b_t), GM experiment with alternative functional forms of βt such as:

$$\beta_t + \beta_0 + \beta_1 t + \beta_2 t^2 \ldots$$

iv) The equation, which is finally chosen to derive the scale of the unreported economy, incorporates estimates for β_0 and β_2, and is as follows:

$$IN_t = -7782.27 + (0.7909 + 0.001203 * t^2) * RY_t$$
$$+ 2637.72 * IT_t + 11856 \, IP_t$$

Where $R_2 = 0.996$; $F = 1238.08$;
IN_t = Gross electricity generation in million Kwh;
RY_t = GDP at factor cost in 1970–71 Rs crore;
t = Time trend (it is also the proxy for technology change);
IP_t = Ratio of gross value added in the secondary sector to gross value-added in the primary sector of the economy.

On the basis of this equation, GM obtain the following estimates for the unreported economy (they present their results as per cent shares of total GDP; here they have also been converted into per cent shares of reported GDP):

Year	As per cent of total GDP	As per cent of reported GDP
1964–65	2.7	2.8
1974–75	12.1	13.8
1978–79	16.4	19.8

A Critique

The first point that needs to be made about GM's methodology is that their write-up does not seem to be complete. Their estimated equation yields values for β_t any given year. But β_t is a product of two parameters, a and b_t; and it is only the latter which yields a numerical measure for the unreported economy. To go from β_t to b_t requires either independent knowledge of the value of a, or, alternatively, the value of a can be derived by assuming that the unreported economy is non-existent in some base year (in which case b becomes unity by hypothesis and $\beta_0 = boa$ gives an estimate of a. Presumably GM adopted the latter approach, but it is not spelt out in their chapter.

Aside from this apparent omission, GM's methodology is questionable on a number of grounds. Most of these relate to GM's assumption of a fixed coefficient relationship between power consumption and national output (abstracting from changes due to technical change and output-mix). While this assumption may be plausible for a technical process or even an industrial plant, it is much less so at the economy-wide level.

First, value-added (whether accounted or not) in service sectors, such as trade, can expand (or contract) greatly with relatively little change in the demand for electricity. The same is true for much of agriculture. Note that the issue here is not of the output-mix of total value added; rather it is a denial of any fixed coefficient, or linear relationship between power consumption and value added in certain major sectors of the economy. Once this is admitted, not much significance can be read into the observed changes in the ratio of total electricity consumption to measured GDP.

A second reason for doubting the significance of changes in this ratio is that electricity is not just an intermediate input in production. Much of residential demand, and perhaps some of commercial demand, falls into the category of final consumption. Such consumption can vary with changes in income, the relative price of electricity, the spread of electricity-using consumer goods and so on. The simple point is that changes in final (that is, as a consumer good) consumption of electricity can powerfully influence the aggregate ratio of total electricity consumption to measured GDP, and thus undermine the interpretation of that ratio as an input-output production relation. Sometimes, the growth of final consumption of electricity may be the result of deliberate government policy. The period 1960–61 to 1978–79 witnessed massive increases in rural electrification; while much of this increase could be classified as intermediate consumption of electricity associated with higher production, much could also be categorised as final consumption, which improved the quality of rural life.

A third weakness of GM's method is that it assumes total electricity production to equal total electricity consumption except for transmission losses which are assumed to be a constant proportion. In fact, with the growing emphasis on rural electrification, the proportion of transmission losses may have been increasing over time.

Fourth, while GM allow, in principle, for changes in electricity demand due to technology change and shifts in the composition of output, their actual modelling of these factors is unconvincing. Technical change is modelled through a simple time trend, which could just as well be interpreted as a proxy for any number of factors ranging from the growth of rural electrification to secular increases in final electricity consumption, stemming from growth of per capita incomes and generalised 'electrification' of the society. As for the output-mix variable, IP_t, its role in explaining changes in electricity consumption turns out to be statistically insignificant. This may be more a comment on the variable used than on the underlying theory. It leaves the tertiary sector wholly out of the account. Moreover, at its high level of aggregation, the variable is incapable of reflecting the effect of output shifts *within* the broad sectors, primary and secondary.

Finally, for those who fall credulous prey to high values of R^2 and F statistics, it is worth emphasising that GM's estimated equation permits alternative interpretations to the one that they have used. GM interprets the estimated β coefficients as indicators of the unreported economy. They could just as easily be interpreted as indicators of electricity-intensification in the economy as it modernises over time and adopts more power-intensive techniques of production in all sectors. Or, the coefficients may be interpreted to represent growing final consumption of electricity commensurate with increasing per capita income, rapid rural electrification and the spread of electricity-using consumer goods. The point is that statistical 'goodness of fit' cannot substitute for weaknesses in the underlying assumptions and theory.

To sum up, GM have made a novel and intriguing attempt to apply a physical input approach to estimating the size of the unreported economy. Unlike the estimates of GG, the results obtained by GM are not, in themselves, implausible. But, as the preceding pages have tried to show, GM's efforts to identify 'residual' power consumption and thence to gauge the size of the unreported economy are vulnerable to too many questions and doubts to merit confidence.

VI: National Accounts Approach: Estimates by Ghosh, *et al.*

The Estimates

As the title says, the main purpose of the chapter by Ghosh, Bagchi, Rastogi and Chaturvedi (1981) is to analyse and explain 'Trends in Capital Formation, Growth of Domestic Product arid Capital-Output Ratios (1850–51 to 1978–79).' In particular, Ghosh *et al.* dwell on the 'intriguing phenomenon of the high observed rates of capital formation not being reflected in higher output growth.' As one of the possible explanations to the puzzle, Ghosh *et al.* consider the possibility that the official data for GDP may reflect significant under-estimation. It should, thus, be clear that Ghosh *et al.* do not make estimation of the unreported economy the central object of their study, but rather are led to this issue in their search for solutions to the investment-output puzzle.

In providing guestimates of unreported GDP, they do not deploy any complicated 'methodology,' in the normal sense of the word. They simply examine the national accounts, by sector, and suggest some orders of magnitude by which output and value-added may be under-recorded in certain key sectors. Thus, they hazard that the gross value of output from manufacturing is understated by 10 per cent, principally to further the goal of tax evasion. For similar reasons, they suggest that gross value added in trade and other services is under-estimated by 15 per cent. For rental from housing, they note that the national accounts rely on municipal valuations, which may be grossly understated because of, primarily, the prevailing rent control laws. Combining these assumptions they estimated unreported GDP to have been about 7–9 per cent of current market price GDP in the years 1970–71 to 1977–78.

An Assessment

The estimates by Ghosh *et al.* are the most informal of all the ones reviewed thus far. Indeed, part of the reason for including them in this survey is that they serve us a contrast to the more 'technical' methods. Nor are they quite in the category of single number guesses that crop up frequently in newspapers and magazines. These estimates are more in the nature of 'three number guesses'—corresponding to the three rates of undervaluation, in different sectors, which they assume.

The fact remains that these percentages are guesses, unsupported by any independent quantitative information. True, they may reflect informed judgment, since all the authors are well-versed in the strengths and weaknesses of India's national accounts. But they are guesses nonetheless. Aside from suggesting possible (and plausible) orders of magnitude, their principal virtue may lie in provoking other researchers to tackle the issues of under-estimation at a *sectoral* level and confirm (or controvert) the guesses they have advanced.

VII: Estimates of Unaccounted Income: A Numerical Overview

In Table 2.3, the estimates reviewed in this chapter are brought together for easy reference and comparison. The latter activity should be prefaced with the repetition of an important warning, namely, that the concept of unaccounted income is not the same in all the studies. Specifically, Chopra's estimates are based on the notion of tax-evaded income, while the others reviewed in this chapter refer to income which are not reported or measured in official estimates of national income and output. It is not entirely clear which concept of unaccounted income underlies Rangnekar's estimates. In his note of dissent to the Wanchoo report, he appears to adhere to the concept of tax-evaded income, but his recent paper (Rangnekar 1982) updating these earlier estimates is somewhat ambiguous on this score.

It should be said that no attempt has been made to evaluate Rangnekar's estimates in this chapter as it was impossible to obtain a clear understanding of his expenditure methodology from the description provided in both the sources mentioned above. Nevertheless, since his estimates are frequently cited, they have been inducted for purely numerical comparisons.

A few points emerge from an inspection of Table 2.3. First, except for the estimates by Ghosh *et al.*, all the others point towards an unaccounted economy that is growing both in absolute value and in relation to officially estimated GNP.[9] How much should be inferred from this

---

[9] And the principal reason underlying the relatively static estimates by Ghosh *et al.*, is that their assumptions about the percentage of underreporting in various sectors are held constant over time; the changes in the aggregate percentage are attributable wholly to changes in the composition of the GDP.

TABLE 2.3   Alternative Estimates of Unaccounted Income, in Per Cent of GNP or GDP

Year	Chopra's Estimate		Gupta & Gupta's Estimates	Gupta & Mehta's Estimates	Ghosh et al.'s Estimates	Rangnekar's Estimates
	Wanchoo Method	Own method				
1960–61	5.0	6.1	–	–	–	–
1960-62	3.0	4.5	–	–	–	–
1960-63	5.3	4.9	–	–	–	–
1960-64	5.2	7.4	–	–	–	–
1960-65	4.9	6.8	–	2.8	–	–
1960-66	5.1	6.4	–	–	–	9.8
1960-67	3.5	6.1	–	–	–	–
1960-68	4.9	5.7	9.5	–	–	–
1960-69	5.0	4.0	13.6	–	–	8.6
1969–70	5.8	7.4	14.9	–	–	8.4
1970–71	4.8	5.2	22.3	--	7.6	–
1971–72	5.1	3.2	28.7	–	7.8	–
1972–73	4.0	3.8	31.9	–	7.8	–
1973–74	4.9	8.1	27.1	–	7.4	9.9
1974–75	5.9	12.4	20.9	13.8	8.1	9.8
1975–76	5.6	9.9	25.0	–	8.4	10.0
1976–77	5.7	10.2	37.6	–	8.7	11.3
1977–78	–	–	38.4	–	8.7	12.1
1978–79	–	–	48.1	19.8	–	13.5
1979–80	–	–	–	–	–	14.4

Sources: Chopra (1982), Gupta and Gupta (1982), Gupta and Mehta (1982), Ghosh *et al.* (1981), Rangnekar (1982), and Government of India (1982).

Note: Columns (1), (2), (3), (5), and (6) are computed as percentage of GNP at current market prices. Column (4) is computed as a percentage of GDP at factor cost and 1970–71 prices.

common characteristic is not clear. True, the rising trend is in conformity with conventional anxieties about a growing black economy. But given the dubious nature of the underlying methodologies, it would be unwise to infer anything more than a weak presumption of a growing trend. Even that judgment may be more firmly based on casual empiricism than on the estimates reviewed here.

Second, and this highlights the fragility of the various exercises, the estimates of unaccounted income for any given year vary widely across the different studies. Thus, for the year 1976–77, they range from a low of 9 per cent of GNP according to Ghosh *et al.* to a high of 38 per cent estimated by GG.[10] About the only thing these numbers have in common is that they are all positive, and even this virtue would have become a casualty if the results of Sandesara's critical application of the Gutmann method had been included (for 1976–77, it gave an estimate of black income of *minus* 55 per cent of GNP).

VIII: Concluding Remarks

What is one to make of all this? The first and most obvious lesson to draw is that the enterprise of estimating the size of the unaccounted economy is still in its infancy. It has a long way to go before the methods and results can persuade the agnostics, let alone the sceptics. This need not be construed as a counsel of despair. In any new field of empirical enquiry, it is quite natural for the early efforts to be highly vulnerable to criticism. But it is only by beginning, and then responding to legitimate criticisms, that progress can be achieved. Of course, there is no guarantee that this particular field of empirical effort will yield increasingly acceptable results. What one can guarantee is that there can be no improvements in the quality of methods and estimates without some effort.

Second, in judging the quality of studies in this area, it would be unreasonable to expect standards of accuracy that may be prevalent in other applied economic work. The very nature of the phenomena under study defy direct measurement. In principle, attempts could be made to

---

[10] Actually, Chopra's estimate by the 'Wanchoo method' is even lower at 6 per cent of GNP, but his preferred, 'own series' yields a higher estimate of 10 per cent of GNP. Furthermore, the concept of unaccounted income underlying Chopra's (and Rangnekar's?) estimates is not comparable to that used by other authors.

mount direct surveys of unaccounted income and its disposition. But the credibility of such survey responses is likely to be extremely low. Hence, there is likely to be a continuing need to rely on indirect methods and circumstantial evidence.

Finally, an excessive preoccupation with the estimation of the size and trends of the unaccounted economy has its dangers. It can detract from serious exploration of its causal origins, its functioning characteristics, as well is the economic and social consequences of the phenomenon. True, such enquiries will be bedevilled by some of the doubts that plague the estimation efforts. But such doubts should not preclude the deduction of qualitative conclusions backed by piecemeal empirical evidence. For example, often it may be possible to form a sound judgment about whether a particular measure will reduce or increase black economic activity. In particular markets, one may even be able to substantiate such judgments with empirical evidence. Such evidence is likely to be more accessible and better grounded for a small segment of the economy than for the economy as a whole. Indeed, such sector or market-wise studies might yield insights about how to improve the macro-estimation efforts. Put simply, the attempts to estimate the dimensions of the black economy should complement, and not substitute for, analyses of its causes, nature and consequences.

[Author's note: I am grateful to Amaresh Bagchi, M. Govinda Rao and Rakesh Mohan for comments. For all the remaining shortcomings as well as the views presented in this chapter, I alone am responsible.]

References

Chopra, O.P. (1982). 'Unaccounted Income: Some Estimates', *Economic & Political Weekly*, April 24.

Contini, B. (1981). 'The Second Economy in Italy', *Journal of Contemporary Studies*, Summer.

Feige, E.L. (1979). 'How Big Is The Irregular Economy?' *Challenge*, November-December.

Ghosh, A.K., Bagchi, A., Rastogi, L.N. and Chaturveai, D.N. (1981). 'Trends in Capita] Formation, Growth of Domestic Product and Capital-Output Ratios (1950–51 to 1978–79)', *Journal of Income and Wealth*, January.

Government of India (1971), Ministry of Finance, Direct Taxes Enquiry Committee, Final Report, December.

Government of India. (1980). Central Statistical Organisation, 'National Accounts Statistics: Sources and Methods'.

————. (1982). Central Statistical Organisation, 'National Accounts Statistics'. 1970–71 to 1979–80, February.

Gupta, P. and Gupta, S. (1982). 'Estimates of the Unreported Economy in India', *Economic & Political Weekly*, January 16.

Gupta, S. and Mehta, R. (1982). 'An Estimate of Underreported National Income', Mimeo, paper presented at the Indian Association for Research in Income and Wealth, Fourteenth General Conference, January (*Journal of Income and Wealth*, Volume 5, No 2).

Gutmann, P.M. (1977). 'The Subterranean Economy', *Financial Analysts Journal*, November/December.

Kabra, K.N. (1982). *The Black Economy in India: Problems and Policies*, Chanakya Publications, Delhi.

Kaldor, N. (1956), 'Indian Tax Reform; Report of a Survey'.

Kenadijian, B. (1982). 'The Direct Approach to Measuring the Underground Economy in the United States: IRS Estimates of Unreported Income', in V. Tanzi, (1982b).

Laurent, R. (1970). 'Currency Transfers by Denomination', Unpublished Ph.D Thesis, University of Chicago.

Macafee, K. (1980). 'A Glimpse of the Hidden Economy in the National Accounts of the United Kingdom', *Economic Trends*, February.

O'Higgins, M. (1982). 'Assessing the Underground Economy in the United Kingdom', Mimeo, paper presented at the International Conference on the Unobserved Economy, Wassenaar, Netherlands, June.

Rangnekar, D.K. (1982). 'Size and Dimension of the Black Economy', *Man and Development*, September.

Sandesara, J.C. (1983). 'Estimates of Black Income: A Critique of the Gutmann Method', *Economic & Political Weekly*, April 2.

Tanzi, V. (1982a). 'A Second (and More Skeptical) Look at the Underground Economy in the United States', in V Tanzi (1982b).

———— (ed), (1982b). 'The Underground Economy in the United States and Abroad', D. C. Heath and Co.

————. (1983). 'The Underground Economy in the United States: Annual Estimates for 1930-1980', *IMF Staff Papers*, June.

3

Unaccounted Income

Some Estimates

O.P. Chopra

The estimates of unaccounted income in India are available for only selected years. This study fills this gap by providing estimates of unaccounted income for a period of 17 years. There has been a secular rise in unaccounted income. It rose more than ten-fold in a decade and a half.

The objectives of this chapter are two-fold: (i) to provide a series on unaccounted income[1] in India for the period 1960–76, and (ii) to identify some variables which could explain variations in it over time. It may be noted that the available estimates on unaccounted income are only for selected years. This study fills a long-felt gap by providing estimates for 17 years.

It is very well recognised[2] that an estimate of unaccounted income is of enormous importance in any economy. It helps in the analysis of (i) tax potential; (ii) effectiveness of tax administration; (iii) limits to fiscal and monetary policies; (iv) inflation and the phenomenon of increase in prices, particularly in items such as land and goods of conspicuous consumption; and (v) the level of tax morality of the society.

---

[1] This has been defined in literature as income that evades taxation. *See* Direct Taxes Enquiry Committee 1971.

[2] *See* Herschel 1978.

The estimates of unaccounted income provided in this chapter reveal a secular rise in its levels. It rose more than ten-fold in a decade and a half from Rs 716 crore in 1961–62 to Rs 8,098 crore in 1976–77. The magnitude of unaccounted income, according to some experts, is as high as Rs 15,000 crore for the year 1980-81.[3] The rise has been particularly dramatic from 1973 onwards.

Section I contains the methodology of estimating the series on unaccounted income along with underlying assumptions; it also provides estimates for the period 1960-76. Section II gives a summary of findings and fields for further exploration.

I: Methodology

In this study, we have used a macro approach to estimate the unaccounted income using the methodology recommended by Direct Taxes Enquiry Committee referred to as 'the committee' for brevity. The committee estimated the amount of unaccounted income by identifying assessable non-salary income. For this purpose, income originating from different sectors is multiplied by (i) the ratio of non-salary income to the income of the given sector, and (ii) the ratio of non-salary income above exemption limit to the non-salary income of the given sector. The difference between the assessable and the assessed non-salary income is the measure of unaccounted income. Since it is difficult to obtain information on non-salary income actually assessed (this may be assessed during the next five years), the committee assumed the ratio of evaded income to non-salary assessable income to remain constant to the one observed in 1960–61. We have given up this assumption in favour of a relatively less demanding assumption, i.e., the ratio of the sum of assessed non-salary income in different years for the given year to the actually assessed non-salary income of the given year to remain constant. This marks a significant departure from the approach used by the committee, and is responsible for a greater divergence in the two series from 1973 onwards when the assessable non-salary income above the exemption limit registered a significant increase.

We may mention that the steps involved in estimating unaccounted income by us are identical to those followed by the committee, except the last one (assuming the ratio of unaccounted income to assessable non-salary income) and are as follows:

---

[3] *See* Palkhiwala 1981.

i) Obtain the information on contribution to national income from: (a) mining and quarrying; (b) manufacturing; (c) railways and communication; (d) transport; (e) trade and hotels; (f) banking and insurance; (g) public Administration and (h) others, including real estate.

ii) Split this income into salary and non-salary portions based on the information given in Table 3.1.

TABLE 3.1   Ratio of Non-Salary Income to Total Income from Different Sectors (a_{ij}) and Percentage of Non-Salary Income above Exemption Limit (b_{ik})

Y_i	a_{ij}	b_{ik}
Mining and quarrying	0.598	60
Manufacturing	0.55	60
Railway and communication	0.19	Nil
Transport	0.50	60
Trade and hotels	0.80	70
Banking and Insurance	0.268	100
Public administration	0.199	100
Others	1.0	50

Source: Direct Tax Enquiry Committee (1971).

iii) Work out the percentage of this non-salary income above the exemption limit. This has been assumed to be the same as given by the Wanchoo Committee report reproduced in Table 3.1.

iv) Summation of non-salary income above exemption limit for the above eight sectors provides information on assessable non-salary income.

v) The information on assessed non-salary income is obtained from the All India Income Tax Statistics for different years.

vi) The difference between non-salary assessable income and non-salary income actually assessed is the measure of unaccounted income.

$$Thus, \ UI = \sum_{i=1}^{n} Y_{i,ns} = Y_{ns}^{A}$$

Where $Y_{i,ns}$ is the assessable non-salary income of the sector i; and Y_{ns}^{A} is the actually assessed non-salary income of the economy.

$$Y_{i,ns} = Y_i \times a_{ij} \times b_{ik}$$

Where Y_i is the income accruing from sector i, as for example mining and quarrying, manufacturing etc; a_{ij} is the co-efficient of non-salary income to the total income accruing from i, the sector; b_{ik} is the co-efficient of non-salary income above the exemption limit accruing from the ith sector.

The underlying assumptions of the methodology are as follows:

i) Only non-salary income is evaded. This assumption may be true for those who are employed by the government. For other salary earners, additional benefits are given in some other form, such as perquisites. Further, some of these salary earners may be the beneficiaries of unaccounted income and this has not been captured by the measure of unaccounted income.

ii) Taxes other than income tax are evaded and the measure of unaccounted income worked out in this exercise captures only that part of income which is subject to income tax. Thus, the evasion of tax that may be due to (a) non-payment or under-payment of excise duty, (b) sales tax, (c) customs duties, or (d) substituting non-agricultural income for agricultural income is not captured. The redeeming feature of the exercise is that we are interested in measuring the quantum of unaccounted income and not the tax evaded. Further, if direct taxes are evaded, indirect taxes are also evaded.

iii) The reported income as accruing from different sectors represents a correct measure of income actually generated in the economy. Thus, to the extent there is under-reporting of production or payments made to different factors of production, the estimates of unaccounted income are under-estimates.[4]

iv) The ratio of evaded income to non-salary assessable income remains constant. The committee estimated unaccounted income on this assumption, given the non-availability of information. In our exercise, this forms just one set of results. The other measure relaxes this assumption but assumes that the ratio of the sum of non-salary income assessed in different years relating to the given year to that assessed in the given year remains the same. This implies an unchanged efficiency of tax administration. From this, it is clear that our assumption is a relatively less demanding one.

[4] Some writers make an adjustment for this. *See* Sandesara 1981.

v) The ratio of non-salary income to total income accruing from various sectors of the economy remains the same. This was found to be true for two periods for which information was given by the committee. Further, there is not enough reason to suggest that the share of non-salary income to the total income accruing from various sectors has undergone any significant change.

vi) The ratio of non-salary income above the exemption limit has remained the same. A correction for any change in the income above exemption limit would require information on gross income to income assessed for each sector. Despite the changes that have taken place in the sphere of exemptions, on balance, there may not be a significant change.

Finally, unaccounted income generated in the agricultural sector has not been taken into account. It is pretty well known that a part of the unaccounted income is diverted to agriculture to convert it into legal money. Despite the above assumptions and the consequent shortcomings of the measure of unaccounted income, our estimates are fairly consistent with estimates provided by others.[5]

The Series on Unaccounted Income

The series on unaccounted income estimated by us is closely related to the one obtained by following the methodology of the committee. The co-efficient of correlation between the two is as high as 0.9. This is explicable as both the series are based on income originating from different sectors of the economy. However, our series shows wider fluctuations than those observed in the estimates based on the committee's methodology. To identify the degree of change in our series consequent upon a change in the committee's series, we obtained regression co-efficients between them. For every unit change in the committee's series, there is 2.04 change in our series and is statistically significant.

Both the series are crucially determined by national income. This suggests that a buoyant economy offers more opportunities for unaccounted income. During periods of recession, it may be difficult for producers and traders to extract extra money. Further, unaccounted income shows co-variation with the years when a scheme for voluntary disclosure was

[5] *See* Palkhiwala 1981. His estimate of black income is Rs 13,000 crore for 1981, whereas our estimate for the year 1976 is around Rs 8,000 crore.

announced. For example, 1965–66 showed a marginal decline in unaccounted income, and during 1965 the government had announced a voluntary disclosure scheme. Similarly, 1968 was marked by recession in the economy. There was a real spurt in unaccounted income during 1973–74, which coincides with a hike in the price of oil and consequent inflation. The year 1973–76 experienced a fall in unaccounted income, partly because of the political climate prevailing at that time and partly on account of the bearer bond scheme introduced in that year.

A perusal of Table 3.2 shows that there is a wide divergence between the estimates of unaccounted income obtained by us and those based on the methodology of the committee from 1973–74 onwards. Partly, this is on account of a substantial increase in the assessable non-salary income. For example, it rose from Rs 6,284 crore (1972–73) to Rs 9,502 crore (1973–74) to Rs 13,612 crore (1974–75); partly, it is on account of the assumption of the committee that the ratio of unaccounted income to assessable non-salary income remains constant. Over time, this ratio may have gone up because of a change in tax ethics. Our estimates, on the other hand, identify the magnitude of unaccounted income as the difference between assessable and assessed non-salary income.

II: Summary of Findings

In this chapter we have obtained some estimates of unaccounted income using the macro approach on the lines recommended by Direct Taxation Enquiry Committee. We attempted an explanation of this unaccounted income to total income. For this purpose two models were formulated. The results corroborate the hypothesis that tax evasion is more likely the higher the rate of tax. The results also support the hypothesis that increase in prices leads to an increase in unaccounted income. Further, the funds are diverted to agriculture to convert unaccounted income into legal money. Contrary to the general impression that unaccounted money has a self-perpetuating (self-augmenting) characteristic, the lagged variable of unaccounted income did not support this impression. We would have incorporated some index of controls in the economy as an explanatory variable but the absence of some accepted methodology on its computation dissuaded us from attempting this.

[The author is thankful to K. Krishnamurthy for valuable comments, N.A. Kazmi for assistance in programming, and M. Saqib for statistical assistance. Financial grant for a bigger project, of which the present work is a

TABLE 3.2 Unaccounted Income (Own Series), Effective Rate of Tax, Marginal Rate of Tax, Price Index, in Rs Crore

Year	UI (WS) (Rs crore)	UI (OS) (Rs crore)	ERT (Model I)	ERT (Model II)	Price Index, base 1970=100	YA/Y	MRT (Income Tax)	Net National Income, current (Rs crore)	Agriculture Income (Rs crore)	UI/(Y-YA)	UI/Y	TR
1960–61	747	916	25.0	11.75	54.2	49.30	61	13335	6580	13.50	6.9	1460
1961–62	801	716	25.13	12.39	55.5	48.10	61	14085	6776	9.80	5.1	1657
1962–63	897	837	27.69	14.00	57.5	46.40	90	14903	6908	10.40	5.6	1982
1963–64	1008	1452	31.78	15.48	59.6	46.90	90	17089	8019	16.01	8.5	2421
1964–65	1132	1564	30.87	14.40	65.8	48.90	51	20148	9850	15.20	7.8	2694
1965–66	1231	1539	31.33	15.82	71.2	45.80	65	20801	9534	13.50	7.4	3048
1966–67	964	1685	31.22	15.20	79.7	47.40	65	24078	11421	13.30	7.0	3426
1967–68	1563	1816	29.64	13.73	91.7	50.20	65	28312	14224	12.90	6.4	3638
1968–69	1651	1318	28.53	14.24	91.3	47.80	65	28862	13794	8.70	4.6	3923
1969–70	2104	2714	31.35	15.07	93.2	47.50	75	31877	15142	16.22	8.5	4396
1970–71	1908	2062	30.77	15.26	99.0	47.40	75	34519	16354	11.35	6.0	4955
1970–72	2208	1392	31.20	16.32	105.0	45.90	75	36864	16913	6.90	3.8	5790
1970–73	1897	1795	33.00	17.14	113.0	46.00	85	40572	18644	8.19	4.4	6645

1970–74	2869	4757	36.36	16.37	131.6	49.80	85	50749	25284	18.60	9.4	7529
1970–75	4110	8611	40.20	18.60	169.2	45.90	85	59374	27273	26.80	14.5	9444
1970–76	4107	7292	39.93	20.96	175.8	41.80	85	61899	25868	20.20	11.8	11447
1970–77	4551	8098	39.12	20.42	172.4	39.80	70	67120	26692	20.00	12.1	12647

Notes: i) For (1), (2) and (5), National Accounts Statistics, Central Statistical Organisation.

ii) For 3, it is unaccounted income (our series) divided by net non-agricultural income.

iii) For 4, unaccounted income divided by net national income.

iv) UI (WS): Unaccounted income on the basis of the methodology recommended by the committee.

v) UI (OS): Unaccounted income own series with modified methodology.

vi) UI without subscripts stands for our own series.

*part, has been provided by Hindustan Electro-Graphites. The author alone
is responsible for any errors that may persist and for the views expressed.]*

References

Allingham, M.G. and Sandomo A., 'Income-Tax Evasion: A Theoretical
Analysis', *Journal of Public Economics*, Volume I (1972).

Government of India, Central Board of Revenue, Directorate of Inspection
(Research, Statistics and Publications). *All India Income Tax Statistics.*

Government of India, Central Statistical Organisation, (i) *National Accounts
Statistics*; 1960–61 to 1974–75 and (ii) *National Accounts Statistics*: 1970–71
to 1977–78.

Government of India, *Direct Taxes Enquiry Committee, Final Report*, 1971.

Herschel, Frederic S., 'Tax Evasion and Its Measurement in Developing
Countries', *Public Finance*, (1978).

Jha, P.S. 'Black Income and Crime'. *The Times of India*, December 7, 1981.

Mork, Kent Anton, 'Income-Tax Evasion: Some Empirical Evidence', *Public
Finance*, (1975).

Nayak, P., 'Optimal Income-Tax Evasion and Regressive Taxes', *Public Finance*,
(1978).

Palkhiwala, N.A., 'The Tax Law Is Still an Ass', *The Illustrated Weekly of India*,
October 25, 1981.

Pandit, V.N. and Sundram K., 'On Black Money', *Indian Economic Review*,
1970.

————, 'Aggregate Demand under Conditions of Tax Evasion', *Public Finance*,
1977.

Rangnekar, D.K., 'Minute of Dissent', *Direct Taxes Enquiry Committee. Final
Report.*

Sandesara, J.C., 'Black Income: Some Estimates in India and Abroad', *The
Economic Times*, December 18, 1981.

Singh B., 'Making Honesty the Best Policy', *Journal of Public Economics*, July
1973.

Spicer, M.W. and S.B. Lundstreet, 'Understanding Tax Evasion', *Public Finance*,
1976.

Srinivasan, T.N., 'Tax Evasion: A Model', *Journal of Public Economics*, Volume
2, (1973).

Vogel, J., 'Taxation and Public Opinion in Sweden', *National Tax Journal*,
December 1974.

4

Estimates of the Unreported Economy in India

Poonam Gupta and Sanjeev Gupta

This chapter presents estimates of India's unofficial economy on a yearly basis for the period 1967 to 1978. These estimates implicitly revise the GNP, per capita and other related statistics for this period. The technique employed has been recently used to determine the size of the unreported economies in the US and Canada. The results indicate that the unreported activity as a proportion of official GNP has grown from 9.5 per cent in 1967 to nearly 49 per cent by 1978. High taxes have contributed significantly to the growth of the unofficial economy. A 1 per cent increase in overall taxes leads to more than 3 per cent increase in the unofficial economy relative to the official economy.

Despite the general concern, to date, there are no systematic estimates of the 'illegal' economy in India. In this chapter, we attempt to compute its magnitude on a yearly basis for the period 1967 to 1978. By doing this, we implicitly revise the gross national product (GNP), per capita income and other related statistics for India. We employ a technique that has recently been used for estimation of irregular economies in the United States (US) and Canada.

The chapter is organised as follows. We first summarise the method and report the estimates obtained from it for India. These estimates are then compared with those for Canada and the US to put them into proper perspective. In the concluding section, implications of the assumptions of the technique employed are discussed. Finally, the policy relevance of the study is highlighted.

I: Methodology

Gutmann (1977) suggested a simple procedure for calculating the magnitude of illegal activity in the United States. He chose a base period (1937–41) when the incentive to avoid taxes was minimal, because of the low tax rates prevailing at that time. For this period, he estimated the ratio of currency outside banks to demand deposits. He then assumed that this ratio would have remained unchanged *except* for changes induced by the growth of the irregular economy. This was based on the assumption that only cash was employed in illegal transactions. He multiplied this ratio by the 1976 level of demand deposits to give the currency required in 1976 for 'legal' transactions. The difference between the currency required and actual currency held outside banks gave an estimate of cash used for 'illegal' activities. If the amount of income produced by a unit of currency in the unreported sector was identical to the amount of income produced by this unit in the official sector then, he argued, the income generated by the estimate of illegal cash could be easily estimated.

In India, the ratio of currency-to-demand deposits has *decreased* from an assumed base of 1950. It is, however, well known that the absolute size of the black economy has increased. Moreover, payments for 'illegal' purchases can be made by cheques. It is not correct to assume as Gutmann's approach does, that only currency is used as a means of payment in the black economy. Since, Gutmann's method suffers from many shortcomings it has not been used for estimating the size of the unreported economy in India.

Feige (1979) developed a more sophisticated method for estimating the magnitude and growth of the black market. He used Irving Fisher's idea that if all the transactions paid for by cheque and by cash were added up then the value of total transactions would represent total economic activity in any society. Feige assumed that the ratio of total transactions to total income was relatively stable. This proportionality between transactions and income has been extensively used in monetary economics and in the empirical work on demand for money function.

The total volume of transactions includes both legal and illegal transactions. Total income or GNP as officially given measures only legal economic activity. Thus, if a proportional relationship exists between transactions and income then significant increases in this ratio would be due to the growth of illegal activity.

To apply Feige's methodology one needs estimates of the total value of chequing transactions and currency transactions. Transactions supported by cheques are equal to the average stock of demand deposits multiplied with their turnover rate (that is, average number of times the demand deposits turn over). Transactions supported by currency (or cash) can be estimated by calculating the turnover rate of a unit of currency and then multiplying it by the total currency with the public. Once total transactions have been calculated this method requires that a benchmark year be chosen where it can be assumed that there was no irregular activity. For this base year the ratio of transactions-to-GNP is first obtained. Then, we get estimates of the magnitude of legal and illegal activities in the succeeding years by dividing the total volume of transactions in each year by the base year ratio. Subtracting measured GNP leaves estimates of income generated in the black economy in these years. In the following section Feige's procedure is applied to India.

II: Estimates for Indian Economy

For India, the ratios for three years, 1949–50, 1950–51 and 1951–52, were averaged and used as the reference point for estimating the size of the black economy for the years 1967–68 to 1978–79. The period 1949–50 to 1951–52 was chosen because it immediately preceded the planning era and the establishment of numerous controls on various sectors of the economy. We felt that in the pre-planning years the underground economy was relatively small. The choice of the base years was also guided by the division of British India into India and Pakistan in 1947.[1]

The GNP, demand deposits, and currency with the public are available for all years. However, figures for the demand deposit turnover rate were published in only some years. Data for the base years, 1967–68 to 1978–79 and their sources, are given in Table 4.1. Since currency turnover rates or the information, which can be used to calculate them, are not systematically published, we had to use proxies from other studies.

[1] Before Partition, the figures for all relevant variables refer to British India. After Partition, the statistics are given separately for India and Pakistan. So GNP, money supply and other relevant data after 1947 are not comparable with earlier figures because of differences in geographical coverage.

To estimate how frequently currency notes turn over on the average, we needed information on the lifetime transactions and the normal life of currency notes of various denominations. The lifetime transactions are the number of transactions that a unit of currency can sustain before its quality deteriorates and it has to be retired from circulation. Division of lifetime transactions by the average length of life yields an estimate of the currency turnovers performed per year. If the length of life of notes of all denominations in circulation is known, then the estimate of currency turnovers for each denomination can be derived. Currency transactions with Re 1, Rs 2, Rs 5, Rs 10, Rs 20, Rs 50, Rs 100, and other higher denomination notes can be separately estimated by multiplying the turnover rate of each denomination by the value of bills of that denomination in circulation with the public. Individual estimates can then be aggregated to give total currency transactions.

An example can clarify how currency transactions with different denomination bills can be estimated. Consider a note of Rs 10. Suppose its average life is three years and its lifetime transactions are 125. Turnover rate per year would be *(125/3)*. If there are Rs 50 crore worth of such notes in the hands of the public then *50 crore × (125/3)* gives the value of transactions supported by the stock of Rs 10 notes.

Estimates of lifetime transactions used in this study are also given in Table 4.1. Table 4.2 presents the percentages of all denomination notes to the total currency in circulation.

Information on average normal life of notes was not available except for the one rupee note, which is approximately 11 months.[2] We assumed the same lifetime for the Rs 2 note. For Rs 5, Rs 10, Rs 20, Rs 50, Rs 100 and Rs 1,000 notes the estimates for average life were proxied by those for Canadian notes.[3] Mirus and Smith (1981) reported that for $1, $2 and $5 notes the average lifetime is slightly over one year. For a $20 note it is three years, and for $100 notes it is nine years. Thus, we assumed lifetimes of 1.1 years for the Rs 5 notes, three years for Rs 10 and Rs 20 notes, nine years for Rs 50 and Rs 100 notes. For Rs 1,000 and Rs 5,000 notes, we assumed a lifetime of 22 years. This was Feige's estimate for a $100 note in the United States. Rs 10,000 notes were ignored altogether because in all years the percentage of these notes in the total currency in circulation was well below 0.5 per cent.

---

[2] See *Reserve Bank of India Bulletin*, September 1958.

[3] Since the quality of notes world over is more or less the same, this approximation was judged to be satisfactory.

TABLE 4.1   Basic Statistics Used in Estimating the Size of the Black Economy

Year	GNP (a) (market prices) (crore Rs)	Demand Deposits (b) (crore Rs)	Currency with Public (c) (crore Rs)	Demand Deposit Turnover (d)	Lifetime Transactions (e)
1949–50	9806	594.69	1200.24	28.0	125
1950–51	10354	604.03	1205.14	28.0	125
1951–52	10919	592.31	1217.05	28.0	125
1967–68	32036	1779.25	3198.67	46.2	125
1968–69	33024	1927.23	3436.24	47.5	125
1969–70	36580	2186.57	3765.35	48.8	125
1970–71	40177	2700.42	4143.08	50.1	125
1971–72	43266	3130.25	4559.67	51.6	125
1972–73	47750	3771.83	4946.50	51.6	125
1973–74	58863	4498.42	5821.50	52.0	125
1974–75	69755	5229.17	6291.83	52.5	125
1975–76	72698	5893.38	6523.86	52.5	125
1976–77	76937	7093.17	7197.42	52.5	125
1977–78	86860	8419.58	8235.92	52.5	125
1978–79	96080	10319.66	9460.42	52.5	125

Sources: Economic Survey; National Accounts Statistics; *International Financial Statistics*, Washington, DC; *Banking and Monetary Statistics of India*, Reserve Bank of India; *Reserve Bank of India Bulletin*; and Robert Laurent, *Currency Transfers by Denomination*, Unpublished PhD Thesis at the University of Chicago, 1970.

With the above average normal lives of notes and lifetime transactions of 125, the yearly turnover rates are: (125/0.9166) or 136.37 for Rs 1 and Rs 2; (125/1.1) or 113.6 for Rs 5; (135/3) or 41.7 for Rs 10 and Rs 20; (1225/9) or 13.9 for Rs 50 and Rs 100; and (125/22) or 5.7 for Rs 1,000 and Rs 5,000. Since currency notes higher than Rs 100 were demonetised on 12 January 1946, currency transactions with Rs 1,000 and Rs 5,000 notes were not estimated for the base years. Higher denomination notes were however reintroduced by the Reserve Bank of India in April 1954; so, for 1967–68 to 1977–78, currency transactions with Rs 1,000 and Rs 5,000 bills were included. In January 1978, Rs 1,000, Rs 5,000, and Rs 10,000 bills were again demonetised; so, for

TABLE 4.2   Percentages of Notes to Total Currency in Circulation*

Year	Rs 1	Rs 2	Rs 5	Rs 10	Rs 20	Rs 50	Rs 100	Rs 1,000	Rs 5,000
1949–50	0.024	2.0	13.3	36.0	–	–	31.5	–	–
1950–51	0.022	1.8	12.0	34.9	–	–	36.1	–	–
1951–52	0.023	1.9	11.5	34.9	–	–	36.6	–	–
1967–68	5.08	1.2	7.7	38.6	–	–	40.4	1.6	0.6
1968–69	4.8	1.3	7.2	37.0	–	–	43.0	1.3	0.7
1969–70	5.06	1.5	7.0	34.6	–	–	45.8	1.3	0.5
1970–71	4.86	1.5	7.0	34.4	–	–	46.6	1.2	0.3
1971–72	4.75	1.5	6.7	33.8	–	–	47.8	1.0	0.5
1972–73	4.61	1.3	6.4	33.7	–	–	48.8	0.7	0.4
1973–74	4.53	1.2	6.5	30.6	2.7	–	49.6	0.8	0.3
1974–75	4.24	1.2	6.2	29.7	5.7	–	48.2	0.5	0.4
1975–76	4.28	0.8	6.4	29.0	6.1	–	48.5	0.5	0.4
1976–77	4.1	1.6	7.4	26.3	5.9	1.2	47.9	1.2	0.3
1977–78	3.28	1.5	6.4	23.5	6.6	8.8	49.5	1.3	0.2
1978–79	2.95	1.6	6.2	19.8	7.5	10.8	46.7	0.6	0.2

* Inclusive of Rs 43 crore retired from Pakistan.
Notes: The data on currency denomination proportions is collected from the
Reserve Bank of India Bulletin, Bombay (February, 1971) and various issues of
the Report of Currency and Finance Reserve Bank of India, Bombay. For the years
1967/68 to 1978/79, the proportions are for March 1967, March 1968 and so on.
This is because the proportions are decided at the beginning of the financial year.

1978–79, currency transactions supported by Rs 1,000 and Rs 5,000
notes were excluded.

Total currency transactions (sum of transactions supported by each
denomination), total demand deposit transactions, the ratio of economy
wide transactions to GNP, the absolute size of the black market in India
and its proportion to official GNP are given in Table 4.3.

Table 4.3 shows that the absolute size of the black market in India
increased from Rs 3,034.37 crore in 1967–68 to Rs 46,866.86 crore in
1978–79, that is, by more than 15 times. In percentage terms, in 1967–
68 the underground economy formed nearly 9.5 per cent of measured
GNP. By 1978–79 it had jumped to 48.78 per cent. Thus, currently

TABLE 4.3 Size of Black Economy

Year	Currency Transactions (crore Rs) 1	Demand Deposit Transactions (crore Rs) 2	(1)+ (2) (crore Rs) 3	(3) as Per Cent GNP 4	Size of the Black Economy (crore Rs) 5	Percentage of (5) to official GNP
1967–68	127974.475	82272.404	210246.879	6.56	3034.372	9.5
1968–69	133399.314	91582.008	224981.322	6.813	4504.1605	13.64
1969–70	145252.795	106769.96	252022.755	6.89	5458.825	14.92
1970–71	158738.685	135479.90	294218.585	7.323	8900.329	22.15.
1971–72	171925.87	161520.90	333446.77	7.707	12354.812	28.56
1972–73	182731.738	194626.598	377358.336	7.903	15195.511	31.82
1973–74	214030.91	234142.584	448173.497	7.614	15894.881	27.00
1974–75	230685.724	274531.247	505216.971	7.243	14518.056	20.81
1975–76	237077.44	309402.65	546480.09	7.52	18457.978	25.39
1976–77	268784.86	372391.425	641176.285	8.334	30014.841	39.01
1977–78	284537.149	442027.95	726565.099	8.365	34335.179	39.53
1978–79	315184.262	541782.15	856966.412	8.92	46866.858	48.78

Notes: Average of 1949/50 to 1951/52 ratios is 5.995. Division of yearly figures in column (3) by 5.995 and then subtraction of measured GNP gives column (5).

almost half of the official income is being produced outside the 'legal' sector. Not only is the black economy a substantial proportion of the regular economy but it has also grown at a rate faster than that of the official economy.

The last column of Table 4.3 shows that the proportion of black economy to GNP fell in 1974–75. This can be attributed to the fact that the government lowered the marginal income tax rates and also allowed the people to declare unaccounted money without any penalty within a specific time period.

The Wanchoo Committee estimated that for the year 1968–69, the absolute size of the black market in India was Rs 1,400 crore.[4] However, estimates for the same year by DK Rangnekar[5] put the size at twice this figure. Our calculations show that even the latter is an underestimate of the true size, the actual estimate being three times the Wanchoo Committee figure.

Feige (1979) estimated that in the US, income produced in the 'illegal' sector was $225.5 billion (or 13 per cent of GNP) in 1976. For the same year, Minis and Smith (1981) credited the irregular economy in Canada with 21.9 per cent of total economic activity ('legal' plus 'illegal'). In contrast, 39 per cent of GNP was produced in the black economy in India in 1976–77. Canadian and US estimates clearly show that it is not India alone which is characterised by a large unreported sector. Advanced economies, with fewer controls as compared to India, also have a large and growing unofficial economy. As a percentage of measured income, however, the size of this economy is smaller in Canada and the US.

Though a significant proportion of economic activity is accounted for by the underground economies in Canada, India and the US, the nature of this economy is somewhat different in North America as compared to India. The irregular sector in North America includes illegal transactions in narcotics trade, gambling and loan sharking. It has grown partly because of increased income tax burdens and government regulations like unemployment insurance. The provision of liberal unemployment benefits has led to the practice of unemployed persons claiming unemployment insurance but working 'off the books' for cash. In India, trade in prohibited drugs, gambling, etc, forms a negligible portion of the black market. The underground economy has grown due to high taxes not only on income but also on commodities. Extensive controls in all

---

[4] *See* Gupta and Thavaraj 1974: 61.

[5] *See* Gupta and Thavaraj 1974: 61.

sectors of the economy, domestic as well as foreign, have diverted a large part of economic activity to the 'illegal' sector. Black markets in commodities like sugar, oil and in foreign exchange—non-existent in North America—are well known in India.[6]

III: Possible Sources of Under and over-Estimation

The assumption of a constant transaction to GNP ratio is plausible if strictly financial transactions are excluded from the numerator. Inclusion of transactions financial in nature would result in a continuously increasing ratio even if the size of the irregular economy has remained unchanged. Failure to adjust for financial transactions would thus lead to over-estimation of the size of the black market. Financial transactions can be excluded from the estimate of total transactions by choosing an average turnover rate of demand deposits that excludes the turnover in major financial centres. In case of India, this adjustment was not required because the turnover rate in Bombay and Calcutta is not higher than the rate in other cities. Moreover, the turnover in these two centres did not increase substantially overtime.

For India, we chose 1949–50 to 1951–52 as the base period assuming that the irregular economy was close to zero in this period. It is quite doubtful that all the economic activity was confined to the 'legal' sector. If the size of the black economy was positive in the reference period, then by assuming zero size we have under-estimated the subsequent magnitude and growth of the underground economy.

The calculations assume that income velocity in the 'legal' economy was the same as that in the 'illegal' economy. If however, income velocity was higher in the 'illegal' sector, for example, because of possible greater integration, then the resulting estimates of income generated in the subterranean economy would be higher.

In our estimates, the average lifetime transactions a currency can perform was unchanged at 125 between the years 1949–50 and 1978–79. This assumption is plausible if the quality of the paper used was the same, for if there were improvements in the paper used for printing currency then the lifetime transactions would be higher in the later years. For the US, Feige found evidence that from the mid-sixties the

---

[6] For a study on the determinants of the black market exchange rate in India, *see* Gupta 1980. For a discussion on the nature of this market, *see* Gupta 1981.

durability of printing paper had nearly doubled, so that the average lifetime transactions supported by a unit of currency were far greater than 125. For India, we could find no such evidence and therefore no adjustments were made. If we increase the lifetime transactions on the assumption that the quality of paper used in India to print rupees has also improved then this would raise the estimates of the size of the black economy.

The demand deposit turnover data in India is available only up to 1974–75. We assume the same turnover rate for the years up to 1978–79. This assumption underestimates demand deposit transactions for the years 1975–76 to 1978–79 because the turnover was probably higher than the 1974–75 rate, if past trend is a guide to future expected turnover rates. Underestimation of demand deposit transactions results in underestimation of the size of the underground economy for the period 1975–76 to 1978–79.

Feige's method estimates only the size of the monetary component of the subterranean economy. No account has been taken of barter transactions. While these are not probably substantial, nevertheless, their exclusion gives smaller estimates of the black economy.

IV: Concluding Comments

In this chapter, we attempted to estimate the size of the black economy in India on an annual basis. For this purpose, the technique suggested by Feige was employed. Our results show that for the years 1967–68, the black economy constituted 9.5 per cent of the official GNP. However, by 1978–79 the size had jumped to nearly half of the official GNP. These estimates tend to reflect the extent and severity of taxes and controls in the Indian economy.

Given the size of the unreported economy in India, it would seem that policymakers and researchers while employing official statistics should adjust for its magnitude. The official growth rate statistics, for example, are biased downwards, especially when the black economy is growing at a rate faster than the official economy. Furthermore, depending on the tax laws and severity of controls, some economic activity is likely to shift in and out of the 'legal' sector from time to time. All this implies that statistical agencies in India must prepare estimates of reported and unreported sector for an accurate picture of the economy. To this end, they could use or refine the method used in this study.

Finally, the results presented in this study should paradoxically comfort the Indian policymaker. After all, the economy has not done all that badly when the irregular activity is taken into account.

[The authors wish to thank J.P. Agarwal and J.B. Donges for helpful suggestions.]

References

Feige, Edgar L. (1979): 'How Big is the Irregular Economy?' *Challenge*, November-December, pp 5-13.

Garcia, Gillian (1978): 'The Currency Ratio and the Subterranean Economy', *Financial Analysts Journal*, November-December, pp 64-66.

Gupta, Meena and Thavaraj, M.J.K. (1974): 'Tax Evasion and Development', *The Economic Times*, Annual volume.

Gupta, Sanjeev (1980): 'An Application of the Monetary Approach to Black Market Exchange Rates', *Weltwirts-chaftliches Archiv*, 116, 235-252.

Gupta, Sanjeev (1981): 'Black Market Exchange Rates', JCB Mohr (Paul Siebeck) Tubingen.

Gutmann, Peter M. (1977): 'The Subterranean Economy', *Financial Analysts Journal*, November-December, pp 26-28.

————. (1978): 'Professor Gutmann Replies', *Financial Analysts Journal*, November-December, pp 67-69.

————. (1979): 'Statistical Illusions, Mistaken Policies', *Challenge*, November-December, pp 14-17.

Laurent, Rober D. (1970): 'Currency Transfers by Denomination', Unpublished Ph D thesis at the University of Chicago.

————. (1979): 'Currency and the Subterranean Economy', *Economic Perspectives*, Federal Reserve Bank of Chicago, March-April, pp 3-6.

Minis, Rolf and Smith, Roger S. (1981): 'Canada's irregular Economy', Paper Presented at the Canadian Economics Association, Annual Meetings, Halifax, NS, May 25-27.

5

Estimates of Black Income

A Critique of Gutmann Method

J.C. Sandesara

The Gutmann method based on a certain manipulation of components of money supply yields negative estimates of black income in India for a fairly long recent period. Clearly, the assumptions of the method are irrelevant in the Indian context and the method is too simplistic.

I: The Method

The Peter Gutmann method involves a manipulation of currency into illegal and legal currency. The results of this manipulation, together with the data on deposits, are then applied to gross national product (GNP) at market prices to bifurcate it into illegal and legal, or black and white GNP. The exercise has, of course, a number of assumptions.

Gutmann's initial premise is that high taxation and restrictions are the parents of black income. The first step in the estimation is, therefore, to fix the benchmark period when taxation was light and restrictions minimal. This then is the period when black income is absent. The problem is one of estimating black money for later years.

The second and the third assumptions are: transactions in the black market are exclusively through currency; and income velocity of currency in the black sector is the same as that of currency and deposits in the white sector.

The fourth and final assumption is that changes in the ratio of currency to deposits, in relation to this ratio in the benchmark period, are induced exclusively by the growth of black money.

The basic data required are components of money supply for the benchmark period and for the year for which estimates are made, and the GNP for the latter year. The computation of black income is illustrated by the following data (*see* Table 5.1).

TABLE 5.1 Some basic numbers in the estimation (Rs crore)

Year	Currency	Deposits	Money supply	GNP
Benchmark period (1950–51, 1951–52, 1952–53)	1281	569	1851	–
Year of estimate (1953–54)	1289	539	1828	10.392

Source: Table 5.2.

  i) Work out the currency-deposit ratios for the benchmark period and for 1953–54:

$$\left(\frac{1281}{569}\right) = 2.25; \text{ and } \left(\frac{1289}{539}\right) = 2.39$$

 ii) Deduct the former from the latter:

$$-2.25 + 2.39 = 0.14$$

iii) Multiply the above and the value of deposits in 1953–54, and get the value of illegal currency:

$$0.14 \times 539 = 76$$

 iv) Deduct the above from money-supply of 1953–54, and get the value of legal currency plus deposits for that year:

$$-76 + 1828 = 1752$$

  v) Work out the ratio of illegal currency to money supply for 1953–54:

$$76 \div 1828 = 0.04$$

vi) Multiply the above and GNP for 1953–54, and get the value of black income:

$$0.04 \times 10392 = 416$$

Thus, of the GNP of Rs 10,392 crore in 1953–54, Rs 416 crore or 4 per cent represented black income.

II: Data

A property of the benchmark period is that it is a 'clean' year. Since high taxation and more restrictions are a post–1942 phenomena in the United States (US), Gutmann took the period of 1937–41 as the initial period.

It was not possible to base our estimates on that early period for various reasons: (a) India prior to 1947 was undivided India, comprising, since Independence in that year, what became India and Pakistan. This major political development led to wide-ranging structural changes; (b) 1939–45 was a period of the Second World War. This period and the ensuing few years were marked by inflation. Also, the period around 1947 was marked by heavy bloodshed in many parts and unparalleled transfers of population from one area to the other. Any period during 1939–49 therefore, would, not satisfy an essential property of normalness relevant for the benchmark period; (c) The official estimates of GNP begin to become available from 1948-49 onwards. In view of these considerations, the choice had to fall on 1950–51 through 1952–53 as the benchmark period. This was also the period when taxes and restrictions were in general less than that during later years. GNP data are no problem. However, a few clarifications in regard to money supply statistics are warranted.

Gutmann goes by money supply in the sense of M1: currency and demand deposits. We also use the same concept. It comprises currency with and deposit money of the public. The former includes notes in circulation plus circulation of rupee coins and of small coins minus cash on hand and with banks, and the latter demand deposits with banks and other deposits with the Reserve Bank of India.

Over the last 30 years, there have been some changes in respect of exclusion/inclusion of some minor items in the currency component, and in the apportionment of saving bank deposits as between demand

and time deposits.[1] While these changes are not major, they do inject an element of non-comparability in the M1 series through time. Fortunately, a comparable series covering the period 1950–51 through 1978–79 has recently become available. We have gone by this series.[2]

III: Estimates

Columns (9) and (11) of Table 5.2 give, in relative and absolute terms, estimates of black income in India for 1953–54 through 1978–79.

The period covered in the table divides itself in two neat parts: 1953–54 through 1963–64 and 1964–65 onwards. During the first period, black income varied from Rs 35 crore or less than one per cent of the GNP in 1956–57 to Rs 1,943 crore or 13 per cent of the GNP in 1960–61. For the second period, the method becomes a problem, as black income is negative throughout.

This is the hardest of all the assumptions to swallow. A number of factors account for the demand for currency in relation to money. Philip Cagan's[3] list includes, of course, personal taxation along with the opportunity of cost of holding currency, expected real income per capita, volume of retail trade, volume of travel per capita and degree of urbanisation. Among the other factors of special relevance in the Indian context are: degree of monetisation, size of the unorganised/informal sector, spread of banking habits, etc. Clearly, a full-scale investigation linking these factors with currency deposits ratios over time is called for. The factors are too many and varied, and it is almost impossible to offer

---

[1] It may be clarified that the deposits included in M1 do not, by and large, carry interest, and may therefore be taken as close substitutes of currency. Only a very small percentage of these deposits may have been paid low or nominal interest for some time in the past. On the advice received from the more knowledgeable persons, I am satisfied that this point is most unlikely to alter noteworthily the lesson suggested by the estimates presented here.

[2] Vasudevan, A. (1980, July–September). Money Stock and Its Components in India, 1950–51 to 1979–80: A Statistical Account. *Indian Economic Journal*. Bombay. Columns (2) (3) and (4) of Statement I of this paper which has been relied upon here, are self-explanatory. Column (5) entitled money supply with public is M1.

[3] National Bureau of Economic Research. (1958). The Demand for Currency Relative to Total Money Supply. *Occasional Paper 62*. New York.

TABLE 5.2 Components of Money Supply (M3) and of Gross National Product in India, 1950–51 to 1979–80

Year	Currency	Demand and other deposits and time deposits	M3 (2+3)	2/3	(5)-(1.42)	Illegal Currency	Legal Currency and Deposits (4-7)	7/4	Gross National Product		
									Total	Black (9*10)	Other (10-11)
1	2	3	4	5	6	7	8	9	10	11	12
Average for 3 years: 1950–51 to 1952–53	1281	900	2181	1.42	Nil	Nil	2181	Nil	9801	–	9801
1953–54	1289	911	2200	1.41	–.01	–9	2209	–.N	10392	–42	10434
1954–55	1377	1002	2379	1.37	–.05	–50	2429	–.02	9804	–196	10000
1955–56	1571	1112	2683	1.41	–.01	–11	2694	–.N	10323	–41	10364
1956–57	1623	1246	2869	1.30	–.12	–150	3019	–.05	11765	–588	12353
1957–58	1674	1489	3163	1.12	–.30	–447	3610	–.14	12060	–1683	13748
1958–59	1792	1684	3476	1.06	–.36	–606	4082	–.17	13451	–2287	15738
1959-60	1931	1952	3883	0.99	–.43	–839	4722	–.22	13824	–3041	16865
1960–61	2098	1866	3964	1.12	–.30	–560	4524	–.14	14946	–2092	17038
1961–62	2201	2043	4244	1.08	–.34	–695	4939	–.16	15879	–2541	18420
1962–63	2379	2174	4553	1.09	–.33	–717	5270	–.16	16991	–2719	19710

1963-64	2606	2431	5037	1.07	-.35	-851	5888	-.17	19544	-3322	22866
1964-65	2769	2729	5498	1.01	-.41	-1119	6617	-.20	22897	-4579	27476
1965-66	3034	3100	6134	0.98	-.44	-1364	7498	-.22	23948	-5269	29217
1966-67	3197	3620	6817	0.88	-.54	-1955	8772	-.29	27432	-7955	35387
1967-68	3376	4084	7490	0.83	-.59	-2410	9870	-.32	32036	-10252	42288
1968-69	3682	4624	8306	0.80	-.62	-2867	11173	-.35	33024	-11558	44582
1969-70	4010	5327	9337	0.75	-.67	-3569	12906	-.38	36580	-13900	50480
1970-71	4383	6205	10588	0.71	-.71	-4406	14994	-.42	40109	-16846	56955
1971-72	4822	7492	12314	0.64	-.78	-5844	18158	-.47	43240	-20323	63563
1972-73	5444	9071	14515	0.60	-.82	-7438	21953	-.51	47717	-24336	72053
1973-74	6336	10616	16952	0.60	-.82	-8705	25657	-.51	58863	-30020	88883
1974-75	6378	12405	18783	0.51	-.91	-11289	30072	-.60	69337	-41602	110939
1975-76	6737	14504	25241	0.46	-.96	-13924	35165	-.66	73671	-48623	122294
1976-77	7910	18039	25049	0.44	-.98	-17678	43627	-.68	79913	-54341	134254
1977-78	8693	22722	31415	0.38	-1.04	-23631	55046	-.75	88884	-66663	155547
1978-79	10316	27727	38043	0.37	-1.05	-29113	67156	-.77	96079	-73980	170059
1979-80	11767	32779	44546	0.36	-1.06	-34746	79292	-.78	NA	–	–

Source: For Columns (1), (2) and (3), A Vasudevan: 'Money Stock and its Components in India, 1950–51 to 1979–80: A Statical Account, The Indian Economic Journal, July-September, 1980, Bombay, Statement 1, Column (2), (3 + 4 + 6) and (7) pp 6-7; For column (10) Central Statistical Organisation, Department of Statistics; Ministry of Planning, Government of India, New Delhi, National Account Statistics for different years.

Notes: i) Rupee is the Indian currency, equivalent 11 U.S. cents, and a crore is 10 million.
    ii) N-Negligible (less than .01), NA: Not Available

any hunch in a general way. However, three observations may be permitted here: (i) Gutmann exaggerates, perhaps out of all proportions, the importance of personal taxation as a causal factor; (ii) Other factors may be far too important causally to be wished away; (iii) If the proof of the pudding is in the eating, the negative estimates yielded by the method support these two propositions.

To sum up: A realistic consideration of the points involved in the first three assumptions suggests that black income in India may in fact be higher than the amounts suggested by the statistics. It is indeed extremely difficult to evaluate even roughly the influence of the factors enumerated in the discussion on the fourth assumption. Obviously, factors other than taxation are far more important. It is perhaps because of them that the estimates for the later years on M1 have turned out to be negative.[4] It is a moot point whether, taking one thing with the other, the method would have fared better even in the limited sense that the estimates would have been more than negative. Perhaps not, for the estimation of black money at any rate for India, is far too serious a business to be handled exclusively by the tool of currency-deposit ratio, and/or to be left to monetary statisticians/economists.

IV: Conclusion

The Gutmann method, which is based on a certain manipulation of the components of money supply, yields negative estimates of black income in India for a fairly long period. The estimates are of course absurd, and point to the irrelevance of the method in the Indian context. Clearly, estimation of black income, at any rate in India, is too complex a problem to be tackled in a simplistic way as in this method.

[The author is grateful to Peter M. Gutmann, D.R. Pendse and Damodar Gujarati for their comments on the draft; to P.R. Brahmananda, D.M. Nachane and A. Vasudevan for discussions on the concepts; and to T.R. Bishnoi for statistical assistance.]

[4] Also, all estimates on M3.

6

Estimating Unaccounted Income in India

Using Transport as a Universal Input

Sacchidananda Mukherjee and R. Kavita Rao

An alternative methodology to measure the scale of unaccounted income in India (shadow economy) using transport as the universal input is developed. Based on input–output tables and National Accounts Statistics, annual demand for road freight transport is estimated. Correspondingly, annual supply of road freight transport is obtained based on availability of diesel for road freight transport, stock of goods carriages, average freight transport capacity per vehicle, average annual distance travel, and average fuel efficiency per vehicle. The mismatch of supply and demand is broadly considered the unaccounted for portion of the gross domestic product. The methodology is tested for two successive input–output tables and three consecutive financial years. Since the analysis is based on assumptions, a comparative static analysis is carried out to check the sensitivity of estimates to changes in the assumptions.

I: Introduction

The present chapter proposes to use 'road freight transport' as the universal input on the basis of which unaccounted incomes in the economy can be measured. The rationale for using road freight transport as a 'global indicator' can be summarised as follows:[1]

i) Road freight transport services are used as inputs by all sectors of the economy.

ii) Services of the transport sector cannot be stored. Whenever there is demand for transport, it is supplied. Therefore, if one can measure supply credibly, it can be taken as a measure of demand for the service. Further, since demand for road freight transport is a derived demand, we can infer the output produced in the rest of the economy from these estimates of size of road freight transport sector.

iii) The strong relationship between transportation output and economic growth has been established in literature (Lahiri *et al.* 2003; Norwood and Casey 2002). Lahiri and Yao (2006) show that the transportation sector plays an important role in propagation of business cycles in the United States (US) economy. The study finds one-to-one correspondence between cycles in the transportation sector and those in the aggregate economy. Often the transportation sector output index is used to forecast economic growth cycles (Lahiri *et al.* 2003). Brookings–Financial Times Tracking Indexes for the Global Economic Recovery (TIGER) considers electricity consumption and freight volumes to track manufacturing activity in 20 countries (Prasad and Foda 2015).

The input-output (I–O) table for the Indian economy presents sectoral interactions (commodity to commodity flow matrix) across 130 sectors, which covers all sectors of the economy. All sectors used land transport as an input. The only exceptions being ownership of dwellings and public administration. This establishes universality of land (road) transport as an input for income generation. When electricity is already established as a universal input for estimation of unaccounted income (Kaufman and Kaliberda 1996; Gupta and Mehta 1982), this approach has been criticised on a number of counts: first, since electricity demand would be expected to vary across sectors in the economy, any change

---

[1] Global indicator methods, in which unaccounted incomes or non-measured production is modelled in terms of a single variable (usually a physical indicator) with which it is believed to be highly correlated, electricity consumption being the most commonly used.

in the sectoral composition of GDP would induce changes in electricity demand quite unrelated to the extent of unaccounted incomes in the economy. It has also been pointed out that for sectors such as electricity, the relationship might be unstable—more related to the weather condition than to actual output. Moreover, given the gap between demand and supply (deficit) in the availability of electricity, this may not be the only source of energy in some countries—a fact that can significantly undermine the applicability of such an approach.

The proposed approach using road freight transport as the universal input has two advantages over the electricity-based approach. First, it does not rely on changes in the relation between GDP and the universal input over time. It provides an estimate for a given year from information available for that year alone. Second, unlike in electricity, the demand for services will be exactly equal to the supply of the services. Thus, this approach can provide an alternative way of looking at unaccounted incomes.

II: Methodology

This methodology, as mentioned earlier, is based on the idea that since transport services are not storable, the supply of transport services would necessarily be equal to the demand for the same. Any difference between the supply and the revealed demand therefore can be treated as unaccounted demand for transport services which in turn would be a reflection of unaccounted incomes in the rest of the economy. To derive the extent of unaccounted incomes therefore, we need to estimate demand for and supply of road freight transport services. The methodology adopted for deriving the estimates of demand and supply are discussed below.

Supply of Road Freight Transport

The supply of road freight transport services in a year can be derived from the stock on road goods carriages (G_{ki}) for that year (say, i^{th} year), their average freight transport capacity (C_k), and their average annual distance travelled (S_k).[2] If we assume that there are n types of goods

---

[2] Following Government of India (2010), we assume that average daily distance travel of medium and heavy commercial vehicle (M&HCV) is 151km and light commercial vehicle (LCV) is 55 km.

carriages on road, the supply of road freight transport services (in tonne kilometre) could be written as:

Supply of Road Freight Transport (T_s) for the year $= \sum_{k=1}^{n} G_{ki} C_k S_k$

[Equation 6.1]

where,

G_{ki} is the stock of on road goods carriages of kth category of goods carriages in the ith year, C_k is the average freight transport capacity of kth category of goods carriages, and S_k is the annual average distance travelled by k^{th} category of goods carriages.

To arrive at the stock of goods carriages on the roads, we need a benchmark on the average age of trucks in India. Existing studies do not provide any estimates of the average age of trucks on Indian roads.[3] To attempt an iterative estimate, we consider 15 years as the average life of a goods vehicle. Then estimated stock of goods carriages would be 22.52 lakh of medium and heavy commercial vehicles (M&HCVs) and 31.47 lakh of light commercial vehicles (LCVs) (as on 31 March 2012). With some assumptions on annual distance travelled and goods carried, the supply of road freight transport services would be 2,988 billion tonne kilometre (BTKM).[4] However, for these goods carriages to ply, the estimated annual demand for diesel would be 46.21 billion litres.[5] The total demand for diesel in road transport would be 69.13 billion litres (including 22.92 billion litres from road passenger transport). However, the availability of diesel for road transport in 2011–12 is only 47.32 billion litres and it is not adequate to meet the mentioned demand for diesel.

Given this difficulty, we use an alternative approach where, availability of diesel is used to determine supply of road freight transport services. By matching the physical demand (D_d) and supply of diesel (D_s) for road

[3] While some reports claim that life of goods carriage in India is up to 20 years (World Bank 2005; MoRTH 2011a), there are no studies that establish an age for trucks on Indian roads.

[4] The assumption on average annual distance travel is based on Government of India (2010) and assumption on capacity of goods carriages is estimated based on category-wise vehicle sales data.

[5] Estimated average fuel efficiency for M&HCVs is 3.2 km/litre and for LCVs is 8.5 km/litre.

freight transport (Equation 6.2), we get the maximum years' stock of goods carriages that could be supported by the available supply of diesel. In other words, given S_k and F_k we estimate G_{ki}, by matching demand and supply (availability) of diesel for road freight transport.

$$D_s = D_d = \sum_{k=1}^{n} G_{ki} S_k F_k \qquad \text{[Equation 6.2]}$$

Demand for Road Freight Transport

Demand for road freight transport for a point of time can be estimated as follows:

$$\text{Demand for Road Freight Transport} = \sum_{j=1}^{m} TI_j \times V_j \dots \quad \text{[Equation 6.3]}$$

TI_j is the transport intensity of the jth sector, and it is the ratio of demand for road freight transport to total output for the sector and V_j is the value of output of the jth sector.

Transport intensity here is measured with respect to output and not value added, since the latter would be more sensitive to changes in relative prices. Transport demand should be related to the physical movement of goods which would be related to outputs rather than value added *per se*.

Since value of output for services sectors is not available from the National Accounts Statistics (NAS), for services sectors we have estimated the value of output as follows:

$$V_s = GDP_s \times \frac{TO_s}{GVA_s} \qquad \text{[Equation 6.4]}$$

where, V_s is the value of output of the sth service sector, GDP_s is the GDP of the sth service sector (available from NAS), TO_s is the total output of the sth service sector (available from I–O table) and GVA_s is the gross value added by the sth service sector (available from I–O table).

We have compressed I–O table 2007–08 (commodity to commodity) from the original 130 commodities and services to 17 sectors. This compression is done for ease of handling. The 17 sectors considered are: one sector for agriculture and allied activities, including mining and quarrying, 14 sectors for manufacturing, and two services sectors—one sector for services other than road transport services (including railways) and one for road transport services (including via pipeline). The rationale for working with a greater disaggregation in manufacturing can be explained as follows: demand for road transport (as percentage of total output) is not only higher for the manufacturing sector as compared to the other two sectors (agriculture, including mining and quarrying and services sector, other than road transport services) but also transport intensity (as measured by the demand for road transport as percentage of total output) varies across manufacturing sub-sectors substantially (coefficient of variation is 0.43). Therefore, to capture the dynamics of road freight transport demand in the manufacturing sector, we have taken 14 sub-sectors.

In our analysis, we have assumed that in sectors other than services sectors, the demand for road freight transport is same as the input road transport services as given in the I–O table.[6] For the services sectors, it is assumed that the demand for freight services is derived from their demand for input goods. This is estimated as follows:

$$DLT_s = \Sigma_g SLT_g \times X_{gs} \; where \; SLT_g = \frac{DLT_g}{TO_g} \qquad \text{[Equation 6.5]}$$

where, DLT_s is the demand for road freight transport in s^{th} category of service sector; DLT_g is the demand for road freight transport in g^{th} category of goods sector; SLT_g is the share of road freight transport in total output of gth category of goods sector; TO_g is the total output of gth category of goods sector; X_{gs} is the demand for g^{th} category of goods sector by s^{th} category of the services sector.

It may be noted that since the I–O table shows the relationship between inputs and outputs for the year for which it is constructed, to avoid problems related to changes in relative prices, the analysis is undertaken in 2007–08 prices.

Finally, if estimated supply of road freight transport is greater than demand, it is considered evidence of under-reported demand. Corresponding to this unreported demand, there would be under-reported GDP.

III: Results

Estimation of Supply

Sector-wise consumption of diesel (high speed diesel oil, HSDO) is available from the *Indian Petroleum and Natural Gas Statistics 2010–11*

---

[6] In other words, it is being assumed that the entire demand for road transport services for the goods producing sectors is for freight services alone.

TABLE 6.1   Sector-wise Consumption (End Use) of Diesel ('000 tonne)

	2007–08	2008–09	2009–10	2010–11	2011–12
Railways	2,036 (4.27)	2,166 (4.19)	2,261 (4.02)	2,371 (3.95)	2,559
Aviation and shipping	622 (1.3)	747 (1.44)	670 (1.19)	562 (0.94)	607
Agriculture	9,330 (19.57)	6,153 (11.9)	6,829 (12.14)	7,337 (12.23)	7919
Power generation	3,243 (6.8)	4,316 (8.35)	4,686 (8.33)	4,890 (8.15)	5278
Mining and quarrying	925 (1.94)	1,025 (1.98)	1,248 (2.22)	1,366 (2.28)	1474
Manufacturing industry*	2,368 (4.97)	4,264 (8.25)	4,754 (8.45)	4,946 (8.24)	5338
Miscellaneous and unknown end use	3,558 (7.46)	2,160 (4.18)	1,956 (3.48)	2,171 (3.62)	2343
Private sales and private imports	31 (0.07)	62 (0.12)	94 (0.17)	112 (0.19)	121
Road transport	25,556 (53.61)	30,817 (59.6)	33,744 (60.0)	36,235 (60.4)	39110
Total	47,669	51,710	56,242	59,990	64750
Availability of diesel for road transport (in billion litre) (1 tonne=1210 litre)	30.92	37.29	40.83	43.84	47.32

Sources: MoPNG (2012).
Notes: * Manufacturing industry includes chemical and fertilisers, civil engineering, electricals/electronics, mechanical, metallurgical, textile, and other consumer and industrial goods. Figure in the parentheses show the percentage share in total diesel sales.

(MoPNG 2012). The availability of diesel for road transport is residually determined in Table 6.1 by first excluding the bulk sales of diesel (railways, industry, etc) and then other sectoral uses of diesel from the total sales of diesel for a year. Since sector-wise diesel sales data is not available for 2011–12, we have estimated the sectoral consumptions of diesel for 2011–12 based on total sales of diesel in 2011–12 (that is,

64,750 thousand tonne) and sector-wise percentage share in total sales for 2010–11.[7]

Road transport consists of road passenger transport and road freight transport. Since reliable estimate on demand for diesel in road passenger transport is not available, we have derived the same based on a few assumptions (Table 6.2).[8]

Using data on category-wise number of registered motor vehicles, the demand for diesel in passenger road transport is estimated based on some assumptions on the share of vehicles run on diesel and the consumption of diesel by these vehicles (Table 6.2).[9]

Given the availability of diesel for road transport, that is, 47.32 billion litres in 2011–12, only 24.40 billion litres (or 51.56 per cent of total available supply for road transport) is available for road freight transport. However, the demand for diesel in road freight transport is derived based on stock of goods carriages (as on 31 March 2012), category-wise average fuel efficiency and average annual distance travelled of goods carriages. These estimates are derived for alternative assumptions on the average age of the vehicles.

In Table 6.3, we present the stock of goods carriages (as shown in second and third columns) by varying the average age of the vehicles ranging from 1 year to 10 years and the corresponding demand for diesel. Table 6.3 shows that the availability of diesel is not enough to meet the demand for diesel for six years' cumulative stock of goods carriages. Once physical availability (supply) and demand for diesel for road freight transport is matched, we estimate the supply of road freight transport based on category-wise average gross vehicle weight and average distance travelled per annum by goods carriages. The estimated supply of road freight transport in 2011–12 is 1,537.51 BTKM: 1,513 BTKM from

[7] Petroleum Policy Analysis Cell (PPAC). Retrieved October 8, 2014, from http://bit.ly/2f35sk7.

[8] We have compiled data on category-wise number of registered motor vehicles for All India and Delhi from 31 March 1996 (1995–96) to 31 March 2012 (2011–12). The data is published by the Ministry of Road Transport and Highways (MoRTH) and is also available in www.indiastat.com website.

[9] Though in a few metros taxis, three-wheelers and jeeps are running on alternative fuels (like LPG, CNG), reliable estimates of their percentage share in total stock of vehicles and their average daily consumption of fuels is not available to us. Therefore, we have not attempted to make any guesstimate and reduce the demand for diesel in passenger road transport.

TABLE 6.2 Estimation of Demand for Diesel in Passenger Road Transport, 2011–12

Category of Passenger Vehicle	Number of Registered Vehicles		Annual Diesel Consumption (billion litre)	Annual Diesel Consumption (litre/vehicle)	Average Distance Travelled (km/day)
	Period	NoS (A)			
Buses (on road stock of vehicles: 13 years)*	1999–2012	8,42,496	10.03 @	21,080	258
Taxis (9 years)*	2003–12	11,37,015	4.15 **	3,650	179
Three wheelers (13 years)*	1999–2012	27,66,100	5.05 @@	1,825	175
Passenger cars (9 years)	2003–12	1,09,75,380	2.02 #	918	45
Jeeps (9 years)	2003–12	8,07,041	1.06 $	1,314	45
Omni vans/buses (9 years)*	2003–12	1,39,949	0.61 $	4,380	120
Total			22.92		

Note: *Excluding Delhi, as all commercial public transport vehicles (including taxis, three wheelers and Omni vans/buses) are run on CNG.

@ We assume that 13% of the stock of buses is public buses, and 87% buses are private buses, and private buses are run half the distance an average public bus runs in a day (assumption based on MoRTH 2011b).

We assume that 20% of total passenger cars are run on diesel (following Chugh and Cropper 2014).

$ In India, except in Delhi, jeeps and omni vans/buses are mostly run on diesel.

**For taxis, we assume that the daily diesel consumption is @10 litre/day (informal interviews with taxi drivers).

@@ For three-wheelers, we assume that the daily diesel consumption is @5 litre/day (informal interviews with auto-rickshaw drivers).

TABLE 6.3 Estimation of Demand for Diesel in Road Freight Transport, 2011–12

Stock of Goods carriages (in year)	Stock of Goods carriages (as on 31 March 2012) (in lakh)		Diesel Demand in Road Freight Transport (in billion litre/year)*			Diesel Demand in Passenger Road Transport (in billion litre/year)*	Total Demand for Diesel in Road Transport (billion litre)	Annual Diesel Availability for Road Transport in 2011–12 (billion litre)
	M&HCVs	LCVs	M&HCVs	LCVs	Total			
1 year	2.96	2.98	5.10	0.70	5.80	22.92	28.72	47.32
2 years	5.52	6.74	9.51	1.59	11.11	22.92	34.03	47.32
3 years	7.09	9.08	12.22	2.14	14.36	22.92	37.28	47.32
4 years	8.90	11.67	15.33	2.76	18.09	22.92	41.01	47.32
5 years	11.12	14.28	19.15	3.37	22.52	22.92	45.44	47.32
6 years (+1)	11.05	21.17	19.03	5.00	24.03	22.92	46.96	47.32
7 years (+2)	13.38	22.89	23.05	5.41	28.46	22.92	51.38	47.32
8 years (+3)	16.84	22.26	29.01	5.26	34.26	22.92	57.19	47.32
9 years (+4)	17.97	23.70	30.95	5.60	36.55	22.92	59.47	47.32
10 years (+5)	20.54	26.30	35.38	6.20	41.59	22.92	64.51	47.32

*Estimated based on methodology described in Equation 1.

Source: Estimated by authors.

TABLE 6.4 Estimation of Supply of Road Freight Transport, 2011–12

Age of Vehicle	Stock of Vehicles (in lakh) (as on 31st March 2012)		Annual Distance Travelled (in lakh km)		Annual Freight Transported (in billion tonne km)		
	M& HCVs	LCVs	M& HCVs	LCVs	M& HCVs	LCVs	Total
1 Year	2.96	2.98	447	164	360	24	384
2 Years	5.52	6.74	834	371	671	54	725
3 Years	7.09	9.08	1071	499	862	73	935
4 Years	8.90	11.67	1344	642	1082	93	1175
5 Years	11.12	14.28	1679	785	1351	114	1466
6 Years	11.05	21.17	1669	1165	1343	170	1513
7 Years	13.38	22.89	2021	1259	1626	183	1810
8 Years	16.84	22.26	2543	1224	2047	178	2225
9 Years	17.97	23.70	2714	1303	2184	190	2374
10 Years	20.54	26.30	3102	1447	2496	211	2707

Source: Estimated by authors.

six years' cumulative stock of goods carriages (Table 6.4) and additional 24.51 BTKM from goods carriages having vintage more than six years.[10]

Estimation of Demand

We have compiled the GDP (2004–05 series) for all the 17 sectors (both at current and constant 2004–05 prices) from NAS (CSO 2012, 2013). Except for services sectors, we have also compiled the gross value of output (at constant 2004–05 prices) from NAS database (CSO 2013). Based on the methodology described in equations 3–5, we have estimated the demand for road freight transport for all the 17 sectors in Table 6.5. For 2011–12, total demand for road freight transport services is estimated

---

[10] We get 1,513 billion tonne km from six years' stock of goods carriages for which entire demand for diesel is met by the available of supply, and another 24.51 billion tonne km from a few goods carriages (having vintage more than six years) for which additional 0.36 billion litre of diesel (over and above meeting the demand for six years' stock of goods carriages) is available.

TABLE 6.5 Estimation of Demand for Road Freight Transport for 2011–12, based on 2007–08 Input–Output Table

Sector Description	Value of Output (at 2007–08 prices) (Rs crore) 2011–12	Demand for Road Freight Transport/ Total Output 2007–08	Demand for Road Freight Transport (Rs crore) (at 2007–08 Prices) 2011–12
A	B	C	(D) = (B*C)
Agriculture and mining	14,41,219	0.016	22,844
Food products	6,66,714	0.029	19,067
Beverages and tobacco products	74,467	0.032	2,372
Textile products	4,72,864	0.067	31,775
Wood and wood products, furniture, fixture, etc	1,02,092	0.042	4,246
Paper and printing, etc	1,38,355	0.061	8,472
Leather and fur products	51,051	0.044	2,269
Rubber, petroleum products, etc	7,31,878	0.014	10,357
Chemical and chemical products	5,01,795	0.042	21,118
Non-metallic products	2,00,528	0.055	11,110
Basic metals	7,29,126	0.029	20,946
Metal products and machinery	5,23,334	0.028	14,442
Electrical machinery	2,62,118	0.031	8,143
Transport equipment	4,68,308	0.030	13,824
Other manufacturing	2,55,890	0.078	19,938

(Cont'd)

TABLE 6.5 *(Cont'd)*

Sector Description	Value of Output (at 2007–08 prices) (Rs crore) 2011–12	Demand for Road Freight Transport/ Total Output 2007–08	Demand for Road Freight Transport (Rs crore) (at 2007–08 Prices) 2011–12
A	B	C	(D) = (B*C)
Non-land transport services as input	59,07,936	0.006	32,572
Land (road) transport services as input	8,21,589	0.007	5,441
Total			2,48,936

*Estimated value of output (at 2007–08 prices) for 2011–12 (Rs crore) = value of output (at 2004–05 prices) for 2011–12 (Rs crore) * (GDP at current prices for 2007–08/GGDP at constant 2004–05 prices for 2007–08).

Sources: Column C: Input – Output Transaction Table for 2007–08 (CSO 2012).

to be Rs 2,48,936 crore (in 2007–08 prices). The table also establishes the universality of road transport as an input for income generation. The value of demand for road freight transport (as we estimate in Table 6.5) is converted into physical units (in BTKM) by using average tariff rate of road freight transport (in rupees per tonne km). The average tariff of road freight transport for 2011–12 is derived from available information and a few assumptions. The estimated average road freight rate is converted to 2007–08 prices by using Road Freight Index of Transport Corporation of India Limited (TCIL). In Table 6.6, we have estimated the demand for road freight transport in physical unit for 2009–10 to 2011–12 using the I–O table of 2007–08.

Unaccounted GDP for India (2011–12)

Here, we compare the physical demand and supply of road freight transport (in BTKM) and estimate the unaccounted supply of road freight transport (Row G in Table 6.7). Corresponding to this unaccounted supply of road freight transport, we have also estimated unaccounted GDP (Row H in Table 6.7) and it is 25 per cent of total (accounted and unaccounted) GDP for 2011–12. In other words, the estimated

TABLE 6.6 Estimation of Demand for Road Freight Transport (Based on I–O Table 2007–08)

Description	2011–12
Demand for road freight transport (in Rs crore) (prices in 2007–08) (A)	24893
Road freight index (RFI) deflator (B)*	1.048
Road freight rate (Rs per tonne km) (respective year's prices) (C)#	2.275
Road freight rate (Rs per tonne km) (prices in 2007–08) (D) [C*(1/B)]	2.171
Demand for road freight transport (in billion tonne km) (E) [A/(D*100)]	1147

* - e.g., RFI2011–12/RFI2007–08.
# - For details estimation method see Appendix II.
Source: Estimated by authors.

TABLE 6.7 Estimation of Unaccounted GDP for India (Based on I–O Table 2007–08*)

Description	2011–12
Demand for road freight transport (in Rs crore) (prices in 2007–08) (A)	248936
Demand for road freight transport (in billion tonne km) (B) (source Table 6.6)	1147
Gross domestic product (in Rs crore) (prices in 2007–08) (C)	6143246
GDP supported by per unit of road freight transport (Rs crore/billion tonne km) (prices in 2007–08) (D) [C/B]	5355.93
Estimated supply of road freight transport (in billion tonne km) (E)	1537.51
Unaccounted supply of road freight transport (F) [(E-B)/E*100] (%)	25.40
Estimated GDP (Rs crore) (prices in 2007–08) (G) [D*E]	8234789
Estimated share of unaccounted GDP (H) [(G-C)/G*100] (%)	25.40

Source: Computed by authors.

unaccounted GDP is 34 per cent of official estimate of GDP for 2011–12 (Table 6.7).

Supply of road freight transport provided by the present stock of goods carriages ideally should be equal to the demand for road freight transport and any discrepancy between them could be due to under-reporting of road freight transport in GDP. Since there is no incentive for an individual entity to under-report the rate of freight (in rupees per tonne km transported) there are always incentives for under or non-reporting of goods (freight) carried through road. Since the transport sector is kept out of the present value added tax (VAT) system, claiming input tax credit against input goods and services is not permissible. Therefore, non-reporting sales are the ideal strategy for transporters, as depending on their sales income tax liability is calculated. However, since transporters cannot issue VAT invoices, there is no incentive for others to report engagement of transport services. If there is under-reporting in road freight transport (which is the most important means of transporting goods from one place to another), there is the possibility of under-reporting in production or output too. Income generated from unreported production/output is also kept out of books of accounts.

Given the presence of a large unorganised sector in the Indian economy and a vast market for locally produced consumer goods, selling goods in cash (without invoice) is not impossible. Therefore, there are incentives for some firms to under-report raw materials and corresponding production (output) and the process leads to generation of unaccounted income. If a sector's output is predominantly used for final consumption, the possibility of not reporting purchase of raw materials and corresponding output would be higher.

A compilation of previous estimates of unaccounted income of India is presented in Table 6.8. The table shows that estimates vary across methods of estimation. As compared to old estimates, current estimates show less variation across methods. Our estimate is in line with other estimates of unaccounted income in India.

IV: Conclusions

This chapter develops a methodology for estimation of unaccounted GDP based on road freight transport as a universal input. The methodology captures economic activities which are not fully accounted in the official estimate of GDP. The chapter estimates the size of the unaccounted

TABLE 6.8 Alternative Estimates of Black Income of Indian Economy (as Percent of GNP or GDP)

Year	Chopra (1982) Estimates		Gupta & Gupta (1982) Estimates*	Gupta & Mehta (1982) Estimates#	Ghosh et al. (1981) Estimates*	Rangnekar (1982) Estimates*	NIPFP (1985) Estimates	Schneider (2005) Estimates	Chaudhari et al. (2006) Estimates	Schneider (2004) Estimates	Kumar (2013) Estimates
	Wanchoo Method	Own Method									
1970–71	4.8	5.2	22.3	–	7.6	–	–	–	–	–	
1971–72	5.1	3.2	28.7	–	7.8	–	–	–	–	–	
1972–73	4.0	3.8	31.9	–	7.8	–	–	–	–	–	
1973–74	4.9	8.1	27.1	–	7.4	9.9	–	–	–	–	
1974–75	5.9	12.4	20.9	13.8	8.1	9.3	–	–	–	–	
1975–76	5.6	9.9	25.0	–	8.4	10.0	15–18	–	–	–	
1976–77	5.7	10.2	37.6	–	8.7	11.3	–	–	–	–	
1977–78	–	–	38.4	–	8.7	12.1	–	–	–	–	
1978–79	–	–	48.1	19.8	–	13.5	–	–	–	–	
1979–80	–	–	–	–	–	14.4	–	–	–	–	
1980–81	–	–	–	–	–	–	18–21	–	–	–	
1983–84	–	–	–	–	–	–	19–21	–	–	–	
1990–2000	–	–	–	–	–	–	–	20.6	–	–	

2000–01	–	–	–	–	–	–	21.8	20.3	23.1
2001–02	–	–	–	–	–	–	23.1	–	24.2
2002–03	–	–	–	–	–	–	–	–	25.2
2013	–	–	–	–	–	–	–	–	50.0

* Estimates are in percentage of GNP at current market prices. # – Estimates are in percentage of GDP at factor cost and 1770–71 prices. Other estimates are in percentage of GDP.

Source: NIPFP (1985); Government of India (2012); Schneider (2004, 2005); Chaudhuri *et al.* (2006).

GDP (as percentage of total GDP: unaccounted and accounted) in India. However, activities like bribe-taking and kickbacks are transfers and not accounted either in the official estimate of GDP or in our estimation of unaccounted GDP. To capture the dynamics of the relationship between inputs and outputs and structural changes of the economy, the methodology is tested by using two different I–O tables (2003–04 and 2007–08) and estimating the results for three consecutive years (2009–10 to 2011–12).

The results show that for reasonable assumptions, fairly consistent estimates of unaccounted GDP can be derived. The actual level of unaccounted incomes in the country can be calibrated by incorporating estimates of the adulteration in diesel and estimates of overloading in trucks. It should be mentioned here that the estimate of unaccounted incomes derived here can be interpreted as an estimate of the extent to which GDP estimates of economic activity are under-reported. This interpretation has two limitations: first, these estimates by themselves cannot be related to incomes not reported for purposes of taxes. Second, any incomes which are generated for illegal activities and/or from activities which are not part of value addition in the economy will not be reflected in this approach. For instance, suppression of incomes from capital gains from the sale of real estate property will not be reflected in this estimate since this is considered a transfer in the methodology for measurement of the GDP.

References

Acharya, S. (1983): 'Unaccounted Economy in India: A Critical Review of Some Recent Estimates,' *Economic & Political Weekly*, Vol 18, No 49, pp 2057–68.

Ahumada, H., F. Alvaredo and A. Canavese (2007): 'The Monetary Method and the Size of the Shadow Economy: A Critical Assessment,' *Review of Income and Wealth*, Vol 53, No 2, pp 363–71.

Aigner, D., F. Schneider and D. Ghosh (1988): 'Me and My Shadow: Estimating the Size of the US Hidden Economy from Time Series Data,' *Dynamic Econometric Modeling*, W.A. Barnett and H. White (eds), Cambridge: Cambridge University Press, pp 224–43.

Ardizzi, G., C. Petraglia, M. Piacenza and G. Turati (2014): 'Measuring the Underground Economy with the Currency Demand Approach: A Reinterpretation of the Methodology, with an Application to Italy,' *Review of Income and Wealth*, Vol 60, No 4, pp 747–72.

Bagachwa, M.S.D. and A. Naho (1995): 'Estimating the Second Economy in Tanzania,' *World Development*, Vol 23, No 8, pp 1387–99.

Bajada, C. (1999): 'Estimates of the Underground Economy in Australia,' *Economic Record*, Vol 75, No 4, pp 369–84.

Bajada, C. and F. Schneider (2005): 'The Shadow Economies of the Asia-Pacific,' *Pacific Economic Review*, Vol 10, No 3, pp 379–401.

Capasso, Salvatore and Tullio Jappelli (2013): 'Financial Development and the Underground Economy,' *Journal of Development Economics*, Vol 101, March, pp 167–78.

Caridi, P. and P. Passerini (2001): 'The Underground Economy, the Demand for Currency Approach and the Analysis of Discrepancies: Some Recent European Experience,' *Review of Income and Wealth*, Vol 47, No 2, pp 239–50.

CSO (2008): 'Input-Output Transactions Table 2003–04,' Central Statistical Organisation, Ministry of Statistics and Programme Implementation, Government of India, New Delhi.

———— (2012): 'Input-Output Transactions Table 2007–08,' CSO, Ministry of Statistics and Programme Implementation, Government of India, New Delhi.

———— (2013): 'National Account Statistics 2013,' Ministry of Statistics and Programme Implementation, Government of India, New Delhi.

Chaudhuri, K., F. Schneider and S. Chattopadhyay (2006): 'The Size and Development of the Shadow Economy: An Empirical Investigation from States of India,' *Journal of Development Economics*, Vol 80, No 2, pp 428–43.

Chopra, O.P. (1982): 'Unaccounted Income: Some Estimates,' *Economic & Political Weekly*, Vol 17, Nos 17–18, pp 739–44.

Chugh, R. and M. Cropper (2014): 'The Welfare Effects of Fuel Conservation Policies in the Indian Car Market,' RFF Discussion Paper Nos 14–33, Resources for the Future, Washington, DC.

Contini, B. (1982): 'The Second Economy in Italy,' *The Underground Economy in the United States and Abroad*, V Tanzi (ed), Boston: DC Heathe and Co, pp 199–208.

Eilat, Y. and C. Zinnes (2002): 'The Shadow Economy in Transition Countries: Friend or Foe? A Policy Perspective,' *World Development*, Vol 30, No 7, pp 1233–54.

Feige, E.L. (1979): 'How Big Is the Irregular Economy?' *Challenge*, Vol 22, No 5, pp 5–13.

Frey, B.S. and W.W. Pommerehne (1984): 'The Hidden Economy: State and Prospects for Measurement,' *Review of Income and Wealth*, Vol 30, No 1, pp 1–23.

Frey, B.S. and H. Week-Hannemann (1984): 'The Hidden Economy as and 'Unobserved' Variable,' *European Economic Review*, Vol 26, Nos 1–2, pp 33–53.

Ghosh, A.K., A. Bagchi, L.N. Rastogi and D.N. Chaturvedi (1981): 'Trends in Capital Formation, Growth of Domestic Product and Capital-Output Ratios (1950–51 to 1978–79),' *Journal of Income and Wealth*, Vol 5, No 1, pp 1–27.

Government of India (2010): *Report of the Expert Group on a Viable and Sustainable System of Pricing of Petroleum Products*, Government of India, New Delhi.

———— (2012): 'Black Money: White Paper,' Central Board of Direct Taxes, Department of Revenue, Ministry of Finance, Government of India, New Delhi, May.

Gupta, P. and S. Gupta (1982): 'Estimates of the Unreported Economy in India,' *Economic & Political Weekly*, Vol 17, No 3, pp 69–75.

Gupta, S. and R. Mehta (1982): 'An Estimate of Under-reported National Income,' *Journal of Income and Wealth*, Vol 5, No 2, pp 109–113.

Gutmann, P.M. (1977): 'The Subterranean Economy,' *Financial Analysis Journal*, Vol 33, No 6, pp 24–27.

Hanousek, Jan and Filip Palda (2004): 'Mission Implausible III: Measuring the Informal Sector in a Transition Economy Using Macro Methods,' William Davidson Institute Working PaperNo 683, May.

Kaufmann, D. and A. Kaliberda (1996): 'Integrating the Unofficial Economy into the Dynamics of Post-socialistEconomies: A Framework of Analysis and Evidence,' Policy Research Working Paper Series 1691, The World Bank, Washington, DC.

Kumar, Arun (2013): 'Indian Economy since Independence: Persisting Colonial Disruption,' New Delhi: Vision Books.

Lahiri, K., H. Stekler, W. Yao and P. Young (2003): 'Monthly Output Index for the US Transportation Sector,' *Journal of Transportation and Statistics*, Vol 6, Nos 2–3, pp 1–27.

Lahiri, K. and V.W. Yao (2006): 'Economic Indicators for the US Transportation Sector,' *Transpiration Research Part A*, Vol 40, No 10, pp 872–87.

MoPNG (2012): *Indian Petroleum and Natural Gas Statistics 2010–11*, Ministry of Petroleum and Natural Gas, Government of India, New Delhi.

MoRTH (2011a): 'Review of the Performance of State Road Transport Undertakings (SRTUs) (Passenger Services for April 2010-March 2011),' Ministry of Road Transport and Highways, Government of India, New Delhi.

———— (2011b): 'Report of the Sub-Group on Policy Issues,' Ministry of Road Transport and Highways, Government of India, New Delhi.

NIPFP (1985): 'Aspects of the Black Money in India,' National Institute of Public Finance and Policy, New Delhi.

Norwood, Jenet and Jamie Casey (2002): 'Transporation Indicators of Economic Growth,' *Key Transportation Indicators: Summary of a Workshop*, Norwood, Jenet and Jamie Casey (eds), Washington, DC, National Academy Press, pp 22–27.

OECD (2002): 'Measuring the Non-observed Economy: A Handbook,' Organization of Economic Cooperation and Development, France.

Planning Commission (2011): The Working Group Report on Road Transport for the Eleventh Five Year Plan, Government of India, Planning Commission, New Delhi.

Prasad, Eswar and Karim Foda (2015): 'The World Economy Remains Adrift in Choppy Waters,' *Brookings*, 4 October, https://www.brookings.edu/opinions/the-world-economy-remainsadrift- in-choppy-waters/.

Rangnekar, D.K. (1982): 'Size and Dimension of the Black Economy,' *Man and Development*, September.

Schneider, Friedrich (2004): 'The Size of the Shadow Economies of 145 Countries All over the World: First Results over the Period 1999 to 2003,' IZA DP No 1431, Discussion Paper Series, The Institute for the Study of Labor (IZA), Bonn, Germany, December.

——— (2005): 'Shadow Economies around the World: What Do We Really Know?' *European Journal of Political Economy*, Vol 21, No 3, pp 598–642.

Tanzi, V. (1983): 'The Underground Economy in the United States: Annual Estimates, 1930–80,' *IMF Staff Papers*, Vol 30, No 2, pp 283–305.

TCI IIMC (2012): 'Operational Efficiency of Freight Transportation by Road in India,' Transport Corporation of India, Gurgaon, Haryana.

World Bank (2005): 'India: Road Transport Service Efficiency Study,' Energy and Infrastructure Operations Division, South Asia regional Office, The World Bank, Washington, DC.

III

BLACK MONEY AND TAX EVASION

(a) The International Ramifications of Tax Evasion

Chapters in this section deal with tax evasion in the business sector and its relationship with the generation and storage of black money. The effort here is to cover ground on the multiple forms of evasion practiced by big business houses.

We begin with how globalisation created newer avenues for tax evasion. Dev Kar's chapter, published in 2011, was a study of capital flight from India between 1948 and 2008. D. Ravi Kanth's chapter, published in 2014, asked if disproportionate focus was placed by policy on Swiss banks as the storehouse of Indian black money, while much of the black money was parked in other financial centres like Dubai and Singapore. S.S.S. Kumar's article, published in 2015, examined if participatory notes in the Indian financial market were used for speculative purposes. He found that the major determinant of participatory note-based capital inflows was the rupee–dollar exchange rate. Paranjoy Guha Thakurta, Shinzani Jain and Advait Rao Palepu's article published in 2017 used a case study method to document a case of customs duty evasion worth Rs 1,000 crore that involved the Adani Group.

7

An Empirical Study on the Transfer of Black Money from India

1948–2008

Dev Kar

This chapter provides an in-depth analysis of the drivers and dynamics of black money transfers (illicit financial flows) from India since the first full year after Independence until 2008. It is estimated that a total of $213.2 billion was shifted out of India between 1948 and 2008, or about 17.7 per cent of India's GDP at end-2008. Applying rates of return on these assets based on the short-term US Treasury bill rate, the total gross transfers of illicit assets by Indian residents amount to $462 billion at the end of 2008. Over this period, illicit flows grew at a compound nominal rate of 11.5 per cent per annum while in real terms they grew by 6.4 per cent per annum. An important finding is that illicit flows from India are more likely to have been driven by a complex interplay of structural factors and governance issues than they are by poor macroeconomic policies. There are reasons to believe that the cumulative loss of capital is significantly understated because economic models can neither capture all sources for the generation of illicit funds nor the various means for their transfer.

I: Introduction

A number of recent scams and intense attention in the media on the governance deficit that enabled these scams has heightened public awareness of the need to improve governance and curb the generation of black money. However, the spate of news reports and discussions in the public domain that followed indicate that many politicians and journalists have conflicting notions about the nature and extent of black money in the Indian economy and the factors that drive its generation. Even academics have bandied about outrageously high estimates of the amount of black money transferred from India since Independence or have equated illicit flows (or the cross-border transmission of black money) with the underground economy. This chapter shows why such contentions and interpretations are fallacious.

In an effort to clear the air, this chapter provides an in-depth analysis of the drivers and dynamics of black money transfers (or illicit financial flows) from India since the first full year after Independence until 2008, the latest year for which complete data is available. In analysing the long-term evolution of illicit flows from India, we ask whether the dynamics of illicit flows can be adequately represented by a simulation model and whether the model can shed light on the main drivers of such flows from India.

According to a recent study, India lost between $11.6 billion and $14.3 billion annually in illicit financial flows during 2000–08, making it one of the top exporters of such capital from Asia (Kar and Curcio 2011). Substantial as these outflows are, they are likely to be understated given that economic models cannot capture all channels through which illicit capital can leave the country. An earlier version of this report received significant media attention in India in the run-up to the 2009 general elections as political parties jostled to take the initiative on this long-festering issue. Reports in the Indian media claimed that Indians held close to $1.4 trillion in illicit funds in foreign accounts. We present a systematic study of whether such claims can be supported by empirical analysis.

The chapter is organised as follows. Section 2 presents the methodology underlying the estimation of illicit flows (transfers of black money). We then present a synopsis of an econometric model of illicit financial flows in Section 3 in order to highlight the main drivers of these flows that were confirmed through model simulations. Section 4 presents the main findings of the chapter.

II: Methodology to Estimate Illicit Financial Flows

The method used in this chapter departs from traditional capital flight models in the treatment of illicit inflows. While the traditional method nets out illicit inflows from outflows, the change in external debt (CED) and the trade mispricing adjustments are based on gross outflows only with illicit inflows set to zero. Thus, when the use of funds exceeds the source, or when trade mispricing indicates export over-invoicing and import under-invoicing, such inward transfers of illicit capital are set to zero for that year.

The evolution of illicit flows from India is examined in two parts—for the entire period 1948–2008 and the behaviour of flows before and after economic reform started in earnest in 1991. Figure 7.1 traces how these flows have behaved over the 61-year-period to 2008, the last year for which complete macroeconomic data are available for India. A total of $213.2 billion was shifted out of India over 61 years between the first full year of India's Independence and 2008. This gross transfer of illicit external assets (a term that is more accurate than the stock of capital flight since the stock is net of withdrawals on which no data are available) needs to be revalued taking account of rates of return. A common proxy for the rate of return on external assets has been the United States treasury bill rate (short-term). In calculating the compound interest on these assets, the current period's interest rate is applied to the sum of the preceding years' accumulated illicit flows and half of this year's flows.

The rationale is that all illicit flows do not arrive at the same time at the beginning of the year; rather we assume that illicit flows are evenly spread out so that only half of the current year's flows earn interest at the current rate. Using this method, results show that the adjusted gross transfer of illicit assets by residents of India amount to about $462 billion as of end-December 2008. This is a huge loss of capital which, if it were retained, could have liquidated all of India's external debt totalling $230.6 billion at the end of 2008 and provided another half for poverty alleviation and economic development.

There are reasons to believe that the present value of illicit assets transferred abroad is significantly understated. For one, the rates of return based on short-term US treasury bill rates fall far short of the rates of return on many types of assets such as hedge funds, real estate, precious metals, and art objects. For another, the principal itself is understated because as we pointed out earlier, economic models can neither capture all sources for the generation of illicit income nor the myriad ways the proceeds can be transferred abroad.

Extrapolating from the estimates provided in Gupta and Gupta (1982), the size of India's underground economy should be at least 50 per cent of the GDP or about $640 billion based on a GDP of $1.28

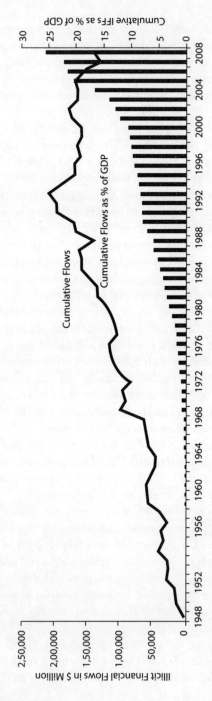

FIGURE 7.1 Cumulative Illicit Financial Flows and as a Percentage of GDP (1948–2008)

trillion in 2008. This means roughly 72.2 per cent of the illicit assets comprising the underground economy is held abroad while illicit assets held domestically account for only 27.8 per cent of the underground economy (Figure 7.2). We assume that although illicit assets held abroad can be brought back to the country, a substantial portion is again trans-ferred abroad once gains from 'investments' are realised. In any case, drawdowns are offset by the transfer of new illicit capital so that, on balance, the share of accumulated transfers abroad is not too far off our estimate. The larger share of illicit assets held abroad confirms Baker's (2005) contention that illicit flows are driven by a desire for the hidden accumulation of wealth.

On an average per annum basis, illicit flows from the country over the period 1948–2008 amounted to about 1.5 per cent of India's GDP or 22.8 per cent of its exports. Over this period, illicit flows grew at a compound nominal rate of 11.5 per cent per annum while in real terms they grew by 6.4 per cent per annum. The growth rates per annum were calculated based on the coefficient of the log linear trend line fitted for the period in question. We will now consider developments in capital flight from India before and after the major economic reform policies which were implemented starting in June 1991.

Ascertaining where economic reform actually started is difficult because reform in this sense represents the totality of policies devoted to freeing up markets from government controls and are typically

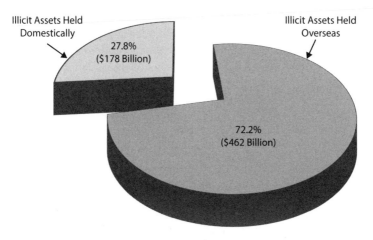

FIGURE 7.2 India: Composition of Underground Economy at 50% of GDP

undertaken in phases. For instance, certain aspects of economic reform such as import liberalisation were a salient feature of India's economic policies shortly after Independence. Nevertheless, the slew of policies aimed at freeing up markets from government controls that started with the P.V. Narasimha Rao government in May 1991 still stands out as a landmark in India's economic history. We find that outflows of illicit capital grew faster after reform than before (nearly 19.0 per annum compared to 15.8 per cent). However, the illicit flows to GDP ratios declined during the post-reform period because reform succeeded in boosting economic growth much more than it did illicit flows. In real terms, outflows of illicit capital accelerated from an average annual rate of 9.1 per cent before reform to 16.4 per cent in the period after.

III: A Block Recursive Dynamic Simulation Model

We developed a dynamic simulation model to examine the complex interactions between macroeconomic, structural, and governance factors that drive illicit flows from India. The model has two parts—an upper block of five equations that examines the interactions between fiscal and monetary policies and a single-equation lower block that seeks to explain the behaviour of illicit outflows from India. The upper block presents a test of the thesis that government expenditures tend to respond faster to inflation than do government revenues, because government outlays are typically subject to inflation adjustment while taxpayers seek to defer tax liabilities in an inflationary environment (thereby allowing inflation to reduce tax burdens). If the resulting deficits are largely financed through central bank credits (or quantitative easing), this leads to an expansion of the money supply which not only generates further inflation but widens the fiscal deficit in a vicious cycle. The purpose of the upper block of equations is to examine whether interactions between fiscal and monetary policies resulted in government deficits and inflation which help to explain illicit flows from India.

The simulated inflation and the fiscal deficit resulting from dynamic simulation in the upper block of the model are then used in conjunction with certain structural and governance variables to explain the behaviour of illicit flows in the lower block. The model as a whole is block-recursive in that it seeks to explain only the macroeconomic portion in a fully endogenous upper block of equations while it treats structural and governance factors as exogenous. This is because structural factors like income inequality and faster growth rates and governance factors as represented by the underground economy, are almost impossible to model endogenously. The complete model represented below was developed and tested equation by equation.

$$\log P_t = -\alpha\beta_0 - \alpha\beta_1 \log Y_t + \alpha\beta_2 \pi_t - (1-\alpha)\log(M/P)_{t-1} + \log M_t$$

$$\log G_t = a_0 + a_1 \log Y_t + a_2 \log P_t$$

$$\log R_t = \lambda_0 + \lambda_1 \log GDP_t$$

$$\log M_t = b_0 + b_1 \log(G-R)_t$$

$$\pi_t = \mu\Delta\log P_t + (1-\mu)\pi_{t-1}$$

$$\psi_t = f([\hat{G}_t - \hat{R}_t], \widehat{\Delta P}_t, \text{Reform}, \text{Underground}_{t-1},$$

$$\text{Trade Openness}, \dot{Y}_t, \text{Gini})$$

The variables in the above model are *P*, *WPI*, *Y*, the real GDP, *G* and *R* the central government expenditures and revenues respectively, *M* the money supply, π_t the expected rate of inflation, Reform, a dummy variable (with zero for the pre-reform period 1952–90, and one for the post-reform years, 1991–2005), ψ_t are illicit outflows based on the *CED+GER* method, $\hat{G}_t - \hat{R}_t$, and ΔP_t are the simulated government expenditures, simulated government revenues, and simulated inflation respectively so that $[\hat{G}_t - \hat{R}_t]$ is the simulated fiscal deficit. The other variables in the model are $\dot{Y}_t$, the real rate of growth, trade openness (defined as the ratio of exports and imports of goods and services to GDP which captures the impact of trade liberalisation on growth of the traded sector), Gini, a measure of income distribution, and underground, a measure of the size of the underground economy which serves as a proxy for the overall state of governance in the country.

While a great deal of information is available with respect to structural factors, governance indicators for the period 1948–2008 are scarce. For example, traditional sources such as indicators compiled by the World Bank or Transparency International's Corruption Perceptions Index only cover a fraction of this period. A review of the literature suggests that the underground economy not only acts as a proxy for governance, it grows by absorbing illicit inflows and provides the funds for cross-border transfers of illicit capital.

A time series on the size of the underground economy was developed assuming that it was 0 per cent at Independence and grew to 50 per cent of the GDP by the end of 2008, as found by a number of researchers. The series was subject to spline interpolation using these boundary conditions and ensuring that estimates for intervening years, 1967–68 to 1978–79, correspond to those found by Gupta and Gupta (1982) using the monetary approach. According to this measure, the post-reform period is characterised by a much larger underground economy (averaging 42.8 per cent of the official GDP compared to just 27.4 per cent in the pre-reform period). The one period lag, rather than the current size of the underground economy, was found to be more statistically significant in explaining larger illicit flows from the country since reform.

In an effort to identify the root cause of illicit flows from India, the above block-recursive dynamic simulation model captures three sets of complex drivers—macroeconomic factors like government deficits, inflation, and inflationary expectations; structural factors such as increasing trade openness and faster rates of economic growth and their impact on income distribution; and overall governance as captured by a measure of the underground economy. As complex as these factors are, illicit flows are also driven by the desire to hide ill-gotten wealth, a motivation that is extremely difficult to model and test.

Keeping these caveats in mind, model simulations provide some interesting insights into the drivers and dynamics of illicit flows from India. The following system of equations achieved convergence in dynamic simulation using the Newtonian method in E-Views:

$$\log P_t = -0.232 - 0.038 {}^* \log Y_t + 0.916 {}^* \pi_t$$
$$\qquad (-0.84) \quad (-0.73) \qquad 50(11.15)^{**}$$
$$\qquad -0.858 {}^* \log (M/P)_{t-1} + 0.930 {}^* \log M_t$$
$$\qquad (-16.59)^{**} \qquad\qquad (49.92)^{**}$$
$$\qquad\qquad \text{Adj. } R^2 = 0.99; \text{ standard error (SE)} = 0.03$$
$$\log G_t = 4.213 + 0.301 {}^* \log Y_t + 1.638 {}^* \log P_t$$
$$\qquad (2.79) \quad (1.90)^* \qquad (15.21)^{**}$$
$$\qquad\qquad \text{Adj. } R^2 = 0.99; \text{ SE} = 0.20$$
$$\log R_t = 4.342 + 0.236 {}^* \log \text{GDP}_t + 1.486 {}^* \log P_t$$
$$\qquad (3.56) \quad (1.84)^* \qquad\qquad (6.96)^{**}$$
$$\qquad\qquad \text{Adj. } R^2 = 0.99; \text{ SE} = 0.16$$
$$\log M_t = 0.599 + 1.132 {}^* \log (G_t - R_t)$$
$$\qquad (1.85) \quad (39.74)^{**}$$
$$\qquad\qquad \text{Adj. } R^2 = 0.96; \text{ SE} = 0.45$$

$$\pi_t = 0.9{*}\Delta\log P_t + 0.1{*}\ \pi_{t-1}$$

$$\psi_t = -6720.99 - 0.27{*}[\hat{G}_t - \hat{R}_t] + 737.58{*}\widehat{\Delta P}_t, - 9645.0{*}Ref$$
$$(-2.18) \quad (-6.55){**} \qquad (0.91) \qquad\quad (-8.40){**}$$
$$+ 0.12{*}UG_{t-1} + 7615.46{*}TO + 1796.20{*}\dot{Y}_t + 155.45{*}Gini$$
$$(8.60){**} \qquad (0.40) \qquad\quad (0.57) \qquad\quad (1.99){**}$$
$$Adj.\ R^2 = 0.89;\ SE = 1956.0$$

The statistics reported above are the values of the estimated coefficients and the ratios of the coefficients to the respective standard errors in parentheses. Variables marked by two stars are significant at the 95 confidence interval while those marked with a single star are significant at the 90 per cent level. All five equations tested have excellent goodness-of-fit and most variables are significant and have the correct sign except the fiscal deficit which unexpectedly has a negative coefficient. The finding that a contracting deficit stimulates capital flight corroborates those of Chipalkatti and Rishi (2001). On the one hand, if contracting deficits are interpreted as reductions in liquidity to the private sector such views may collectively induce flight capital. On the other, larger budget deficits may end up crowding in private investments thereby reducing the incentive for illicit transfers. So the link between fiscal deficits and illicit flows is not unambiguous as shown by previous studies.

Macroeconomic Policies and Outflows

We find scant evidence that imprudent macroeconomic policies drove illicit flows from the country. While government fiscal operations led to persistent deficits which were largely financed through central bank credits, the deficits and inflation did not drive illicit outflows. In fact, central government deficits have been rather limited and under certain conditions discussed above, they may have actually curbed illegal capital flight. The reason that changes in the deficit and inflation do not adequately explain illicit outflows is probably because macroeconomic drivers have a far stronger influence on *licit* capital movements (involving private portfolios) than on flows that are *illicit*.

There are two caveats with regard to the findings on government deficits and inflation as drivers of illicit capital from the country. First, lack of comprehensive data on consolidated government revenue and expenditure (i.e., including state and local governments and not merely the central government) did not allow an assessment of larger deficit financing on inflation and the impact of larger deficits themselves on driving illicit flows. Second, the shifting list of items subject to price controls and the varying intensity of implementation detracts from the quality of the wholesale price index as a measure of inflation.

It should be noted that the monetary impact of financing the deficit would probably have been higher in the earlier periods when the private financial markets, including the market for government bonds, were shallow and the government had to rely more on credits from the monetary authorities to finance its budgetary deficits which fuelled inflation. In the latter period, particularly after reform policies launched in 1991 were well under way, financial liberalisation would have fostered financial deepening, thereby offering the monetary authorities a viable alternative to inflationary finance. To the extent that the government was able to take recourse to private markets to finance its deficits, the link between changes in deficits and high-powered money would be broken.

There are two reasons why we did not find evidence of a strong vicious cycle interaction between government deficits and inflation in India. First, the increasing recourse of the government to financing its budget deficit through bond finance rather than quantitative easing particularly in the post-reform period, effectively short-circuited the deficit-inflation cycle to some extent. Second, model simulations confirm that the speed of adjustment of expenditures to inflation was not that much higher than revenues and this limited their asymmetrical response to inflation.

The model strongly indicates that the causes of illicit outflows from India lie in a complex web of structural and governance issues rather than unstable macroeconomic policies. The results show that reform itself had a negative impact on illicit flows in that liberalisation of trade and general deregulation led to an increase in illicit flows rather than their curtailment. The result is counter-intuitive in that one would typically expect economic reform to dampen illicit transfers as economic agents gain more confidence in the domestic economy. In order to explain this result, it is necessary to analyse how the 'by-products' of reform, namely, economic growth and income distribution, and increasing trade openness relate to illicit flows. Because these structural by-products of reform behaved quite differently during the pre (1948–1990) and post-reform (1991–2008) periods, the report examines their relationship to illicit flows by splitting the sample period into those two phases. Collapsing the two periods and simulating the model over the entire period 1948–2008 obscured the effects of the variables so that they no longer seem significant in explaining capital flight. At the same time, the longer sample period was imperative for testing the robustness of the model.

There was no statistically significant link between trade openness and misinvoicing in the years prior to reform. However, in the years since 1991, when economic reform led to increasing trade openness (as the size of external trade to GDP more than doubled from 10.8 per cent in the pre-reform period to 21.7 per cent after reform), results show openness to be statistically significant and positively related to trade misinvoicing.

It seems that trade liberalisation merely provided more opportunities to related and unrelated companies to misinvoice trade, lending support to the contention that economic reform and liberalisation need to be dovetailed with strengthened institutions and governance if governments are to curtail capital flight. Otherwise, deregulation will merely provide an added incentive for those seeking to transfer illicit capital abroad. That deregulation needs to be accompanied by stricter oversight is nothing new—we now know that deregulation without adequate oversight of financial institutions on Wall Street has helped, not hindered, their abuse.

Data also confirm that economic reform since 1991 has fostered a faster pace of economic growth. However, analysis shows that more rapid economic growth in the post-reform period has actually led to deterioration in income distribution. The rising trend towards greater income inequality during a period of rapid economic growth is corroborated by Sarkar and Mehta (2010), Sengupta *et al.* (2008), and others. In the post-reform period, there are clear indications that faster economic growth seemed to go hand-in-hand with larger, not smaller, illicit flows and a worsening of income distribution. In fact, we find a statistically significant correlation between larger volumes of illicit flows and deteriorating income distribution. Thus, while reform has fostered a faster pace of economic expansion, the resulting growth has not been inclusive and the higher income inequality has driven larger illicit flows from India particularly since 2000.

A more skewed distribution of income implies that there are many more high-net-worth individuals (HNWIs) in India now than ever before. Based on the capacity to transfer substantial capital, it is the HNWIs and private companies that are the primary drivers of illicit flows from the private sector in India (rather than the common man). This is a possible explanation behind our findings that reform has led to faster growth which has not been inclusive in that the income distribution is more skewed today, which in turn has driven illicit flows from the country. This result does not hold in the pre-reform period when growth rates were low, and income distribution was more equitable.

Another limitation of the data is the lack of a time series on a consistent deposit rate of interest for the period 1948–2008. The result of this limitation is that it is not possible to test how interest differentials impact the volume of illicit outflows. By the same token, a consistent time series on the real effective exchange rate (REER) which could have acted as a proxy for the expected rate of depreciation (indicated by a real effective exchange rate that is out of alignment with international competitiveness) could not be included. The want of a comprehensive measure of unit labour costs is the main reason why there is no REER series for 1948–2008 (a CPI, consumer price index or WPI, wholesale price index is not the best measure to capture unit labour costs).

The dummy variable for reform (0 pre-reform 1948–1990; 1 post-reform 1991–2008) was found to be significant at the 5 per cent level indicating that liberalisation of financial markets and general deregulation led to an increase of illicit flows rather than a curtailment. Reform led to increasing trade and financial sector openness as well as higher rates of economic growth. However, while the results confirm that both trade openness as well as growth contributed positively to illicit outflows, the variables were not statistically significant for the entire period 1948–2008. In order to understand why, it is necessary to examine the link between these variables and illicit flows in the pre and post-reform periods. Collapsing the two periods and simulating the model over 1948–2008 obscures the effects of the variable so that they are no longer significant in explaining illicit flows.

The actual and simulated variables are plotted in the accompanying chart (Figure 7.3). Convergence of the model in dynamic simulation meant that the necessary and sufficient conditions for stability of the model were met for the period 1953–2008. The charts tracking the simulated government expenditures, government revenues, price level, and money supply against actual values show that the model performed very well.

Dispelling Some Myths Regarding Black Money

There are certain myths surrounding the transfer of black money that have been circulating in the Indian media. These should be dispelled not only to clear the air but to allow well-focused policy discussions on curtailing the generation and transmission of illicit capital. First, we find media

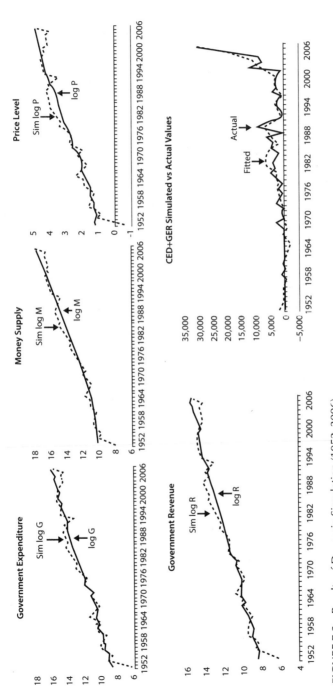

FIGURE 7.3 Results of Dynamic Simulation (1952–2006)

reports floated by some academics that Indian nationals hold around $1.4 trillion (PTI 2010) in illicit external assets to be wildly exaggerated. This is because the back-of-the-envelope method used to derive the $1.4 trillion is deeply flawed—the figure was based on Global Financial Integrity's (GFI) estimated average illicit outflows of $22.7 billion per annum (over the period 2002–06) in the original GFI report multiplied by 61 years since Independence (Kar and Cartwright-Smith, 2008). Of course, it is totally erroneous to apply annual averages to a long time series when illicit flows are fluctuating sharply from one year to the next. To illustrate, India's GDP amounted to slightly less than $22 billion in the six years 1950–55, which would imply that more than 100 per cent of the GDP was transferred out as black money in each of those years—an absurd proposition.

Another interpretation by Bhalla (2011) of our finding that the amount of black money in the Indian economy represented some 7.5 per cent of the GDP was found to be totally erroneous. According to him, this 7.5 per cent figure is too high because he estimates that the amount of black money as a result of tax evasion in India amounts to around 1.5 per cent of the GDP. This argument is wrong because the 7.5 per cent figure he cites is based on our estimate of the *change* in the size of the underground economy as a percentage of the GDP. The confusion arises from trying to equate cross-border flows of black money with the flows of black money into the entire underground economy. The underground economy consists of illicit assets that are not only derived from tax evasion but all sorts of illegal activities such as drug trafficking, cross-border smuggling, same-invoice faking, hawala type currency swaps, sex trade, human trafficking, etc, on which the question of paying taxes does not arise. It would be a pure assertion to say tax evasion is the major component of the underground economy which, according to internationally accepted definitions, includes the proceeds of all illegal activities. We estimate that cross-border transfers of black money, which includes the proceeds of tax evasion, amount to some 1.5–2.2 per ceent of the GDP, which is not inconsistent with Bhalla's estimate on tax evasion alone with a caveat that estimates of illicit flows are *likely to be significantly understated* because economic models cannot capture the proceeds of all illegal activities most of which are settled in cash.

Getting the Money Back?

Finally, there continue to be sporadic reports in the Indian media of 'getting the money back' from various tax havens around the world. This too is sensationalism with scant regard for the legal and other challenges involved. Illicit assets are typically lodged in secrecy jurisdictions behind a tight wall of opacity. Moreover, complex financial instruments such as derivatives and trust companies are structured in such a way that tracing the ultimate beneficiary of such investments is next to impossible. Furthermore, proving that a certain individual received illicit funds from a specific source for a specific illegal activity (as a result of bribery, kickbacks, drug trafficking, etc.) and then transferred those funds on a specific date to a specific account in a secrecy jurisdiction is almost impossible to do in a court of law. To make matters more difficult, offshore centres, tax havens, and even developed country banks would not permit any government agency to go on a 'fishing expedition' by allowing them to trawl through their accounts in search of illicit funds. Hence, the legal challenges involved in linking illicit funds to specific account holders would be almost impossible to surmount.

There are other equally dubious proposals to get the money back. The first involves a government amnesty for offenders to bring back their money by a certain date failing which a huge penalty and jail term is promised. The second involves a unilateral declaration by the government that all illicit assets held abroad by Indians now belong to the government as of a certain date. It is unlikely that there would be many seeking an amnesty for the return of illicit assets. This is because tax amnesty programmes will do nothing to encourage criminals and others who have transferred illicit funds abroad since those funds are not subject to income taxes anyway. The government's attempts to confiscate illicit funds through a unilateral declaration of ownership will fall flat because as far as owners of illicit capital are concerned, the government declaration does not bring about a material change in their situation. The funds continue to be illicit as before and owners continue to have access to their illicit funds outside the country in full cooperation of secrecy jurisdictions without any knowledge of the Indian authorities. Indeed, if matters were so simple, then such unilateral declarations by governments would have ensured that there were no illicit funds left in the world.

IV: Conclusions

An important finding in this study is that illicit flows from India are more likely to have been driven by a complex interplay of structural factors and governance issues than they are by poor macroeconomic policies. Hence, in order to curtail such flows policymakers must address these entrenched issues through a combination of tax reform and other redistributive policies to ensure more inclusive growth. They must ensure that customs reform and other regulatory oversight lead to significant improvements in governance necessary to shrink the underground economy. For their part, developed countries must hold banks and offshore financial centres to greater accountability regarding transparency so as not to facilitate the absorption of illicit funds.

Using the World Bank Residual Model adjusted for gross trade mispricing (i.e., illicit inflows through export over-invoicing and import under-invoicing are set to zero), we found that a total of $213.2 billion was shifted out of India over 61 years between the first full year of India's Independence (1948) and 2008, or about 17.7 per cent of India's GDP at end–2008. If we apply rates of return on these assets based on the short-term US treasury bill rate, we estimate that the total gross transfers of illicit assets by Indian residents amount to $462 billion at the end of 2008. Had India managed to avoid this staggering loss of capital, the country could have paid off its outstanding external debt of $230.6 billion (as of end 2008) and have another half left over for poverty alleviation and economic development. Over this period, illicit flows grew at a compound (nominal) rate of 11.5 per cent per annum while in real terms they grew by 6.4 per cent per annum. There are reasons to believe that the cumulative loss of capital is significantly understated because economic models can neither capture all sources for the generation of illicit funds nor the various means for their transfer.

There are a number of policy implications arising out of this study. We found that the underground economy is an important driver of illicit financial flows. The growth of the underground economy is indicative of the state of overall governance in the country. Generally, one would expect a high correlation between the state of overall governance and the size of the underground economy—countries with strong governance (such as Norway) typically have a small underground economy whereas those with poor governance (such as Nigeria) have a large underground economy.

The policy implication is that measures that shrink the underground economy can be expected to curtail illicit flows, while those that expand it would drive such outflows. As tax evasion is a major driver of the underground economy, efforts to expand the tax base and improve tax collection can be expected to curtail illicit flows. But this is not as easy as it sounds. Improving tax compliance requires a sustained and credible effort by the government whereby economic agents are convinced that the tax burden is distributed fairly and that they are getting their money's worth in terms of the services that the government provides. Taxpayers then become true stakeholders of the economy and tax evasion loses some of its appeal.

Post-script: This chapter does not take account of the impact of subsequent demonetisation of certain high-denomination notes on the official and unofficial Indian economies. For instance, a direct impact of demonetisation would be a significant reduction in the currency in circulation equivalent to a monetary contraction. The secondary impact of this monetary contraction would be a temporary slowdown in GDP growth pending the growth of monetary aggregates as dictated by the Reserve Bank of India. Still, even if we had fed the model with current monetary data reflecting demonetisation, we doubt that the results would significantly alter the main findings of this chapter for the period as a whole. At most, we could expect the model to show a temporary slowdown in the rate of growth of the underground economy in the absence of a sustained improvement in various aspects of governance.

References

Baker, Raymond (2005): *Capitalism's Achilles Heel: Dirty Money and How to Renew the Free Market System* (Hoboken, NJ: John Wiley & Sons).

Bhalla, Surjit (2011): 'No Proof Required: How Black Is My Economy?', *The Indian Express*, 5 February, 2.

Chipalkatti, Niranjan and Meenakshi Rishi (2001): 'External Debt and Capital Flight in the Indian Economy', *Oxford Development Studies*, Vol 29, No 1.

Financial Action Task Force (2010): 'India: Mutual Evaluation Report on Anti-Money Laundering and Combating the Financing of Terrorism'.

Gupta, Poonam and Sanjeev Gupta (1982): 'Estimates of the Unreported Economy in India', *Economic & Political Weekly*, January, 69-75.

International Monetary Fund (2005): 'Regulatory Frameworks for Hawala and Other Remittance Systems', Monetary and Financial Systems Department, Washington, DC, IMF.

Kar, Dev and Karly Curcio (2011): *Illicit Financial Flows from Developing Countries: 2000-2009; Update with a Focus on Asia* (Washington, DC: Global Financial Integrity), January.

Kar, Dev and Devon Cartwright-Smith (2008): *Illicit Financial Flows from Developing Countries: 2002-2006* (Washington, DC, Global Financial Integrity), December.

Kar, Dev, Devon Cartwright-Smith and Ann Hollings-head (2010): 'The Absorption of Illicit Financial Flows from Developing Countries: 2002-2006'.

Nayak, Dinkar (1999): 'Capital Flight from India (1975-1995)', Foreign Trade Review: *Quarterly Journal of the Indian Institute of Foreign Trade*, 34, No 2, 57–73.

Press Trust of India (2010): 'Black-money Debate: Cong Terms BJP Claim Bogus', *The Times of India*, 20 April. Accessed on the web, 14 October 2010, http://timesofindia.indiatimes.com/india/Black-money-debate-Cong-terms-BJP-claim-bogus/ar-ticleshow/4424198.cms.

Sarkar, Sandip and Balwant S Mehta (2010): 'Income Inequality in India: Pre- and Post-Reform Periods', *Economic & Political Weekly*, 45, No 37, September.

Sengupta, A, K P Kannan and G Raveendran (2008): 'India's Common People: Who Are They, How Many Are They, and How Do They Live?', *Economic & Political Weekly*, 43, No 7.

8

On a Wild Goose Chase for Black Money in Switzerland

D. Ravi Kanth

The noisy call to 'bring back black money' from Swiss bank accounts of Indians ignores the larger and growing deployment of illegal wealth in financial centres like Dubai. It is also overlooked that such money is rarely kept in the bank accounts of individuals but is held by trusts which make investments and whose beneficial owners are hidden from public gaze. Is this a serious effort to end tax evasion and capital flight or is it a public drama in which everyone knows no one is serious?

A banking expert on tax havens recently flew down to Dubai to provide investment advice to an Indian group based in the emirate. He was taken around a warehouse and shown a large quantum of funds stored as cash that he was required to inject into unauthorised accounts in Swiss banks. Given the popular image of the Swiss banks as the world's storehouse for illegal funds, the adviser's task should have been easy. That is what many expect to be commonplace as evidenced by the ongoing drama about bringing back black or illegal money stashed in Swiss banks.

During the general elections in May 2014, the Bharatiya Janata Party (BJP) flagged the issue of illegal wealth held by Indians abroad and the need to repatriate it home as one of its main priorities if elected to office. A BJP leader often mentioned a figure of $1 trillion that he said had been siphoned off from India to Switzerland.

But the hue and cry about bringing money back that is now engaging the National Democratic Alliance (NDA) government, the courts and the media seems to be a deliberate attempt at obfuscating the process by which illegal income is generated, how and to what extent it is taken out of the country, how it is deployed, and where it is invested. If the government, the courts and the special investigation team constituted (SIT) to investigate the issue were to focus their efforts on 'bringing back black money from Swiss banks' they might find that their objective would be better realised if they direct their energies elsewhere.

I: Misplaced Focus

The banking expert who went to Dubai declined to enter into any transaction to recycle the rupees into Swiss francs or dollars saying it was a crime to do so under existing Swiss laws. According to the adviser, who did not wish to be identified, 'The Indian government should be focusing on the new financial centres of Dubai, Singapore, British Virgin Islands, Luxembourg, etc., where much of the Indian black money has accumulated over the last two decades rather than on Swiss banks, which are used as a smokescreen to divert attention from the real problem.' These funds in tax havens are often routed back to India through Mauritius, which has a double taxation avoidance agreement (DTAA) with India.

The focus, however, remains on Switzerland. There is no clear estimate of the size of unauthorised funds held by Indian nationals in Swiss banks. The Swiss National Bank (SNB), the central bank, releases data annually on deposits held by foreign nationals, but these are of all funds—both legal and illegal monies. And it is difficult to discern which of these accounts can be treated as declared and which as undeclared funds.

According to the SNB, the deposits held by Indian companies or citizens in the Swiss banks are estimated around Swiss francs (CHF) 1.95 billion in 2013, CHF1.34 billion in 2012, and CHF2.03 billion in 2011. These figures do not tell us whether they are deposits by Indian banks, companies, or individuals, and of course how much of it may be illegal. The CHF 1.95 billion of Indian deposits in Swiss banks is about $2.02 billion, a far cry from the $1 trillion figure that has been bandied about. The informal estimate is that somewhere around $25 billion is what Indians are holding as illegal wealth in Swiss banks.

II: New Centres

Bankers in Europe say that much of the illegal monies held by Indians abroad that have been obtained by over-invoicing of imports/under-invoicing of exports, corruption in defence deals, and from the gold and diamond trade with Dubai, among others, are deployed either in the Asian financial centres or ploughed back into the domestic market. Instead of maintaining unauthorised accounts in the names of individuals, the holders of illegal wealth turn to gold and diamond traders in Dubai who can place them in the market without any trace of identity. The government has abundant financial intelligence to know where the illegal wealth and funds are accumulating, particularly about the role of Dubai and Singapore.

Dubai, of course, is the headquarters for the hawala operators. It is now India's largest trading partner and there are strong reasons to believe that the mysterious growth of India's trade with a non-oil producing emirate is linked to the transfer of illegal monies to this offshore financial centre (Krishnaswamy and Shaw 2014). In short, the bulk of Indian money is in Dubai, Singapore, and within the country. But, by focusing on Switzerland, the government is able to divert attention from real money laundering centres that have emerged during the last few years.

III: Changes in Swiss Rules

That Switzerland has long been the world's financial magnet for attracting foreign deposits and maintaining them under a rubric of confidentiality-cum-secrecy provisions is well known. But growing international pressures from the Paris-based Organisation for Economic Co-operation and Development (OECD), the rich country macroeconomic policy club, and other major trans-Atlantic capitals, particularly Washington, DC, have forced the Swiss government to reform their banking secrecy provisions.

For instance, in 2009 the United States forced the largest Swiss bank, Union Bank of Switzerland (UBS), to share information on nearly 4,500 rich American clients and pay a financial penalty of $780 million. Following the disclosures made by a former UBS official Bradley Birkenfeld, an American citizen, the US government exerted pressure on the Swiss government. Washington declared a commercial war on Switzerland threatening Berne that it would cancel US banking licences to UBS and other Swiss banks if information was not promptly shared.

The Swiss government panicked and chose to act on a war footing. The UBS case led to a largescale reform of Swiss bank secrecy laws and, finally, the Swiss government had to fall in line.

The Swiss government, under international pressure, has also relaxed the 'confidentiality' provisions for sharing information about illegal or unauthorised deposits with all other countries, including India, subject to certain conditions (caveats). In cases not based on 'fishing expeditions'—i.e., searching for information without knowing whether such information exists—it is now relatively easy to get information about unauthorised deposits of foreign account holders from the Swiss banks.

Earlier, any government seeking information about unauthorised deposits held by its citizens in Swiss banks had to provide the names and bank details, including the account numbers, without which the Swiss government refused to share information. Under the new Swiss law, India and other countries, which have entered into DTAAs with Switzerland, can obtain information after providing the account number or the name of the account holder along with legitimate proof or evidence of the account holder having violated domestic tax obligations.

A major change in the Swiss law is that the government can now share information without involving the account holder/client if it is satisfied on the basis of the evidence provided by India or any other country.

The legal work is now cut short but not entirely removed. The foreign account holder, for example, has the right to appeal once—while a decision has to be taken in 30 days. Within those 30 days, the Swiss government can decide whether to share or refuse information case by case on the basis of evidence from the foreign government. But even with all these changes India and other governments will continue to find it difficult to receive information of holders of accounts with unauthorised money based on fishing expeditions.[1]

---

[1] In the odd case, governments have been lucky with fishing expeditions. One such case was the Liechtenstein affair which surfaced in 2008. The Indian government was provided with information about unauthorised account holders which was delivered to the Supreme Court. The German government purchased the information from a former Liechtenstein bank official in the LGT Group, a banking firm owned by the ruling dynasty of Liechtenstein. Based on the information received from Germany, the Indian government began proceedings—without having established a case of tax violation. The 627 names of Indian holders given to the Supreme Court by the Indian government are from the Liechtenstein list.

IV: Forms of Disguise

However, to look for illegal wealth held in 'bank accounts' is looking for something that may not be there. With the increasing difficulties involved in individuals maintaining undeclared accounts, there is a shift towards maintaining funds through a structured company or trust with nameplate addresses often located in Mauritius or other tax havens. By maintaining trusts, it becomes doubly difficult for the Government of India to provide evidence about the real identity of individuals behind these trusts.

But where are these trusts registered? And where do they park their funds? The shell companies and trusts usually look for registration in tax havens like the Cayman Islands, British Virgin Islands, the Isle of Man and of course Dubai, Singapore and Mauritius. There certainly continues to be the occasional spurt of fund flow to Switzerland because of the sophisticated investment advice offered by Swiss banks. Unlike Swiss banks, the banks in Dubai deploy unauthorised deposits in risky products such as reversible convertibles that bet on the movement of equity or basket of equities or currencies. Therefore, there will always be some demand for the services of Swiss banks.

And as everyone knows if the government really was serious about preventing the recycling of black money it would have ended the practice of foreign institutional investors (FIIs) making investments through participatory notes (P-Notes). By not doing so, the government is deliberately allowing undeclared Indian funds to be channelled back into areas like real estate. For decades the government has known that a large chunk of foreign direct investment (FDI) and FII funds coming through Mauritius is Indian black money being laundered back via doorplate companies in the island nation. If the government were to be brave enough to abrogate the DTAA with Mauritius, it should be able to know the identity of individual beneficial owners of trust, offshore companies and family foundations, etc, which are routing funds back to India.

V: Round-Tripping

Big money illegal income is generated by tax evasion in real estate and exports/ imports. It is also generated by corruption in large government procurement orders. A large part of it is used and re-used in the domestic economy, again in real estate, and in smuggling, crime, for payment as bribes, and of course in elections. A part—only a part—is temporarily stashed abroad and invested in various avenues out of the reach of the domestic tax official. But it is rarely kept as 'cash' in accounts in Switzerland or elsewhere. This illegal income is turned into illegal wealth but it keeps getting recycled back into the domestic economy through illegal hawala trade or legally through the Mauritius FDI/FII/PI route.

All this brouhaha about bringing back illegal monies parked in Swiss banks has come back to embarrass the Bharatiya Janata Party (BJP) government. That the Narendra Modi government came to power by spending an unprecedented amount on elections is as clear as day and night. That the BJP has been heavily funded by, among others, the gold and diamond traders in Surat and Mumbai is also well known. Most of the illegal money held outside India belongs to corporates, owners of family companies and politicians. It is fairly clear why the periodic exercises to 'unearth' or 'bring back' black money resemble a charade which is increasingly looking tired and bored with itself.

References

Krishnaswamy, R and Abhishek Shaw (2014): 'The Puzzle That Is India-UAE Trade', *Economic & Political Weekly*, 18 January.

9

Participatory Note Investments

Do Indian Markets Need Them?

S.S.S. Kumar

Investments through participatory notes in the Indian stock market have been a cause for concern for policymakers. It is argued that P-Notes did play a role in attracting foreign investments, when suitable instruments were unavailable in India. But, today, with new liquid contracts available in Indian equity markets, P-Notes serve no purpose other than providing anonymity to foreign investors, and a potential route for tax evasion. From statistical analysis, it was found that P-Note inflows/outflows seem to be determined by rupee–dollar exchange rate movements, and not by fundamental price-to-earnings ratios, or even sentiment indicators like put–call ratio and advances-to-declines ratio. Policymakers must discourage foreign institutional investors from moving to P-Notes to avoid tax, and in the long term P-Notes must be phased out—the first step could be setting caps on investments through P-Notes at the firm level and at an aggregate level as well.

Portfolio investors in India, also known as foreign institutional investors (FIIs), are entities established or incorporated outside India, but propose to make investments in Indian capital markets. India is one of the countries in Asia (others being China and Taiwan) where, it is mandatory for FIIs to register with the market regulator before investing. In India, it is the Securities and Exchange Board of India (SEBI). Non-resident entities like pension funds, and mutual funds, among other entities, can register as FIIs and invest in India. Registration as an FII requires fulfilling various conditions like track record, financial soundness, and importantly registration with and regulation by the appropriate foreign regulatory authority.

I: Participatory Notes

A non-resident entity can also invest in India in two other ways through a sub-account of a registered FII and also through the derivative instruments issued by registered FIIs. These derivative instruments are commonly known as participatory notes (P-Notes), with the underlying assets being the securities listed on Indian markets. P-Notes are issued by registered FIIs to overseas investors intending to invest in Indian stock markets without registering with SEBI. More specifically, the FII uses its proprietary account to buy stocks and issue a contract (P-Note), which guarantees a return that mirrors the return on the underlying security. Hence, P-Notes are a form of derivatives issued by registered FIIs in India. The size of P-Note investments was Rs 207,639 crore as on 31 March 2014. Yet, there is scant literature on the nature and characteristics of P-Note investments. Although there are chapter that examine the nature and impact of FIIs in India (Chakrabarti 2001; Kumar 2001; Singh 2009; Stigler, Shah and Patnaik 2010; Bose 2012), studies on P-Note investments are conspicuous by their absence. Hence, this study is an attempt to fill this gap.

Policies Governing P-Notes

The issue of P-Notes caught the attention of a significant number of foreign investors because they provide anonymity, which enables certain entities to carry out their operations without disclosing their identity. This same characteristic also became the cause for concern for regulators, as they are not comfortable with the huge inflow of funds through the P-Note route. However, some entities prefer the P-Note route as the process of investing is quick and free from the hassles of registration. This is especially true for investors who invest in Indian markets solely as part of a global diversification strategy, wherein the allocation to the Indian market is not huge. Also some foreign investors, like the hedge funds, are often exempted from the purview of a regulator in foreign jurisdictions and therefore do not qualify for registration with SEBI.

Further, some foreign investors intend to retain anonymity of their trades so as to avoid front-running by local investors. But the regulator and policymakers in India suspect that the P-Note route is misused for money laundering, to avoid tax and compliance issues. This argument gets credence as a significant number of the sub-accounts of FIIs are based out of countries popularly referred to as tax havens (Table 9.1). The advantage of setting up an entity in a tax haven is that not only that the entity pays very little (or nil tax) in that country, but also hardly pays any tax in India by virtue of the double taxation avoidance agreement (DTAA) between India and the other country.

Figure 9.1 shows the proportion of P-Notes in the total assets under the management of FIIs. The average investments in P-Notes were around one-fifth of the assets under the management of FIIs during 2003. Subsequently, there was a steep increase in investments through P-Notes during 2004–07, accounting for nearly half of the assets under FII management. SEBI became uneasy with the magnitude of P-Note

TABLE 9.1 Assets Under Custody (AUC) of FIIs Country-wise (Top 10 Countries) (Rs crore)

Countries	January 2012		January 2013		January 2014	
	FII	SA	FII	SA	FII	SA
Mauritius	76,079	1,75,548	97,262	2,56,151	1,19,197	3,05,854
US	80,753	1,91,972	95,469	2,16,946	91,018	1,96,880
Singapore	36,214	6,952	72,130	10,321	83,173	10,506
Luxembourg	26,456	52,061	31,111	79,100	30,510	82,262
United Kingdom	21,465	28,406	20,395	43,047	24,700	51,929
UAE	34,385	1	42,363	1	46,763	103
Canada	8,656	9,764	12,779	12,709	128	26,793
Netherlands	10,017	4,940	16,582	5,968	21,476	6,395
Japan	1,636	12,898	105	17,159	12,717	15,034
Ireland	1,041	14,468	10,656	10,999	12,309	12,769
Others	34,422	65,191	62,205	80,920	55,610	82,841
Grand Total	3,31,126	5,62,200	4,61,057	7,33,319	4,97,601	7,91,365

Source: SEBI; FII–foreign institutional investor; SA–sub account.

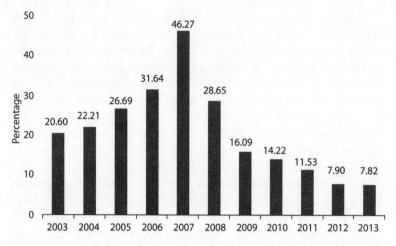

Figure 9.1   P-Note Investments as Percentage of Assets under FII Management

inflows. In October 2007, SEBI circulated a discussion chapter proposing some changes to bring in transparency and identification of the original beneficiaries (or investors) of P-Notes. Following this move, there was a trend reversal in the subsequent months. Not only did the investments via P-Notes start to decline, but outflows were exacerbated by the global financial crisis of 2008. In the last two years of the period of study, P-Note inflows have come down significantly and appear to have stabilised around 7.5 per cent of the assets managed by FIIs. This is partly due to the perceived uncertainties with regard to capital gains tax changes.

Broad Trends of P-Note Flows

Summary statistics of the net FII and P-Note inflows are shown in Table 9.2.

Net FII inflows peaked at Rs 139,931 crore in May 2014, while P-Note inflows peaked at Rs 75,217 crore in June 2007. The P-Note-related inflows into Indian equity markets had two distinct and contrasting phases—August 2006 to October 2007 (investments were net positive), and November 2007 to February 2009 (investments were net negative).

The P-Note inflows were positive and substantial from August 2006 to October 2007. Monthly inflows averaged around Rs 22,053 crore. In fact during this 14-month-period, non-P-Note-related inflows averaged only Rs 13,629.53 crore. Further, P-Note inflows were continuously

TABLE 9.2 Summary Statistics of Foreign Investors' Monthly Inflows during October 2003–May 2014 (Rs Crore)

Item	Non-P-Note FII Inflows	Net-P-Note Inflows
Mean	11,582.6	1,284.02
Median	12,137	2,071
Standard deviation	48,314.6	21,481.8
Range	2,59,967	1,47,108
Minimum	−1,20,036	−71,891
Maximum	1,39,931	75,217

positive except for December 2006 and July 2007. That is when SEBI and policymakers in India became anxious and came up with the discussion chapter requiring the disclosures on the original beneficiaries of P-Notes. Following this, P-Note inflows turned net negative continuously with monthly outflows averaging around Rs 24,292 crore from November 2007 to February 2009, while, during the same period, non-P-Note-related FII outflows averaged Rs 11,155.5 crore. Incidentally, this period coincides with the global financial crisis, and the reasons for the outflow could not be attributed only to the SEBI's discussion chapter on disclosure requirements.

The correlation coefficient between FII inflows and P-Note inflows was 0.5795 indicating that both the investments in levels are reasonably correlated. A month-wise analysis of the inflows indicate that in 13 months P-Note inflows were not only positive, but were also greater than net FII inflows and this was observed mostly during the period 2003–07. When the total foreign investments (both P-Note and non-P-Note-related inflows) were positive, it is noticed that P-Note inflows average (10 per cent trimmed mean) 31 per cent of the inflows and during the outflows period they comprised 29 per cent (10 per cent trimmed mean) of the total foreign outflows.

Table 9.3 shows the number of months in which both flows were in the same direction, and also the number of months in which they moved in opposite directions. In around 65 per cent of the total months observed, both flows are in the same direction. More specifically, almost 47 per cent of the months both net FII and P-Note investments were positive, while 18 per cent of the occasions both are net negative. When the net FII inflows are positive around 23 per cent of the months

TABLE 9.3   Direction of Movement of Monthly FII and P-Note-Related Funds

Direction of Fund Movements	Number of Months
FII investments are positive and P-Note investments are positive	60
FII investments are negative and P-Note investments are negative	23
FII investments are positive and P-Note investments are negative	30
FII investments are negative and P-Note investments are positive	15
Total observations	128

P-Note investments are negative. It emerges out that in general, P-Note investors move in the same direction as those of FIIs. And in general, P-Note investors do not have views contrarian to those of FIIs investing in India. Looking at the size of outflows in relation to FII investments during the periods of withdrawal—either by FIIs or by P-Note investors—it appears that P-Note investors withdraw money in substantial amounts which makes them less desirable for domestic markets.

II: Data Description

Even though India was receiving significant inflows through the P-Note route over the last 20-odd years, time series data on P-Note investments is available on SEBI's website only at a monthly frequency and that too only from September 2003 onwards. SEBI only provides the total outstanding value of P-Notes with underlying Indian securities. The data available is of a stock-variable type, whereas studies like the current one requires flow-type time series data, that is, monthly net inflows. Therefore, using available month-end data, net P-Note inflows data is constructed by taking the difference between the values of P-Notes outstanding at the end of two consecutive months. For instance, the net P-Note inflows during February, in a given year, is taken as the difference between value of P-Note investments outstanding at the end of February and P-Notes outstanding at the end of January. This study employs the monthly data on the nine variables given below during the period September 2003–May 2014:

i) *Net Inflows of p-notes (pnr)*: The net P-Note inflows for a given month computed as above are standardised with respect to the monthly market capitalisation of the National Stock Exchange (NSE). The monthly market capitalisation values are obtained from the *Handbook of Statistics on Indian Securities Market 2013* (SEBI 2014).

$$PNR_t = \frac{Net\ PNote\ Inflows_t}{Market\ Capitalisation_t}$$

ii) *Standard & Poor's (S&P) 500 Index Returns (SP)*: S&P 500 index is considered a proxy for foreign market activity. The index returns are computed as natural log differences, that is: $SP = Ln\left(I_t/I_{t-1}\right)$, where It is the level of the S&P 500 index on day t. Month-end S&P 500 index data was obtained from the Chicago Board Options Exchange (CBOE) website.

iii) *CBOE Volatility Index (VIX)*: The VIX proxies United States (US) stock market volatility. This index, as compiled by the CBOE, is based on the implied volatilities of a weighted range of S&P 500 Index options both calls and puts. Month-end VIX data was obtained from CBOE website (CBOE).

iv) *Dollar Returns (DOLLAR)*: Monthly rupee–dollar exchange rate was used to calculate dollar returns as natural log differences. The monthly exchange rate data was obtained from the Handbook of Statistics on Indian Economy 2013 (RBI 2013).

v) *Nifty Index Returns (Nifty)*: The Nifty index is a market capitalised weighted index of the NSE. The monthly returns are computed as $Nifty = \ln\left(\frac{Index_t}{Index_{t-1}}\right)$.

vi) *Volatility of Nifty Index (VOLNIFTY)*: Monthly volatility is calculated as the standard deviation of the natural log of returns of Nifty indices for the respective period.

vii) *Price–Earnings Ratio (PER)*: The price-to-earnings ratio is an equity valuation multiple defined as market price per share divided by annual earnings per share. In an efficient market, the share price should reflect a firm's future value creation potential, greater value creation can indicate higher future dividends from the company.

viii) *Put–Call Ratio (PCR)*: The PCR is the number of put options traded divided by the number of call options traded in a given period. The average value for the PCR is not 1.00 since equity options traders and investors almost always buy more calls than puts. Hence, on an average the ratio is often less than 1.00 for stock options. When the ratio is close to 1.00 or greater, it indicates a bearish sentiment. A higher than aver-age number indicates more puts being bought relative to calls. This means that more traders are wagering against the underlying, and hence the general outlook is bearish. Conversely, when the ratio is near 0.50 or lesser, it implies a bullish sentiment.

ix) *Advances to Declines Ratio (ADR)*: The advance-to-decline ratio shows the ratio of advancing issues to declining issues. It is calculated by dividing the number of advancing stocks by the number of declining stocks. The ADR gives an indication of the direction of the market. When drawn on a chart, the steepness of A–D line shows if a strong bull or bear market is under way.

Data on variables vi, vii, viii and ix described are obtained from the *Handbook of Statistics on Indian Securities Market 2013*. A positive relationship is expected between Nifty movements and P-Note inflows, and a negative relationship is expected between Nifty volatility and P-Note inflows. A weak rupee will make the Indian market attractive in dollar terms for external investors. Therefore, with a weakening rupee an inflow of P-Notes is expected. However, if the P-Note investors withdraw funds, spooked by a weakening rupee, P-Note outflows will be expected. If the P-Note investors are enticed by fundamental factors, a positive relationship is expected with the PER and sentimental indicators like PCR and ADR might not be significant determinants of P-Note inflows.

III: Methodology

In the first stage of analysis the time series properties of the variables were first checked before proceeding with the choice of estimation methodology; since estimations of the non-stationary series are known to be spurious. In order to check for stationarity and unit roots, Dickey–Fuller generalised least squares (GLS) and Kwiatkowski–Phillips–Schmidt–Shin (KPSS) tests were performed. The results of these tests are given in Table 9.4. Results show that in both tests, all of the variables are stationary at 5 per cent level of significance and hence are integrated of order zero, that is, I(0).

TABLE 9.4 Unit Root Tests

Variable	DF–GLS Test Statistic	KPSS Test Statistics
PNR	−8.914083*	0.183084
Nifty	−9.695387*	0.157381
SP	−7.670801*	0.109264
VOLNIFTY	−5.937510*	0.256352
VIX	−8.296073*	0.079757
Dollar	−9.571583*	0.244486
PER	−2.689258*	0.248391
PCR	−4.972672*	0.203360
ADR	−10.40761*	0.119728

*Significant at 5%.

To study the impact of PNR on the Indian equity market a vector auto-regression (VAR) with exogenous variables (VAR-X) is employed.[1] The VAR methodology is flexible and the most often-employed methodology in the analysis of multivariate time series, since it is a natural extension of the univariate autoregressive model for use with dynamic multivariate time series. The VAR model is a dynamic system of equations that allows for interactions between the variables while imposing minimal assumptions about the underlying structure. A VAR system can be expressed in the following form:

$$Y_t = A_1 Y_{t-1} + \ldots A_p Y_{t-p} + \in_t$$

Where Y_t is a vector of endogenous variables at time t and $A_i = (I = 1 \ldots p)$ are coefficient vectors, p is the number of lags included in the system, and $\in_t$ is a vector of residuals. A VAR-X model is a VAR process that

[1] Given the short-run nature of the data the study does not employ co-integrated VAR methodology.

is affected by other observable variables that are determined outside the system. The VAR-X model can be represented as:

$$Y_t = v + B_1 Y_{t-1} + \cdots + B_p Y_{t-p} + \theta X_t + \in_t$$

Where v is a n-vector, B_i are $n \times n$ matrices, p is the lag length, Y_t is a vector of endogenous variables, θ is a n-vector, X_t is a vector of exogenous variables and $\in_t$ is a vector of residuals. In this study, S&P 500 and CBOE VIX indices returns are considered exogenous variables because FII and P-Note inflows to/from India will not have an impact on these variables.

The lag length for the VAR (p) model may be determined using model selection criteria like Akaike information criteria (AIC), Schwarz-Bayesian information criteria (BIC), and Hannan-Quinn information criteria (HQ). The AIC criterion asymptotically overestimates the order with positive probability, whereas the BIC and HQ criteria estimate the order consistently under fairly general conditions. Hence, in this study BIC is employed to determine the lag length. A maximum lag length of 12 is considered to determine the optimal lag length (since the study employs monthly data, 12 lags is a reasonable period). The VAR analysis is complemented with Granger causality tests.

IV: Results and Discussion

Table 9.5 presents the results from the VAR-X analysis which shows the behaviour of the P-Note investments in Indian equity markets and Table 9.6 presents the residual diagnostics of the VAR-X analysis. It may be inferred from the residual test statistics that the VAR-X analysis is robust as there is no significant serial correlation or heteroskedasticity. It may be noticed that P-Notes are influenced by the US stock market returns and the rupee–dollar exchange rate. Even, the Nifty index has a significant association with the US market. The positive relationship between S&P 500 and Nifty returns mean that the Indian market may only provide limited diversification possibilities for foreign investors.

The P-Note inflows impact Nifty returns but the volatility of Nifty is unaffected by these inflows. The P-Note inflows are influenced by the rupee–dollar exchange rate. Thus far, studies have statistically established the impact of net FII inflows on the Indian equity market. But the

TABLE 9.5 Results of VAR–X Analysis

	PNR	NIFTY	VOLNIFTY	DOLLAR
PNR(-1)	0.106496	3.169601	−0.07928	−0.9312
Std Error	0.10031	1.21524	0.13510	0.49239
t-Statistic	1.06169	2.60820	−0.58679	−1.89118
NIFTY(-1)	−0.01377	−0.20743	0.013109	0.047583
Std Error	0.00796	0.09643	0.01072	0.03907
t-Statistic	−1.72961	−2.15100	1.22279	1.21782
VOLNIFTY(-1)	−0.07829	0.775869	0.516146	−0.09361
Std Error	0.06126	0.74213	0.08251	0.30070
t-Statistic	−1.27813	1.04546	6.25585	−0.31130
DOLLAR(-1)	−0.06534	−0.34191	0.059660	0.060183
Std Error	0.01905	0.23082	0.02566	0.09352
t-Statistic	−3.42960	−1.48130	2.32493	0.64351
C	0.001829	−0.00255	0.006795	0.004664
Std Error	0.00102	0.01232	0.00137	0.00499
t-Statistic	1.79822	−0.20653	4.95908	0.93395
SP	0.048334	0.990538	−0.04958	−0.27821
Std Error	0.01445	0.17508	0.01946	0.07094
t-Statistic	3.34457	5.65754	−2.54716	−3.92173
VIX	0.000550	−0.04131	0.000599	0.009313
Std Error	0.00335	0.04057	0.00451	0.01644
t-Statistic	0.16416	−1.01816	0.13277	0.56656
Adj R-Square	0.233646	0.430279	0.387022	0.244868
F-statistic	**7.402497**	**16.86017**	**14.25898**	**7.809718**

results of this study lead to the inference that P-Note inflows influence Nifty returns in a statistically significant way.

Results from the VAR Granger causality/block exogeneity Wald tests are given in Table 9.7. The important findings that emerge are: the rupee-dollar exchange rate Granger causes P-Note investments, and there is no causation in the reverse direction, that is, PNR does not Granger cause dollar returns. The Nifty index is influenced by net

TABLE 9.6   VAR–X Residual Diagnostic Test Results

Lags	VAR Residual Portmanteau Tests for Autocorrelations					VAR Serial Correlation LM Tests	
	Q-Stat	Prob	Adj Q-Stat	Prob	df	LM-Stat	Prob
1	4.263767	NA*	4.297607	NA*	NA*	13.26346	0.6534
2	21.88839	0.1468	22.20423	0.1367	16	18.05567	0.3206
3	45.06282	0.0626	45.93932	0.0526	32	23.94205	0.0908
4	58.39723	0.1446	59.70738	0.1197	48	13.88324	0.6074
5	78.71105	0.1020	80.85373	0.0758	64	21.61938	0.1559
6	100.5972	0.0596	103.8251	0.0379	80	22.54574	0.1264
VAR Residual Heteroskedasticity Tests	Chi-sq = 292.5574		df = 270			Prob = 0.1652	

P-Note inflows. In the Nifty volatility equation, PNR is not found to be significant. Therefore, it may be inferred that the PNR does not Granger cause market volatility. From the VAR analysis it may be inferred that Nifty volatility is a function of past levels, indicating the persistent nature of volatility in Indian markets.

To examine whether the P-Note investments are influenced by fundamental factors or by sentiment indicators like PCR and ADR, a linear regression is estimated with PNR as the dependent variable and the monthly price-to-earnings ratio (which is considered to proxy the fundamental factors), as one of the independent variables. Also, Nifty returns, Nifty volatility, ADR and PCR are also included as independent variables. The results given in Table 9.8 show that there is a contemporaneous association between P-Note investments and return and risk of Nifty, whereas fundamental factors like PER or sentiment indicators like ADR and PCR are found to be not statistically significant. The same analysis is repeated by replacing (results are not reported here but are available with the author) price-to-earnings with other fundamental factor price–book value ratio (PBR), but the inferences remain the same.

Therefore, the analysis shows that P-Note investments are predominantly 'return seeking,' but neither fundamental factors nor sentiment indicators appear to be statistically significant determinants, therefore leading to the inference that they could be short-term investors.

TABLE 9.7 Granger Causality/Block Exogeneity Wald Tests

Equation/Variable	PNR		NIFTY		VOLNIFTY		Dollar	
	Chi-sq	Prob	Chi-sq	Prob	Chi-sq	Prob	Chi-sq	Prob
PNR	–	–	6.802718	0.0091	0.344326	0.5573	3.576553	0.0586
NIFTY	2.991566	0.0837	–	–	1.495218	0.2214	1.483093	0.2233
VOLNIFTY	1.633621	0.2012	1.092983	0.2958	–	–	0.096906	0.7556
Dollar	11.76213	0.0006	2.194249	0.1385	5.40531	0.0201	–	–

TABLE 9.8   Regression Results (Dependent Variable: PNR)

Variable	Coefficient	Std Error	t-Statistic	Prob
C	0.004205	0.003192	1.317075	0.1904
NIFTY	0.035496	0.005421	6.547855	0.0000
VOLNIFTY	−0.17353	0.052977	−3.27549	0.0014
PER	−0.00015	0.000136	1.07084	0.2864
PCR	0.001464	0.002758	0.530718	0.5966
ADR	−0.00011	0.000288	−0.36981	0.7122
Adjusted R-squared = 0.373362 F-statistic = 15.65711				
D-W stat = 2.078415 Prob(F-statistic) = 0				
Breusch–Godfrey serial correlation LM test				
F-statistic				0.116607
Prob				0.89
Obs*R-squared				0.248797
Prob				0.883
Heteroskedasticity test: white F-statistic				0.178219
Prob				0.9703
Obs*R-squared				0.929386
Prob				0.9681
Scaled explained SS				2.593794
Prob				0.7623

Given the nature of the P-Note investments—evident from the econometric analysis—policymakers in India need to reassess the need for investments through the P-Notes route. The categories of investors who could benefit from P-Notes are two.

The first are foreign investors like hedge funds who invest in Indian markets as part of their global portfolio. As their allocations are rather small, they may not find it worth going through the registration process. With changes in markets and availability of newer products like Nifty futures contracts that trades on the Singapore Exchange (SGX), these investors can meet their portfolio allocations to India by making use of this product. Non-availability of P-Notes is not going to be a serious impediment for this set of investors.

The second are investors who might be using the P-Note route to avoid front-running by other investors in the local markets, and they might be interested in having their trades remain anonymous. Requirements of such investors can also be met by hedging with options and futures contracts that trade on the NSE and Bombay Stock Exchange (BSE) in India. The P-Notes were a pragmatic way to solve the requirements of these categories of investors a few years ago, but with the development and availability of liquid contracts on the stock exchanges, their apparent legitimate needs could be met in alternative ways. Hence, P-Notes are irrelevant in these changed times for these categories of investors.

In fact, P-Notes are suspected to provide an opportunity for possible round-tripping of black money. Further, as P-Notes are denominated in foreign currency, FIIs are also free from exchange rate risks. Hence, there are sufficient grounds for even registered FIIs to invest through the P-Notes route. The recent changes require that P-Notes be issued only to the residents of a country whose securities market regulator is a signatory to the International Organization of Securities Commissions (IOSCO), a multilateral memorandum of understanding, or a signatory to a bilateral memorandum of understanding with SEBI. This may curb the opaqueness surrounding the ultimate beneficiaries of P-Notes.

Yet, P-Notes may be attractive to even registered FIIs because of taxation issues. Moreover, P-Note holders have to pay taxes in their home country while registered FIIs face an uncertain tax regime as they are now subject to minimum alternate tax (MAT). A shift by FIIs to invest in India through the P-Note route may result in a loss of taxes to the exchequer.

In the light of the above, and based on the results of the econometric analysis, policymakers in India may have to reassess the need for foreign inflows in the form of P-Notes. As this money is not driven by fundamental factors, but rather by the allure of higher returns, this type of capital may not be in the long-term interest of Indian equity markets. Policymakers may have to consider discouraging existing FIIs from moving their funds in to the P-Note form in order to avoid taxes. Additionally, a long-term plan must be articulated to phase out investments through this route. At the least, caps must be set, both for each registered FIIs, as well as at an aggregate level.

V: Conclusions

This study attempts to fill in a gap in the FIIs–Indian markets literature by focusing on the P-Note investments-specific component of FII investments. The P-Notes are a kind of derivative instruments issued by registered FIIs in India to those who wish to invest in India anonymously. Investing through P-Notes is effortless, and hence has gained popularity amongst investors like hedge funds. These have attracted the attention of not only market participants, but the size of inflows into Indian stock markets through this route is making regulators uncomfortable due to the possibilities of misuse and tax avoidance.

This study finds that during the 14-month period from August 2006 to October 2007, P-Note investments were positive and significant while during the period between November 2007 and February 2009 P-Note-related investments were substantially negative. A monthly analysis of the direction of FII and P-Note inflows shows that in general, P-Note investors move in the same direction as those of FIIs. And P-Note investors do not have views contrarian to views of FIIs investing in India. But the size of outflows in relation to FII investments during periods of withdrawal either by FIIs or by P-Note investors show that P-Note investors withdraw money in substantial amounts.

The important findings from the econometric analyses are that the rupee–dollar exchange rate is the chief determinant of P-Note inflows to India. From the findings of the study, coupled with the fact that a large number of sub-accounts are based in tax havens, it might be inferred that some of these flows could be attempting to bypass capital account restrictions that disallow exploiting exchange rate movements. It was also found that the Nifty index is influenced by P-Note inflows. P-Note investments are guided by Nifty returns, i.e., contemporaneous values are positively related to Nifty returns and negatively related to volatility. More importantly, fundamental factors like PER or sentiment indicators like PCR are not significant determinants of P-Note inflows. This suggests that market advances will lead to inflows, and when the markets decline a reversal will lead to substantial P-Note outflows. In view of these characteristics, P-Note investments are less desirable considering the nimbleness of inflow and outflow, and size of P-Note-related investments.

Therefore, the concerns of policymakers in India especially with regard to P-Note inflows are not unfounded. This study argues for discouraging existing FIIs from shifting their current investments into the P-Note form, just to avoid taxes. Additionally, a long-term plan must be articulated to phase out investments through this route, and these intentions should be communicated by specifying caps both at the registered FII form level as well as at the aggregate level.

References

Bose, S. (2012): 'Mutual Fund Invetments, FII Investments and Stock Market Returns in India,' *Money and Finance*, September, pp 89-110.

Chakrabarti, R. (2001): 'FII Flows to India: Nature and Causes,' *Money and Finance*, Vol 2, No 7, pp 61-81.

CBOE (nd): 'VIX Options and Futures Historical Data,' Chicago Board Options Exchange, http://www.cboe.com/micro/vix/historical. aspx.

Kumar, S.S.S. (2001): 'Does the Indian Stock Market Play to the Tune of FII Investments: An Empirical Investigation,' *IUP Journal of Applied Finance*, Vol 7, No 3, pp 36-44.

RBI (2013): *Handbook of Statistics on Indian Economy (2013)*.

SEBI (2014): *Handbook of Statistics on Indian Securities Market 2013*, Securities and Exchange Board of India (SEBI)

———— (nd): 'Statistics: Foreign Portfolio Investors Investments,' SEBI, http://www.sebi.gov.in/ sebiweb/investment/statistics.jsp?s=fii.

Singh, B. (2009): 'Changing Contours of Capital Flows to India,' *Economic & Political Weekly*, Vol 45, No 43, pp 58-66.

Singh, Manmohan (2007): 'Use of participatory notes in Indian Equity Markets and Recent Regulatory Changes,' IMF Working Papers, WP/07/291, available at http://ssrn.com/ab-stract=1078796.

Stigler, M., A. Shah and I. Patnaik (2010): 'Understanding the ADR Premium,' NIPFP Working Paper No 71, http://www.nipfp.org.in/media/ medialibrary/2013/04/wp_2010_71.pdf.

10

Did Adani Group Evade Rs 1,000 Crore Taxes?

Paranjoy Guha Thakurta, Shinzani Jain and Advait Rao Palepu

The corporate conglomerate headed by Gautam Adani has been accused by the directorate of revenue intelligence (DRI) of having allegedly evaded taxes and laundered money to the tune of around Rs 1,000 crore while trading in cut and polished diamonds and gold jewellery. The DRI has claimed that companies in the Adani Group misused export incentives and indulged in high-velocity circular trading through a complex web of front companies located in different parts of the world. The government seems strangely reticent about filing a review petition in the Supreme Court that could protect its revenue interests.

For more than a decade now, the directorate of revenue intelligence (DRI) has been investigating how a clutch of companies in the Adani Group led by Gautam Adani allegedly evaded taxes and laundered money while trading in cut and polished diamonds and gold jewellery. The DRI, which is an investigative wing of the department of revenue in the ministry of finance, has issued a number of showcause notices to firms in the group alleging evasion of taxes to the tune of roughly Rs 1,000 crore. Adani is considered to be close to Prime Minister Narendra Modi.

While the allegations against the Adani Group have meandered through various tribunals and courts of law, questions are being raised as to whether the ministry of finance is deliberately dragging its feet in moving a review petition before the Supreme Court that could safeguard its revenue interests. Four detailed questionnaires were sent by the *Economic & Political Weekly* (*EPW*) to (i) finance minister Arun Jaitley and five of his senior officials; (ii) the minister of state for commerce and industry Nirmala Sitharaman and the director-general of foreign trade; (iii) law minister Ravi Shankar Prasad; and (iv) Adani himself. These questionnaires were emailed and also sent by regular post on 18 November 2016. Whereas spokespersons of Adani and the law minister responded, Jaitley, Sitharaman and officials in their respective ministries did not answer the questions more than a month and a half after those were sent to them.

Here is the story in a nutshell. A set of firms in the Adani Group apparently misused various export incentive schemes through a complex web of front companies located in different parts of the world. These shell companies, which indulged in high-velocity 'circular trading' among related corporate entities, were also used to launder money, the DRI has claimed. All the corporate entities were directly or indirectly controlled by, or associated with, Adani Enterprises Limited (AEL), a flagship firm of the Adani Group which was called Adani Exports Limited before 2007. The DRI has alleged that AEL flagrantly misdeclared the freight on board (FOB, also called free on board) values of cut and polished diamonds (CPD) and gold jewellery.

The investigative agency has also claimed that group companies and their associates indulged in circular trading to 'artificially' inflate exports and 'fraudulently' avail of financial benefits from vaious export promotion schemes initiated by the directorate-general of foreign trade (DGFT) in the ministry of commerce and industry (MCI). Such schemes included the incremental export promotion scheme (IEPS) introduced by the DGFT in 2003–04 under which came the target plus scheme (TPS) introduced in the Foreign Trade Policy 2004–09. Responding to the *EPW*'s questionnaire, a spokesperson of the Adani Group denied these allegations. Copies of the various showcause notices issued by the DRI to group companies are with the *EPW* and material from these notices has been drawn for this chapter.

I: Misuse of Export Promotion Schemes

Among the different export promotion schemes initiated by the MCI, a particular scheme sought to provide certain corporate entities exporting goods or services called 'trading houses' to avail of benefits that are proportionate to the quantum of exports achieved. Trading houses are ranked on the basis of their total annual exports and the highest exporters are designated 'star trading houses.' For 2003–04, the DGFT announced a scheme called the duty free credit entitlement (DFCE) scheme.

Under the DFCE, certain benefits were provided to trading houses recognised by the government as star trading houses or 'status holders.' Specific exporters were recognised as status holders 'on the basis of the FOB (freight on board)/NFE (net foreign exchange) value of goods and services ... as well as on the basis of services rendered by the service provider during the preceding three licensing years or the preceding licensing year, at the option of the exporter.' Under the DFCE scheme, a status holder would receive financial benefits equal to 10 per cent of the total incremental exports achieved in 2003–04 over the exports in the previous financial year, that is, 2002–03, provided the incremental growth was at least 25 per cent.

AEL and its group/associate companies had earlier been exporting various commodities from foodgrains to textiles. The Adani Group had a relatively small export turnover of just over Rs 400 crore in 2002–03. The DRI has claimed that after the announcement of the DFCE scheme, AEL formed a consortium with different corporate entities to 'artificially inflate' its exports to take advantage of the scheme. These five group companies were Hinduja Exports Private Limited (HEPL), Aditya Corpex Private Limited (ACPL), Bagadiya Brothers Private Limited (BBPL), Jayant Agro Organics Limited (JAOL) and Midex Overseas Limited (MOL). It is further alleged that in addition to these five Indian companies, AEL directly and indirectly managed and controlled 45 overseas corporate entities.

In 2003–04, the total export turnover of AEL suddenly jumped more than eleven times, to be precise, by 1,181 per cent. The turnover of HEPL rose by as much as 160 times (16,624 per cent), ACPL's by over 150 times (15,819 per cent) while that of MOL rose more than seven times (765 per cent) in these two years (Table 10.1).

Besides the DFCE, other export promotion schemes that were introduced by the DGFT included the TPS in September 2004 which offered incentives to status holders varying between 5 per cent and 15 per cent of the incremental growth in the turnover of exports (Table 10.2). Initially, studded gold jewellery and CPD were permitted to be included while calculating the FOB figure and therefore, towards claiming incentives under the TPS.

TABLE 10.1   Rise in Export Turnover of Adani Group of Companies between 2002–03 and 2003–04, in Rs Crore

	Adani Exports	Hinduja Exports	Aditya Corpex	Midex Overseas	Adani Group (Total)
2002–03	377.44	4.15	2.68	28.26	412.53
2003–04	4,838.53	694.07	426.63	244.60	6,203.83
% increase	1,181.93	16,624.58	15,819.03	765.53	1,403.85

Source: https://indiankanoon.org/doc/1510260/.

TABLE 10.2   Incentives under the Target Plus Scheme

Percentage Incremental Growth	Duty Credit Entitlement (% of incremental growth)
20% and above but below 25%	5%
25% or above but below 100%	10%
100% and above	15% of 100%

Source: DGFT.

II: DGFT Notifications

On 31 March 2007, the DRI issued a showcause notice pointing out that there had been a sudden and unprecedented increase in the Adani Group's export turnover of CPD, gold jewellery, rough diamonds and third party exports (all of which could be included at that time in calculating the figure of 'incremental' growth of exports for availing benefits from the DGFT) between 2003–04 and 2004–05. According to the notice, the bulk of these exports took place after September 2004 when the TPS was introduced.

The following year, the group's exports came crashing down. In 2005–06, the total exports of the Adani Group were barely a third of that achieved in the previous year. Exports of CPD and articles of gold came down sharply. Why? Simply because the benefits were withdrawn after the government realised that the export promotion schemes were being misused. As the MCI became aware of the misuse of the IEPS, some amendments were made to the Exim policy. In January 2004, the DGFT issued a number of notifications clarifying that exports of precious metals in any form, including plain jewellery and rough, uncut and semi-polished diamonds and third-party exports would not be permitted for inclusion in calculating the FOB figure.

The amendments were opposed by AEL and other exporters. They contended that the notifications were seeking to withdraw benefits already given to exporters. On 7 February 2004, AEL filed a petition in the Gujarat High Court challenging the validity of the notifications issued on 28 January that year. On 23 July, the court [in *Adani Exports Limited v Union of India (UoI)*] ruled against AEL and others upholding the validity of the notifications. AEL then filed a special leave petition (SLP) in the Supreme Court. The DGFT also filed an SLP against the order of the high court. Appeals were also filed by other firms and the government in similar cases against the orders of various high courts— such appeals included ones filed by Kanak Exports, the UoI and the DGFT challenging an order of the Bombay High Court.

The Exim policy was later further amended (through notifications issued on 23 February 2005 and 20 February 2006) to exclude studded gold jewellery and certain categories of products (diamonds and other precious, semi-precious stones) from the list of items entitled to receive export benefits under the TPS.

III: Findings by Supreme Court

In October 2015, the Supreme Court upheld the appeals filed by the DGFT and the UoI, dismissing the appeals filed by others. It was pointed out that there had been a spectacular rise in the turnover of two firms, Rajesh Exports and Kanak Exports, between 2002–03 and 2003–04 (Table 10.3). The more than 2,000 per cent rise in exports came entirely in the form of gold coins and jewellery. For Adani Exports, over 80 per cent of its export turnover came from diamonds and supplies from status holders. In other words, the Adani Group would not have met the minimum turnover and growth criteria that had been laid down in the Exim policy and the amended DFCE scheme (Table 10.4).

It is evident from Figure 10.1 that the export turnover of AEL rose sharply from Rs 377 crore in 2002–03 to Rs 4,657 crore the following year and further to Rs 10,808 crore in 2004–05. This sudden spurt in turn-over occurred during the period AEL availed of benefits from the DFCE scheme and the TPS. Subsequently, when in 2004 the DGFT issued notifications clarifying that the particular items would not be eligible for export incentives under the DFCE scheme (in 2004) and the TPS (in 2005 and 2006), AEL's export turnover collapsed. The Supreme Court

TABLE 10.3 'Exports' of Relevant Exporters

Name of Firm	Turnover 2002–03	Turnover 2003–04	% of growth	Share of gold coins and plain jewellery in total exports (%)
Rajesh Exports, Bengaluru	112	2372	2017	100
Kanak Exports, Mumbai	27	1070	3816	100

Source: http://www.advocatekhoj.com/library/judgments/announcement.
php?WID=6714.

TABLE 10.4 Export Turnover of Adani Exports Limited, Ahmedabad, during 2003–04

Item	Exports (crore)
Total	4657
Rough, and re-exported polished diamonds	2475
Supplies taken from status holders not meeting the minimum turnover and growth criteria	1316
Share of categories (I) and (II) in the total exports	81.4

Source: http://www.advocatekhoj.com/library/judgments/announcement.
php?WID=6714.

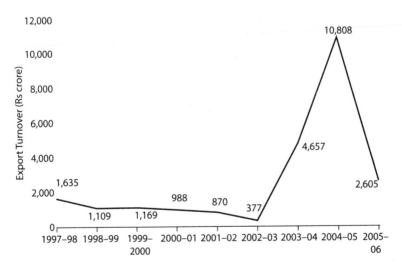

FIGURE 10.1 Export Turnover of Adani Exports Ltd (1997–2006) (Rs Crore)

pertinently observed that there was a 1,135 per cent surge in AEL's exports during 2003–04, whereas the company's exports had declined in the preceding six years.

The division bench of the apex court comprising Justices A.K. Sikri and Rohinton F. Nariman used very harsh language to highlight how the firms 'misused' benefits by 'fraudulently' inflating export turnover, citing 'conclusive' evidence of how AEL increased its exports of rough diamonds despite the fact that India is not a rough diamond producing country. The order read:

> The same set of diamonds were rotating and these never entered the Indian domestic territory or to the end consumers abroad. The value of such exports in the past two years may exceed Rs 15,000 crore... Many of these exporters exported to their own counterparts in Dubai and Sharjah. The jewellery attracted a 5 per cent import duty at Dubai; the consignments were declared as jewellery in India but were declared as scrap in Dubai to avoid the import duty. (DGFT *and Another v Kanak Exports and Another 2015*)

Setting aside the direction of the Bombay High Court granting the exporters benefits of incentive schemes that had accrued in the past, the Supreme Court bench concluded:

> It was pernicious and blatant misuse of the provisions of the scheme and periscopic viewing thereof establishes the same. Thus, the impugned decision reflected in the notifications dated 21 and 23 April 2004, did not take away any vested right of these exporters and amendments were necessitated by overwhelming public interest/considerations to prevent the misuse of the scheme. Therefore, we are of the opinion that even when (the) impugned notification issued under section 5 could not be retrospective in nature, such retrospectivity has not deprived the writ petitioners/exporters of their right inasmuch as no right had accrued in favour of such persons under the scheme. This court, or for that matter the high court in exercise of its writ jurisdiction, cannot come to the aid of such petitioners/exporters who, without making actual exports, play with the provisions of the scheme and try to take undue advantage thereof.

IV: DRI Investigations Against Adani Group Firms

The network of the Adani Group is worth mapping. Adani Enterprises Limited (which was earlier Adani Exports Limited, or AEL) is a public limited company in which Gautam Adani and his brothers Rajesh Adani and Vasant Adani are directors. With Samir Vora (Gautam Adani's brother-in-law) at the helm of affairs, ACPL and HEPL (partnership firms that were taken over by the Adani Group) played the role of the proverbial knights on the chessboard while MOL, JAOL and BBPL were the pawns. Background checks on these pawns conducted by the DRI indicate that their main activities used to be exports of molasses, soybean, castor oil, rice and other agricultural products.

While HEPL entered into a memorandum of understanding (MoU) with JAOL and BBPL, ACPL signed one with MOL. The MoUs stated that the entire export-oriented operations in CPD were to be handled by HEPL and ACPL in order to achieve the required increment in export turnover, thus enabling the Adani Group to obtain benefits under the TPS. Pursuant to these MoUs, Deven Mehta (director, HEPL) was appointed as the authorised signatory for BBPL and JAOL while Saurin Shah and Vishwas Shah (employees of AEL) were appointed as signatories for MOL. The alleged 'collusion' among the firms and their representatives resulted in accrual of benefits to HEPL and ACPL under the TPS and to the signatories of AEL who allegedly gained between 2 per cent and 2.5 per cent of the FOB value in an unauthorised manner, the DRI has claimed in its showcause notice (Table 10.5).

The DRI has alleged that the import and export operations of all six companies were handled by Vora. The DRI went on to claim that total

TABLE 10.5 Export of CPD by Adani Group Companies, in Rs Crore

Year	AEL	ACPL	HEPL	MOL	JAOL	BBPL	Total
2002–03	20.31	0.00	0.00	0.00	0.00		20.31
2003–04	1,465.27	0.00	94.23	0.00	0.00	0.00	1,559.23
2004–05	5,626.67	662.31	1,064.15	329.34	201.79	162.78	8,047.04
2005–06 (up to Jan 2016)	1,193.64	1,311.27	2,258.80	849.86	544.37	296.26	6,454.20

Source: Showcause notice issued by the DRI.
Abbreviations: AEL—Adani Enterprises Limited (earlier Adani Exports Limited); HEPL—Hinduja Exports Private Limited; ACPL—Aditya Corpex Private Limited; BBPL—Bagadiya Brothers Private Limited; JAO- Jayant Agro Organics Limited; and MOL—Midex Overseas Limited.

exports of CPD by the Indian companies in the Adani Group in 2004–05 were worth $1,643.02 million, out of which goods worth $1,314.19 million (or 79.98 per cent of the total) were exported to eight specific companies situated in the United Arab Emirates (UAE), Hong Kong and Singapore. Similarly, during 2004–05, out of the total imports worth $1,641.68 million, imports worth $1,304.13 million (79.44 per cent) were from only seven companies in the countries mentioned. Similar patterns emerged for 2005–06 as well. Two Hong Kong-based companies—Kwality Diamonds and Seven Stars—and four UAE-based companies—Excel Global, Jewel Trade, Crown Diamonds and KVK Diamonds—acted as suppliers and buyers of the CPD to and from AEL and its group companies. In addition, eight companies—Wingate Trading, Sphere Trading, Global Enterprises, Top Rich (all in Hong Kong), Planica Exports Private Limited, Emperor Exports Private Limited, Gracious Exports Private Limited and Orchid Overseas Private Limited (in Singapore)—were all incorporated after September 2004 after the introduction of the TPS. Wingate Trading, Sphere Trading, Top Rich and PNJ Trading stopped their business activities in 2005.

This, according to the DRI, suggests a clear link between the way in which trading malpractices took place and the timing of the DGFT notifications.

Further, the proprietor of three companies, namely, Wingate Trading, Sphere Trading and PNJ Trading, was one Nishaben Vijay Gandhi. While PNJ Trading exported CPD to Indian firms from Hong Kong, Wingate and Sphere imported CPD from the same set of Indian companies. These transactions took place among the firms at profit margins varying between 5 per cent and 10 per cent and would return full circle at a remarkable velocity. According to the DRI, goods imported were often exported out of India on the same day! Theoretically, the same goods could have been exported more than 100 times in a year and in terms of the various slabs of incentives under the TPS, an unscrupulous exporter could have earned a phenomenal Rs 1,500 for every Rs 100 invested, the DRI has calculated.

The story was no different in Singapore. There was a common set of five directors shared across AEL's trading partners. Email messages reproduced in the DRI's showcause notice that were retrieved by the directorate of forensic sciences (DFS) indicated that AEL controlled and managed its trading partners in Dubai, Hong Kong and Singapore.

Circular Trading of Studded Gold Jewellery

In 2009, the DRI issued a fresh set of two showcause notices alleging that AEL and its associate companies—HEPL, ACPL and MOL—that had allegedly availed of extraordinary benefits under the TPS, also indulged in fraudulent 'circular trading' by importing gold bars of 995 purity from the UAE and then exporting the goods in the form of crude studded gold jewellery purity back to the UAE. The jewellery was subsequently melted down and imported back to India in the form of gold bars to boost the group's export turnover. What is remarkable is the rate at which these activities took place: between September 2004 and February 2005, the firms in the Adani Group exported over 59,500 kilograms (kg) of what is supposed to be studded jewellery valued at over Rs 3,843 crore ($861.40 million).

The entire trading operations involving first, import of gold jewellery into the UAE and export of gold bars from the UAE; second, receipt of funds for the exports into accounts of dummy exporters of the gold bars; and finally, payments of funds from the accounts of dummy importers of studded gold jewellery, were controlled and managed by the employees of Adani Global FZE, Dubai, which is a subsidiary of Adani Exports and GA International. Adani Global FZE, Dubai is a company owned and managed by Vinod Shantilal Shah, also known as Vinod Shantilal Adani, the elder brother of Gautam Adani.

Interestingly, these export orders comprised gold bangles weighing anywhere between 100 grams (g) and 240 g and pendants weighing over 70 g each. Studded jewellery of such dimensions, using gold with 995 purity, is rare in the jewellery business due to the inability of pure gold to hold precious stones. This has been argued by the DRI. The lengths of the production cycle and the export cycle of this jewellery were unbelievably short: more than 100 kg of the goods were manufactured within 2–3 days of the receipt of gold by the workers and the goods were then promptly exported. In particular instances, the export consignment each weighed as much as 500 kg, which is reportedly unusual. Moreover, the Indian firms charged an exorbitant 7 per cent as 'making charges' to artificially inflate the value of the goods exported, the DRI has alleged.

The investigation also unearthed that Adani Global FZE had insured itself against the risk of storage and transport of the jewellery and gold bars. This insurance policy was bought from Oman Insurance Company, Dubai. The fact that Adani Global FZE obtained an insurance policy covering not only itself but other importers and exporters in these operations, which included the refinery where the gold scrap was melted down and converted into gold bars, speaks of the 'dubious' nature of these transactions, the DRI has alleged. At the time when Adani Global FZE bought the insurance policy, it had neither imported any gold jewellery nor exported gold bars. Further, after the DGFT issued notifications amending the Exim policy in February 2005, the companies abruptly stopped exporting studded gold jewellery. The value of export incentives obtained by the Adani Group companies in this specific instance was more than Rs 575 crore ($130.68 million).

Abuse of the DFCE Scheme

Permission for setting up private or public bonded warehouses was obtained by AEL from the customs department in July 2003 after the introduction of the IEPS. This, in effect, meant that goods imported, stored, manipulated and exported from these warehouses would be exempt from payment of customs duty. In accordance with the TPS, AEL imported CPD and re-exported the same after value addition of 5 per cent. This has been shown in the company's books of accounts. The Adani Group firms obtained DFCE certificates from the DGFT and utilised these for importing gold and silver without paying duty, that is, by claiming exemption from payment of duty under the IEPS. In its application to the DGFT, AEL also acknowledged that it did not take into account the re-export of imported goods while computing the value of exports.

The DRI notice issued seeks to establish that exports of CPD made by AEL were squarely covered as re-export of imported CPD. Further, these imported gold bars, after conversion into 100 g bars, were sold in the open market. Hence, the gold and silver bars imported without payment of duty under the DFCE scheme cannot be accounted as inputs for the CPD exported by AEL and would be liable for payment of customs duty. The DRI has alleged that this was done intentionally in circumvention of the July 2004 order of the Gujarat High Court prohibiting the inclusion of gold exports in the DFCE. This order of the Gujarat High Court was upheld by the Supreme Court in the case of Kanak Exports. The DRI notice proposed confiscation of the seized 250 gold bars (of 1 kg each) imported by AEL and confiscation of around 25,000 kg of gold bars and 31,000 kg of silver bars together valued at more than Rs 4,000 crore.

Artificial Value Addition

There are a few thousand instances of circular trading that have been detailed in the DRI's notices. The firms claimed value addition of 5–10 per cent in their official books of account although all that was done was to sort, sieve and clean the diamonds by boiling them in water. Such activities do not involve great technical expertise and, if the DRI is to be believed, raise doubts about the genuineness of the transactions that have been recorded. The imports and exports of diamonds took place in small dingy rooms measuring 10 feet (ft) by 12 ft inside the bonded warehouse where manufacturing activities are disallowed, the DRI has alleged.

After the DRI issued showcause notices, in an adjudication order issued in January 2013, the commissioner of customs, imports (Mumbai) held that:

i) No processing was carried out by any of the six notices to achieve value addition of 5–10 per cent.

ii) The notices have not shown how simple processes of boiling, sieving and assortment, if carried out, can result in value addition of 5–10 per cent.

iii) The FOB value declared in the shipping bills by simply adding 5–10 per cent of the CIF (cost, insurance and freight) value is artificial and hence, the export value declared should be rejected under Section 14 of the Customs Act, 1962.

The commissioner then imposed a penalty of Rs 25 crore on AEL and penalties of Rs 2 crore each on the five other companies. Additionally, it imposed heavy penalties on the directors of all six companies, including Gautam Adani's brother Rajesh Adani and brother-in-law Samir Vora. The commissioner upheld the charges made in the DRI's notices that tax benefits to the tune of Rs 1,000 crore had been fraudulently obtained by the Adani Group companies.

To recapitulate, the DRI had from 2007 onwards alleged that the companies had misdeclared the FOB value of export goods in contravention of the Foreign Trade (Development and Regulation) Act, 1992 and Foreign Trade (Regulation) Rules, 1993; that the group through its directors had entered into a 'conspiracy' with people and entities based in Singapore, Dubai and Hong Kong to undertake 'dubious' imports and exports of diamonds to take undue benefits of the TPS; entered into

MoUs with group companies for claiming incremental exports; misde-clared value addition of 5–10 per cent by assortment, boiling, sieving and repacking without any manufacturing/processing or change in the form of the cut and polished diamonds; and failed to declare details of com-mission payable in shipping bills. It was estimated that benefits worth Rs 679.62 crore were claimed by AEL and its associate companies in 2004–05 and an additional Rs 218.16 crore were claimed in 2005–06.

V: The Reversal: CESTAT Order

A development then took place that shocked the DRI. The order of the commissioner of customs was set aside by the Mumbai bench of the Customs, Excise and Service Tax Appellate Tribunal (CESTAT), Western Zone. By an order dated 9 April 2015, which was issued more than four months later on 26 August that year, CESTAT members Anil Choudhary and PS Pruthi summarily dropped all the charges against the Adani Group. The tribunal chose to accept the FOB value declared by the companies and disagreed with the DRI's claim that there had been circular trading. The CESTAT disagreed with the commissioner that 'no process' had been carried out in the bonded warehouse since the diamonds were sorted, sieved and boiled. It disagreed with the commissioner that these 'processes' could not have added value to the extent of 5 per cent. The tribunal was of the view that the 'transac-tion values' of the CPD were 'genuine' and that foreign exchange had been 'fully realised' through the sales proceeds. The allegedly fraudu-lent intentions with which the value of exports were misdeclared and artificially inflated as well as the claims of circular trading were all effectively ignored by the CESTAT.

The tribunal ignored the evidence that the DRI had adduced to its showcause notices to indicate circular trading. One such piece of evidence was an email exchange between different employees of group companies, including Adani Global. The first names of these employees were Asha, Mary, Rakesh, Tejal and another employee was SM Shah. According to the DRI, these email exchanges indicate that the same set of diamonds would be imported, exported, imported again and re-exported from and to India, Dubai and Singapore in a cyclical manner.

The CESTAT also chose to ignore a letter dated 26 May 2015 writ-ten by the additional DGFT to the joint secretary (drawback), Central Board of Excise and Customs in the finance ministry which stated,

...there are cases of circular trading and many other types of mischief reported under the target plus scheme ... Such petitioners do not become eligible for such shipping bill claims as per the judgment of the Supreme Court. So, any claims arising on account of such shipping bills may be disallowed. Therefore, (the) department of revenue and (the) DRI are requested to give the complete list of exporters along with details of ship-ping bills who have misused under both the schemes (the DFCE and/or the target plus scheme).

Officials in the income tax department and the enforcement direc-torate (who spoke to the lead author of this chapter on the condition that they will not be identified) said that no investigations had been conducted nor action initiated by their respective departments. A senior customs officer based in Mundra port (through which many of the consignments of diamonds were imported and exported and which is part of the Adani Group) said a number of disputes relating to alleged misuse of export benefits were pending with the DGFT. 'The Adani cases are among the many hundred revenue sensitive matters on which DGFT has not taken a decision and this is because there is no audit of, or accountability in, the proceedings of the DGFT,' said this person.

A senior official of DGFT, who too spoke to the lead author of this chapter on the condition of anonymity, explained:

...the best course of action will be to ensure that no benefits are given under the TPS scheme and the benefits that have already been availed of under the DFCE scheme (for exports in 2003–04) be declared void *ub initio*. Since the exports of CPD have been held to be fraudulent by the Supreme Court in the Kanak Exports case, the benefits under the DFCE already issued to AEL should also be disentitled. It is unfortu-nate that there are no clear guidelines for expeditious action in such cases of fraud.

VI: A Systemic Problem

On 31 March 2016, the Reserve Bank of India (RBI) relaxed the rules applicable to importers of rough cut and polished diamonds. It per-mitted banks to approve a 'clean credit' facility extended by foreign suppliers to Indian importers of CPD beyond the stipulated 180-day period. Clean credit refers to the credit facility extended by foreign suppliers to Indian importers without imposing the requirement of the need to furnish a letter of credit or a fixed deposit to serve as an underlying guarantee.

While it is contended that this move is intended to ease operational difficulties faced by importers, experts monitoring the diamonds trade suggest that this could be an invitation to fresh trouble. One such person said that these provisions can be easily abused by importers to launder money, that it is quite easy to create an offshore corporate entity that could import goods from an Indian exporter and delay remittances, or worse still, default on payment. This expert apprehended that such malpractices could undermine the financial positions of banks. On one side, the trading firm's books of accounts would show higher receivables as a part of its balance sheet which may serve as a premise to obtain more credit from Indian banks even as the unscrupulous trader would by then have encashed the proceeds from the sale of the diamonds in, say, Hong Kong, to move the assets out of India.

The systemic nature of such fraud is worth noting. A report by the Financial Action Task Force, released in October 2013, titled *Money Laundering and Terrorist Financing through Trade in Diamonds* stated that India, which accounts for more than 90 per cent of the total business of CPD in the world, has seen instances of companies grossly overvaluing the goods they exported. The report explained how such activities are conducted and operationalised to transfer sums of foreign exchange outside India, giving examples of diamonds round-tripping back to India at inflated prices.

In its judgment in the Kanak Exports case, the Supreme Court highlighted another instance of misutilisation of export incentives relating to Reliance Industries Limited (RIL) and its group company IPCL (formerly India Petrochemicals Corporation Limited). The court said that RIL and IPCL 'manipulated' export turnover to maximise export benefit entitlements under the DFCE scheme and the TPS. It held that IPCL had artificially inflated its export performance in 2003–04 and was hence not eligible for benefits under the DFCE scheme. The court observed that goods worth Rs 2,127.18 crore manufactured by RIL were exported in the name of its group company IPCL to claim extra benefits under the DFCE scheme. A DRI report had earlier stated that RIL lowered its export turnover for 2003–04 by a similar amount to show that it had achieved a rate of growth of exports above 100 per cent (between 2003–04 and 2004–05) to claim TPS benefits at the rate of 15 per cent. The Supreme Court upheld the DRI's contention in this instance.

VII: Conclusions

The DRI filed an appeal against the CESTAT order in the Supreme Court on 6 April 2016, which was eventually disposed of on 22 July 2016. The ministry of finance now has to file a review petition against this decision. The question that remains unanswered: what has dissuaded the ministry from filing this review petition even though more than nine months have gone by?

According to a Delhi-based lawyer familiar with the case who (like the others) spoke to the *EPW* on condition of anonymity, 'the entire argument of the DRI is premised on a DGFT notification which was upheld by the Supreme Court in 2015 in the Kanak Exports judgment.' The advocate added that this case is of great significance since it is the first relating to circular trading which has reached the doors of the country's apex court. He said that if the revenue department fails to convince the Supreme Court about its case against the Adani Group through its review petition, the 'consequences could well be disastrous for the government as this could affect all circular trading cases that are in the pipeline.'

A questionnaire was sent by the *EPW* to Ravi Shankar Prasad, union minister for law and justice, seeking to enquire if his ministry would recommend a review of the Supreme Court's decision on the DRI's appeal against the CESTAT order. A response came from Saurabh Kumar, additional private secretary to the minister, who said the questions should be sent to the finance ministry and the MCI.

As already stated, a detailed questionnaire sent on 18 November 2016 to finance minister Arun Jaitley, copies of which were marked to the revenue secretary, the chairman, Central Board of Excise and Customs, the chairman, Central Board of Direct Taxes, the director, Enforcement Directorate and the director-general, DRI, were not replied to. On the same day, another questionnaire was sent to minister of state for industry and commerce Nirmala Sitharaman and the director-general, foreign trade, which also went unanswered.

In response to the *EPW*'s questionnaire, Jatin Jalundhwala, chief legal officer for the Adani Group stated that the CESTAT had dealt with all the allegations made by the DRI, including those relating to circular trading and the relationships with overseas buyers and suppliers, and had set these aside. He stated that the CESTAT had held that all the exports and imports of CPD by the Adani Group were 'genuine' and 'thus, (the) FOB value of CPD exported cannot be re-determined.' Jalundhwala added that the Supreme Court by dismissing the appeal filed by the customs department also 'affirmed the validity/genuineness of transactions of imports and exports...'

Post-script: Details of the follow-up investigations after the original article was published as well as related documents may be found at www.theafiles.in.

References

Financial Action Task Force (2013): 'Money Laundering and Terrorist Financing through Trade in Diamonds,' *FATF Report*, October, http://www.fatf-gafi. org/media/fatf/documents/re-ports/ML-TF-through-trade-in-diamonds. pdf.

III (b) The Hindu Undivided Family Act

This section deals with the clauses in Indian income tax laws that have allowed Hindu Undivided Families (HUF) to freely avoid tax. The chapter, by I.S. Gulati, a doyen of Indian public finance studies, was published in 1973. In this chapter, Gulati questions the very need for a HUF in the income tax act, despite numerous adverse comments on it in the reports of the Raj Committee and the Wanchoo Committee.

11

HUF Tax Avoidance Revisited

I.S. Gulati

One of the most important areas for tax base reform in the present system of direct taxation in India is the treatment of the Hindu Undivided Family (HUF) for purposes of income and capital taxation. It was with this in view that, more than a decade ago, an estimate was attempted of income tax avoidance taking place through use of the present provisions of the lax law relating to the Hindu Undivided Family, for the years 1957–58 and 1958–59.[1] This chapter seeks principally to bring those estimates up to date. In addition, attempts to quantify the gains to revenue likely to accrue from adopting either the Raj Committee's recent recommendation for a total derecognition of the HUF as a tax entity or the Wanchoo Committee's recommendation made more than one year ago for higher rates on HUF incomes.

I: Introduction

The tax situation of the Hindu Undivided Family (HUF) and its members has remained as favourable as it was in the 1960s. The HUF and its members continue to enjoy the privilege of being treated as separate taxable units. Also the HUF, as such, can be divided and sub-divided into smaller units of HUFs, each such unit comprising a separate taxable entity. Further, the HUF continues to have access to, what is called, the technique of partial partition, so that, while the HUF properties can

[1] Gulati, I.S. & Gulati K.S. (1962). *The Undivided Hindu Family: A Study of its Tax Privileges.* Bombay: Asia Publishing House.

be partially divided among its individual members, the HUF can still retain itself as a distinct unit.[2] Thus, where a family partitions some of the properties among its members, while the income of the partitioned properties is added to the income of the individual members to whom the properties are allotted from their self-acquired property or from sources unrelated to family assets, the income from the undivided properties can be shown separately as HUF income for tax purposes and the law provides no means of assessing the two incomes together even if they are received and enjoyed by the same individual.

Assessment Units

What is no less important to note, in this context, is that persons who are parties to the original partition—partial or complete—can further reunite into one or more HUFs as and when desired. It is not necessary that such reunion/s be between all such members (viz., those who were parties to the original partition), or that the reunion/s be with respect to *all* the assets received by these reuniting members at the time of original partition. We are advised that, under the existing law, a small HUF consisting of a widower father and three adults—but unmarried—sons can form as many as ten HUF assessment units and at the same time have four individual assessment units. The 10 HUF units may thus be formed as follows:

A (Father)

B   C   D

Constitution of HUF in terms of membership		Property held by each unit
1	ABCD	Dunlop
2	ABC	Goodyear
3	ACD	CEAT
4	BCD	Premier
5	AB	Madras Rubber
6	AC	Burmah Shell
7	AD	Esso
8	BC	Indian Oil
9	BD	Hindustan Motor
10	CD	Indian Iron

[2] The definition of 'partition' in the IT Act 1961 though intended to impart some rigour is really no obstacle to families intending to go through the motion of partition (*vide* Section 171 of IT Act 1961).

(The choice of scripts is illustrative; the important thing to note is that each HUF unit holds distinct property.)

As a separate taxable unit, each HUF is entitled to a separate exemption limit, which is higher than that allowed to an individual taxpayer and regardless of whether or not the members of the HUF have their own separate incomes/wealth, their share of the HUF income/wealth is of no relevance in the determination of tax liabilities of the members as individuals.

But an individual could have the income from his self-acquired assets assessed to tax as part of HUF income if he decided to throw his self-acquired property into the family common stock—or what is commonly referred to as the family hotchpot—and the act of throwing could not be regarded as 'transfer.' It is held by the courts that, for a Joint Hindu Family to come into being, there is no need for a nucleus of property to exist originally. It was because of this provision that new HUFs could spring up even without a previous base of family hotchpot, and it is only in this respect that an attempt was made in 1970 (Taxation Laws Amendment Act) and again in 1971 (Finance Act Number 2) to prevent abuse. These amendments, however, have the extremely limited and narrow purpose of requiring the 'clubbing' of that income of the individual with his wife and minor children, which is attributable to the interest of the wife and minor children in the HUF in respect of assets thrown by the individual in the family hotchpot after 31 December 1969. The amendments, it must be noted, do not prohibit, or even restrict, the creation of new units on the basis of ancestral assets. Nor do they affect the position of the existing units with respect to non-ancestral assets thrown in the hotchpot before 1 January 1970.

Official Reports

It must be admitted that, while the tax situation of the HUF has remained more or less as favourable as when the first attempt was made at highlighting the magnitude of tax avoidance through the use of the provisions concerned of the tax laws in the country, there is far greater awareness of this situation today than existed ten years ago. As late as in 1967, S. Boothalingam, in his *Final Report on Rationalisation and Simplification of the Tax Structure*, conceded that 'there has always been some scope to use the institution of the HUF as a means of lowering the tax liability of individuals' but did not appear to consider it worth the government's while, on revenue grounds at least, to take measures to rectify the situation.[3] By December 1971, when the Direct Taxes Enquiry Committee, more popularly known as the Wanchoo Committee, came out with its final report, the verdict had substantially changed to: '*the institution of the HUF is widely used for tax avoidance.*'[4] Most recently, the Raj Committee on Taxation of Agricultural Wealth and Income has not only endorsed the Wanchoo Committee's observations in this context but gone further to observe that '*the continued recognition of (HUF) is likely to affect seriously the effectiveness of all direct taxes including those on agriculture.*'[5]

Unfortunately, neither the Wanchoo Committee nor the Raj Committee has published any estimates of the amount of tax avoidance that might actually be taking place by the use of the various devices open to the taxpayers in this respect. The Wanchoo Committee did arrange for studies of five or six big families to be undertaken in each of certain selected commissioners' changes. These studies are stated, in the report, to have revealed:

> ...firstly 'that tax avoided by the members of these families was quite substantial' and secondly that 'the number of income tax files in respect of each family was [found to be] more than the total number of members in the family.

II: Estimates of Avoidance

As stated at the very outset, more than ten years back (i.e., in 1961–62) an attempt was made by the present writer, in collaboration with K.S. Gulati, to find an answer to such a question. Estimates of income tax avoidance were attempted for the two years, 1957–58 and 1958–59, on the basis of available income tax data.

In making those estimates of income tax avoidance for the earlier period, we had proceeded on the assumption that a genuine undivided Hindu family would have paid tax on its total income without trying

---

[3] Boothalingam did, no doubt, suggest two possible methods 'to restrict or diminish the tax benefits' of the HUF but he felt that the question 'which of these methods is adopted for none at all on the ground that it may not just be worthwhile on revenue grounds is mainly a matter for administrative decision'. See his Final Report: 43–4.

[4] See Wanchoo Committee Report p. 74, para 3.23.

[5] See Raj Committee Report, p. 97, para 6.14.

to split itself up by resorting to partial partition. This assumption was made in full awareness that, in actual practice, almost all the families (HUFs) appearing on tax roll were likely to be resorting to partial partition with a view to avoiding tax. This is now confirmed by the Wanchoo Committee when it observes that the HUF as a unit of assessment is retained only to avoid taxes and not out of 'consideration of sentiments.'

Estimates of income tax avoidance were attempted by calculating what the income tax revenue would have been had an HUF paid tax on its total income without claiming partial partition and what the income tax revenue would be had the original HUF property been distributed between one HUF and four individual members, the latter rejoining into a registered firm. On the above basis, the amount of income tax avoided was placed at Rs 132 crore for 1957–58 and Rs 147 crore for 1958–59. The corresponding figure for 1967–68, based on the 1972–73 rates, works out to Rs 201 crore. Table 11.1, which presents these latest calculations, has been constructed on exactly the same lines as the corresponding tables done for the earlier estimate.[6] For the earlier study, estimates were also worked out for various other types of partial partition but those have not been attempted now.[7]

It is important, however, to enter a warning at this stage, viz., that these above estimates are not estimates of what the government could hope to reclaim through possible tax avoidance measures. When it comes to making an estimate of the possible gain to revenue, a different type of calculation has to be made. In an exercise of this sort, consideration has to be given to the question of what exactly tax provisions relating to HUFs would be replaced by. For instance, in attempting the earlier estimates of income tax avoidance, consideration was not given to the possibility that *all HUF income would, as a result of tax base reform, be divisible among its members and taxable in the hands of the members.* Such an assumption would have yielded a different, and distinctly smaller, estimate of tax avoidance for the simple reason, that *the HUF income would then be taxable not in one lot but in several lots,* though the number of these latter lots would still be less than if the same HUF income could, for tax purpose, be divided into a number of HUF units as well as individual units. However, in the context of the policy recommendation then made by the authors, as a minimum necessary step towards preventing the

---

[6] See pp. 76 and p. 78 of Gulati and Gulati, 'The Undivided Hindu Family, A Study of Its Tax Privileges'.

[7] See *Economic & Political Weekly*, May 15, 1971.

TABLE 11.1 Estimated Total Loss to Revenue Due to Avoidance of Income Tax through Partial Partition (One HUF, One Registered Firm) in 1967–68

The Income Group as shown in the Official Statistics	Number of Assessees in each Income Group	Actual Tax Assessed from this Group	Corresponding True Income of the Original HUF	Total Tax Payable by HUFs on True Income after Partial Partition	Total Loss to Revenue on Account of Partial Partition of True Income	Tax Loss Co-efficient (3/5)	Total Actual Loss to Revenue (6*7)
(1) (Rs)	(2) (1000s)	(3) (Rs lakhs)	(4) (Rs)	(5) (Rs lakhs)	(6) (Rs crore)	(7) (Rs crore)	(8) (Rs crore)
60001–75000	16.91	22.16	40000	33.83	16.47	0.65	10.70
75001–10000	14.32	59.86	50000	57.27	21.40	1.04	22.26
10001–15000	15.45	141.42	60000	61.80	30.07	2.29	68.86
15001–25000	12.99	293.86	100000	279.22	51.48	1.05	54.05
25001–50000	6.14	484.22	200000	653.16	47.12	0.74	34.87
50001–100000	1.33	360.62	500000	628.51	17.64	0.57	10.05

Notes: While the data used in columns 2 and 3 are taken from the published figures for 1967–68, the calculations in columns 5, 6, and 8 are based on the income tax rates applicable in 1972–73; 2) The tax loss co-efficient seeks to remove any over or understatement that might result in the total tax payable by HUFs after partial partition due to the choice of the true income of original HUF in each income group in column 4.

erosion of the base of income taxation, *what was attempted at that time, too, was an estimate of the possible gain to revenue on account of withdrawal of recognition from partial partition of HUF.* This gain was placed at Rs 16 crore for 1958–59.[8]

While it was then felt by us that, as a very minimum, the government should withdraw forthwith the recognition given to the partial partitioning of the HUF for tax purposes, this would still have been a half-house measure. The HUF would still have been a separate unit of assessment and its members would have continued to be taxed on their own incomes without regard to their respective shares of the family income.

As has been stated above, the Wanchoo Committee was the first ever official expert body to recognise the serious tax avoidance implications of the present HUF provisions of our tax laws. The committee also made a specific recommendation, aimed at rectifying the existing situation, which fell far short of a complete derecognition of the HUF as a distinct taxable entity.

The Wanchoo Committee recommended that higher rates of income tax (and also wealth tax) should apply to any HUF if any of its members had independent income above the exemption limit. On the face of it, this recommendation could be considered very radical. The rates suggested by the committee for HUFs are, as can be seen from Table 11.2, drastically higher than those suggested by the committee for individuals at the lower slabs of income. But, as the Raj Committee puts it, 'The higher rates of tax would be effective only if the income and wealth of the HUFs are large enough and if there are no ways open to it for splitting them.'

The Wanchoo Committee's suggestion seems to ignore that, so long as one does not assume that all scope for dividing and sub-dividing the HUF income/wealth has already been exhausted, all that the HUFs have really to do in order to offset the impact of the recommended increase in rates for HUFs is to resort to further sub-division. Again, to quote from the Raj Committee's report, 'Since an HUF can be divided and subdivided into smaller units of HUFs—each such unit comprising a separate taxable entity in addition to the main HUF—the incidence of the higher rates proposed can in fact be avoided quite easily, particularly

---

[8] See p. 92 of Gulati and Gulati, 'The Undivided Hindu Family'.

TABLE 11.2   Wanchoo Committee's Recommended Rates of Income Tax

Income slab (Rs)	Rates of Tax (Per cent)	
	Individuals	HUFs
0–5000	Nil	Nil*
5001–10000	10	15
10001–15000	15	25
15001–20000	20	35
20001–25000	25	
25001–30000	35	45
30001–40000	45	
40001–50000	50	55
50001–60000	55	
60001–70000	60	65
Over 70000	65	

Source: Wanchoo Committee Report, p. 20 and p. 75.
Notes: Surcharge at 15 per cent in respect of incomes over Rs 15,000.
* It is presumed that the exemption limits for HUFs will remain at the present level of Rs 7,000, therefore, for the HUF the next effective income slab would be Rs 7,001-10,000.

if the main HUF had not been divided earlier into the maximum permissible number of HUFs.'[9]

Another aspect of the apparently radical recommendation of the Wanchoo Committee is that, even though the proposed rates applicable to HUF income in the earlier slabs are substantially higher than those suggested for individuals (and also compared to 1972–73 rates for individuals as well as HUFs), the new rates would still be lower than those marginal rates which would have applied to the undivided (or unpartitioned) income. After all, there is no way of knowing that an HUF, which for purposes of income tax assessment falls in the lower income slabs, may have members who on the basis of their independent income—not to speak of their total income including shares from various HUFs of which they may be members at the same time—belong to the very highest of income slabs. That is to say, the absence of any provision for their aggregation along with any income which they may

[9] See Raj Committee Report, p. 97.

be earning on their own, the members' taxable capacity, or ability to pay, cannot be measured merely from the figure of incomes of the respective family or families of which they are members.

III: Loss of Revenue

More recently, however, thinking on the subject of tax avoidance and broadening of the tax base has been in terms of a total withdrawal of recognition now accorded to the HUF, as a separate unit of assessment to tax.[10]

The Raj Committee, while recommending the adoption of the family as the unit of assessment for agricultural holdings tax, observed that 'recognition given to HUFs should be totally withdrawn for tax purposes, and the income and wealth of each HUF considered divisible among the nuclear families constituting it and treated as part of the income and wealth of each such family while assessing the tax on them.'[11]

Thus, when we attempted the earlier estimates of possible gain in revenue, based on the data for 1958–59, the assumption we made was that, while partial partition of HUF would be completely disallowed, the HUF would continue to exist as a distinct taxable entity. *The much more relevant assumption to be made in the present context, however, would be that HUF would cease to exist as a distinct taxable entity and that the entire HUF income is divisible among its members who in turn are liable on their respective shares as part of their respective taxable incomes as individuals.*

What has been attempted now, therefore, is an estimate which not only is much more recent but also more pertinent from the point of view of policy formulation today. The estimate is still confined to only gain in revenue from income tax. Again this estimate, too, has been attempted on the basis of the information available for 1967–68 with respect to the number of HUF assessments and the distribution of income among these units but using the 1972–73 rates of income tax.

It is important to bring out that, in making this estimate, the procedure we have followed is to measure income tax avoidance with reference, to what HUFs are liable to pay *qua* HUF by way of income tax and what individual members of an HUF would have been called upon

---

[10] See the author's own article, 'Agenda for Tax Base Reform', *Economic & Political Weekly*, May 15, 1971.

[11] See Raj Committee Report, p. 97.

to pay had the HUF income been deemed divisible among its members, entitled to ask for partition, and taxable in their individual hands. Also, it is assumed that, the income due to wife and minor children, from the HUF pool, is agreeable with the income of the husband. Such an estimate of income tax avoidance can also be regarded as an estimate of the gain to revenue should the HUF be de-recognised for tax purposes.

Although the procedures followed in making calculations are broadly the same as were adopted for the earlier estimates of tax avoidance, it must be said that, a few departures have been made therefrom. The principal departure made by us from the procedure followed in the earlier study is that, in making our estimate of tax avoidance, and by inference of the gain to revenue on account of the derecognition of the HUF for tax purposes, we assume partial partition of the original HUF to take place in such a way that, as a result, only one HUF remains on the tax roll and the other newly created HUFs fall below the exemption limit. This procedure, it was felt, would help interpret the available data much more meaningfully than was possible under the procedure followed for the earlier study, when the division of the original HUF into more than one taxable HUF was postulated.

Table 11.3 presents the estimate referred to above. Using 1967–68 data but 1972–73 rates, the amount of income tax avoidance works out to between Rs 22 crore and Rs 45 crore. The lower figure of Rs 22 crore assumes that only one partial partition takes place within a family resulting in one HUF and four individual assessments. The higher estimate of Rs 45 crore assumes the creation of four HUFs in addition to four individual assessments.

The observations of the Wanchoo Committee on this subject could be said to support the impression that, not only is splitting up of an HUF quite common among the high-income taxpayers, but also that the splitting takes place in quite some *depth*. The observations relevant in this context were made by the committee, on the basis again of the studies of the selected big families referred to above. The committee observed that (a) the tax avoided through the use of HUF provisions by the families studied was quite substantial; (b) the income tax avoided in one case was as high as 60 per cent; and (c) in all cases the number of income tax files for each of these families was larger than the number of members in the family. It was, in fact, on the basis of such findings as these that the Wanchoo Committee must have felt obliged to make the assertion that the HUF, as a unit of tax assessment, existed largely for the purposes of tax avoidance and little for 'consideration of sentiment.'

TABLE 11.3 Estimated Total Loss to Revenue through Partial Partition (1967–68 data at 1972–73 rates)

Income Group	Numbers of Assessees in each Income group	Total loss to Revenue (Rs crore)				Correction Term	Corrected Total Loss to Revenue (Rs crore)			
		Case I	Case II	Case III	Case IV		Case I	Case II	Case III	Case IV
7501-10000	14318	2.20	3.31	4.41	5.35	.88	1.93	2.91	3.88	4.71
10001-15000	15450	2.38	4.40	5.72	6.91	1.03	2.45	4.53	5.89	7.12
15001-25000	12987	5.53	7.93	10.34	13.00	.99	5.47	7.85	10.24	12.87
25001-5000	6139	9.32	11.79	14.26	16.73	.89	8.29	10.49	12.69	14.89
50001-100000	1333	4.32	5.13	5.93	6.74	.72	3.11	3.69	4.27	4.05
100001- 200000	273	1.19	1.36	1.54	1.71	.71	.84	.96	1.09	1.21

Source: All India Income Tax Statistics, 1967–68.

Notes: 1) 'Correction term' has been applied with a view to removing any over or understatement implied in the choice of the assessed income in each group.

2) Cases (i) The original HUF breaks up into one HUF and one firm of 4 partners. (ii) The original HUF breaks up into 2 HUFs (one HUF having an asset of Rs 7,000) and one firm of 4 partners, (iii) The original HUF breaks up into 3 HUFs (two each having an asset of Rs 7,000) and one firm of 4 partners. (iv) The original HUF breaks up into 4 HUFs (three each having an asset of Rs 7,000) and one firm of 4 partners.

What the calculations in Table 11.3 bring out clearly is that, were the government to accept the Raj Committees recommendation for the total withdrawal of recognition from the HUF as a tax entity, the gain in terms of income tax revenue alone could be in the vicinity of Rs 45 crore a year. It bears repetition to say that the total gain should be much higher if one were also to take into account the impact of this particular tax base reform on revenues from: wealth tax, gift tax and estate duty.

IV: Conclusions

The solution to the tax avoidance problem created by the HUF provisions in the present tax laws lies clearly in a simple and straight-forward step, whereby the present recognition to the HUF as a separate unit of assessment is totally withdrawn and all members are as a consequence obliged to report their share of the HUF income/wealth as part of their total income/wealth for purposes of taxation.

It will be necessary, alongside of this withdrawal of recognition to HUF, to make the shares of the wife and minor children in the HUF income/wealth aggregable—or clubbable to follow the current tax jargon—with the husband's income/wealth.

Although the Wanchoo Committee shied away from recommending the clubbing of family income/wealth for tax purposes, the case for doing so is no less strong. *But it ought still to be noted that, the suggestion made here is a limited one relating to the clubbing of the HUF shares which, if not acted up on alongside the proposed withdrawal of recognition from the HUF as a unit of assessment, will leave open considerable scope for income and wealth splitting and, therefore, tax avoidance.*

As pointed out at the very outset, some limited 'clubbing' for HUF purposes has already been introduced in the tax law, but that relates only to the income from self-acquired property thrown in the family hotch-pot. What is being proposed by us here is the extension of this 'limited' clubbing to all the property and its income, whether self-acquired or ancestral, kept until now in the name of the HUF or HUFs.

It must be noted, in conclusion that *the withdrawal of recognition from the HUF for tax purposes, does not and need not affect the present laws of inheritance which may continue to apply as before. But there is no doubt that it would amount to terminating an important, and well-entrenched, privilege of the rich and wealthy*—a privilege whose continuation cannot be justified on any score, sentimental, social, or economic. Also, from the larger point of view of broadening the base of direct taxes—a reform that is simply crying out for action—withdrawal of recognition to the HUF deserves the highest priority for the simple reason that its continued recognition is a major factor responsible for the erosion of the tax base.

III (c) Excise Duty Evasion: Case Study

The chapter by Gopinath Pradhan and M. Govinda Rao, published in the *EPW* in 1985, discussed the ways in which excise duty was evaded in one industry: cotton textiles. They noted two major routes of evasion: (i) inter-sectoral misclassification of the output, and (ii) intra-sectoral misclassification, which also involves understatement of production and undervaluation.

12

Excise Duty Evasion on Cotton Textile Fabrics

Gopinath Pradhan and M. Govinda Rao

The few studies that exist of tax evasion in India have been largely confined to direct taxes, particularly personal income tax, and there is hardly any empirical study of evasion of commodity taxes. Given that commodity taxes predominate in the government's tax revenues, this is an obvious lacuna. Study of excise duty evasion is especially opportune now for many reasons. First, the needs of resource mobilisation for the Seventh Plan call for minimising such evasion. Further, there is a belief that central excise duties are better administered than states' sales taxes and this argument is sometimes extended to suggest expansion of the list of items covered under additional excise duties. It would, therefore, be interesting to examine the extent of tax evasion in respect of a commodity on which the states have surrendered the right to levy sales tax in lieu of additional excise duties.

In spite of the importance of the subject in policymaking, very few studies have been conducted in India on tax evasion. Further, the few studies that exist have been largely confined to the evasion of direct taxes, particularly personal income tax, and hardly is there any important empirical study on the evasion of commodity taxes. Given that the yield of commodity taxes predominate in the tax revenues of the developing countries, this is an obvious lacuna. It is hoped that this study of excise duty evasion in cotton textile fabrics would partially fill the gap.

I: Cotton Textiles Industry: Important Features

An important feature of the growth of the textiles industry during the last 30 years is the phenomenal growth of powerlooms. The number of looms registered an average growth rate of 10.5 per cent from 23,800 in 1951 to 483,000 in 1982. The corresponding growth rate of looms in both the mill sector and the handloom sector were very low at 0.2 per cent and 1.1 per cent respectively. A similar trend is seen in the ease of cloth output also. Even the official estimate of the powerloom output, which is known to be biased downward, shows the share of powerlooms to have gone up from about 2 per cent in 1956 to 35 per cent in 1982 (Table 12.1).[1] The annual rate of growth in the official estimate of powerloom output was as high as 11.9 per cent during the period. As against this, the output of the composite mill sector declined substantially even in absolute terms and that of handlooms increased at a much slower rate of 2.3 per cent per annum.

The powerlooms are spread throughout the country in clusters of varying sizes and a large number of them are unauthorised. This can give rise to enormous evasion of duty on the output of the powerloom sector.

Admittedly, the trend in the growth of the different sectors of the industry is the outcome of government policy in terms of banning the expansion of weaving capacity in the mill sector since 1956, and the discriminatory levy of excise duties on the output of the mill sector *vis-à-vis* the powerlooms and the handlooms. Coupled with this is the greater possibility of evasion of duty in the powerloom sector than in the mills.

Flows between Different Sectors of Textiles Industry

In order to locate the major avenues of evasion, it is necessary to understand the inter-linkages among the different sectors of the textiles industry and to identify the different points of levy. The manufacture

---

[1] It should be noted that official estimates understate the production of powerlooms significantly, for it is believed that a large pan of the hank yarn is consumed by power-looms. The official estimates understate powerloom output also for other reasons. First, on the basis of a survey, it is known that about 7–10 per cent of hank yarn is used by the powerlooms in the manufacture of certain categories of cloth like saris. Second, a kilogram of yarn yields 15 metres of cloth for higher counts of yarn (more-than 41s) as against 8 metres for lower counts. As the proportion of higher count yarn consumed by the powerlooms is larger, the official estimates are understated. On this, see Mazumdar 1984.

TABLE 12.1 Estimated Cotton Cloth Production in Different Sectors (in million metres)

Year	Mills	Powerlooms	Handlooms	Total
1956	4285 (74.8)	151 (2.3)	1483 (22.9)	6486 (100.0)
1960	4616 (68.4)	491 (7.3)	1642 (24.3)	6749 (100.0)
1971	3957 (53.8)	1419 (19.3)	1980 (26.9)	7356 (100.0)
1976	3881 (48.8)	1734 (21.8)	2330 (29.3)	7945 (100.0)
1977	3223 (46.7)	1638 (23.7)	2040 (29.6)	6901 (100.0)
1978	3251 (44.4)	1884 (25.7)	2190 (29.8)	7325 (100.0)
1979	3206 (42.5)	2014 (26.7)	2320 (30.8)	7540 (100.0)
1980	34.76 (47.8)	2268 (27.3)	2570 (30.9)	8314 (100.0)
1981	3147 (38.5)	2453 (30.2)	2520 (31.0)	8120 (100.0)
1982	2347 (30.2)	2721 (34.9)	2720 (34.9)	7788 (100.0)

Sources: For column (1): Indian Cotton Mills Federation—Handbook of Statistics on Cotton Textile Industry, Bombay, 1983; For column (2): Indian Cotton Mills Federation—Handbook of Statistics on Cotton Textile Industry, Bombay, 1983 (Estimated on the basis of figures pertaining to delivery of hank yarn.)
Notes: 1) Figures in parentheses indicate percentages of total
2) Figures in column (2) are estimated by deducting volume of handloom cloth from that of total cotton cloth production in the decentralised sector.

of cotton cloth involves three main stages, namely, (i) spinning of yarn from cotton, (ii) weaving of the yarn into grey cloth, and (iii) processing and finishing of the grey cloth. While spinning is done by spinning and composite mills, weaving into grey cloth is done by composite mills, powerlooms and handlooms. Processing and finishing of the fabrics is done by composite mills as well as independent processing units run either with the aid of power or steam or manually.

The direction of input-output flows according to types of mills and the inter-linkages among the different sectors of the textiles industry along with the points of levy of excise duty are shown in Figure 12.1. It is seen that the yarn produced in spinning mills is woven in composite mills, powerlooms as well as handlooms. Similarly, the yarn produced in the composite mills is woven in handlooms and powerlooms besides composite mills themselves. Again, all woven cloth can be processed in composite mills or independent processing units run either with the aid of power or steam or manually. It is thus seen that there is a two-way

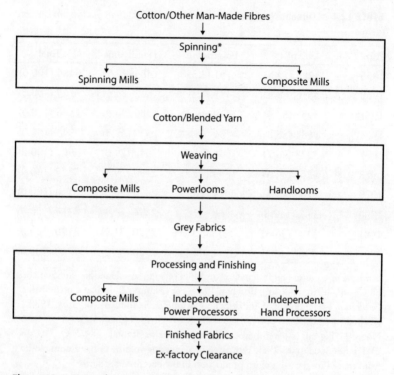

Figure 12.1 Manufacturing Stages and Types of Units
Note: * Handspinning done for the production of Khadi cloth is ignored here.

flow between the organised mill sector and the decentralised weaving and processing sector.

II: Excise Duty Structure

For reasons of data availability, we have taken 1978–79 as the reference year for our study. There are, however, no reasons to believe that the degree of evasion in later years would be any lower than our estimate.[2]

---

[2] The changes in the tax structure introduced in the later years have not substantially altered the avenues of tax evasion. For details see Rao and Pradhan 1984.

Two features of the levy on cotton yarn as existing in 1978–79 are important from our point of view. First, the labour-intensive handloom sector was sought to be encouraged by exempting cotton yarn in hank form on the presumption that this is necessarily used only in handlooms. However, the beneficiary of this policy has turned out to be largely the powerlooms. It is known that the powerlooms do weave some items such as saris and dhotis from yarn received in hank form (Anand 1979). Besides, powerlooms are known to purchase sizeable quantities of hank yarn and rewind it into cones or pirns in order to evade excise duty on yarn (Jain 1983).

The second important feature of the excise duty on yarn is its differentiated rates. Progressivity in the structure was sought to be brought about by levying higher rates of tax on higher counts of yarn. As the conversion of yarn from hanks into cones or pirns, noted in the previous paragraph, involves a cost, it becomes economical to do so for yarns of higher counts and, thus, diversion of yarn and consequent evasion of the duty is beneficial only in respect of higher counts of yarn. Another important consequence of this is the tendency of the spinning mills, in order to avoid higher taxes, to spin lower counts of yarn even though they could spin higher counts from long-staple cotton. It may be noted that this results in lower cloth output as the yield of cloth per kilogram of yarn is lower for lower counts of yarn.

For the purpose of the central excise tariff, 'cotton fabrics' were defined to include all varieties of fabrics where cotton predominated by weight and contained more than 40 per cent by weight of cotton and 50 per cent or more by weight of non-cellulosic fibres or yarn or both. In the case of fabrics such as embroidery in piece, fabrics impregnated and coated, these percentages referred to the base fabrics.

A brief description of the rate structure prevailing in 1978–79 in the mill, the powerloom and the handloom sectors is given in Table 12.2. Three important features of the tax structure are relevant for our purposes and hence, may be noted. First, discriminatory rates of taxation of the fabrics produced in different sectors were imposed. Second, differentiation in the rate structure was made to depend upon both the yarn counts used in the manufacture of the fabric as well as the price of the fabric. Third, differential rates of tax were levied on the fabrics termed as sound, fents and rags. These features have important implications for the method and quantum of evasion and hence call for further elaboration.

TABLE 12.2 Rates of Excise Duty on Cotton Fabrics Sector-wise (1979–80)

Sl No.	Description	Mill Made	Handloom Fabrics Process Processed by Independent Processors		Powerloom Fabrics Processed by Independent Processors
			Approved by Govt.	Not approved by Govt.	
1	Cotton fabrics (including fents and rags) in which the average count of yarn is 41s or more	15	5 without prnting or dyeing or both 9 with printing or dyeing or both	8** 12	8 12
2	Cotton fabrics (other than those in which the average count of yarn is 41s or more)* whose value per square metre				
	a) Does not exceed Rs 4	2	0.80	1.40	1.40
	b) Exceeds Rs 4 but does not exceed Rs 6	3	1.20	2.10	2.10
	c) Exceeds Rs 6 but does not exceed Rs 7	4	1.60	2.80	2.80
	d) Exceeds Rs 7 but does not exceed Rs 8	6	2.40	4.20	4.20
	e) Exceeds Rs 8 but does not exceed Rs 9	8	3.20	5.60	5.60
	f) Exceeds Rs 9 but does not exceed Rs 10	10	4.00	7.00	7.00
	g) Exceeds Rs 10 but does not exceed Rs 11	12	6.00	9.00	9.00
	h) Exceeds Rs 11 but does not exceed Rs 12	14	8.00	11.00	11.00
	i) Exceeds Rs 12	15	9.00	12.00	12.00

3	Fents and rags with average count of yarn less than 41s				
	a) Does not exceed Rs 4	2	0.80	1.40	1.40
	b) Exceeds Rs 4 but does not exceed Rs 7	3	1.20	2.10	2.10
	c) Exceeds Rs 7 but does not exceed Rs 9	6	2.40	4.20	4.20
	d) Exceeds Rs 9 but does not exceed Rs 12	10	4.20	7.00	7.00
	e) Exceeds Rs 12	15	9.00	12.00	12.00

Sources: 1) Government of India, Ministry of Finance, Department of Revenue, Report of Expert Committee on 'Tax Measures to Promote Employment, 1980, New Delhi; 2) Census Publications, Census Central Excise Tariff, 1978–79, New Delhi.

Notes: * Cotton fabrics of this group when classified under 'controlled cloth' variety, are subject to a tax rate reduced by 50 per cent.

** In the budget proposal effective from 1.3.1979 the duty was increased from 8 per cent to 12 per cent. It was subsequently reduced to 11 per cent with effect from 24.4.1979.

Possible Avenues of Evasion

The structure of excise on cotton textile fabrics and the production pattern of the commodity would indicate the following major methods of evasion: evasion through (i) inter-sectoral misclassification of the output; and (ii) intra-sectoral misclassification which also involves understatement of production and undervaluation.

The existence of inter-sectoral rate differences could provide avenues of evasion through inter-sectoral misclassification of output. It may be difficult to misclassify the output of the mill sector, for, it being an organised sector, evasion by this means has a higher probability of being detected. On the other hand, misclassification of powerloom output as handloom output can be done with less fear of detection, for, it is not possible to monitor production flows in units in the decentralised sector. Even the estimates of their production figures are based on yarn deliveries, hank yarn being taken to be entirely used in the handlooms. Given that hank yarn is exempt from excise duty, evasion of the tax by rewinding hank yarn into cones or pirns and using them in powerlooms would be beneficial so long as the duty evaded exceeds the cost of rewinding. As higher rates of duty are levied on higher counts of yarn, this is specifically viable for yarn counts higher than 40.[3] Thus, in the process of evading the duty on yarn, powerloom output is misclassified as handloom output.

Another inter-sectoral avenue of evasion of the tax arises from the misclassification of fabric processed by independent processors using power, as hand-processed fabrics are exempted from the excise duty whereas those processed with use of power are required to pay tax—the rates ranging from 1.4 per cent to 12 per cent. Given the unorganised nature of the industry, it may not be difficult to misdeclare power-processed fabrics as hand-processed and claim exemptions. It should be noted that the hand-processing machinery is identical to the power-processing machines and hence the products would not be different. Each such unit processes about 20,000 metres of cloth per day (GoI 1980). It is common knowledge that in some places hand-processing and power-processing units do operate in adjacent sheds in benami names making it easier to indulge in misdeclaration. Sometimes, the same unit is run on power usually, but is manually operated at the time of inspection.

[3] The Mill Owner's Association (1982) contends that the cost of rewinding hank yarn into cones is around 1–2 per kg of yarn. As the excise duty on yarn of 40 counts is Rs 1.63 per kg, conversion becomes economical for yarn of counts higher than 40.

Given the structure of excise duties, we can trace an optimal path of excise evasion wherein a producer can evade the tax throughout the production flow, both on the yarn and on the cloth. A producer can purchase hank yarn which is exempted, rewind it into cones or pirns and weave it on the powerlooms. Grey cloth produced by the power-looms is exempt. This grey cloth would be processed in independent hand-processing units whereby the duty is avoided. However, duty is evaded when it is processed in power-processing units and misclassified as hand-processed.

However, evading of the tax in the way mentioned above requires coordination of the activities of different sectors of the textiles industry. It is in this context that we have to understand the role of the traders. Traders occupy a prominent place in almost all the activities of textile manufacturing. They buy the hank yarn, rewind it into cones or pirns by paying appropriate charges, weave it in the powerlooms by paying a rental to the powerloom owner, and process them in independent processing units. Subsequently, they illicitly stamp inflated prices on the cloth as well as trademarks of reputed mills and sell it in wholesale and retail outlets.

Evasion arising out of the intra-sectoral tax rate differential can be classified under two categories, namely, (i) suppression of quantity of cloth produced in a sector, and (ii) undervaluation of the cloth produced. Under the latter, we may include the misclassification of the higher priced categories as lower priced, misclassification of the count of yarn used, misclassification of sound fabrics as fents or rags, tie-in-sales and such other methods usually employed in the trade to evade taxes. Although it is possible, it may not be very probable that the mill sector evades taxes by suppressing the quantity of output. The probability of getting detected by suppressing output in the organised sector would be high and therefore employment of this method to evade taxes may not be frequent. On the contrary, given the graded nature of the tax structure, the evasion of the tax through undervaluation could be sizeable.

Evasion through Inter-Sectoral Misclassification

Evasion of Duty on Yarn

We have already mentioned that the exemption of hank yarn from excise duty leads to evasion of the yarn duty through illicit rewinding of hank yarn into cones or pirns and weaving them on powerloom. As the rate of duty is higher on the higher counts of yarn, tax evasion on such yarn becomes especially tempting. Subsequently, as the official estimates of handloom and powerloom production depend of the yarn deliveries in hank and non-hank form respectively due to the diversion, the official estimate of handloom production is overstated and powerloom production estimates are understated.

A Planning Commission study by Anand (1979) places the misclassification at 500 million metres for the year 1975. Jain (1983) similarly estimates that 840 million metres of powerloom cloth would have been misclassified as handloom cloth in 1981. The Mill Owners' Association places the misclassified quantity of cloth at 600 million metres in 1981. It thus seems that the diversion of hank yarn and the consequent evasion of yarn duty arising therefrom is considerable.

We have attempted to estimate the amount of yarn diversion and cloth misclassification by independently estimating the production figures. An estimate of production is arrived at by adding the consumption of handloom cloth to the exports of such cloth. Estimates of household consumption of handlooms are available in *Consumer Purchases of Textiles*, an annual publication of the textiles committee, market research wing, ministry of commerce. We have adjusted calendar year data given in this publication proportionately to correspond to the fiscal year 1978–79. Adjustments had to be made in the reported export figures also, for, although data on the export of handloom cloth are available in both quantities and values, data on the export of handloom manufactures are available only in value terms. Assuming the price per metre of the latter, we have estimated the quantity of handloom manufactures.

The estimated misclassification of yarn is presented in Table 12.3. It is seen that total household consumption of handloom cotton cloth

TABLE 12.3 Misclassified Handloom Cloth, 1978–79, in million metres

Household consumption	962.59
Non-household consumption	520.19
Export of handloom cloth	84.60
Export of handloom cloth manufactures (value of Rs 28.91 crore at the rate of Rs 7.42 per metre)	38.95
Total estimated production	1606.33
Official estimated production	2119.23
Misclassified cloth	512.91

in 1978–79 amounted to 962.59 million metres. *Consumer Purchases of Textiles* gives us the estimated non-household consumption of cotton fabrics, but the handloom component is not separately available. However, the Planning Commission's study (Anand 1979) estimates non-household consumption of handloom for the year 1975 at 300 million metres, which in that year formed 63.5 per cent of total non-household consumption (institutional purchases). Assuming the proportion to remain the same in 1978–79, we have estimated the non-household consumption of handloom in the year at 520.19 million metres. The estimated total consumption of handloom in 1978–79, thus, is placed at 1,482.78 million metres.

During the year, the export of handloom cotton cloth was 84.6 million metres having a value of Rs 628 million. Besides this, handloom manufactures worth Rs 289.1 million were also exported. If the price per metre of cloth of the former (Rs 7.42) is assumed, the exported quantity of cotton manufactures would amount to 38.95 million metres.

By adding the estimated consumption to estimated exports, we get an estimate of the production of cloth which comes to 1,606.33 million metres for the year 1978–79. Estimation made on the basis of hank yarn deliveries, however, places handloom production at 2,119.23 million metres. Thus, 512.91 million metres of powerloom cloth seem to have been misclassified as handloom cloth.

To arrive at the amount of duty loss due to yarn diversion, we have to estimate the diversion of cloth and yarn of various counts. However, certain assumptions are called for as the data in the required disaggregation are not available. We have assumed that there would be no misclassification of cloth through the diversion of yarn for cloth up to 20 counts because for such cloth the cost of rewinding the yarn would far exceed the benefit from excise evasion. Further, it is assumed that the misclassification of cloth of the remaining count groups would be proportional to the estimated production of cloth (derived on the basis of yarn deliveries).[4] By applying an appropriate cloth-yarn conversion ratio to the misclassified cloth production estimates, we have obtained an estimate of yarn diversion in different count groups (Table 12.4). By applying appropriate rates of duty on the diverted yarn, the amount of duty evaded can easily be derived. As seen in the table, the duty thus

---

[4] It may be mentioned that this assumption leads to a very conservative estimate of evasion, for, given the structure of excise duty, the diversion of yarn would be disproportionately high for higher count categories.

TABLE 12.4 Estimate of Yarn Diversion and Evasion of Duty (1978–79)

Count Groups	Hank Yarn Deliveries (in thousand kgs)	Cloth Produceable Per Kg of Yarn	Estimate of Cloth Production on the basis of Yarn Deliveries (million metres)	Our Estimate of Cloth Production (million metres)	Misclassified Production (million metres)	Estimated Yarn Division (million kgs)	Average Duty (Paise/kg)	Basic Amount of Evasion		
								Basic	Special (Rs million)	Total
1–10s	54673.50	8	437.39	437.39	0	0	–	0	0	0
11–20s	72994.25	8	583.95	583.95	0	0	–	0	0	0
21–30s	26991.75	10	269.92	143.82	126.10	43.25	43.25	5.45	0.27	5.72
31–40s	36633.75	10	366.34	195.20	171.14	88.00	88.00	15.06	0.75	15.81
41–60s	20061.75	15	300.93	160.34	140.59	234.25	234.25	21.95	1.10	23.05
61–80s	7649.75	15	114.75	61.14	53.61	387.75	387.75	13.84	0.69	14.53
Above 80s	3064.25	15	45.00	24.49	21.47	668.00	668.00	9.55	0.48	10.03

Notes: 1) We have assumed that the yarn upto 20 counts will not be diverted and hence our estimates and the estimates based on yarn deliveries has been distributed among the different count groups in proportion to the estimated production of cloth of different counts derived from yarn delivery figures.

2) The figures in column (2) which represent the hank yarn delivery according to fiscal year 1978–79 adjusted from the calendar year data given in the Indian Cotton Mills' Federation, Handbook of Statistics on Cotton textile on Cotton Industry, Bombay.

3) The information on Cloth Produceable per kg of yarn given in column (3) is taken from Mazumdar (1984).

evaded amounts to Rs 6.92 crore which forms about 8 per cent of the actual collections. Collection of this amount would have resulted in the total excise collection from yarn of Rs 94.79 crore and evasion on this account as a proportion of the total works out to 7.3 per cent.

Evasion of Duty on Cloth

As stated earlier, the diversion of hank yarn to evade yarn duty also results in the evasion of duty on cloth. We have already estimated that about 513 million metres of powerloom cloth were misclassified as handloom cloth in 1978–79. There is no reason to expect that excise duty would have been paid on this cloth.

Evasion of the cloth duty can be included in a more general form of evasion—misclassifying power-processed fabrics manufactured in powerlooms as hand-processed. This, as we have already mentioned earlier, leads to enormous misclassification of power-processed fabrics as hand-processed and hence evasion of duty.

We do not have any estimate of the misclassification of powerloom cloth processed by processors using power or steam as having been hand-processed. Therefore, although we believe that the tax evasion under this category would be considerable, we are unable to estimate it.

In any case, there is no reason to believe that on the misclassified powerloom cloth, duty would have been paid. Further, given that these are likely to be passed on to consumers as mill fabrics, one may presume that they would have been processed by power but misclassified as hand-processed. Duty loss on account of this has been estimated by using the information on prices as given in the Dandekar Committee and price range-wise distribution as given by the Mill Owners' Association. The computations detailed in Tables 12.5 and 12.6 show that aggregate loss of duty on account of misclassification of the cloth amounts to Rs 12.66 crore. These form 8.71 per cent of the actual collection of excise duty on cotton textile fabrics.

Evasion of excise duty arising from the intra-sectoral tax differences is confined to the composite mill sector. As mentioned earlier, we can identify two broad types of evasion under this category, namely, (i) evasion through suppression or understatement of the quantity of cloth produced; and (ii) evasion through undervaluation of fabrics; under the latter, we may include, besides direct undervaluation, methods such as misclassification of count groups, price groups and sounds into fents and

TABLE 12.5 Evasion of Excise Duty on Misclassified Cloth

Variety	Quantity of Misclassified Cloth (in million metres)		Ex-factory Price Per Sq. Metre	Value of Misclassified Cloth (Rs million)	Total Tax Payable		
	Linear Metres	Sq Metres			Basic	Additional Plus Special (Rs million)	Total
Medium B	126.10	132.38	3.15	417.00			
Medium A	171.14	179.66	4.05	727.62	21.18	3.18	24.36
Fine	140.59	147.59	5.55	819.13			
Superfine	75.08	78.82	3.70	291.63	88.86	13.33	102.19

Source: For Col (3): Government of India, Ministry of Finance, Department of Revenue, Report of the Expert Committee on Tax Measures to Promote Employment (1980), p. 83.

Notes: On the basis of a survey, we found that the average width of the cloth is 1.0498 metres.

TABLE 12.6 Evasion of Excise Duty on Misclassified Cloth of Med-B and Med-A Varieties

Price Ranges	Quantity of Misclassified Cloth Belonging to Med-B and Med—A Categories (million sq metres)	Value of Cloth (Rs million)	Price/Sqm	Tax Rate Applicable (Basic) (%)	Tax Payable (Basic Rs million)
Upto Rs 4/sqm	57.29	119.84	2.09	1.4	1.68
Rs 4-6/sqm	114.21	358.38	3.14	1.4	5.02
Rs 6-7/sqm	66.62	262.80	3.94	1.4	3.68
Rs 7-8/sqm	30.39	138.16	4.55	2.1	2.90
Rs 8-9/sqm	15.66	80.58	5.15	2.1	1.69
Rs 9-10/sqm	12.17	69.83	5.74	2.1	1.47
Rs 10-11/sqm	4.87	30.79	6.32	2.8	0.86
Rs 11-12/sqm	4.34	29.99	6.91	2.8	0.84
Above Rs 12/sqm	6.49	54.25	8.36	5.6	3.04

Notes: i) 1 The value of 226.41 million sq metres or fine and superfine cloth was estimated at 1110.76 million rupees. At 8 per cent of basic tax rate, which is levied on these varieties of powerloom cloth, the total basic tax payable would be 88.86 million rupees.

ii) While distributing the quantity and value of Med-B and Med-A powerloom cloth varies in price ranges, the pattern given in the memorandum submitted by the Mill Owners' Association, Bombay, to the Tripartite Committee, 1982 has been followed.

rags, tie-in-sales and such other methods usually employed to understate the value of the cloth.

In order to examine whether the composite mills in fact indulge in largescale suppression of output to evade excise duty, we have attempted to independently estimate the yarn and cloth production on the basis of the availability of the basic raw material, namely, cotton. Applying the norms stipulated by textile technologists for the conversion of cotton into yarn and yarn into fabrics, we have estimated the amount of yarn and fabrics that could, in fact, have been produced. These estimates are then compared with the cotton and yarn consumption figures reported in the mill sector to examine the possibility of suppression of yarn and cloth output in this sector.

We have estimated cotton availability for spinning as follows: production estimates of cotton are added to the net imports (imports minus exports) and changes in the stock of cotton to arrive at the total cotton available in the year. By adjusting this for other uses of cotton and cotton used in hand-spinning (the production of khadi), we have estimated the cotton available for spinning and composite mills.

In the manufacture of yarn from cotton, certain wastages are involved primarily due to the existence of trash in mixing, blowroom droppings, gutter losses, semi-high production card waste and unaccounted losses such as those arising from comber waste, sweepings, clean waste, hard waste and invisible losses. The Ahmedabad Textile Industry's Research Association (ATIRA) gives the norms for wastages under each of these heads for different warp and weft count groups of yarn. Taking into account these norms, we have obtained the estimates of cotton that is reported to have been consumed in the mill sector. For blended yarn, we have estimated the cotton component at 35 per cent based on our discussions with some manufacturers. By comparing cotton availability with the estimated cotton consumption, we have estimated the quantity of suppressed yarn (Table 12.7).

We have attempted also to estimate the extent of suppression of cloth output by the mill sector in the year 1978–79. These estimates are detailed in Table 12.8 and largely these are self-explanatory. Given that the suppression of yarn output is negligible, we have arrived at the estimated yarn that would have been consumed in the mill sector by merely adding the reported cotton yarn consumption to changes in stocks. By applying the norms of loss involved in converting yarn into cloth, possible cloth output from yarn availability is estimated.

TABLE 12.7 Wasted and Yarn Realisation (As Percentages of Cotton Consumed)

Mixing	Carded				Combed				
Warp count group (Ne)	4-9	10-13	14-25	26-34	28-34	35-44	45-70	71-99	100-140
Corresponding weft counts	4-9	10-13	14-29	30-39	30-38	39-49	50-70	80-109	110-140
Trash in mixing* (%)	11.0	10.0	7.0	5.0	5.0	4.0	3.0	2.0	2.0
Wastes (%)									
Blowroom droppings	12.0	11.0	7.7	5.4	5.4	4.4	3.2	2.2	2.0
Gutter loss	1.2	1.1	0.8	0.5	0.5	0.4	0.3	0.3	0.2
SHP card waste**	4.2	4.2	4.4	4.5	4.5	4.3	4.3	4.3	4.4
Unaccounted loss (%)									
Comber waste	–	–	–	–	9.0	10.9	12.0	13.0	14.0
Sweepings	2.0	1.8	1.6	1.6	1.4	1.2	1.0	1.0	1.0
Clearer waste	0.6	0.5	0.4	0.4	0.4	0.4	0.2	0.2	0.2
Hard waste	0.6	0.5	0.4	0.3	0.3	0.3	0.3	0.3	0.3
Invisible loss	1.8	1.7	1.6	1.5	1.5	1.3	1.3	1.3	1.3
Yarn realisation (%)	77.6	79.2	83.1	86.0	77.0	76.9	77.4	77.4	76.4

Notes: * If trash is less by one per cent, yarn realisation increases by one per cent and vice-versa.

** SHP = Semi-high production cards with high production cards, the yarn realisation improves by about 0.4 per cent owing to about 0.4 per cent owing to about 0.5 per cent less waste extracted at cards with tandem carding, the yarn realisation is reduced by about 0.9 per cent compared to SHP cards. Source: Ahmedabad Textile Industry's Research Association 'Norms for the Textiles Industry', Ahmedabad, 1982, p. S 28.

TABLE 12.8   Expected Consumption of Yarn Cotton in Spinning and Composite Mills, 1978–79

Count Groups Yarn	Production of Yarn Cotton Blended (million kgs)		Yarn realisation*	Expected Consumption of Cotton (million kgs)		Total Consumption
				Cotton Yarn	Blended Yarn**	
1-10s	103.75	1.50	76.60	133.70	0.68	134.38
11-20s	274.50	14.75	81.90	335.16	6.30	341.46
21-30s	233.00	48.00	84.30	275.74	19.88	295.62
31-40s	205.25	83.50	77.00	266.56	37.96	304.52
41-60s	63.75	45.75	77.00	82.79	20.79	103.58
61-80s	27.00	17.25	77.00	35.06	7.84	42.90
Above 80s	14.75	4.75	77.00	19.16	2.16	21.32
Total	922.00	215.50		1148.17	95.61	1243.78

Source: For columns (2) and (3): Government of India, Ministry of Commerce, Office of the Textile Commissioner, Indian Textile Bulletin, Bombay, 1980.
Memorandum Items: (i) Availability of cotton for mill consumption: 1263.95 mn kgs ; (ii) Reported cotton consumption by the mill sector derived on the basis of the yarn produced: 1243.78 mn kg; (iii) Difference: 20.17 mn kgs
Notes: * Based on the norms of Ahmedabad Textile Industry's Research Association (1982).

　　** Assuming that the cotton component in blended yarn is 35 per cent. This consistsofproductionavailableformilsectorconsumption(74.18lakhbalesof170 kgs) and change in stock (0.17 lakh bales of 170 kgs each).

According to the ATIRA norms, the losses involved in weaving yarn at winding, warping, sizing and other stages should aggregate about 3 per cent. This, however, is the minimum wastage involved and, in actuality, the wastage could indeed be higher. On the basis of our discussion with textile technologists, we have taken the wastage at 5 per cent and estimated the expected consumption of yarn. The difference between the yarn that would have been consumed and the actual consumption indicates the extent of understatement of cloth production.

Our estimates as may be seen from the table do not indicate significant understatement of cloth output. The underestimation seems to be of the order of only 1 per cent of the cloth production. This again cannot definitively be attributed to tax evasion as our assumption regarding the cotton content in blended fabrics and the wastage norms may be subject to some margins of error.

Undervaluation and Evasion of Duty

Undervaluation for evasion of the excise duty can be done in many ways. Given that the tax rates levied on the fabrics are graded in terms of counts of fabrics and their prices, undervaluation can easily be done by both misclassifying the fabric count and the price of the fabric. Other methods of undervaluation brought to our notice include tie-in-sales[5] and misclassification of sound fabrics as fents and rags. Again, there can also be understatement of the manufacturing sale price.[6] As it may not be possible to monitor the distributive channels as much as the production flows, the probability of detecting evasion would be lower when these methods are employed and, therefore, we have hypothesised that, under this method the evasion could indeed be significant.

To estimate the extent of evasion, we have to proceed through various steps which are detailed in Table 12.9. The *Consumer Purchases of Textiles* (GoI 1978, 1979) gives us the price range-wise details on household purchases of categories of cloth such as dhotis, saris, drill, shirting, coating, suiting, ladies' dress materials, bedsheet, bed cover, *chaddar*, long cloth and sheeting. These together constitute 67 per cent of total quantity and 71 per cent of the total value of cloth consumed. From total consumption, we have excluded the consumption of handloom and khadi cloth purchases, the data on which are available in *Consumer Purchases of Textiles*. Also, we have excluded the quantity and value of control-led cloth consumption from the mill sector on the basis of the data on controlled cloth packed during the period as given by the textile commissioner's office. The value of controlled cloth has been estimated

---

[5] When a dealer buys fabrics of two different prices, the volume of purchases of the fabric of lower price may be overstated and that of higher price correspondingly understated. This method is called 'tie-in-sales'.

[6] It is very difficult to draw a distinction between evasion and avoidance in such cases. It is well known that the invoice price of the cloth is generally almost 15–25 per cent lower than the stamped price. While the retailer recovers the sale margins at various stages of the transaction added to the stamped price including the excise duty thereon from the consumer, the government receives a much lower amount of excise revenue.

TABLE 12.9 Difference between Declared and Estimated Yarn Consumption, 1978–79

Quantity of cloth and Yarn Counts*	Declared Cotton Yarn Consumption of Mills (million kgs)	Declared Cotton Cloth Production Mills		Estimated Yarn Consumption*** (million kgs)	Difference between declared and Estimated yarn consumption (million kgs)
		Million Metres	Million Kgs**		
Coarse (1-16s)	116.90	435.00	92.05	96.89	20.01
Med –B (17-25S)	137.60	921.25	116.91	123.06	14.54
Med –A (26-40s)	161.75	1675.50	182.46	192.06	–30.31
Fine (41-60s)	10.75	80.75	10.09	10.62	0.13
Superfine (61s and above)	10.00	127.25	9.21	9.68	0.32
Total	437.00	3239.75	410.72	432.31	4.69

Notes: * Data on count-groups of yarn are available in the intervals of MOs, ll*20s, etc. Therefore, to get the count-groups l-16s, 17-25S, etc, which correspond to the variety of cloth (like coarse, Med-B, etc), we have assumed uniform distribution of yarn within the intervals 1-10s, 11-20s, etc, and arrived at the above count-groups.

** For converting the cloth data given in metres into kilograms we have taken the equivalents averaged for five years (1969-1973) on the basis of the data given in National Productivity Council (1976). The computed equivalents per 100 metres, of coarse Medium B, Medium A, fine and superfine cloth are 21.16 kgs, 12.69 kgs, 10.89 kgs, 12.50 kgs, and 7.23 kgs, respectively.

*** In the process of weaving the cloth, the estimated loss of yarn is about three percent (ATIRA) to five per cent. In the above figures five per cent loss is assumed.

on the basis of the information on prices of the mill sector cloth of different qualities available in the *Report on Tax Measures to Promote Employment* (GoI 1980), adjusted for the subsidies assuming constant subsidy per square metre of controlled cloth.

The third important adjustment pertains to the exclusion of power-loom cloth consumption. This necessitates estimation of both the quantity and value of the consumption of powerloom cloth. Assuming that the change in stocks is zero, consumption of powerloom cloth would be equivalent to its production *minus* exports. However, as worked out earlier, official production estimates of powerloom cloth are understated to the tune of 513 million metres as these have been misclassified as handloom cloth. Therefore, we have added this to the production estimates of powerloom cloth given in the *Report on Tax Measures to Promote Employment*, to arrive at the quantity of powerloom cloth production. The report gives the estimates in terms of different qualities, namely, coarse, medium-B and medium-A, fine and superfine. The misclassified quantity of cloth can also be easily disaggregated into these categories. The report also gives the average producers' prices of each of the five qualities of cloth on the basis of which we have arrived at the estimated ex-mill value of production of powerloom cloth. Estimates of the quantity and value of consumption of powerloom cloth have been obtained by deducting the quantity and value of exports from the relevant production estimates. The value of consumption in retail prices has been estimated by adding the margins estimated by us on the basis of the replies to the questionnaire circulated among the textile mills.

To calculate the tax potential in respect of the categories of fabrics considered by us, we require information on the purchases of mill fabrics of more than 41 counts and less than 41 counts, the latter disaggregated further in terms of different ex-mill price ranges corresponding to the tax rate categories. We have separated the consumption of cloth of below 41 counts in proportion to the production estimates of coarse, medium-A and medium-B fabrics given in the *Report on Tax Measures to Promote Employment*. Correspondingly, the proportion of fine and superfine cloth production is applied to the total consumption to arrive at the consumption of cloth above 41 counts. The values of these categories have been obtained by multiplying the quantities with retail prices.

As the rates of excise duty on cotton fabrics of below 41 counts vary according to the price of the fabric, we have to obtain the quantities and values of these fabrics in terms of different price ranges corresponding to tax rate categories. Fortunately, *Consumer Purchases of Textiles*

TABLE 12.10 Estimation of Consumption of Mill Cloth of Different Varieties

Varieties	Consumption per Household		Total Consumption		Controlled Cloth		Handloom Textiles	
	Q	V	Q	V	Q	V	Q	V
	1	2	3	4	5	6	7	8
Dhoti	11.662	61.865	1171.762	6216.194	66.688	278.521	153.332	690.596
Sari	16.205	105.355	1628.270	10586.05	44.859	197.855	274.811	1744.626
Shirting	10.129	71.491	1017.737	7183.330	103.35	330.098	31.651	312.793
Coating/suiting	1.358	13.121	136.421	1318.381	4.442	27.600	12.962	113.240
Ladies' dress material	8.224	59.899	826.353	6018.662	-	-	6.029	61.895
Bed sheet/bed cover	1.918	117.721	192.740	1780.637	-	-	7.034	71.240
Long cloth	5.293	27.024	531.868	2715.358	108.39	431.300	4.120	17.383
Total	54.789	356.477	5505.151	35818.62	337.73	1265.375	489.938	3011.723

Notes: Q = Quantity in million meters; V = Value in rupees
i) Columns 1, 2 are calculated from *Consumer Purchases and Price Trends of Textiles*, monthly bulletins.
ii) Total consumption both quantity and value columns 3 and 4 is derived by taking total number of households (=100479500) in 1978–79
iii) Controlled cloth columns 5 and 6 is from textile commissioner's office and relates to packing of controlled cloth.
iv) Columns 7, 8, 9 and 10 are arrived at by multiplying the total number of households with the per household data available in consumer's purchases.

Varieties	Khadi Textiles		Powerlooms and Mill Sector		Consumption considerate of Powerlooms		Powerloom Value at Rental Price	Consumption of Mill Sector	
	Q	V	Q $3-(5+7+9)$	V $4-(6+8+10)$	Q Price	V value at EX-factory		11-13	12-15
	9	10	11	12	13	14	15	16	17
Dhoti	15.474	64.809	936.269	5182.262	301.745	1149.629	1547.952	634.523	3634.361
Sari	4.924	4.952	1303.677	8632.625	419.974	1915.349	2729.831	883.703	5902.794
Shirting	9.968	4.952	872.765	6444.481	281.222	1429.952	1889.812	591.543	4554.670
Coating/suiting	15.474	117.26	93.543	1060.281	30.189	235.448	329.664	63.354	730.617
Ladies' dress material	10.018	91.235	810.307	5865.531	261.145	1300.853	1781.009	549.102	4084.522
Bed sheet/bed cover	6.099	36.474	179.607	1672.923	57.850	370.780	514.865	121.757	1158.053
Long cloth	-	-	419.351	2266.675	135.034	502.658	668.418	284.317	1598.257
Total	61.956	416.68	4615.518	31124.78	1487.159	6904.645	9461.551	3128.359	21663.234

v) After taking total production of powerlooms from the report of the Export Committee on Tax Measures to Promote Employment (GoI 1980), the quantity of cloth due to diversion of hank yarn from handloom sector was added to get actual quantities of power-loom cloth. From the total production, quantity of powerloom cloth exported was deducted to get the quantity available for home consumption. The value of the powerloom cloth available for home consumption was derived from the price data available in the above mentioned report. Taking 67 per cent of the quantity and 71 per cent of the value, the distribution in each category was made in the same proportion of columns 11 and 12 for quantity and value of powerloom cloth respectively.

(GoI 1978, 1979), gives us data on the price range-wise purchases of different varieties of cloth considered by us. We have apportioned the mill consumption of less than 41 counts according to the data in these price range-wise purchases. This does not impart a significant bias in the estimation, as cloth of less than 41 counts constitutes almost 92 per cent of the quantity of cloth purchases and 91 per cent of the value of purchases. An additional assumption involved in this exercise is that the purchases of the cloth of the decentralised sector would fall into a pattern similar to that of the mill sector's cloth.

All the price ranges and values so far derived are in retail prices. To estimate the tax potential from these, we have to convert them into ex-factory prices. Similarly, the quantities are in terms of linear metres whereas the tax rates are specified per square metre. As mentioned earlier, on the basis of the response received from the mills to a questionnaire circulated to them, we have obtained both the average width of the cloth of different varieties considered by us and the average margin of increase of retail prices over the ex-factory prices. On these, by applying the relevant rates of taxation, we have estimated the excise tax potential in respect of the categories of mill cloth considered by us.

It is seen from our analysis that the categories considered by us should have yielded excise revenue amounting to Rs 93.71 crore from the levy of only the basic duty and another Rs 14.06 crore from the levy of special and additional duties. As mentioned, the categories considered by us constitute only 75.7 per cent of the value of total consumption of textiles. Assuming that the tax potential varies proportionately with the amount of cloth, the total excise duty potential in respect of cotton fabrics of the mill sector would increase by the same proportion. This would amount to Rs 140.51 crore. But the actual collection in 1978–79, as given in the *Statistical Year Book of Central Excise* (GoI 1984), amounted to only Rs 100.97 crore (Rs 87.80 crore basic duty + Rs 13.17 crore special and additional).[7] Thus, the estimated excise duty evasion by means of undervaluation of mill sector fabrics alone amounted to Rs 39.54 crore in 1978–79. This formed as much as 28.1 per cent of the excise duty collection from cotton textile fabrics.

The evasion of duty on cotton cloth through inter-sectoral misclassification was estimated earlier at Rs 12.70 crore. The loss of revenue to

---

[7] Again, it should be noted that taking actual collections rather than the duty liability from declared production makes an implicit assumption that the amount of arrears in the year has not changed from the previous year.

the exchequer by means of undervaluation in the mill sector fabrics has been estimated at Rs 39.54 crore. Thus, in the aggregate about Rs 52.24 crore seem to have been evaded. Had this amount been collected, the aggregate excise duty from cotton textile fabrics would have amounted to Rs 184.85 crore. Thus, the extent of evasion works up to as much as 28.3 per cent. In other words almost 47.2 per cent of the actual duty collection from cotton text fabrics seems to have been evaded.

[The chapter is extracted from the report on 'Excise Duty Evasion in Cotton Textile Fabrics' submitted to the Central Board of Excise and Customs in November, 1984. The authors wish to record their gratitude to Raja J. Chelliah and Shankar N. Acharya for enlightening discussions. Research assistance was provided by Satya Pal.]

References

Anand, Ritu (1979): 'Choice of Technology in Textile Industry', Government of India, Planning Commission, Project Appraisal Division, 1978–79.

Ahmedabad Textile Industry's Research Association (1982); 'Norms for the Textile In-dustry', ATIRA, Ahmedabad.

Desai, Ashok V. (1981): 'Technology, and Market under Government Regulation' (mimeo), National Council of Applied Economic Research, New Delhi.

Government of India (1976): The Report of the Expert Group on Textiles, Collectorate of Excise, Bombay.

——— (1978): Market Research Wing, Textile Committee, Ministry of Commerce, 'Consumer Purchases of Textiles', Bombay.

——— (1978): Market Research Wing, Textile Committee, Ministry of Commerce, *Consumer Purchases and Price Trends of Textiles*, Monthly Bulletin, Nos 88-99, Bombay.

——— (1979): Market Research Wing, Textile Committee, Ministry of Commerce, 'Consumer Purchases of Textiles', Bombay.

——— (1979): Market Research Wing, Textile Committee, Ministry of Commerce, *Consumer Purchases and Price Trends of Textiles*, Monthly Bulletin, Nos 88-99, Bombay.

——— (1980): Ministry of Commerce, Report of the Working Group on Hand-Printing Industry and Hand-Processing Industry, New Delhi.

——— (1980): Ministry of Finance, Department of Revenue, Report of the Expert Committee on Tax Measures to Promote Employment, New Delhi.

——— (1980a): Office of the Textile Commissioner Ministry of Commerce, *Indian Textile Bulletin*, Annual Number, Vol XXVI, No 5, Bombay.

——— (1984): Directorate of Statistics and Intelligence, Central Excise & Customs, 'Statistical Year Book, Central Excise', Vol 1, New Delhi.

Jain, L.C. (1983): 'Handlooms Face Liquidation', *Economic & Political Weekly*, Vol XVIII, No 35.

Mazumdar Dipak (1984): 'The Issue of Small versus Large in the Indian Textile Industry—An Analytical and Historical Survey', World Bank Staff Working Papers, No 645,

Mill Owner's Association (1982): Memorandum Submitted by the Millowners' Association, Bombay, to Tripartite Committee, Bombay.

National Productivity Council (1976): 'Productive y Heads in Cotton Textile Industry in India', New Delhi.

Rao, M.G. and Pradhan, G. (1984): 'Excise Duty Evasion in Cotton Textile Fabrics', NIPFP. New Delhi.

III (d) Black Money and Politics

Corruption and black money has historically fed into the election processes in India. Jagdeep S. Chhokar's chapter in this section covers the relationship between politics and black money. It is a participant-activist's account of the struggle of the civil society against this unholy nexus. Chhokar also comments on the intransigence of the two major political parties of India—the Bharatiya Janata Party (BJP) and Congress—with regard to ensuring transparency in election finances.

13

Black Money and Politics in India

Jagdeep S. Chhokar

The issue of black money in politics in India is multifaceted. A number of questions about its role in politics, how it is generated, its volume, its ill effects, and how it can be eliminated do not have answers that are always specific or clear-cut, and are often interlinked. A few of the answers can at best be partial or anecdotal and circumstantial. This chapter is an attempt to clarify some of these issues.

Since 8 November 2016, when the Prime Minister announced that currency notes of Rs 1,000 and Rs 500 would be taken out of active circulation, with the ostensible objective of removing all 'black' money from the economy and society, the issue of use of black money in politics has been part of the public discourse. The bulk of the discussion has centred on money spent during elections but that is only part of the story, though a significant part.

The issue of black money in politics in India is multifaceted. Some of the questions that arise about this are: Why is black money used or required in politics? What role does it play? Where does it come from, or how is it generated? How much money is involved? Is use of black money in politics harmful? If yes, what is the harm or how does it harm, and who does it harm? Can something be done to eliminate or reduce the use of black money in politics? How can that be done, and who will, or can, do it? Answers to these and similar questions are not always specific or clear-cut, and are often interlinked. A few of the answers can at best be partial and or anecdotal and circumstantial. This chapter is an attempt to clarify some of these issues.

Black Money

Why should 'unaccounted' or 'undeclared money' be used in politics? A simple and logical answer is that such money is, and has to be, used when unaccountable and undeclarable activities are undertaken. And if it is used, then it follows that such activities are indeed undertaken, or have to be undertaken, as some will say, while being involved in competitive political and electoral processes. Just in case any reader has the slightest doubt, a former chief election commissioner provides a list of 40 'types of illegal expenses [undertaken] during election.'[1] The author goes on to say, 'every year more ingenious methods of distributing cash come to light,' and refers to these as 'ever-evolving.'

The Evidence

And if the above are considered random views without any basis, here is some hard data. Every candidate contesting the election to the Lok Sabha is required to submit a statement of the expenditure incurred to the Election Commission of India (ECI) in a sworn affidavit after the election.[2] For the 2009 Lok Sabha election, the limit on expenditure, as laid down under Rule 90 of the Conduct of Election Rules, 1961,[3] was Rs 25 lakh.

The Association for Democratic Reforms (ADR),[4] an organisation working on improving governance and democracy in the country, analysed the election expenditure affidavits of 6,753 candidates who contested the 2009 Lok Sabha election. Only four candidates of the 6,753 said that they had exceeded the limit for expenditure and 30 said they

---

[1] Quraishi, S.Y. (2014). *An Undocumented Wonder: The Making of the Great Indian Election* (pp. 265-327). New Delhi: Rupa.

[2] Section 77(1) of the Representation of the People Act, 1951, prescribes this. Sub-section (3) of the same Act reads '(3) The total of the said expenditure shall not exceed such amount as may be prescribed.' The act can be seen at http://bit.ly/2f35sk7. Retrieved January 11, 2017.

[3] See http://bit.ly/2j4hQVd. Retrieved January 11, 2017.

[4] ADR (www.adrindia.org) works on improving democracy and governance in the country, focusing on electoral and political reforms.

had spent around 90–95 per cent of the limit. The remaining 6,719, about 99.5 per cent of the candidates, said under oath that they had spent only 45–55 per cent of the limit.

The above figures need to be seen in the context of the complaint by candidates and political parties that the limit set for election expenditure is too low and needs to be increased. The limit has been raised from time to time. It started with Rs 25,000 in 1951, moved up to Rs 1 lakh in 1979, to Rs 4.5 lakh in 1994, to Rs 15 lakh in 1997, to Rs 25 lakh in 2003, and to Rs 40 lakh in 2011. It was raised to Rs 70 lakh in February 2014.[5]

Some indirect evidence comes from the increase in assets of members of Parliament (MPs) and members of legislative assembly (MLAs) obtained from comparing the assets declared by them in their affidavits in consecutive elections. In the 2014 Lok Sabha election, there were four MPs whose assets increased more than 1,000 per cent from 2009 to 2014—the figures, in descending order, are 5,649 per cent, 2,081 per cent, 1,700 per cent, and 1,281 per cent. There were 22 MPs whose increase in assets ranged 500–999 per cent.[6]

The situation involving MLAs is even more revealing. There are four MLAs whose assets have increased from one election to the next by more than 10,000 per cent. The figures, in descending order, are 39,439 per cent, 39,367 per cent, 35,736 per cent, and 13,350 per cent, and the states to which these MLAs belong are Meghalaya, Rajasthan, Arunachal Pradesh, and Bihar. And there are 92 MLAs whose assets increased between 1,000 per cent and 9,999 per cent from one election to the next. The assets of 136 MLAs increased by 500–999 per cent.[7]

Identifying Sources of Political Funds

Given that nothing of consequence or significance was done by governments or the political parties, it was left to a civil society group to try and identify where political parties were getting their money from. To this end, the ADR filed a right to information (RTI) application to the

[5] Anon. (2014, February 28). Govt clears Election Commission Proposal, Candidates can Spend More on Campaign. Press Trust of India. Retrieved January 11, 2017, from http://bit.ly/2xavCMw

[6] Compiled from ADR reports.

[7] Compiled from ADR reports.

Central Board of Direct Taxes (CBDT) on 28 February 2007 seeking the following information:

i) Whether the political parties mentioned in the RTI application have submitted their income tax returns (ITRs) for the years 2002–03, 2003–04, 2004–05, 2005–06, 2006–07.
ii) Permanent account number (PAN) allotted to these parties.
iii) Copies of the ITRs filed by the political parties for the afore-mentioned years along with the corresponding assessment orders, if any.

The CBDT transferred the application to nine chief commissioners of income tax (CCITs) all over the country. All except two CCITs declined to divulge the information citing various reasons. Because of the denial of information citing frivolous reasons, the ADR filed nine 'first appeals' to the appropriate appellate authorities at nine cities. All the first appeals were rejected.

The ADR then filed on 31 July 2007 nine 'second appeals' to the Central Information Commission (CIC) as provided in Section 19(3) of the RTI Act. These appeals were heard over several hearings. The CIC also issued notices to all 19 political parties about whom information had been sought. All the major political parties were represented by senior advocates and they submitted written responses opposing the disclosure of their income tax returns. The CIC considered all the written responses as also the oral arguments, and finally gave a decision on 29 April 2008:[8]

> The commission directs that the public authorities holding such information shall, within a period of six weeks of this order, provide the following information to the appellant: income tax returns of the political parties filed with the public authorities and the assessment orders for the period mentioned by the appellant in her RTI application dated 28 February 2007.

This is how copies of ITRs came to be in the public domain. Scrutiny of copies of ITRs revealed that political parties declare even crores as income in the ITRs but do not pay any income tax. A search for the reason for this led to Section 13A of Income Tax Act, which makes 'special provision relating to incomes of political parties.'[9]

---

[8] Central Information Commission (2008). Order No CIC/OK/A/2007/01407. Retrieved December 25, 2016, from http://bit.ly/2j1OMxP
[9] Income Tax Act, 1961.

13A: Any income of a political party which is chargeable under the head 'income from house property' or 'income from other sources' or 'capital gains' or any income by way of voluntary contributions received by a political party from any person shall not be included in the total income of the previous year of such political party:

Provided that—

  i) such political party keeps and maintains such books of account and other documents as would enable the assessing officer to properly deduce its income therefrom;
 ii) in respect of each such voluntary contribution in excess of twenty thousand rupees, such political party keeps and maintains a record of such contribution and the name and address of the person who has made such contribution; and
iii) the accounts of such political party are audited by an accountant as defined in the *Explanation* below sub-section (2) of Section 288: Provided further that if the treasurer of such political party or any other person authorised by that political party in this behalf fails to submit a report under sub-section (3) of Section 29C of the Representation of the People Act, 1951 (43 of 1951) for a financial year, no exemption under this section shall be available for that political party for such financial year.

Explanation—For the purposes of this section, 'political party' means a political party registered under Section 29A of the Representation of the People Act, 1951 (43 of 1951).

What is important in the above is the second proviso which, when read in conjunction with Section 29C of the Representation of the People Act, 1951, in effect says that if a political party does not submit a statement of donations of more than Rs 20,000 each to the ECI, it will not get the 100 per cent exemption from income tax that Section 13A of the Income Tax Act permits.

This provison led the ADR to file an RTI application to the ECI seeking copies of the lists of donations of more than Rs 20,000 submitted by political parties. Once these lists were available, the total amount of donations of more than Rs 20,000 received by a political party in a specific year were compared with the total income declared by the same political party for the same year in its income tax return.

The above comparison revealed that on an average across all political parties, the donations of more than Rs 20,000 each explained only

20–25 per cent of the total income of the political parties. What this meant was that around 75–80 per cent of the declared income of political parties, on an average, is from unknown sources.

Attempt to Communicate with Political Parties

Once it was discovered that the bulk of the declared income of political parties was from unknown sources, the ADR sent RTI applications to the six national parties (Bharatiya Janata Party, BJP; Congress; Bahujan Samaj Party, BSP; Nationalist Congress Party, NCP; Communist Party of India, CPI; and Communist Party of India—Marxist, CPI(M) requesting them for the following information.

i) Sources of the 10 maximum voluntary contributions received by your party from financial year 2004–05 to financial year 2009–10. (a) The modes of these donations (cheque, cash, demand draft, etc). (b) The amounts of these donations. (c) The financial years in which these contributions were made.

ii) Sources/names of all voluntary contributors along with their addresses who have made single contributions of more than Rs 1 lakh to your party from financial year 2004–05 to financial year 2009–10.

The parties declined to give the information saying they were not under the purview of the RTI Act and therefore did not need to respond to RTI applications.

The ADR then approached the CIC requesting that the six national political parties be declared public authorities under the RTI Act. The CIC initially declined, saying that there was not enough data and asked the ADR to provide more data if it could gather that. The ADR spent almost two years, collecting data about the six national political parties by filing around 2,000 RTI applications to various government authorities seeking information about how much of public funds were spent on services and facilities provided to political parties. All these data were presented to the CIC.

A full bench of the CIC conducted a number of hearings where the political parties were represented by senior lawyers. Some of the hearings were also attended by senior leaders of political parties. The lawyers and leaders both opposed the ADR's request. After all the hearings, the CIC finally declared on 3 June 2013 'that AICC/INC, BJP, CPI(M),

CPI, NCP and BSP are public authorities under Section 2(h) of the RTI Act.'[10]

The CIC, in its decision of 3 June 2013, also said:

The presidents, general/secretaries of these political parties are hereby directed to designate CPIOs and the appellate authorities at their headquarters in 6 weeks time. The CPIOs so appointed will re-spond to the RTI applications extracted in this order in 4 weeks time. Besides, the presidents/general secretaries of the above mentioned political parties are also directed to comply with the provisions of Section 4(1) (b) of the RTI Act by way of making voluntary disclosures on the subjects mentioned in the said clause.

None of the six political parties complied with the decision of the CIC. They neither designated CPIOs nor appellate authorities, nor did they supply the information that had been sought in the original RTI applications. The ADR then filed a complaint of non-compliance of its decision to the CIC. The complaint was heard by a fresh full bench of the CIC. In the first hearing, the CIC decided to issue notices to the political parties asking them for reasons for non-compliance. Once again, none of the six parties responded to the notice of the CIC.

In the next hearing, the CIC decided to send showcause notices to all the six political parties and asked them to be present to explain not complying with the CIC's decision of 3 June 2013. All the six parties ignored the showcause notice of the CIC. They neither attended the next hearing nor responded to the notice. After repeated hearings and notices, the CIC, in a decision announced on 16 March 2015,[11] finally expressed its inability to get its own order implemented.

The CIC stated:

(a) the respondents are not in compliance with the commission's order of 3 June 2013 and the RTI Act. The respondents, as public authorities, have *not implemented the directions contained in the commission's order and there is no evidence of any intention to do so* (emphasis added); …

---

[10] Central Information Commission (2013, June 3). File No. CIC/SM/C/2011/001386; CIC/SM/C/2011/000838. Retrieved December 25, 2016, from http://bit.ly/2vLXgPp

[11] Central Information Commission (2015, March 1). File No. CIC/CC/C/2015/000182. Retrieved December 25, 2016, from http://bit.ly/2eGbuq4

(e) the complainants are at liberty, in view of the facts and circumstances of this case, to approach the higher courts for appropriate relief and redressal.

It was after this that the ADR and Subhash Chandra Agrawal, who had also submitted similar but independent applications and complaints to the CIC, filed a public interest litigation (PIL) in the Supreme Court requesting it to get the CIC's lawful order implemented.[12] The PIL named the Union of India, the ECI, and the six national political parties as respondents.

Interestingly, but not perhaps surprisingly, the very first response filed in response to the petition was by the Union of India,[13] even before any of the six political parties responded. Once again, not surprisingly, the union said in its affidavit that political parties should not be under the RTI Act. The matter is still under consideration of the Supreme Court.

This effort 'to identify the sources of political funds' started in February 2007 and it is now 2017, but the end is not yet in sight. The nexus between the political class, political parties, and politicians continues. While there were 125 MPs with pending criminal cases in the 2004 Lok Sabha, the corresponding figure for the 2009 Lok Sabha was 162 and for the 2014 Lok Sabha was 186.[14]

Additional Evidence

Much against the solemn protestations of political parties that they do not do anything wrong, there is at least one example where the wrongdoing has been pronounced judicially.

Having discovered that an electoral trust had made significantly large donations to both the BJP and Congress, the ADR decided to find out more about that particular trust. The trust had been set up jointly by three companies registered in India. Attempts to find out what could be the reasons for three companies in different sectors to set up an electoral trust jointly revealed that all the three companies were 100 per cent fully-owned subsidiaries of a company registered in the United Kingdom (UK).

[12] Association for Democratic Reforms (2015, May 19). Public Interest Litigation. Retrieved December 27, 2016, from http://bit.ly/2vMch3Y

[13] Government of India (2015, August 21). Response to PIL. Retrieved December 27, 2016, from http://bit.ly/2xPliXq

[14] Compiled from ADR reports.

This meant that the money donated by the electoral trust and accepted by the BJP and Congress was, following the legal principle of 'lifting the corporate veil,' actually controlled by a foreign entity.

This had a serious problem. The Foreign Contribution (Regulation) Act (FCRA) was enacted in 1976 to regulate receipt of foreign funds by Indian entities. Section 4(1)(e) of the FCRA specifically prohibits political parties from accepting any foreign contributions,[15] saying, '(1) No foreign contribution shall be accepted by any—(e) political party or office-bearer thereof.' This act was replaced in 2010 by the FCRA, 2010. Section 3(1)(e) of it also read as follows: 'No foreign contribution shall be accepted by any ... (e) political party or office-bearer thereof.'[16] In view of the above, the acceptance of funds that were controlled by a company registered in a foreign country was a clear violation of the FCRA.

The ADR and another petitioner filed a PIL in the Delhi High Court, asking for action to be taken against both the parties for having violated the FCRA. The defence put forward by the BJP and Congress was that the majority shareholder of the British entity was an Indian citizen. The high court was not persuaded by this argument in view of the well-established principle of law that a company is a legal entity different from the owner or promoter.[17]

After hearing arguments from all sides, the Delhi High Court said in its judgment of 28 March 2014:[18]

> For the reasons extensively highlighted in the preceding paragraphs, we have no hesitation in arriving at the view that *prima facie* the acts of the respondents *inter se*, as highlighted in the present petition, clearly fall foul of the ban imposed under the Foreign Contribution (Regulation) Act, 1976 as the donations accepted by the political parties from Sterlite and Sesa accrue from 'foreign sources' within the meaning of law.

[15] Foreign Contribution (Regulation) Act, 1976. Retrieved January 17, 2017, from http://bit.ly/2eLJzcj

[16] Foreign Contribution (Regulation) Act, 2010. Retrieved January 17, 2017, from http://bit.ly/2eGlVtX

[17] Delhi High Court (2014, March 28). WP(C) 131/2013. Association for Democratic Reforms & Anr vs Union of India & Ors. Retrieved January 16, 2017, from http://bit.ly/2wGnYrx

[18] Chhokar, Jagdeep S. (2015, December 28). Govt wants to amend FCRA Act rather than punish Congress, BJP for violating it. *Firstpost*. Retrieved January 16, 2017, from http://bit.ly/2vMHjZy

The Delhi High Court also ordered that the directions 'shall be complied within a period of six months from date of receipt of certified copy of the present decision.'

The ECI wrote to the ministry of home affairs (MHA) saying that since the MHA was the administering authority under the FCRA, it should take action against the two parties under law. The MHA wrote letters to the ministry of corporate affairs, which also responded, but all this correspondence did not lead to any action.[19]

Meanwhile, as the end of six months approached, both the BJP and Congress filed appeals in the Supreme Court against the judgment of the Delhi High Court. It is worth noting that the Supreme Court did not stay the judgment of the high court, and that a stay was not asked for. While this was going on, the Government of India made two attempts to amend the FCRA, both of which did not succeed. Finally, it brought in a 'surreptitious' amendment by slipping in a paragraph in the Finance Bill of 2016.[20]

Something very peculiar transpired in the next hearing of the appeals in the Supreme Court on 22 November 2016. The lawyers for the BJP and Congress said that they would like to withdraw their appeals because in the light of the amendment of the FCRA, the Delhi High Court judgment, and consequently the appeals, had become infructuous. It was pointed out to the court that the 'surreptitious' amendment brought in through the Finance Bill amended the FCRA 2010 and that the Delhi High Court had stated:

> Since the writ petition drew attention to donations made to political parties for the period up to the year 2009, we record at the outset that our concern is not with the Foreign Contribution (Regulation) Act, 2010, which has come into force on 26 September 2010. Our discussion of the legal position would be with respect to the Foreign Contribution (Regulation) Act, 1976.

In view of this observation, the 'surreptitious' amendment of the FCRA 2010 did not have any effect on the violation of the FCRA 1976 declared by it. On learning about this, the lawyers for the BJP and the

---

[19] Chhokar, Jagdeep S. (2016, April 11). Surreptitious FCRA Amendment: The Empire Attempts to Push Back. The Wire. Retrieved January 16, 2017, from http://bit.ly/2xPom5P

[20] Chhokar, Jagdeep S. (2016, April 11). Surreptitious FCRA Amendment: The Empire Attempts to Push Back. The Wire. Retrieved January 16, 2017, from http://bit.ly/2xPom5P

Congress sought time to seek instructions from their clients about the next course of action. At the next hearing, both the BJP and Congress withdrew their petitions and the Supreme Court decided the appeals to be 'dismissed as withdrawn.'[21]

Both the petitioners, the ADR and EAS Sarma, have written to the MHA to take action now that the Delhi High Court judgment has been reaffirmed, in a way, by the Supreme Court with the legal challenge to that judgment being 'withdrawn.'[22] At the time of writing this, there was no information in the public domain about the MHA having taken or even initiated any action.

Demonetisation, Budget 2017–18, and After

A public statement by the revenue secretary on 16 December 2016 was revealing. The highest bureaucrat in the finance ministry said publicly that while common citizens will be questioned about the source of banned higher denomination currency notes, more so if they deposited more than Rs 2.5 lakh, political parties were free to deposit any amount of cash in old currency notes and no questions would be asked of them. When questions were raised about this undue favour being extended to political parties, none less than the finance minister stepped in to clarify that the government had not changed any rules related to political party finance and everything was being done according to existing rules.

What the finance minister seems to have conveniently overlooked is that 'existing rules' still have only these provisions—filing of annual income tax returns by political parties and 100 per cent exemption from income tax under Section 13A of the Income Tax Act, and submitting a list of donations above Rs 20,000 to the ECI under Section 29C of the Representation of the People Act, 1951. The existing law has no provisions for old and new currency.[23] The statement of the revenue secretary seemed

[21] Chhokar, Jagdeep S. (2016, December 9). Time to Get Real About Foreign Money and Black Money in Politics. *The Wire*. Retrieved January 16, 2017, from http://bit.ly/2vMyIGj

[22] Chhokar, Jagdeep S. (2016, December 12). FCRA: Are political parties unique organisations, and thus above the law? *Firstpost*. Retrieved January 16, 2017, from http://bit.ly/2wIMHdf

[23] Anon. (2017, February 1). Union Budget 2017: Full speech of Finance Minister Arun Jaitley. *The Times of India*. Retrieved February 7, 2017, from http://bit.ly/2vMzsLe

to be an open invitation to political parties to convert their, possibly unaccounted, cash stored in old currency notes into new currency without any adverse impact, with which people at large were threatened.

Just as this article was being written came the news of the 2017–18 budget of the central government. The following portion in the budget speech of the finance minister created quite a stir:[24]

165....(a) In accordance with the suggestion made by the Election Commission, the maximum amount of cash donation that a political party can receive will be Rs 2,000 from one person.

(b) Political parties will be entitled to receive donations by cheque or digital mode from their donors.

(c) As an additional step, an amendment is being proposed to the Reserve Bank of India Act to enable the issuance of electoral bonds in accordance with a scheme that the Government of India would frame in this regard. Under this scheme, a donor could purchase bonds from authorised banks against cheque and digital payments only. They shall be redeemable only in the designated account of a registered political party. These bonds will be redeemable within the prescribed time limit from issuance of bond.

What is being claimed to be a reduction from Rs 20,000 to Rs 2,000 is completely untrue.[25] There was no law limiting cash donations to Rs 20,000. The political parties only had to declare donations above Rs 20,000. This limit of Rs 20,000 still remains the same even after the budget. A new provision has been introduced to put a limit of Rs 2,000 of cash contributions which do not necessarily have to be declared.

The other supposedly big announcement is about 'electoral bonds.' How effective these bonds might be in ensuring transparency in political funding can be seen from the following statement of the finance minister in a post-budget media interaction:[26]

[24] Government of India (2017). The Finance Bill 2017. Ministry of Finance. Retrieved February 7, 2017, from http://bit.ly/2w9qOSH

[25] Anon. (2017, February 2). Present system has failed, we are experimenting with a new system, says Arun Jaitley. *The Indian Express*. Retrieved February 7, 2017, from http://bit.ly/2gJfGWI

[26] Anon. (2017, February 2). Present system has failed, we are experimenting with a new system, says Arun Jaitley. *The Indian Express*. Retrieved February 7, 2017, from http://bit.ly/2gJfGWI

[T]here is a provision of electoral bonds which requires an amendment to the RBI Act. A notified bank will be issuing those bonds. Any donor can buy those bonds using cheque or digital money. These bonds can be given to the political party. Every recognised political party will have to notify one bank account in advance to the Election Commission and these can be redeemed in only that account in a very short time. These bonds will be bearer in character to keep the donor anonymous.

That 'political parties will be entitled to receive donations by cheque or digital mode from their donors' is very surprising. Does it mean that political parties were earlier not 'entitled to receive donations by cheque or digital mode from their donors?'

The disparities between what the budget speech says and what the Finance Bill has show unambiguously that the government of the day does not have any intentions to bring transparency in political funding.

IV

DEMONETISATION AND THE INDIAN ECONOMY

(a) The Rationale for Demonetisation

Chapters included in this section deal with papers that questioned the economic rationale for demonetisation as offered by the government and the RBI after 8 November 2016. Prior to 2016, there were two demonetisations in India: the first in 1946 and the second in 1978. The key differences between the demonetisations of 1978 and 2016 are discussed by J. Dennis Rajakumar and S.L. Shetty, which was published in November 2016.

In a December 2016 article, Vineet Kohli and R. Ramakumar questioned the economic rationale of demonetisation from the standpoint of five claims put out by the government: that it would eliminate counterfeit currency; that it would unearth significant amounts of black money; that it would reduce interest rates in the banking system; that it would expand the fiscal space of the government; and that it would help formalise the informal sector of the Indian economy.

In a first and exclusive, this volume publishes an invited chapter by Amitava Bandyopadhyay, Ranjan Sett and Dipak K. Manna, the authors of the famous report of the Indian Statistical Institute, Kolkata on the extent of counterfeit currency in circulation in the economy.

The last two chapters are contributions that comment on the debate on creating a cashless—or a less-cash—economy. C.P. Chandrasekhar, in a very interesting contribution in March 2017, asked if negative interest rates (which is supposedly made possible by a cashless economy, according to a section of economists) can either drive up credit growth or improve growth rates of GDP. A second contribution to the debate was by Atul Sood and Ashapurna Baruah in January 2017. They argued that the nationalist fervour unleashed by the government after demonetisation was also the inauguration of a new moral political project in India. Here, every citizen was either 'a patriot or a criminal' while the state epitomised virtue and stood above everyone else.

14

Demonetisation

1978, the Present and the Aftermath

J. Dennis Rajakumar and S.L. Shetty

In the context of the demonetisation of Rs 500 and Rs 1,000 notes, the issuance of currency and its different denominations are traced over time, while also tracking key macroeconomic features of India's changing economy over the decades. Further, the possible immediate and longer term economic effects of demonetisation are discussed.

It is now widely acknowledged that the public at large is suffering due to the 8 November announcement to demonetise the Rs 500 and Rs 1,000 notes. An overwhelming proportion of the population has been directly punished by this decision that aims to tackle the black economy. Such extreme steps are resorted to only in response to situations of hyperinflation or some form of financial crisis. No such situation exists now. India's previous experience with demonetisation was when the President of India promulgated the High Denomination Bank Notes (Demonetisation) Ordinance on 16 January 1978, demonetising the Rs 1,000, Rs 5,000 and Rs 10,000 currency notes with the objective of eliminating 'the possible use of such notes for financing illegal transactions' (RBI 1977–78: 77). At that time, demonetisation received limited public attention and had little impact on the daily lives of people. High-denomination notes demonetised then, formed just a minuscule fraction—about 0.6 per cent—of the total currency in circulation (*see* Table 14.1). Further, the demonetised notes were of significantly high value,

TABLE 14.1 Issue of Bank Notes (Rs in billion)

Year	Denomination of Bank Notes							
	Rs 50	Rs 100	Rs 500	Rs 1000	Rs 5000	Rs 10000	Total denominations	HD Notes
1970–71		22.1 (12.3)	–	0.450	0.215	0.010	42.2	0.7
1971–72		24.8 (14.7)	–	0.36 (–20.0)	0.197 (–8.6)	0.137 (1293.	40.4 (–4.3)	0.7 (2.7)
1972–73		28.5 (12.9)	–	0.43 (19.4)	0.190 (–3.5)	0.100 (–26.8)	106.2 (163.1)	0.7 (3.8)
1973–74		32.2 (2.1)	–	0.35 (–18.6)	0.250 (31.6)	0.260 (160.1)	281.1 (164.8)	0.9 (19.5)
1974–75		32.9 (4.2)	–	0.35 (0.0)	0.240 (–4.0)	0.216 (–17.1)	40.8 (–85.5)	0.8 (–6.3)
1975–76	0.9	34.2 (4.2)	–	0.88 (151.4)	0.230 (–4.2)	0.013 (–94.2)	345.4 (747.5)	1.1 (39.3)
1976–77	7.3 (753.5)	37.3 (8.9)	–	1.05 (19.3)	0.180 (–21.7)	0.239 (1793.7)	884.1 (156.0)	1.469 (30.8)
1977–78	10.0 (35.6)	43.0 (15.5)	–	0.550 (–47.6)	0.180 (0.0)	0.001 (–099.5)	129.0 (–85.4)	0.7311 (–50.2)
2000-01	328.2	1081.4	529.5	37.2			2124.6	566.7
2001-02	356.0 (8.5)	1180.4 (9.2)	685.1 (29.4)	71.8 (93.0)			2673.7 (25.8)	756.9 (33.6)
2002-03	351.9 (–1.2)	1153.9 (–2.2)	938.1 (36.9)	159.7 (122.5)			3033.8 (13.5)	1,097.8 (45.0)
2003-04	330.3 (–6.1)	1214.4 (5.2)	1229.4 (31.0)	274.7 (72.0)			3341.6 (10.1)	1,504.1 (37.0)

2004–05	299.4 (–9.3)	1232.8 (1.5)	1527.3 (24.2)	420.8 (53.2)		3647.2 (9.1)	1,948.1 (29.5)
2005–06	278.4 (–7.0)	1346.4 (9.2)	1823.3 (19.4)	643.5 (52.9)	4284.3 (17.5)		2,466.8 (26.6)
2006–07	279.5 (0.4)	1354. 4 (0.6)	2254.0 (23.6)	936.8 (45.6)	5042.5 (17.7)		3,190.8 (29.3)
2007–08	265.1 (–5.2)	1345.8 (–0.6)	2631.1 (16.7)	1412.2 (50.8)	5960.6 (18.2)		4,043.3 (26.7)
2008–09	244.4 (–7.8)	1370.3 (1.8)	3083.0 (17.2)	1917.8 (35.8)	6908.3 (15.9)		5,000.9 (23.7)
2009–10	210.6 (–13.8)	1383.6 (1.0)	3644.8 (18.2)	2382.5 (24.2)	7973.9 (15.4		6,027.3 (20.5)
2010–11	159.8 (–24.1)	1402.4 (1.4)	4453.1 (22.2)	3027.1 (27.1)	9504.4 (19.2)		7,480.2 (24.1)
2011–12	174.4 (9.1)	1411.9 (0.7)	5128.1 (15.2)	3468.8 (14.6)	10598.3 (11.5)		8,596.9 (14.9)
2012–13	173.1 (–0.8)	1442.1 (2.1)	5359.5 (4.5)	4299.0 (23.9)	11696.6 (10.4)		9,658.5 (12.3)
2013–14	172.4 (–04)	1476.5 (2.4)	5702.5 (6.4)	5081.4 (18.2)	12875.8 (10.1		10,783.9 (11.7)

(Cont'd)

TABLE 14.1 (Cont'd)

Year	Denomination of Bank Notes						Total denominations	HD Notes
	50	100	500	1000	5000	10000		
2014–15	174.4 (1.1)	1502.7 (1.8)	6563.9 (15.1)	5612.5 (10.5)			14332.7 (11.3)	12,176.4 (12.9)
2015–16	194.5 (11.6)	1577.8 (5.0)	7853.8 (19.7)	6325.7 (12.7)			16482.8 (15.0)	14,179.4 (16.5)
As % to total 1970–71	–	52.4	–	1.1	0.5	0.0	100.0	1.6
1977–78	7.7	33.3	–	0.4	0.1	0.0	100.0	0.6
2000–01	15.4	50.9	24.9	1.8			100.0	26.7
2010–11	1.7	14.8	46.9	31.8			100.0	78.7
2011–12	1.6	13.3	48.4	32.7			100.0	81.1
2012–13	1.5	12.3	45.8	36.8			100.0	82.6
2013–14	1.3	11.5	44.3	39.5			100.0	83.8
2014–15	1.2	10.5	45.8	39.2			100.0	85.0
2015–16	1.2	9.6	47.6	38.4			100.0	86.0

Source: Based on data extracted from Reserve Bank of India (2016b), *Handbook of Statistics on Indian Economy 2015–16.*
Notes: HD notes refer to high-denomination notes of Rs 500 and above.
Figures in paranthesis are annual percentage change.

having little use for common people. The current situation is different, the demonetised 500 and 1,000 notes constitute over 85 per cent of total notes in circulation by value.

The authorities in 1978 seemed to have been prompted to act against the holdings of high-denomination notes due to quantum jumps in such currency holdings in 1975–76 and 1976–77 (*see* Table 14.1). After the 1978 demonetisation, Rs 100 notes remained the highest denomination in circulation for about a decade. In October 1987, the Reserve Bank India (RBI) issued Rs 500 banknotes, apparently with a view to meeting higher transaction needs arising from inflation. Later, the Rs 1,000 note was reintroduced in November 2000.

There is another aspect of the 1978 experience that needs to be noted. A large portion—45 per cent of the high-denomination notes in circulation or about 53 per cent of the high-denomination notes tendered for conversion—were with banks and government treasuries and not with the public (*see* Table 14.2). This time, however, only Rs 96,080 crore or just about 5 per cent of the total notes in circulation were with banks and

TABLE 14.2 Profile of 1978 Demonetisation

	Total notes on 16 January 1978 (crore)	Note tendered for conversion to RBI (crore)	Amount passed for exchange for lower denomination (crore)	Col (2) as % of Col 1	Col (3) as % of Col 1
Total value of HD notes	145.42	124.45	116.31	85.6	80.0
Of which held by: (1) Banks and government treasuries	64.94	64.94	61.24	100.0	94.3
(2) Public	80.48	59.51	55.07	73.9	68.4
Public as % of total	55.3	47.8	47.3		

Source: Reserve Bank of India, Annual Report 1977–78, p. 38.
Notes: HD notes refer to high-denomination notes comprising Rs 1,000, Rs 5,000 and Rs 10,000. Cols (2) and (3) are based on notes tendered for conversion to the Reserve Bank of India, as on 30 June 1978.

government treasuries. In the first week of November 2016, when the current demonetisation took place, about 95 per cent of such currencies were with the public.[1]

Another fundamental difference between the 1978 measure and the current one relates to the motivation behind the actions taken. The reason this time, according to the RBI, is that there has been an increased incidence of fake notes in higher denominations, and that these notes are used by terrorists and by those hoarding black money (RBI 2016c).

However, the RBI's recent annual reports have shown how counterfeit notes detected in the banking system (excluding counterfeit notes seized by the police and other enforcement agencies) have been rising, but not alarmingly. Counterfeit notes have generally constituted less than or around 0.002 per cent of the notes in circulation.[2]

In accordance with international practice, the process of withdrawal of old notes, of the pre–2005 series in India, began in May 2013, but 'in phases to preclude any inconvenience to the public' (RBI 2016a: 92). While such notes remained legal tender, the facility for their exchange remains available only at RBI offices. This was done in a routine manner through banks. Initially, the exchange window was made available till January 2015, with the RBI taking utmost care not to cause inconvenience to the public. 'Banks were sensitised to ensure the withdrawal in a smooth and non-disruptive manner without causing any inconvenience to the public' (RBI 2014: 108). The exchange facility was however extended till December 2015 'to ensure withdrawal of the remaining pre-2005 old design banknotes with least inconvenience to members of the public' (RBI 2015: 110). The principle of indirect demonetisation is thus achieved through gradual withdrawal of specific older series of notes. This seems to have brought, among other things, some reductions in the detection of counterfeit notes during 2012–13 and 2013–14 (RBI 2014: 109).

---

[1] This is evident from the fact that total currencies with banks and government treasuries were worth above Rs 96,080 crore, while the high denomination notes in circulation alone in March 2016 were of the order of Rs 14,17,940 crore. Total non-public holdings of all currencies were then only 6.4 per cent of high-denomination currencies in circulation.

[2] Authors' estimates based on data extracted from Table VIII.8 of RBI *Annual Report 2015–16* (p. 92).

I: Currency Holdings Since 2001–02

Phenomenal changes have taken place in the economy during the past decade and a half. There has been considerable diversification in favour of the services sector in total gross domestic product (GDP), which obviously absorbs higher amounts of currency. Liberal economic policies included sizeable reductions in marginal tax rates, impetus for trade, easing of controls on foreign direct investment (FDI), as also portfolio investment in share markets, liberalisation of commodity trading, and opening up of large numbers of organised retail outlets. All of these have created a liberal economic environment which has given impetus to people to hold large amounts of cash. Over time, due to persistence of inflation, the value of the rupee has also eroded.

In such an environment, the authorities responded by reintroducing high-denomination notes for ease of trade and general economic activities. Until the introduction of Rs 500 notes in October 1987 and reintroduction of Rs 1,000 notes in November 2000, Rs 50 and Rs 100 notes had held sway (*see* Table 14.1). In 2000–01 about 65 per cent of the notes in circulation were in the form of Rs 50 and Rs 100 notes and by 2015–16, their share dwindled to just about 10 per cent. The Rs 500 and Rs 1,000 notes have increased in share: Rs 500 notes from about 25 per cent in 2000–01 to 47 per cent in 2015–16, and Rs 1,000 notes which were issued in 2000–01 grew to 38 per cent in 2015–16. Thus, the two together accounted for as much as 86 per cent of the total notes in circulation, which showed that transactions in India have been preponderantly through these two denominations.

II: Currency and GDP Growth

A comparison of the growth of note issuances with other macroeconomic indicators such as growth rate of the GDP at market price and the inflation rate produces interesting results (*see* Table 14.3).

First, the rate of increase in high-denomination notes outpaced the increase of total bank notes throughout the post-Independence period. Second, the annual growth rates in total currency as well as those in high-denomination notes have been much higher than the nominal GDP growth (which could be partly due to monetisation). For instance, the annual average of high-denomination notes growth during the eight-year period from 2005–06 to 2012–13 worked out to 22.2 per cent, which has been much higher than the average annual GDP growth of

TABLE 14.3 Growth Rate of Bank Notes, HD Notes, GDP and Inflation Rates

	HD Notes	Total Bank Notes	GDP (Current)	GDP (Constant)	GDP Deflator	WPI	New CPI (Combined)
GDP 2004–05 series							
2005–06	26.6	16.8	13.9	9.3	4.2	4.5	
2006–07	29.3	17.6	16.3	9.3	6.4	6.6	
2007–08	26.7	17.2	16.1	9.8	5.8	4.7	
2008–09	23.7	17.1	12.9	3.9	8.7	8.1	
2009–10	20.5	15.7	15.1	8.5	6.1	3.8	
2010–11	24.1	18.7	20.2	10.3	9.0	9.6	
2011–12	14.9	12.5	15.7	6.6	10.5	8.9	
2012–13	12.3	10.6	12.2	4.7	5.3	7.4	10.1
GDP 2011–12 series							
2012–13	12.3	10.6	13.9	5.6	7.9	7.4	10.1
2013–14	11.7	10.2	13.3	6.6	6.2	6.0	9.3
2014–15	12.9	11.4	10.8	7.2	3.3	2.0	5.9
2015–16	16.5	14.9	8.7	7.6	1.1	-2.5	4.9

Source: Based on data extracted from Reserve Bank of India (2016b), Handbook of Statistics on Indian Economy 2015–16.
Notes: HD notes refer to high-denomination notes of Rs 500 and above; GDP refers to gross domestic product at market price.

15.3 per cent in nominal terms. Even the average growth of total currency issues at 15.8 per cent has been somewhat higher than the average GDP growth. This was as per the 2004–05 series of GDP estimates. According to the 2011–12 GDP series, high-denomination notes grew at 12.3 per cent in 2012–13, which was 0.9 times of the GDP growth rate. By 2015–16, high-denomination notes grew at 16.5 per cent, surpassing the GDP growth rate of 8.7 per cent, that is, 1.9 times higher. A similar trend is noticed when we compare growth of issue of bank notes to the GDP growth rate (See Figure 14.1). An increase in the issue of high-denomination notes and total bank notes have taken place in spite of lower order of inflation rate during the last few years. Normally, the impetus for currency expansion comes from high inflation.

III: High Cash and Demand Deposits

Has the phenomenal rise in the issue of bank notes, particularly high-denomination notes, altered the behaviour of money supply in the economy? In India, both narrow (M1) and broad money (M3) concepts are used. M1 consists of currency with the public, demand deposits, and other deposits with the RBI, while M3 additionally includes time deposits. M1 has expanded during the last few years essentially due to

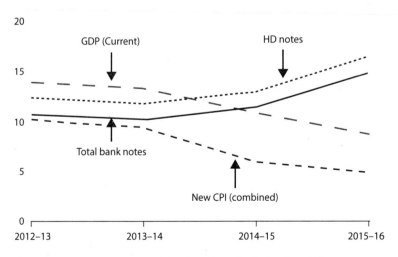

Figure 14.1 Currency Notes, GDP Growth and Inflation Rate (%)

sizeable increases in currency with the public, while demand deposits have grown at high rates in some years (*see* Table 14.4). M3 mostly comprises time deposits, a little over three-fourths, though a marginal reduction is seen during the last two years. Amongst the components

TABLE 14.4 Movements in Money Supply and Its Components

	Currency with public	Demand deposits	Other deposits with RBI	M1	Time Deposits	M3
Outstanding as on March 31 (in crore)						
2006	3,56,314	2,86,998	6454	6,49,766	15,95,887	22,45,653
2016	5,98,095	9,97,021	15,451	9,97,021	90,43,773	19,94,042
Absolute variations (in crore)						
2005–06	55,810 (15.7)	1,20,425 (42.0)	389 (6.0)	1,76,624 (27.2)	2,97,217 (18.6)	4,73,841 (21.1)
2006–07	70,730 (17.2)	70,181 (17.2)	624 (9.1)	1,41,535 (17.1)	4,49,009 (23.7)	5,90,544 (21.7)
2007–08	85,556 (17.7)	1,00,768 (21.1)	1,560 (20.9)	1,87,884 (19.4)	5,19,933 (22.2)	7,07,817 (21.4)
2008–09	97,040 (17.1)	10,316 (1.8)	−3,494 (−38.7)	1,03,862 (9.0)	6,73,059 (23.5)	7,76,921 (19.3)
2009–10	1,02,042 (15.3)	1,29,282 (22.0	−1,727 (−31.2)	2,29,597 (18.2)	5,78,325 (16.4)	8,07,922 (16.9)
2010–11	1,44,344 (18.8)	4,886 (0.7)	153 (−4.0)	1,49,077 (10.0)	7,52,341 (18.3)	7,52,341 (18.3)
2011–12	1,11,834 (12.3)	−11,954 (−1.7)	−831 (−22.7)	99,049 (6.0)	7,81,666 (16.1)	8,80,715 (13.5)
2012–13	1,17,391 (11.5)	42,323 (6.0)	418 (14.8)	1,60,132 (9.2)	8,44,856 (15.0)	10,04,988 (13.6)
2013–14	1,04,758 (9.2)	58,753 (7.8)	−1,275 (−39.4)	1,62,236 (8.5)	9,65,331 (14.9)	11,27,567 (13.4)
2014–15	1,40,363 (11.3)	79,654 (9.8)	12,625 (642.5)	2,32,642 (11.3)	8,00,140 (10.7)	10,32,782 (10.9)
2015–16	2,11,913 (15.3)	1,05,389 (11.8)	861 (5.9)	3,18,163 (13.9)	7,86,009 (9.5)	7,86,009 (9.5)

(*Cont'd*)

TABLE 14.4 *(Cont'd)*

	Currency with public	Demand deposits	Other deposits with RBI	M1	Time Deposits	M3
Variations as % to M3						
2005–06	11.8	25.4	0.1	37.3	62.7	100.0
2006–07	12.0	11.9	0.1	24.0	76.0	100.0
2007–08	12.1	14.2	0.2	26.5	73.5	100.0
2008–09	12.5	1.3	−0.4	13.4	86.6	100.0
2009–10	12.6	16.6	−0.2	28.4	71.6	100.0
2010–11	16.0	0.5	0.0	16.5	83.5	100.0
2011–12	12.7	−1.4	−0.1	11.2	88.8	100.0
2012–13	11.7	4.2	0.0	15.9	84.1	100.0
2013–14	9.3	5.2	−0.1	14.4	85.6	100.0
2014–15	13.6	7.7	1.2	22.5	77.5	100.0
2015–16	19.2	9.5	0.1	28.8	71.2	100.0

Source: Based on data extracted from Reserve Bank of India (2016b), *Handbook of Statistics on Indian Economy 2015–16*
Note: Figures in parantheses are percentage variations.

of M1, currency with the public is the primary one. Although the ratio of currency with public to M3 (also known as currency ratio) has been declining over the years, except in the last two years, demand deposits as a ratio has remained nearly the same. The percentage variation of M1 was higher than that of M3 in recent times due to sluggish growth in time deposits. In the overall expansion of M3, the share of M1 has doubled from 14.4 per cent in 2013–14 to 28.8 per cent in 2015–16, with simultaneous reduction in the share of time deposits. Within M1, the share of currency with the public has gone up from 9.3 per cent to 19.2 per cent, and demand deposits went up from 5.2 per cent to 9.5 per cent between 2013–14 and 2015–16. Thus, the bulk of increase in money supply (that is, liquidity generated) during these years is attributable to the huge rise in currency with the public and demand deposits.

TABLE 14.5   Income Velocity of Money and Its Components

	GDP/ Currency	GDP/Demand Deposits	GDP/ M1	GDP/Term Deposits	GDP/ M3
GDP 2004–05 Series					
2004–05	9.63	12.51	5.40	2.13	1.53
2005–06	9.59	11.31	5.15	2.12	1.50
2006–07	9.52	10.69	5.00	2.05	1.46
2007–08	9.64	10.58	5.01	1.91	1.38
2008-09	9.16	10.85	4.94	1.76	1.30
2009–10	9.08	10.77	4.91	1.68	1.25
2010–11	9.15	11.34	5.05	1.74	1.29
2011–12	9.30	13.65	5.52	1.69	1.29
2012–13	9.32	14.47	5.66	1.65	1.28
GDP 2012 Series					
2011–12	9.02	13.23	5.36	1.64	1.25
2012–13	9.17	14.24	5.57	1.63	1.26
2013–14	9.44	14.84	5.76	1.60	1.26
2014–15	9.47	14.87	5.77	1.58	1.24
2015–16	9.21	14.74	5.63	1.56	1.22

Source: Based on data extracted from Reserve Bank of India (2016b), *Handbook of Statistics on Indian Economy 2015–16.*
Notes: Worked out using money supply (average for financial year).

IV: Falling Velocity of Money

The income velocity of money is normally measured as a ratio of nominal GDP to money supply.[3] The view that the issue of bank notes was done to meet the transaction motive of money can be well examined if we observe a rise in the GDP to currency (*see* Table 14.5). The income velocity of currency has marginally come down from 9.63 in 2004–05

[3] This follows from the simple quantity theory of money which is expressed as $M^*V = P^*Q$; where M is the total money supply, V is the velocity of money, P is the price level and Q is the output. In fact, P^*Q is the monetary value of goods and services produced in the economy, represented by the GDP. The income velocity (V) can be worked out by rearranging this equation as P^*Q/M.

to 9.08 in 2009–10, but this has gone up to 9.32 in 2012–13. This observed trend is based on GDP as per 2004–05 series. Considering GDP 2011–12 series, it is seen that income velocity of currency has marginally risen from 9.02 in 2011–12 to 9.44 in 2013–14, only to decline to 9.21 in 2015–16. A near similar trend is witnessed in the ratio of the GDP to demand deposits as well. Overall, the GDP-to-M3 ratio has consistently fallen from 1.26 in 2013–14 to 1.22 in 2015–16. In view of a larger rise in the money supply relative to GDP growth, the income velocity has declined. Reduction in income velocity has also occurred at a time when the inflation rate has been slowing. But the behavioural change demonstrated by the velocity has been largely explained by the income velocity of currency and demand deposits.

Does the increased use of currency reflect the failure of electronic payments to expand? As per RBI data, retail electronic payments as a percentage of nominal GDP have risen only nominally; it fell from 127.5 per cent in 2013–14 to 123.4 per cent in 2014–15 and then increased to 130.9 per cent in 2015–16.[4] It thus explains the persistence of relatively higher growth in bank notes and high-denomination notes in the last two years. We may attribute this to the public's propensity to treat money also as a store of value, apart from being a medium of exchange. What is more, these are years in which the inflation rate was lower than earlier years and hence the public would have viewed minimum erosion in the value of money, which in turn would have increased their propensity to view currency as a store of value. That alone does not justify demonetisation unless such currency holdings are largely illegal or have large unaccounted sources.

V: Expected Outcomes

Whether demonetisation this time will achieve its stated purpose can be understood only when more statistics become available. The extent of demonetised high-denomination currency that finally fails to be exchanged for new notes or be deposited in banks will be an important indicator.

Economic consequences of the demonetisation measure have many dimensions. Short-term can be further divided into two parts: disruptions

---

[4] Authors' estimates based on data extracted from Table IX.I of RBI *Annual Report 2015–16* (p. 95).

in the lives and day-to-day activities of people, and the shock leading to contractions in consumption, trading and household incomes. Savings are unlikely to be affected as currency holdings will be converted into bank deposits, though no doubt such actions will have medium-term implications, particularly on interest rates.

The tremors that demonetisation has sent across the economy were clearly visible in the course of the last many days with trading activities crumbling. One may treat this as a shock. But this has to be absorbed to prevent it from precipitating a further crisis. The shock absorbers include stepping up private and public investment, and global demand for domestically produced goods.

The interest rates are expected to go down due to a surfeit of liquidity in the banking system with the public depositing high-denomination notes and withdrawing only limited amounts. This is very unlikely to boost private investment as firms anyway would have excess capacity. Global demand cannot be expected to drive domestic production and employment as the global economy still trails. Demand for imported goods can go down due to a depressed price situation and want of liquidity in the market. This can make the dollar cheaper (or rupee stronger) which will further weaken export competitiveness (unless of course the demand for the dollar increases due to other reasons).

Based on the prediction of money market equilibrium models, we know that any inward shift in the money supply curve (which demonetisation can easily do) will put pressure on the interest rate, if there is no discernible shift in the money demand curve. Due to the inconvenience caused and for want of currency for transaction purposes, the money demand curve could shift downward, thus leaving interest rates unaffected, but having adverse effects on the level of output. In other words, withdrawal of high-denomination notes will certainly have a short-term impact on market transactions and hence output level in the economy. That is, aggregate demand in the economy gets adversely impacted in the short run, which perforce implies that the price level in the economy would go down in the next few months (if reflation is not a public policy choice). If aggregate demand falls due to reduction in money supply with a simultaneous fall in prices, inventories will build up, which firms may not want due to the opportunity costs involved, and this can eventually impact production. Adjustments in outsourcing firms, and small and medium enterprises would be exposed to a higher order of demand risk affecting employment in that segment. Thus, the short-term impact could have far-reaching consequences. Conceding to this line of reasoning would mean that the recent demonetisation has clearly set a stage for an economic crisis that is sure to affect the economy unless public spending increases.

Increasing public spending is perhaps doable in the current scenario. Currency notes issued are liabilities of the RBI, and to the extent demonetised notes do not get surrendered, the liabilities of the RBI could be expected to go down unless these liabilities are not extinguished. If such liabilities are extinguished, the most likely result would be a corresponding addition to the RBI's accrued income as part of 'other liabilities and provisions' on the liabilities side to begin with. As per practice and statute, such surplus income eventually becomes part of the annual transfer to the central government. Hence, it could augment the government's revenue. Given this expected improvement in the fiscal position arising from demonetisation, public spending may be viewed as the sole shock absorber.

VI: Public Policy and Public Pain

Studies on corruption practices in India have shown that the system of bribes, underhand dealings and use of dubious means to get things done, are rampant. These practices, it cannot be denied, are all pervasive. The abundant supply of Rs 2,000 notes, a poorly thought-out move, will gravitate towards those interested in unaccounted transactions, once again encouraging illegal transactions.

The malaise of unaccounted transaction ought to have been addressed at its root, that is, by closely examining high value transactions to uncover their sources of financing; for instance by raiding real estate and jewellery sector operators. It is not for nothing that a study by the World Bank staff has placed India at the top of emerging market economies as moving the highest share of shadow economy in total GDP (22.2 per cent) as compared with China's 12.7 per cent and Japan's 11 per cent. Further, there is a need to monitor conspicuously high levels of expenditure in India and even abroad, on marriages and other such extravaganzas. Besides, if any administration is sincere about attacking the phenomenon of unaccounted money, it has to strictly regulate political party funding. When all these fairly straight-forward alternatives exist, the government machinery did not have to inflict such hardships on the public.

References

Reserve Bank of India (1977–78): *Report on Currency and Finance 1977–78*, Mumbai: RBI.

——— (1978): *Annual Report 1977–78*, Mumbai: RBI.

——— (2005): *History of the Reserve Bank of India (1967–1981)*, Volume 3, Mumbai: RBI.

——— (2014): *Annual Report 2013–14*, Mumbai: RBI.

——— (2015): *Annual Report 2014–15*, Mumbai: RBI.

——— (2016a): *Annual Report 2015–16*, Mumbai: RBI.

——— (2016b): *Handbook of Statistics on Indian Economy 2015–16*, Mumbai: RBI.

——— (2016c): *Frequently Asked Questions Withdraw-al of Legal Tender Character of the Existing Bank Notes in the Denominations of Rs 500 and Rs 1,000* (Updated as on 18 November 2016), accessed at the https://www.rbi.org.in/Scripts/FAQView. aspx?Id=119, on 21 November 2016.

Schneider, F., A. Buehn and C.E. Montenegro (2010): 'Shadow Economies All over the World New Estimates for 162 Countries from 1999 to 2007,' Policy Research Working Paper 5356. Washington, DC: World Bank.

15

Economic Rationale of Demonetisation

An Analysis of the Claims of the Government

Vineet Kohli and R. Ramakumar

In this chapter, we examine the government's claims on the benefits of demonetisation. We argue that (a) the extent of circulation of counterfeit notes in the Indian economy is exaggerated; (b) the claims of unearthing large amounts of black money is unfounded and based on a poorly informed view of what constitutes black money; (c) no improvement in government finances may be expected due to demonetisation; (d) it is unlikely that interest rates in the economy may fall as a consequence of demonetisation; and (e) the movement into a less-cash economy may neither lead to the shrinkage of the shadow economy nor reduce corruption, and, instead, may open up new spaces of surveillance and assaults on the personal freedoms of citizens.

On 8 November 2016, Prime Minister Narendra Modi announced the demonetisation of Rs 500 and Rs 1,000 notes with effect from the next day. Through the 50 days after 8 November, the government has made a set of claims with regard to the objectives and outcomes of the demonetisation scheme. In this note, we wish to examine the economic rationale and logic behind a few of these claims.

The *first* claim is that demonetisation would plug terror financing. The Prime Minister asked: 'Have you ever thought about how these terrorists get their money? Enemies from across the border run their operations using fake currency notes ... Many times, those using fake five hundred and thousand rupee notes have been caught and many such notes have been seized' (PMO 2016).

The *second* claim is that demonetisation would help unearth 'black money.' Clearly, the Prime Minister was referring to black money hoarded in cash; he asked: 'Which honest citizen would not be pained by reports of crore worth of currency notes stashed under the beds of government officers? Or by reports of cash found in gunny bags?' (PMO, 2016). There are two ways in which this is supposed to happen: one, unaccounted cash is not returned to the banking system due to fear of detection; and two, when unaccounted cash that enters the banking system is either detected by tax authorities or voluntarily disclosed by the depositors.

The *third* claim is that the unearthed black money would expand the fiscal space of the government. One, when unaccounted cash is not returned to the banking system, the Reserve Bank of India (RBI) can use the savings to pay the government a dividend. Two, unaccounted cash that is voluntarily disclosed would be subjected to a 50 per cent tax as per the Taxation Laws (Second Amendment) Bill 2016. Unaccounted cash not voluntarily disclosed but detected by tax authorities would be subjected to a 75 per cent tax. Further, the declarant would have to deposit 25 per cent of the undisclosed income into the Pradhan Mantri Garib Kalyan Deposit Scheme 2016, which would be used to finance 'programmes of irrigation, housing, toilets, infrastructure, primary education, primary health, livelihood, etc.'[1]

The *fourth* claim is that demonetisation would help reduce interest rates in the banking system. According to Arun Jaitley, minister for finance, 'banks are now flushed with funds ... and ... these low-cost funds are going to be lent at a much lower rate.'[2] In his address to the nation on 31 December 2016, the Prime Minister further claimed that demonetisation would reduce inflation in the economy.

The *fifth* claim is that demonetisation would help formalise India's informal economy, reduce the extent of transactions in cash and help create a 'less-cash economy.' In fact, between November 2016 and December 2016, the slogan of demonetisation has shifted from being

---

[1] Government of India (2016). Taxation Laws (Second Amendment) Bill, 2016. Retrieved February 7, 2017, from http://bit.ly/2gJ1Nrt

[2] Anon. (2016, November 18). Demonetisation will redefine new normal for Indian economy: Arun Jaitley. *The Economic Times*. Retrieved February 7, 2017, from http://bit.ly/2x7c7EB.

an attack on black money into a facilitator of transformation into digital transactions. A number of incentives have been offered to induce people to use digital transactions.

I: Counterfeit Currency

The circulation of counterfeit currency in the economy is a fact. However, there is no accurate estimate of the quantum of circulation of counterfeit notes. There are two major sources of data on fake Indian currency notes (FICN): one, the data released by the RBI on FICN 'detected by the banking system;' and two, the data released by the National Crime Records Bureau (NCRB) on FICN 'seized' by the police.

- The share of FICN 'detected' by banks in the total number of Rs 500 notes in circulation was 0.000022 per cent in 2013–14, 0.00002 per cent in 2014–15 and 0.000016 per cent in 2015–16. The share of FICN in the total number of Rs 1,000 notes in circulation was 0.000021 per cent in 2013–14, 0.00002 per cent in 2014–15 and 0.00002 per cent in 2015–16 (RBI 2016).[3]
- The share of FICN seized by police in the total number of Rs 500 notes in circulation was 0.0037 per cent in 2013, 0.0025 per cent in 2014 and 0.0019 per cent in 2015. The share of FICN seized in the total number of Rs 1,000 notes in circulation was 0.0038 per cent in 2013, 0.0031 per cent in 2014 and 0.0028 per cent in 2015.[4]

In 2012, the government had entrusted the Indian Statistical Institute (ISI), Kolkata with a study on counterfeit notes. The results of the study were reported in the written answer to a question in the Rajya Sabha in August 2015.[5] According to the answer, 'the face value of FICN in

[3] As regards earlier years, a reply to the Rajya Sabha by the then finance minister in 2009 had stated: 'the Reserve Bank of India has informed that they have received very few complaints of counterfeit currency notes found in the notes issued by banks during the period 2006–07 to 2008–09' (Answer to Avtar Singh Karimpuri, by Pranab Mukherjee, finance minister, Starred question no: 379, answered on December 15, 2009, Issue of Counterfeit Currency by Banks).

[4] Answer to P.C. Mohan, by Arjun Ram Meghwal, minister of state for finance, Unstarred question no: 3285, Lok Sabha on August 5, 2016, available at http://bit.ly/2wKb2iN.

[5] See reference in foot note number 3.

circulation was found to be about Rs 400 crore' and 'the value remained constant for the last four years.'

Media reports also quoted the ISI study as concluding that 'the existing systems of seizure and detection are enough to flush out the quantum of FICN being infused.'[6]

Thus, it is unclear if the quantum of FICN is anything significant to warrant overarching measures like demonetisation.

II: Black Money

A crucial assumption in the demonetisation exercise is that 'black money' is hoarded as cash. Such a view is not just narrow, but also serves to defeat the larger purpose of preventing illegal creation and storage of unaccounted money. To begin with, it is necessary to distinguish between three concepts: 'black economy', 'black money' and what we may refer to as 'black cash'.

The term 'black economy' may simply refer to a broad set of economic activities that generate *production and income flows* that are under-reported or un-reported or result from economic illegality. A portion of incomes generated in the black economy, when saved, adds to the stock of black wealth or, what we may call 'black money'. Because savings that financed the acquisition of black money were themselves undisclosed, black money has been defined officially as 'assets or resources that have neither been reported to the public authorities at the time of their generation nor disclosed at any point of time during their possession' (GoI 2012a).

A part of the black money is held as 'black cash'. According to estimates in NIPFP (1985), cash was a 'very significant' form of holding black money in only less than 7 per cent of the cases. The prominent forms of holding black money were: (a) under-valued commercial and residential real estate; (b) under-valued stocks in business; (c) benami financial investment; (d) gold, silver, diamonds and other precious metals; and (e) undisclosed holdings of foreign assets. More recently, open economy policies, free trade arrangements and financial liberalisation policies have expanded the scope for holding black money in newer forms.

[6] Chauhan, Neeraj. (2016, May 11). Fake notes worth Rs 400 crores in circulation. *The Times of India*. Retrieved March 31, 2017, from http://bit.ly/2eHXFaF

However, the very concept of black money is nebulous (NIPFP 1985). This is because the same person who earns black income also typically generates income in white. He may choose to declare his savings by claiming them to be a portion of his legitimate income. There may be, in other words, black incomes but little or no black savings! No wonder then that economists are not very fond of estimating the size of black money. In fact, we are not sure if there could be any realistic estimate of black money in India. A commonly cited estimate puts the size of the 'black economy' between 19 per cent and 21 per cent of the GDP (NIPFP 1985). Some other estimates note higher shares; according to Kumar (2016), the size of the black economy amounted to about 62 per cent of the GDP in 2012.

In fact, the idea that only illegal holdings of cash lubricate the black economy is itself misplaced. This presumption has not only infiltrated the public discourse but has also seeped into some of the academic work on the subject. In his much-quoted work on the 'subterranean economy' of the United States (US), Gutmann (1977) chose a base period in which he considered the size of the black economy to be negligible. The currency-to-deposit ratio of the base period was then applied to the deposits in 1976. Such a method gave him an estimate of the legitimate currency requirement in 1976. The ratio of GDP-to-legitimate money (legitimate currency *plus* deposits) multiplied by the currency stock in excess of its legitimate requirement, then, gave Gutmann his measure of black income in the US.

The problem, however, is that transaction balances used for generating black income need not be undeclared or illegal. For example, a firm can declare cash in its balance sheet and then use it to procure inputs at inflated prices from an associated firm that operates from a low tax jurisdiction. The profits can then be ploughed back into the firm, say, *via* the foreign investment route. The expansion of liabilities that results may, at least temporarily, cause the firm to hold even larger amounts of cash. In this case, there is nothing illegal about the original holdings of cash or their subsequent augmentation. In fact, since transaction balances are held legally as cash, they could well be held as deposits. The example, therefore, shows that bank deposits can also finance black activities. This, of course, goes against the very grain of what Gutmann suggests and what the current Indian government would have us believe.

In the example we constructed above, black incomes are generated in the country but received in a foreign land. But are not incomes from corruption (and many other forms of illegalities) received as cash within the country? Would not demonetisation reduce these to worthless pieces of paper? It would, but only to the extent that the recipients of such incomes were foolish enough to continue to hold them as illicit cash. They could, in the first place, choose to consume these incomes. But even when such incomes are saved, they need not be held as cash. The savings can take the form of land, gold/bullions or financial shares. Besides, there are ways to launder illicit cash. For example, 'bill masters' may be engaged to sell fake bills to those firms that wish to inflate their expenses (GoI 2012b). Illicit cash can then be shown as a receipt for sales that never took place and, in this manner, made perfectly legitimate.

Thus, only a small section, which stores cash in large amounts either for future use or as revolving cash in business/trade transactions, is adversely affected by demonetisation. As we explained above, even here, a big portion of cash might actually be legal or made legal through myriad innovative ways. In sum, no significant unearthing of illegal cash may be expected by demonetisation, even if it might halt or slow down illegal cash-based operations for a while.

III: Fiscal Space

In the days soon after 8 November, the buzz in policy circles was that demonetisation would extinguish close to Rs 3 lakh crore of RBI's currency liabilities. The enlarged net worth of the RBI, it was hoped, could then be transferred to the government in the form of a special dividend. The legal permissibility of such a transfer was a matter of speculation for almost a month after the announcement. However, two points may be noted in this context. First, the transfer of extinguished currency as dividend to the government was ruled out by the RBI itself. Urjit Patel, the RBI governor, clarified on 7 December that 'the withdrawal of legal tender characteristic status does not extinguish any of the RBI balance sheets ... They are still the liability of the RBI.' Second, as on 10 December, an amount of Rs 12.44 lakh crore in the old series of notes had already entered the banking system. The public had time till 30 December to deposit old notes with banks, and they could continue to submit old notes to the RBI until around March 2017. In other words, there is likely to be very little money left with the RBI to extinguish.

Given that the dividend route is closed, the government would bank on the second version of the income disclosure scheme (IDS) to improve tax collections and enlarge the kitty of the Pradhan Mantri Garib Kalyan

Deposit Scheme 2016. However, one wonders why such a scheme could not have been announced without demonetisation. Perhaps, demonetisation has armed the government with evidence on big ticket deposits that it can use to confront tax evaders. Yet, why would anyone deposit a large sum into a bank after 8 November and invite scrutiny from tax authorities? According to news reports, people may have split their large hoards of cash into smaller parcels before converting them into deposits. The tax authorities now have the unenviable task of establishing the trail from the original hoards of cash to multiple small-ticket deposits in the millions of accounts spread across tens of thousands of bank branches.

What is likely to be the net revenue gain from demonetisation? As an illustration, let us assume that Rs 1.6 lakh crore are voluntarily disclosed (which is more than two and a half times the amount disclosed in the first income disclosure scheme). A 50 per cent tax on this amount would result in an addition of Rs 80,000 crore to government's tax kitty. Besides, declarants are supposed to provide an interest free loan equal to one-fourth of the disclosed amount to the government for a period of four years. Assuming a 6 per cent interest rate on borrowings, the government would then save Rs 2,400 crore in each of the next four years. The present discounted value of this income stream comes to Rs 8,430 crore. The total revenue gain is then Rs 88,430 crore.

On the other hand, the government would also lose money. It will end up spending about Rs 17,000 crore on printing and distributing currency and, conservatively, another Rs 6,000 crore as the interest cost (*see* next section) of managing the excess liquidity with banks. Let us assume that 2 per cent of the nominal GDP is shaved off due to demand contraction; instead of growing at, say, 11.5 per cent per annum, the nominal GDP would grow at 9.5 per cent per annum. Taking the nominal GDP (at market prices) of Rs 135 lakh crore in 2015–16 and a tax-to-GDP ratio of 17 per cent, the combined loss of tax revenue to the centre and the states due to economic contraction would amount to Rs 45,900 crore. The total loss of revenues due to demonetisation would then be about Rs 68,900 crore. This does not include the compensation that government may have to provide for toll operators (about Rs 922 crore, as per estimates in the media) and the loss of revenue from the sops announced on digital payments. The net revenue gain to the government would then be Rs 19,530 crore. Even if we are generous and assume that the government actually gains Rs 40,000 crore from the entire exercise, it would still work out to just 1.3 per cent of the combined revenue receipts of central and state governments in 2015–16.

In other words, it is hard to think of demonetisation as a game-changer for government finances.

IV: Interest Rates and Inflation

According to Arun Jaitley, and a few media commentators, demonetisation would expand credit supply and reduce interest rates in the economy. Such a claim betrays an incorrect understanding, not only of India's credit markets, but even more worryingly, of the process of demonetisation itself.

Before dealing with this issue in detail, we need to, right at the outset, dispel a claim made by the Prime Minister in his 31 December 2016 address. He had said: 'The excess of cash was fuelling inflation and black-marketing. It was denying the poor, their due. Lack of cash causes difficulty, but excess of cash is even more troublesome.'[7] What may drive inflation, besides a sustained escalation of costs, is an excess of demand over supply. Demand, of course, is backed by access to a means of payment, which may be held as cash or deposits. It is thus conceptually erroneous to claim that a mere conversion of cash into deposits will deprive economic agents of the means of payments to demand commodities. However, as a matter of fact, after 8 November 2016, the poor, who are under-served by banks and mostly receive and make payments in cash, were forced to spend less due to the denial of their rightful cash. The 'success' in controlling prices, in other words, was achieved by squeezing the consumption budget of the poor.[8]

---

[7] Modi, Narendra. (2016, December 31). PM's address to the nation on the eve of New year 2017 . Pmindia.gov.in. Retrieved March 31, 2017, from http://bit.ly/2f8sshF

[8] According to available estimates, on a year-on-year basis, consumer prices in India increased by 4.2 per cent in October 2016 and 3.6 per cent in November 2016, which was 'the lowest inflation rate since November 2014' [see Ferreira, Joana (2017, August 14). India Inflation Rate. *Trading Economics*. Retrieved August 15, 2017, from http://bit.ly/2eA2jHT]. In the monetary policy statement released on 7 December 2016, the RBI had also noted the possibility of 'abrupt compression of demand in November due to the withdrawal of sbns'. See Reserve Bank of India. (2016, December 7). Fifth Bi-monthly Monetary Policy Statement, 2016-17 Resolution of the Monetary Policy Committee (MPC), Reserve Bank of India [Press release]. Retrieved March 31, 2017, from http://bit.ly/2wOyICQ.

The claim that demonetisation would result in lower interest rates can be rationalised through a simple money multiplier process. Suppose Rs 10 of cash in the hands of the public is converted into deposits. Let us further assume that out of every Rs 10 that banks issue as deposits, they are required to hold Rs 1 as cash reserve. As a result, banks will now have Rs 9 worth of 'excess cash,' which they lend to public and, which, assuming that the public is discouraged from holding cash, returns as deposits. The cycle would then start afresh: deposits will increase by Rs 9, cash reserves by Rs 0.90 and loans by Rs 8.10. When all is said and done, deposits, reserves and loans would have increased by Rs 100, Rs 10 and Rs 90 respectively. Another way to understand this process is to simply assume that the banks hold no more than their required reserves by crediting Rs 90 to the deposit account of their borrowers. Of course, such an expansion of credit cannot come without a reduction in its price and demonetisation has raised hopes that the interest rate on loans may fall in the near future.

There is, however, a fly in the ointment. What we are witnessing in India today is not a permanent conversion of currency into deposits but a temporary measure that would last only till the limits on withdrawals exist. Once the convertibility of deposits into cash is restored, the multiplier process sketched above would start working in the reverse direction. As deposits worth Rs 10 are converted into cash, the banks, now holding less cash than they are required to, would be compelled to extinguish loans worth Rs 90 (and the corresponding sums in the deposit accounts of their borrowers) from their balance sheets. Any increase in credit on account of demonetisation would therefore be completely temporary.

There is more. The textbook money multiplier mechanism assumes that banks fix the overall quantity of credit and its price is determined in the marketplace. In the real world, just the opposite happens: banks fix the price of credit and its quantity is determined in the marketplace by the activities of borrowers. To borrow a terminology developed by Polish economist Michal Kalecki, the quantity of bank credit is demand-determined whereas its price is cost-determined. Commercial banks can always expand their lendable resources by borrowing funds from the RBI at the repo rate fixed by the latter. The repo rate, in turn, sets the floor for lending rates to various bank borrowers.[9] It is only

---

[9] The mark-up added by banks on the floor fixed by the RBI varies with the risk profiles of borrowers. Typically, smaller borrowers pay higher rates than larger borrowers. The mark-up may also depend on the quantum of excess

when the stock of eligible securities with banks, which the RBI requires as collateral in repo transactions, begins to run thin that one can realistically talk in terms of a quantity constraint on their credit-creating capacity.

Surely, there was no quantity constraint for Indian banks before demonetisation. As on 28 October 2016, the stock of government and other approved securities with banks stood at Rs 28,956 billion; this was about 29 per cent of the demand and time liabilities issued to the non-bank public, a figure well in excess of the 20.75 per cent statutory liquidity ratio (SLR) that the banks are required to maintain.[10] There was no constraint on the credit-creating capacity of banks to begin with, and the finance minister's claim that demonetisation would result in an expansion of credit appears grossly exaggerated.

Since the RBI acts as a price fixer in money markets, it seeks to mop up the enlarged cash reserves of banks either by activating its reverse repo window or through the outright sale of government securities.[11] Between 30 November 2016 and 6 December 2016 alone, the RBI had mopped up more than Rs 4 lakh crore from the commercial banking system.[12] The impact of expanded deposit base would, therefore, be not so much to enlarge credit to private borrowers as to shift the ownership of G-Secs and T-Bills from the RBI's balance sheet to that of the banks.

It is hard, then, to see how interest rates in the banking system would fall due to demonetisation; any decline in interest rates would only be transient.

On the other hand, excess liquidity situation, while doing little to improve credit supply, will actually have adverse fiscal implications. This is because the RBI, a public institution whose profits are transferred to the central government budget, will lose its income earning assets

---

reserves held by banks. However, since the current surge in reserves is purely temporary, any reduction in the rate of interest due to demonetisation would be short-lived. In any case, the RBI can directly use the repo rate to influence interest rate structure in the economy. Demonetisation of 86 per cent of the country's currency stock is indeed a curious way of reducing interest rate.

[10] The calculations were made using the data provided by the RBI's *Weekly Statistical Supplement*.

[11] Otherwise, short-term money market rate would fall below the reverse repo rate and undermine RBI's policy stance.

[12] The calculations were made using information from the RBI's press releases.

to commercial banks. Moreover, to the extent that market stabilisation bonds are used to mop up excess reserves from the banking system, interest payments will have to be made directly from the central government budget. The exact magnitude of these costs is anybody's guess at the moment. But if Rs 12 lakh crore is mopped up by the RBI for a period of just one month, assuming an annual interest rate of 6 per cent paid over 12 equal monthly instalments, the total interest outgo of the central government would be about Rs 6,000 crore.[13]

V: Less-Cash Economy

Given the inordinate delay in the printing of new currency, the government has begun a campaign for less-cash banking. It is argued that less-cash banking would formalise a large share of India's informal economy by bringing more firms into the tax net.

To begin with, there is no clear relationship between the currency-to-GDP ratio and what we call as the 'shadow economy,' which is a more appropriate concept to use than informal economy.[14] India had a currency-to-GDP ratio of 12.5 per cent in 2015 (Rogoff 2016). The size of India's shadow economy—using one definition—is estimated at about 21 per cent of its GDP (Schneider, Buehn and Montenegro 2010). Let us take three countries where the currency-to-GDP ratio was either higher or comparable to India's: Japan at 18.6 per cent, Hong Kong at 14.7 per cent and Switzerland at 11.1 per cent. The size of the shadow

[13] Rs 12.44 lakh crore is roughly the amount that returned to the banking system in the form of old notes, as on 10 December 2016. The final amount would, in all probability, be close to Rs 14 lakh crore or Rs 15 lakh crore. From this, we should deduct the amount of new currency that is withdrawn by public. About Rs 4.61 lakh crore was issued in new notes to the public as on 10 December 2016. But the process of releasing new currency has been painfully slow and may continue for many months forcing the banks to hold excessive cash on their balance sheets. Moreover, if demonetisation induces an economic slowdown and a decline in credit offtake, the RBI may well end up mopping up an even higher amount of cash reserves from the banking system.

[14] Schneider, Buehn and Montenegro (2010: 5) define the shadow economy as 'all market-based legal production of goods and services that are deliberately concealed from public authorities' to avoid payment of taxes and social security contributions, to avoid meeting labour market standards and regulations and to avoid complying with administrative requirements of governments, such as filling up of forms.

economy relative to GDP in 2012 was only 8.8 per cent in Japan, 15 per cent in Hong Kong and 7.6 per cent in Switzerland (Schneider, Buehn and Montenegro 2010; Schneider 2011). Now, let us take five countries that had lower currency-to-GDP ratios than India in 2015: South Africa and Brazil at 3.4 per cent, Chile at 3.6 per cent, Indonesia at 4.1 per cent and Mexico at 5.7 per cent. All these countries had a large-sized shadow economy relative to GDP in the second half of the 2000s: 26.8 per cent in South Africa, 38.5 per cent in Brazil, 18.5 per cent in Chile, 19.1 per cent in Indonesia and 28.5 per cent in Mexico.

A higher share of cash in total payments does not necessarily indicate a larger shadow economy. According to a Deutsche Bank study in 2016,

> ... surveys and estimations for different countries show that *a high share of cash in total payments does not always indicate a large shadow sector.* Germany and Austria are cash-intensive countries with relatively small shadow economies. In Sweden, cash payments have become rare but the country still has a mid-sized shadow economy. However, in many cases the degree of cash usage and the size of the shadow economy do seem to be related: Spain, Italy and Greece are characterised by intense cash usage and large shadow economies while countries with relatively low cash usage tend to show low levels of shadow activity (Anglo-Saxon countries as well as Switzerland, the Netherlands or France). Given these diverse findings, it becomes clear that *cash is scarcely the reason for conducting shadow activities* (Mai 2016: 7-8; emphasis added).

Similar, again, is the relationship between corruption and cash. There are cash-intensive countries with lower perceived corruption and less cash-intensive countries with higher perceived corruption. The Corruption Perceptions Index of Transparency International represents the perceived level of public sector corruption on a scale of 0 (highly corrupt) to 100 (very clean). In 2015, the index was higher for many economies with higher currency-GDP ratios (75 for Japan and Hong Kong; 86 for Switzerland; 81 for Germany; 76 for Austria) and lower for many economies with lower currency-GDP ratios (44 for South Africa; 38 for Brazil; 35 for Mexico; 36 for Indonesia).[15]

There are also many reasons why cash is preferred by firms, particularly small and micro-enterprises. Transaction costs in cash transactions are low; in particular, costs of book-keeping are minimised by relying on

---

[15] Transparency International. (2016, February 1). *Corruption Perceptions Index 2015.* Retrieved March 31, 2017, from http://bit.ly/2gPfatY

cash. The use of digital transactions is, on the other hand, expensive as each transaction invites a 2–3 per cent tax. Cash transactions may also be convenient because of the immediacy of realisation without delays of bank transfers. In many cases, informal credit is available to small and micro-enterprises only as cash, and needs to be repaid too as cash. In other words, forcefully formalising a fragile informal sector may actually end up eliminating the minuscule margins on which these firms survive.[16]

Finally, cash leaves no trail, while digital payments leave a trail. For this reason, the potential for state surveillance, violation of privacy and abuse of civil liberties rise significantly with the replacement of cash payments with digital payments. New sources of metadata on everyday transactions of citizens are emerging; big data analytics is increasingly becoming big business. Such personal data of citizens turn into commodities in the grey markets, resulting in a breakdown of trust between the state and its citizens. While strong laws on privacy and cyber-security exist in many western economies, the Indian legal system is marked by the absence of such legal safeguards. The introduction of Aadhaar, and its expansion into the Orwellian idea of India Stack and the JAM (Jan Dhan–Aadhaar–Mobile) trinity, present new threats to the freedoms of Indian people that have not been adequately appreciated in the public discourse on cashless transactions.

VI: Conclusions

In this brief note, we tried to examine the government's claims on the benefits of demonetisation. We argued that (a) the extent of circulation of counterfeit notes in the Indian economy is exaggerated; (b) the claims of unearthing large amounts of black money is unfounded and based on a poorly informed view of what constitutes black money; (c) no improvement in government finances may be expected due to demonetisation; (d) it is unlikely that interest rates in the economy may fall as

---

[16] This is a point also made by Rogoff (2016), who notes that '… for emerging markets and developing economies, it is far from clear that measures to reduce the size of the informal economy by reducing the use of cash will be a net benefit. A great deal of informal employment makes use of workers with low human capital who could not clear the threshold for employment in the formal sector and could not be easily absorbed by firms required to bear the costs of dealing with weak government institutions.'

a consequence of demonetisation; and (e) the movement into a less-cash economy may neither lead to the shrinkage of the shadow economy nor reduce corruption, and, instead, may open up new spaces of surveillance and assaults on the personal freedoms of citizens.

Thus, one finds it extremely difficult to locate any economic logic in the conception and implementation of demonetisation.

References

GoI (2012a), 'Black Money: White Paper', Ministry of Finance, Government of India, New Dehi, May.

GoI (2012b), 'Measures to Tackle Black Money in India and Abroad', Report of the Committee headed by Chairman, Central Board of Direct Taxes (CBDT), Ministry of Finance, Government of India, New Dehi.

GoK (2016), 'Interim Report of the Committee to Study the Impact of Demonetisation on the State Economy of Kerala', Kerala State Planning Board, Government of Kerala, Thiruvananthapuram, December.

Gutmann, P. (1977), 'The Subterranean Economy', *Financial Analysts Journal*, 33 (6), pp. 26-34.

Kumar, Arun (2016), 'Estimation of the Size of the Black Economy in India, 1996-2012', *Economic & Political Weekly*, 51 (48), 26 November.

Mai, Heike (2016), 'Cash, Freedom and Crime', *EU Monitor*, Deutsche Bank AG, Deutsche Bank Research, Frankfurt, November.

NIPFP (1985), 'Aspects of the Black Economy in India', Report submitted to the Ministry of Finance, Government of India, National Institute of Public Finance and Policy, New Delhi.

PMO (2016), 'PM's Address to the Nation', available at http://www.pmindia.gov.in/en/news_updates/prime-ministers-address-to-the-nation, accessed on 17th December 2016.

RBI (2016), *Annual Report 2015–16*, Chapter 8, Reserve Bank of India, Mumbai.

Rogoff, Kenneth S. (2016), *The Curse of Cash*, Princeton University Press, Princeton and Oxford.

Schneider, F., Buehn, A. and Montenegro, C.E. (2010), 'Shadow Economies All Over the World: New Estimates for 162 Countries from 1999 to 2007', Policy Research Working Paper 5356, Development Research Group, World Bank, Washington.

Schneider, F. (2012), 'Size and Development of the Shadow Economy of 31 European and 5 Other OECD Countries from 2003 to 2012: Some New Facts', Unpublished Note, available at http://www.econ.jku.at/members/Schneider/files/publications/2012/ShadEcEurope31.pdf.

16

The Problem of Fake Indian Currency Notes

A Process Oriented View

Amitava Bandyopadhyay, Ranjan Sett and Dipak K. Manna

The system for containment of FICN problem is reviewed. It is argued that effective solution mechanism lies in process view of the problem with appropriate governance model for continuous monitoring.

Currency counterfeiting is a dangerous crime. More so in India as national security agencies suspect that fake Indian currency notes (FICN) are used for terror financing. Making counterfeiting difficult by improving security features; increasing public awareness to make transactions difficult; flushing out fake notes quickly through improved detection; and restricting entry to the Indian economy at the outset through improved vigil are some of the steps introduced by the government to contain the problem. However, the quantum of FICN in circulation needs to be estimated to assess the effectiveness of these measures and to assess security risk realistically.

The estimates on the value of FICN in circulation have been judgmental, bereft of quantitative method, with sharply divided opinions across different agencies. Some estimates were alarmingly large. An *India Today* report pegged the quantum at Rs 90,000 crore with a scary comment that 10–20 per cent of the currency notes in circulation could be fake (Bhupta, 2009). Unfortunately, even policy debates regarding FICN were dominated by anecdotes rather than systematic compilation and analyses of data.

Under these circumstances, the Economic Intelligence Unit (EIC) formed a working group in 2013 to examine the FICN problem more objectively. Members from different agencies like National Investigation Agency (NIA), Central Bureau of Investigation (CBI), National Crime Records Bureau (NCRB), Central Economic Intelligence Bureau (CEIB), Directorate of Revenue Intelligence (DRI), Department of Economic Affairs (DEA), Financial Intelligence Unit (FIU), and Reserve Bank of India (RBI) were co-opted. The NIA was identified as the nodal agency and the Indian Statistical Institute (ISI) was inducted for estimation and methodology development.

After much deliberation on alternative approaches, their feasibility and risks, the job was entrusted to the ISI towards the end of 2014. The ISI was mandated to study the system and develop a methodology to address the FICN problem in its entirety (covering aspects like data capture, regular analysis and initiation of timely corrective action) within a stipulated time. The other agencies were expected to provide data, offer valuable experience and comments, examine the assumptions critically and assess feasibility. The ISI was represented by the present authors.

In this chapter, we review the system for containment of the FICN problem and look at the way ahead. It is primarily based on the authors' experience gained during the study.

The Problem in Perspective

Containing FICN problem requires controlling both its inflow and circulation on a continual basis. *Seizing* counterfeit currency before it enters the economy; *detecting* these notes quickly; and *using* performance measures to strengthen the seizure and detection systems judiciously are the major activities to address the problem.[1] Clearly, this problem does not have a one-shot solution. It must be understood

---

[1] Seizure refers to discovery of fake notes generally in bulk, aided most often by intelligence input, before it gets into circulation along with genuine notes in the economy. Detection applies to identification of fake note(s) during regular transaction typically a few in numbers. Both seizure and detection together is referred to as recovery.

that the problem demands continuous monitoring. In other words, the problem should be recognised as a process in operation over time seeking actions for improvement. Deming's plan–do–study–act (PDSA) cycle (Moen and Norman 2010) is an important management tool, and is proposed here to design the solution system. Accordingly, the activities listed above are identified and connected as a process using PDSA cycle (Figure 16.1).

Improper implementation of any of these activities weakens the structure of the solution system and reduces its effectiveness. Such failure is attributable more to governance than technical issues. Estimation of the value of FICN in circulation, though important, is just one activity of the entire solution system. Absence of a proper governance structure is the major issue—far more likely to exacerbate the problem than technical issues related to just estimation.

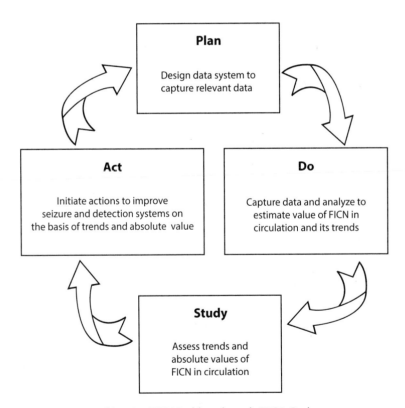

FIGURE 16.1 Addressing FICN Problem through PDSA Cycle

System Study

Examination of the prevailing system for FICN problem with respect to PDSA cycle uncovered ample opportunities for improvements in areas like data system design, methods of compilation and estimation, trend analysis and initiation of actions.

Data System

Recovery of FICN is being carried out by a number of organizations. The CBI, Border Security Force (BSF), NIA and state police from the ministry of home affairs and DRI, customs and CEIB from the ministry of finance carry out seizures while commercial banks and the RBI are the primary detection agents. However, many other agencies like post offices, railway reservation counters, etc, handling large volumes of cash were found to be missing from the prevailing system. Inclusion of the same was kept at abeyance for the time being due to lengthy underlying administrative procedures.

Review

The data capture system lacked periodic review to ensure its continuing suitability and effectiveness.

Data Compilation, Estimation and Trend Analysis

The system did not have provisions to compile local recovery data to get quick assessments of possible risky situations. This was pointed out but could not be addressed due to implementation complexities at that instant. Further, an institutional system to carry out in-depth analysis periodically was absent. Even the ISI study appeared to be a one-time affair. In the absence of an institutionalised system, effectiveness of policy actions like improving security features of currencies cannot be judged meaningfully.

Data Flow

Retaining NCRB as the data warehouse, an unambiguous data system for capturing and reporting recovery was developed (Figure 16.2). This involved (a) elimination of inconsistencies in the direction of data flow

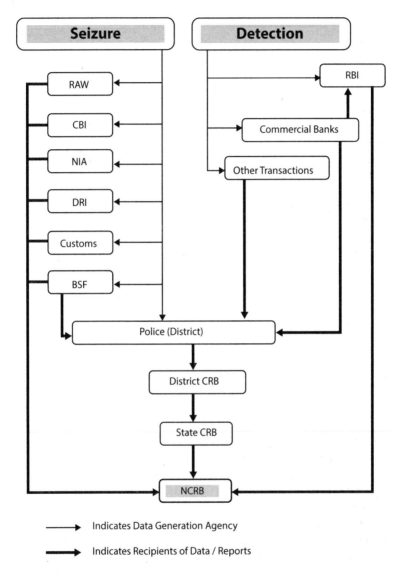

FIGURE 16.2   Proposed System for FICN Seizure and Detection Data

(by design, NCRB was practically kept excluded from getting seizure data), (b) resolution of some issues connected to non-reporting or irregular reporting, (c) prevention of mix-up between seizure and detection data, and (d) designing new formats for data capturing and reporting.

Estimation Methodology

The volume of seizure indicates the intensity of current counterfeiting activity. It is true that with an efficient seizure system, there is likely to be very little FICN left in the circulation. However, information on the current stock of fake currency circulating in the economy is extremely important as it measures the efficacy of the seizure system. This leads us to examine the detection data for estimation of fake currency in circulation.

Towards this, US Treasury (2000) is possibly the pioneer proposing two methods: 'parts-found-in-processing (PFP)' and 'life-of-counterfeit (LOC).' Chant (2004) enumerates the strengths and weakness of these methods and develops a composite method (COMP) by taking advantage of both to provide estimates for 2001 in Canada. Bose and Das (2013) examine the above methods including others for possible application in India. They note that '... (they) are having certain obvious limitations,' and proceed on to propose an *inverse sampling* method for the purpose.

This method was deliberated in the working group, but was found to be unsuitable. Consequently, a new methodology for FICN problem is called for.

Counterfeit notes, under circulation, are transacted like any genuine currency. Their movement is likely to be random (till detection) and in the long run the notes would be spread equally across across different sectors of the economy. Detection data, captured at the present only by commercial banks and the RBI (Figure 16.2), may be examined to provide a scientific estimate.

A pictorial representation of the process of detection of counterfeit notes by (commercial) banks and the RBI (central bank) is given in Figure 16.3. It is noted that some counterfeits may remain undetected while passing through the banks establishing that detection efficiency is strictly less that 100 per cent. Further, some notes in circulation may not get into the banking system at all in a given period of time while some others may enter more than once.

Taking these into account, a new methodology has been developed for estimation of FICN in circulation. Its salient features are as follows:

- The method applies to currency notes of any denomination of interest;
- Meaningful estimates can be obtained from the prevailing data system in the banking sector;

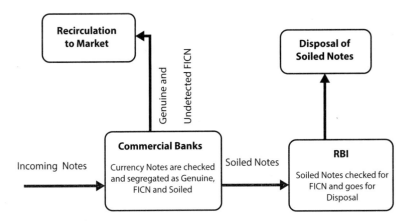

FIGURE 16.3 Flow Diagram of FICN Detection by Commercial Banks and RBI

- Detection efficiency at the RBI, while processing the soiled notes, is considered to be 99 per cent;
- Detection efficiency at bank is unknown, but less that 100%. This efficiency can be estimated denomination-wise.

Estimates

FICN of lower denominations being extremely rare, the interest had been on the denominations of Rs 100, Rs 500 and Rs 1,000. Based on five years' data starting from 2010–11, the estimates were worked out (Table 16.1).

Required input data from the banks and RBI were generally clean except for heavily under-reported detection data from the public sector

TABLE 16.1 FICN Estimates

Year	FICN Rate (PPM)	Value of FICN (Rs crore)
2010–11	232	291.55
2011–12	265	405.90
2012–13	262	426.88
2013–14	229	382.35
2014–15	235	414.94

banks, and lack of readily available data on cash transactions at the banks. Redress of the same would lead to higher reliability of the estimates.

Discussion and Conclusion

We have reviewed the system for controlling FICN problem. Now, we discuss the way forward.

Implication of the Estimates

With Rs 13.68 lakh crore of *notes in circulation* (NIC) during 2014–15, FICN turned out to be just 0.03 per cent of the total volume of cash. Putting another way, the average loss is less than Rs 4 per Indian resident in the year. Further, seizure data suggested that the rate of attempted infusion of FICN to be Rs 70 crore or about 0.005 per cent of the NIC. Thus, both the value of FICN in circulation and that being infused are minuscule compared to the size of the Indian economy.

As seen in the Table 16.1, the value of FICN in circulation during the period of study is about Rs 400 crore—an insignificant figure indeed, which looks totally in disagreement with *India Today's* report in 2009. The very finding is now corroborated by RBI (2017) after demonetisation. Incidentally, at about the same time, a section of media (e.g., Nayak 2017 in *Economic Times*, Jain 2017 in *Jagran*) put forward the corresponding figure at Rs 23,235 crore, out of nowhere, without disclosing either the source or the method of estimation. A back-of-the-envelope calculation suggests that it translates to getting on the average 3 FICN in every 200 notes (i.e., two bundles of any denomination). Since most of us are yet to find a single fake note in our lifetime, this sounds absurd!

The fact that FICN in circulation and that being infused are low does not mean that it is not a threat. In certain regions the rate of occurrence could be alarming. However, the current system does not permit region-wise stratification of data to get an idea about this threat—essentially a governance failure. Further, any laxity on the part of security agencies to intercept and seize FICN may encourage counterfeiting and intensify the problem in the long run.

Immediate Action

As mentioned earlier, a number of cash-intensive sectors like registration offices, post offices, railway reservation counters and cooperative banks, etc, are yet to be included in the FICN data system. Action must be initiated to bring them suitably into the system, and leading to a revision of Figure 16.2 as well as estimation methodology accordingly. Specific data capture systems may be implemented at a few strategic points (banks, post offices, etc, at select locations) to regularly get quick estimates and trends. This is all the more important in the post-demonetisation scenario since counterfeits of newly designed currency of Rs 2,000 have already come to the notice of the Government of India.

Data Quality

A system must be introduced to improve upon data quality, namely, completeness, timeliness, accuracy and configurability.

Lessons Learned

We conclude this chapter with the following final remarks.

- *Continuity:* The FICN problem is ongoing and demands continuous monitoring. Hence, the PDSA cycle is a very important candidate for improvement.
- *Process view:* Providing effective solutions to an ongoing problem like this requires that all the associated entities be connected with the process view (Hammer 1990) rather than a system suffering from a *functional silo syndrome.*
- *Governance:* Three essential issues requiring focus are (i) allocation of resources, responsibilities and authorities (for data capture, analysis, reporting and actions); (ii) review system to ensure continuing suitability and effectiveness of different procedures; and (iii) encapsulation of knowledge to minimise dependence on experts on a regular basis (i.e., development of estimation systems on the basis of data that can be used by non-technical persons).

In short, switching over to a data-based, systemic and ongoing solution rather than the present event management-oriented, expert opinion driven method is likely to bring about huge improvement.

References

Bhupta, Malini. (2009): 'Fake Currency: The New Threat,' *India Today*, 6 February 2009.

Bose, S. and A Das (2013): 'Estimation of Counterfeit Currency Notes in India—Alternative Methodologies,' RBI Working Paper No. 03/2013, Department of Economic and Policy Research, RBI.

Chant, John (2004): 'Counterfeiting: A Canadian Perspective,' Bank of Canada Working Paper 2004-33.

Hammer, M. (1990): 'Reengineering Work: Don't Automate, Obliterate,' *Harvard Business Review*, July-August, pp 104-112.

Jain, Surabhi (2017): 'RBI Annual Report says 762,072 Fake Notes Detected in 2017', Jagran, 31 August 2017.

Moen, Ronald D. and Clifford L. Norman. (2010): 'Circling Back: Clearing the Myths about Deming Cycle and Seeing How It Keeps Evolving,' *Quality Progress*, Vol 43, No 11, pp 22-28.

Nayak, Gayatri (2017): 'Fake Notes More than Double of what was Estimated: RBI', *Economic Times*, 30 August 2017.

Reserve Bank of India (2017): 'Annual Report—VIII. Currency Management', 30 August 2017, https://www.rbi.org.in/scripts/AnnualReportPublications. aspx?Id=1208.

U.S. Department of Treasury (2000): 'The Use and Counterfeiting of United States Currency Abroad,' February 2000.

17

Negative Interest Rates

Symptom of Crisis or Instrument for Recovery?

C.P. Chandrasekhar

A near-unprecedented turn to negative interest rates to trigger a recovery has characterised the monetary policy in several developed countries and in Europe. This is the result of a shift away from a fiscal policy to an almost exclusive reliance on monetary policy, involving quantitative easing and low interest rates, in macroeconomic interventions across the globe. The failure of this macroeconomic stance has led to the phenomenon of negative rates in countries other than the United States, and the first sign of even a partial recovery in that country has been enough to set off a reversal.

A bizarre phenomenon has characterised several developed capitalist economies since 2014—negative interest rates. Depositors, principally banks, holding deposits with central banks in Europe, Japan and elsewhere, as well as retail customers holding deposits in Post Finance, Switzerland's fifth largest commercial bank owned by its postal service,[1] are being penalised rather than being rewarded when they hold deposits. This is unprecedented. Evidence collated by Homer and Scylla (2005) suggests that there is no observed instance of negative interest rates in the 5,000 years preceding its recent occurrence.

---

[1] *See* Atkins 2016.

It is, of course, difficult for commercial banks to impose negative interest rates on their depositors, who may then choose to hold cash. So in the first instance, this penalty tends to be imposed by central banks which set policy rates on banks that choose to hold deposits with the former. The message sought to be sent out is that banks are supposed to use available resources to lend, and not to earn a small return from depositing that money with the central bank. The process was triggered by the European Central Bank (ECB), which in June 2014 reduced its deposit facility rate to –0.1 per cent,[2] to address stagnation and deflation in the region. Since then, many national central banks, such as those in Denmark, Sweden, Switzerland and Japan, have moved the interest 'paid' on part of the deposits with them, to negative territory. This shows that the widespread trend observed after the Great Recession set in around 2008, for policy rates to be cut to stall and reverse the downturn, has gone so far in some countries that rates have breached the zero-barrier. The ECB itself has in three steps cut its deposit rate to –0.2 per cent, –0.3 per cent and –0.4 per cent in September 2014, December 2015, and March 2016 respectively (Figure 17.1, Figure 17.2, Figure 17.3).

I: Implications of Negative Interest Rates

The implications of negative interest rates are obvious. They discourage the holding of deposits by rendering them not just barren like cash, but going further and penalising those who chose to hold deposits rather than use the purchasing power that they represent. So this would push holders of purchasing power who do not want to immediately use it, to either hoard it in the form of cash or invest it in safe assets that offer a positive return. The first port of call for investments we should expect would be risk-free government bonds.

This results in another bizarre development. When depositors are pushed into investing their money in safe assets such as domestic and foreign government bonds that offer positive rates, this causes large increases in bond prices. On the one hand, the current yield on a bond, which is the ratio of a fixed annual coupon payment due on the bond to its current market price, falls as its price rises. On the other, when a bond is held to maturity, the bondholder is repaid not the prevailing

---

[2] Negative rates were to apply also to average reserve holdings in excess of the minimum reserve requirements.

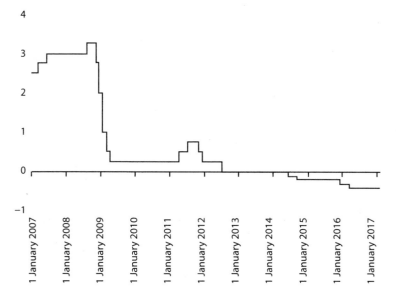

Figure 17.1 ECB Deposit Facility Interest Rate (%)
Source: https://www.ecb.europa.eu/stats/policy_and_exchange_rates/key_ecb_interest_rates/html/index.en.html.

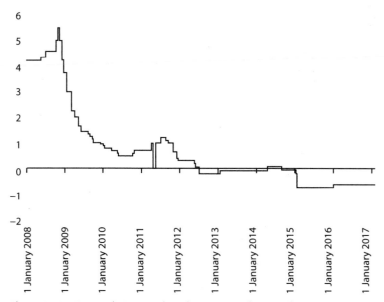

Figure 17.2 Danmarks National Bankrates—Certificates of Deposit (%)
Source: http://nationalbanken.statbank.dk/nbf/99541.

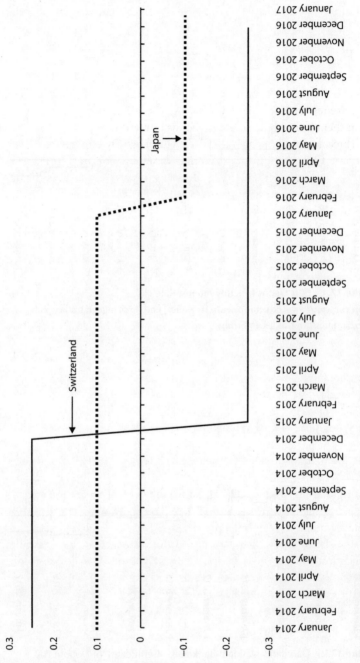

Figure 17.3 Policy Rates of Central Banks in Switzerland and Japan (% pa)

market price, but the par or face value of the bond. So if an investor buys into a bond when its price is ruling high relative to its par value, its yield if held to maturity can be negative since the coupon payments due till maturity and the par value do not cover the high price paid for its acquisition. That is, bond yields turn negative as well. This condition is unprecedented. But bond preference has in recent months been so high that yields in countries like Japan, Germany and France entered negative territory, with investors paying the governments for borrowing from them if they hold sovereign bonds to maturity.

Three factors, among others, explain large investments in bonds in some Organisation for Economic Co-operation and Development (OECD) countries despite the promise of negative yields. First, the late adoption of central bank quantitative easing (QE) policies in Japan and Europe, involving large purchases of government bonds. These countries opted initially for interest rate cuts to spur recovery. This was especially true in Europe, where some members of the monetary union considered it inappropriate for the ECB to buy sovereign bonds of member countries, as they feared it would encourage a lax fiscal stance. It was only in early 2015 that the bond buying policy adopted by the United States (US) and the United Kingdom (UK) in the wake of the Great Recession was followed by the ECB, since it was clear that interest rate reductions had not been successful in addressing stagflation. When the Japanese central bank and the ECB shifted to buying bonds to infuse liquidity, the demand for bonds rose irrespective of yield, raising prices.

Second, the demand for bonds rose because of the uncertainty created by the recession, and the financial turmoil that followed was such that the cost and/or risk of holding deposits, or more cash, was seen as high enough to warrant turning to no-risk or low-risk government bonds and even to investment grade corporate bonds, despite their rising prices.

Third, inflation was at such a low that the real (inflation adjusted) loss of holding negative-yielding bonds may not have been as large even when compared with losses that may have been suffered on positive-yielding bonds in high inflation periods.

The rise in bond prices that results from the increase in demand for bonds leads in turn to a sharp rise in the volume of negative-yielding bonds, especially government bonds, being held by investors. By July 2016, Citi had estimated that around a third of developed country government debt was trading at negative yields (Karaian 2016). That figure was placed at 45 per cent by October 2016 (Reuters 2016). This peculiar feature soon characterised some investment grade corporate bonds as well, as investors bought into them despite higher risks, because they offered a higher positive current yield than government bonds. Estimates of the total market value of negative-yielding bonds vary, since estimation involves identifying such bonds based on some gauge of their prevailing market value (converted into a common currency, if necessary, at some exchange rate). Bloomberg, for example, reports that the total value of such bonds rose from $476 billion in August 2014 to a peak level of $12.2 trillion in June 2016 (Figure 17.4) (Kuntz 2016, 2016a).

As is clear from Figure 17.5, most of these bonds were sovereign bonds, and had been bought in Japan, followed by Europe. As on 30 September 2016, of the total face value of $11.6 trillion of negative-yielding investment grade bonds in the broad Bloomberg–Barclays index, $5.7 trillion originated in Japan and $5.5 trillion in Europe. Further, $9.9 trillion of these bonds, or more than 85 per cent were sovereign bonds (Figure 17.6, Figure 17.7) (Kuntz 2016).

Underlying this trend is a much more proactive role for monetary policy in countering deflationary trends. Thus, in the March 2016 move by the ECB, besides reducing the interest it pays on deposits or the negative rate from –0.3 per cent to –0.4 per cent, it offered zero interest loans to banks, with the promise that if they use that money to lend 2.5 per cent or more than they were previously doing, then the ECB would pay them the equivalent of 0.4 per cent of what they borrowed from it as interest. In sum, the central bank is promising to

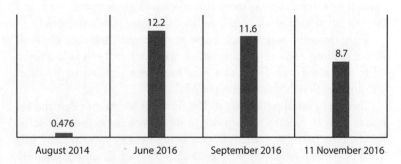

Figure 17.4   Value of Negative Yield Government and Investment Grade Corporate Bonds—Bloomberg ($ trillion)
Source: Bloomberg from Kuntz (2016, 2016a).

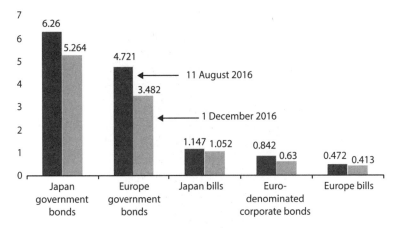

Figure 17.5 Value of Negative Yield Bonds by Type—Fitch ($ trillion)
Source: Fitch ratings from Samson (2016).

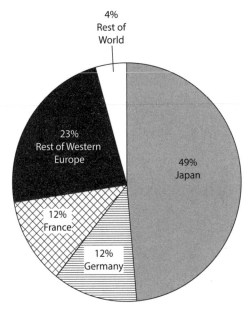

Figure 17.6 Distribution of Negative-yielding Bonds by Location on
30 September 2016
Source: Bloomberg from Kuntz (2016).

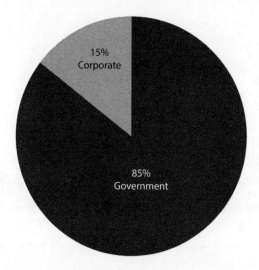

Figure 17.7   Distribution of Negative-yielding Bonds by Type on
30 September 2016
Source: Bloomberg from Kuntz (2016).

pay banks that borrow from it, so long as they increase their lending
to households and firms.

The motivation for negative deposit rates is clearly to pressure or
persuade banks to lend rather than hold on to reserves with the central
bank. This was not the first time that central banks have opted for such
a policy (the Swedish Riksbank had flirted with it in 2009–10). But this
time around, the tendency spread fast, with more countries adopting
action along these lines.

II: From Private Debt to Public Debt

There are two questions to be answered here. The first is why this phenomenon that was initially seen as a freak occurrence—negative interest
rates—has recurred across a wide swathe of developed countries and
persisted for so long. The second is why the US has been relatively free
of this phenomenon, though US interest rates have been near zero for a
considerable period of time.[3]

---

[3] At one point, even Janet Yellen told a Congressional hearing, that the Fed
would, if it found it necessary, consider this option. *See* Smialek 2016.

The answer to the first question seems to lie in two factors, which together account for the spread of the phenomenon across developed countries. One is the mechanism underlying the pre-2008 boom in industrialised countries and the resulting crisis. The other is the nature of the post-crisis stimulus in much of the developed world. During the pre-2008 boom in the developed world, a financial surge triggered real economy growth based on a debt- financed explosion in housing investments and consumption, which fed on itself. Based on the premise that financial innovation led by securitisation had managed to distribute risk and dissolve it, the financial sector not only substantially increased credit provision in the system but also did so by expanding the universe of borrowers and bringing into its ambit those who were unlikely to be able to bear the burden of that debt. In the event, the proportion of potential defaulters in the borrower universe increased substantially, leading to the bursting of the credit bubble. Once the crisis occurred, even if the banks were rescued, unless the government restructured the debt of borrowers, as opposed to only the balance sheet of the lenders (the banks and financial firms), demand would not revive. But little was done to restructure and reduce household debt, and restore employment, incomes and household balance sheets to the pre-crisis situation.

Close examination suggests that as the response aimed at resolving the financial crisis unfolded, the ability of the system to address and deal with crisis of the real economy was subverted. As noted, an important characteristic of capitalist growth in the late 1990s and the first decade of this century was that it was driven by debt-financed private investment (largely in housing) and consumption, riding on a series of asset price bubbles in stock, housing, and real estate markets. The bubbles, by making people feel that they were richer than anticipated, encouraged and fuelled debt-financed consumption. This, of course, served the interests of increasingly dominant finance capital, which could argue that it was serving as the engine of a new economy, while deriving huge returns in various forms from the process.

This trend was accompanied by an ideological push to legitimise the role of private capital in general and finance capital in particular, and delegitimise the role of the State that was increasingly portrayed as being over-intrusive, inefficient and responsible for inflation and slow growth. An important component of such advocacy was the position that the State should substantially limit its tendency to resort to debt-financed public expenditures, partly on the ground that this was inflationary. This had as its corollary, an appreciation of the role of financial expansion in spurring debt-financed private expenditure.

The resulting shift from public expenditure to debt-financed private expenditure as the stimulus for growth, and the defence of that shift in the form of an initially ascendant and now dominant neo-liberal ideology, has had important implications for the ability of the system to deal with the Great Recession. In the first instance, having opposed large unrequited public expenditures, especially bailouts, finance capital had to find ways of justifying the huge demand it had to make on taxpayers' money to save itself. Declaring the financial crisis as being an exceptional, unpredictable, and almost unprecedented event, financial firms (especially those located in the US) garnered for themselves huge support from the State, which in their view, was not supposed to intervene in markets. Even if taxpayers were to bear the burden of this systemic bailout over time, governments in the developed countries had, in the first instance, to borrow heavily, and central banks had to loosen their monetary strings.

This had two implications. On the one hand, public deficits and the public debt to gross domestic product (GDP) ratio shot up, as governments borrowed to finance 'stimulus packages' that were substantial cash infusions to save financial firms. On the other hand, the financial firms being rescued, used access to this zero interest liquidity provided against worthless collateral to buy into this public debt with positive returns, and quickly returned to profitability. So governments got increasingly indebted and the financial firms being rescued accumulated a part of the bonds issued to finance debt. In sum, what was a private debt problem when the crisis began turned into a public debt problem once the financial firms were saved from bankruptcy.

So long as debt was being incurred largely to save finance, all objections to excessive public borrowing were buried. Problems arose when, having saved the banks and financial firms, governments turned their attention to restoring growth and strengthening safety nets for those who had been rendered unemployed and/or were hit badly by the crisis. At this point, the traditional hostility of finance against government deficits and public debt came to the fore, aggravated by the fear that at least some governments that were hit by the crisis might default on their debt.

III: Monetary Policy as Principal Instrument for Recovery

What was surprising was that governments succumbed to the pressure not to use debt-financed fiscal spending as a means of stimulating a recovery. This made monetary policy measures, such as liquidity infusion and interest rate reduction, the principal instruments to combat recession and spur recovery. The US Federal Reserve (Fed) boosted its balance sheet from around $800 million to more than $4 trillion by 2014. Capital was made available at extremely low, near-zero interest rates. Once the crisis spread to Europe, this policy was adopted there as well.

This turn-in policy clearly ignored the lessons from the run-up to the 2008 crisis. As noted earlier, the crisis was the culmination of a trajectory of growth in which debt-financed private investment and consumption provided the demand-side stimulus for growth. As a result, private sector balance sheets were overburdened with debt that firms and households found difficult to service in the midst of a recession. It was unlikely that the private sector would once again be able to increase its borrowing substantially. What was needed, therefore, was more emphasis on raising demand with increased public expenditure, and not a return to monetary policies aimed at creating another bubble.

Implicit in the dependence on monetary policy is the idea that private debt at low interest rates would substitute for public debt to revive demand and growth. The problem is that this expected outcome is not being realised, partly because firms and households already overburdened with debt are not confident of raising earnings to levels needed to service additional debt. The flipside of this is that banks and other financial institutions are less willing to lend because of the fear of default. Since monetary policy is directed in the first instance at these institutions, the reliance on such policies even when they are not effective has had some bizarre effects (Chandrasekhar and Ghosh 2016).

One such effect is the movement of rates to negative territory, reflecting the desperation of governments, which find that deep rate cuts have not had the desired effects of stalling the downturn and ensuring a recovery. One form the tendency takes is for central banks to set their policy rates, which signal their monetary stance, below zero. Thus, negative rates are the consequence of policymakers betting on interest rate cuts to drive growth through multiple channels. To start with, they expect bank lending rates to come down and encourage households and firms to spend and/or invest more, raising demand. Second, investors not wanting to pay governments for holding their money are expected to turn to asset markets like the stock market. That would raise financial asset prices and trigger the oft-cited 'wealth effect.' With the value of paper or real assets rising, holders of those assets would be encouraged to spend more today rather than add further to accumulated wealth, spurring demand. Finally, since low and negative interest rates in a country would discourage foreign investors from investing in bonds and financial assets in the country concerned, the currency can depreciate, improving the competitiveness of exports.[4]

As noted, these expectations are not being realised. Households and firms being still burdened with debt are wary about borrowing more, and banks are cautious of increasing their exposure to them even if pushed by the central bank. Recent evidence suggests that consumers have increased their savings and reduced their debts in Denmark, Sweden, and Switzerland (Pozen 2016). In Japan too, consumers are reportedly saving more. One reason could be that negative interest rates may be seen as a signal of bad times ahead, encouraging individuals and households to forego consumption today to insure themselves against impending hardships. Moreover, lower interest rates are not the best instrument at driving investment, and definitely not during a recession. A study of corporate investment in the US over 1952–2010 has found that: 'Investment grows rapidly following high profits and stock returns but, contrary to standard predictions, is largely unrelated to recent changes in market volatility, interest rates, or the default spread on corporate bonds,' and that adjusting the interest rate by 1 per cent or 2 per cent does not generate a change in the investment behaviour of corporations (Kothari *et al.* 2015).

Finally, even the expectation that capital flows out of a country that is adopting a policy of pushing interest rates below zero, could depreciate its exchange rate, improving export competitiveness and assisting growth, has also been belied. With many countries relying on interest rate cuts, the effective depreciation of currencies, while significant vis-à-vis the dollar, is more or less the same for each of them against the dollar. That neutralises the competitiveness benefits from depreciation relative to the dollar, with little chance of an export boom.

While interest rates cuts, which take them below the 'zero barrier' have had limited or no effect, there is concern about the effect that negative rates can have on financial markets. They could trigger a shift to stocks away from bonds and set off another speculative spiral in stock markets. Negative rates are likely to adversely affect bank profits as well.

---

[4] Rogoff (2016), who as discussed later is a votary of doing away with the 'zero bound' on the interest rate, also sees the advantages of negative rates being delivered through these routes.

While banks need to pay depositors a reasonable rate to attract their savings into deposits, the low interest environment and pressure to lend requires them to cut rates they charge their borrowers. The result is a squeeze on margins. The effect this could have on financial markets is still uncertain. In short, there are grounds to believe that, while negative rates, being the result of the ineffectiveness of interest rate reduction as a means to spur recovery, are themselves ineffective, they can lead to financial instability.

IV: Why Take This Unsual Stance?

Why then are central banks and governments opting for this unusual stance? It is partly because they are trapped by their own macroeconomic stance. In his famous 1943 essay on the 'Political Aspects of Full Employment,' Michal Kalecki had argued that the opposition to government spending in capitalist economies leads to dependence on stimulating private investment through other means such as reducing interest rates or cutting taxes. But this, he noted, can have bizarre consequences. If, for example, the rate of interest or income tax is reduced in a slump (to counter it) but not increased in the subsequent boom (to keep it going),

> ...the boom will last longer, but it must end in a new slump: one reduction in the rate of interest or income tax does not, of course, eliminate the forces which cause cyclical fluctuations in a capitalist economy. In the new slump it will be necessary to reduce the rate of interest or income tax again and so on. Thus in not too remote a time the rate of interest would have to be negative and income tax would have to be replaced by an income subsidy. (Kalecki 1943–71: 143)

In the current context, the problem is not that the interest rate that was reduced during the slump was not raised during an ensuing boom. The problem is that large reductions in policy interest rates when they were in positive territory did not counter the slump. But since governments have forsaken completely the option of relying on the fiscal lever to manoeuvre a recovery, they have no choice but to continue reducing interest rates, which have finally entered negative territory. But that too seems unlikely to trigger growth in the foreseeable future. It is only increasing the prospects of another financial bust.

Yet, there are leading advocates of negative interest rates. Some even have a reason why they make the case, but with no real justification based on how it would work. In a November 2013 speech, Lawrence Summers argued against the 'zero lower bound'—the perception that interest rates once at zero, cannot be reduced further. To quote a summary of his view, 'in a typical slump, the Federal Reserve encourages borrowing by reducing the interest rate to substantially below the rate of inflation, so people are effectively being paid to take out loans. (In economic jargon, that's a 'negative real interest rate.') But interest rates cannot be much below inflation when the inflation rate itself is close to zero, as it is now' (Coy and Philips 2013). Since in Summers' view the interest rate would need to be 2 or 3 percentage points lower than the inflation rate to get the economy going, 'when the inflation rate was just 1.2 per cent and the federal funds rate was kept in the range of 0–0.25 per cent, the economy was bound to be stuck in a rut' (Coy and Philips 2013). Hence, in his view, 'it may be necessary to deal with a world where the zero lower bound is a chronic and systemic inhibitor' (Coy and Philips 2013). Ben Bernanke (2016) too has expressed similar views, arguing in fact that raising the inflation target may not be a good alternative for negative interest rates.

Kenneth Rogoff (2016) also agrees, and his book *The Curse of Cash* is focused on finding ways of mitigating the 'zero bound' or 'taking it off the table.' The zero bound in Rogoff's view is now a major problem, since negative interest rates are the only way of restoring post-recession growth given the consequences (errors?) of monetary policy and the global environment. One of these consequences is the collapse in inflation, because of 'inflation targeting evangelism,' with central banks coalescing around an inflation target of around 2 per cent. This brings down inflation expectations as well, making it difficult to get real interest rates down without breaching the zero bound. Another is a substantial increase in economic volatility in contemporary capitalism, which requires governments to resort to negative interest rates when recessions are deep, as was the case after 2008. A third is that a 'global savings glut' of the kind Bernanke popularised, with blame attributed to China and other emerging markets, which has brought 'normal' real interest rates lower the world over. Using the interest rate mechanism to affect other variables will therefore require reducing nominal rates below zero.

The misuse of the notion of a savings glut to explain the crisis caused by financial deregulation and the speculative frenzy it triggered has been dealt with elsewhere (Patnaik 2010) and need not detain us here. Besides that, the argument seems to be that the volatility generated by the rise of finance and the single-minded dependence on monetary policy should be addressed through monetary measures such as shrinking cash transactions and doing away with the zero bound that can increase instability even more. This is advocated despite the fact that monetary measures that were sacred to neo-liberal macroeconomists such as 'inflation-targeting evangelism' have proved to be a part of the problem and not the solution.

V: The US Puzzle

This brings us to the second question raised earlier as to why the US has not had the same experience as Japan and Europe of being pushed into breaching the zero bound. While the US too has seen a long period during which huge volumes of liquidity have been pumped into the economy and interest rates kept at near zero, unlike Europe and Japan, it has not had to reach a stage where interest rates had to turn negative. This is partly because of the fact that though the 2008 financial crisis broke in the US, and then spread to Europe and elsewhere, it is the one country so affected that has been able to stall the downturn and even ensure a slight recovery.

According to the June 2016 survey of the US economy, the OECD (2016) estimates that relative to the pre-crisis peak (in 2008 Quarter 1 or Q1), US GDP in Q4 of 2015 was 10.6 per cent higher. Over the same period, the euro area's GDP was 0.06 per cent lower and Japan's 0.37 per cent lower. However, even in the US, not all sections have benefited from the recovery. Writing in June 2016, Baker (2016) argued:

> Employment rates are down from prerecession levels even among prime age (25–54) workers with college and advanced degrees. In spite of strong recent job growth, the labour market remains weak. The weakness shows up in wages. The high unemployment of the recession years led to a huge income shift from wages to profits.

This together with the fact that the balance sheets of households and firms are still burdened with debt means that reducing interest rates is not likely to raise demand significantly. However, the access to zero interest credit has not only stabilised the banking system, but set off a boom in the financial assets markets. That boom has been strengthened by the flight to safety to dollar-denominated assets of the world's wealth holders and the appreciation of the dollar that followed. This would trigger an increase in household wealth and affect consumption and investment decisions (OECD 2015).

The US has possibly benefited from this in terms of growth, reducing the pressure to take interest rates to negative territory. The ratio of net worth to disposable income of households and nonprofits in the US, which had fallen sharply from its peak in late–2007, has more or less regained its pre-recession peak (Figure 17.8).

In fact now, low inflation and changed expectations on growth in the US have encouraged the Fed to not just go back on QE, but to raise interest rates as well. On 14 December 2016, the Fed raised the federal funds rate by one quarter of a percentage point, taking its target band for short-term interest rates to between 0.5 per cent and 0.75 per cent. More importantly, it signalled a change in the stance of monetary policy by suggesting that there are likely to be three more rate hikes over 2017, and predicting that the long-term interest rate, which has been in decline, would rise to 3 per cent.

There has been a growing consensus that the Fed has continued with a loose monetary policy, with near zero interest rates and ample liquidity, for far too long. Yet macroeconomic policy in the US has remained trapped in its monetary mire. But politics seems to have offered the Fed an escape route (Chandrasekhar and Ghosh 2017). The real reason that the Fed has chosen this time to go the way it should on the interest rate front is the perception that political circumstances have shifted focus from monetary to fiscal policy when it comes to spurring growth. The source of this conviction is the Donald Trump campaign that promised to cut taxes and boost infrastructural spending to stimulate growth.

If the economic platform that promised such a stimulus, which gave Trump his victory, is implemented, it would amount to a major reversal in the macroeconomic stance adopted by developed countries for quite some time now. Trump claims that what needs to be done is to stimulate demand and incentivise private investment with tax cuts, and drive growth and jobs with substantially enhanced infrastructural spending. The logic of how this strategy could be pushed without a runaway increase in federal deficits and public debt, which financial investors and many in Trump's team would object to, is nowhere near clear. There is little reason to believe that Trump himself would want to displease finance capital by allowing deficits to widen.

That generates much uncertainty on what the economic policy would really look like under the Trump administration. Despite that uncertainty, and leveraging the evidence of recovery in the US, the Fed has

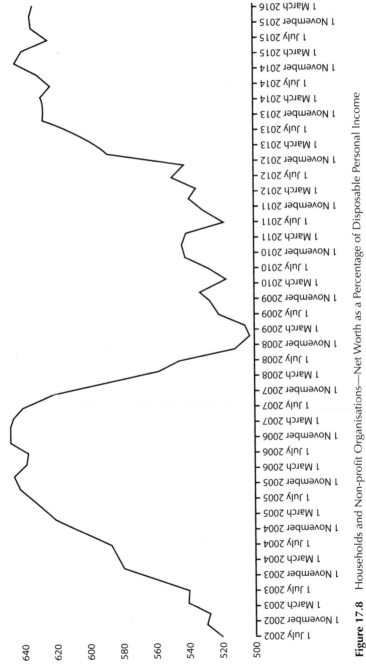

Figure 17.8 Households and Non-profit Organisations—Net Worth as a Percentage of Disposable Personal Income

Source: Federal Reserve Bank of St Louis at https://fred.stlouisfed.org/series/HNONWPDPI.

clearly decided to hand over the task of sustaining and building on that recovery to the fiscal policy that would be pursued by the treasury under Trump. There are no guarantees, however, that the Trump spending programme will be implemented, and whether it will make any difference to the performance of the economy if it is.

Meanwhile, however, the unprecedented medium-term trend of investment in negative-yielding bonds has reversed itself in recent months, influenced initially by changing Fed perceptions on holding down interest rates and the Brexit vote, but gaining momentum especially after the election of Trump as US President. Principally, taking a cue from the Fed, central bankers elsewhere seem to withdrawing support to negative interest rates in bond markets. Central banks in Japan and Germany have signalled that they were not continuing with their bond-buying spree, even when private investors are walking away from these markets where prices are seen as too high.

As Figure 17.4 shows, the Bloomberg estimate of the total value of negative-yielding bonds, which had declined marginally from its peak of $12.2 trillion in June 2016 to $11.6 trillion in September 2016, stood at a much lower $8.7 trillion on 11 November 2016, having fallen by $1.4 trillion from 4 November 2016.

As was expected, the bond sell-off was concentrated in government bonds (Figure 17.5). But this was not because there had been any change in the policy rates that were being charged by central banks (Figure 17.1, Figure 17.2, Figure 17.3). Rather it was because of the changed policy on QE which triggered a sell-off that reduced prices and has begun increasing yields on long-term government bonds (Figure 17.9). As a result, yields on 10-year sovereign bonds have entered positive territory in Japan, German and Denmark since November 2016, coinciding with the election of President Trump. In Switzerland this had begun even earlier.

One implication of this is that bond trades, prices and yields are not driven by the policy rate alone, but by speculation regarding the role that fiscal policy will play. Clearly, expectations are that the Trump era would be one in which debt-financed state expenditure on infrastructure and related areas would be an important instrument to raise growth. This would mean that (i) central banks may choose to retreat from low interest, easy money policies; (ii) new issues of treasury bills would increase sharply, reducing bond prices and raising bond yields; and (iii) demand and prices in the real economy could turn buoyant, heralding a new phase of goods-price inflation. If these expectations

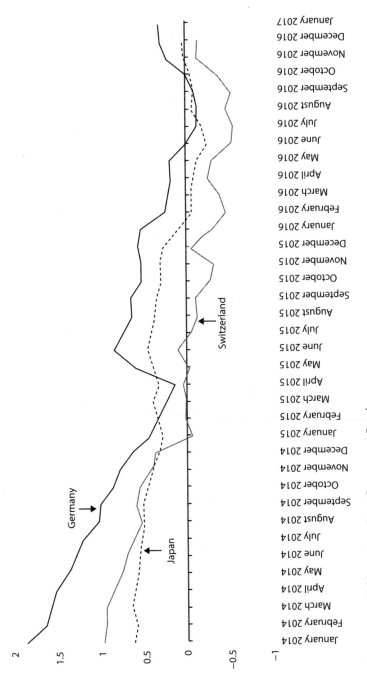

Figure 17.9 Yields on Long-Term Government Bonds

Source: CEIC.

are realised, many of the factors underlying the surge in the demand for bonds and in bond prices may unwind. In addition, opportunities for investment in the real, commodity producing sectors would increase, providing the basis for the rapid exit from negative-yielding bonds.

All this suggests that there is a difference in the factors driving negative policy rates affecting banks, and negative yields in bond prices, with the latter not merely the result of the transmission of the effects of the former. On the one hand, negative policy rates are being adopted by central banks to address the persistent recession in the global economy, and are supported by governments that see this (as opposed to fiscal policy) as the preferred instrument to engineer a recovery. Trump's rhetoric questions this perspective, and has called for a greater reliance on expenditure measures, though how they would be financed is still unclear. Negative bond yields, on the other hand, are a fallout of the deflationary environment (rather than the means to address it).

The mere expectation that Trump's ascendancy could trigger a spending surge, and provide the space for the Fed and possibly other central banks to retreat from their failed monetary stance, which has for too long now been based on QE and low or negative interest rates, shook up bond markets. However, the initial sell-off seems to have abated, and what happens next would depend on whether Trump translates his rhetoric into actual policy.

References

Atkins, Ralph (2016): 'Swiss Bank PostFinance Introduces Charges for Retail Consumer Deposits,' *Financial Times*, 11 November.

Baker, Dean (2016): 'Obama Helped Avert Economic Collapse, But Recovery Is Distant,' *The New York Times*, 29 July, http://www.nytimes.com/roomfordebate/2016/01/12/reflecting-on-obamaspresidency/obama-helped-avert-economic-collapse-but-full-recovery-is-distant.

Bernanke, Ben (2016): 'What Tools Does the Fed Have Left? Part 1: Negative Interest Rates,' *Brookings*, 18 March, https://www.brookings.edu/blog/benbernanke/2016/03/18/what-tools-does-thefed-have-left-part-1-negative-interest-rates/.

Chandrasekhar, C.P. and Jayati Ghosh (2016): 'Has Monetary Policy Lost Its Mojo,' *The Hindu Business Line*, 14 March, http://www.thehindubusinessline.com/opinion/columns/c-p-chandrasekhar/has-monetary-policy-lost-its-mojo/article8352860.ece.

Chandrasekhar, C.P. and Jayati Ghosh (2017): 'What Explains the Bond Market Reversal,' *The Hindu Business Line*, 13 February, http://www.thehindubusinessline.com/opinion/columns/c-p-chandrasekhar/explaining-the-bond-market-reversal/article9539724.ece.

Coy, Peter and Mathew Philips (2013): 'Larry Summers Has a Wintry Outlook on the Economy: The ex-Treasury Boss Says Current Policy Isn't Radical Enough,' Bloomberg, 19 November, https://www.bloomberg.com/news/articles/2013-11-18/larry-summers-current-economic- policy-isnt-radical-enough.

Dobbs, Richard, Susan Lund, Jonathan Woetzel and Mina Mutafchieva (2015): *Debt and (Not Much) Deleveraging*, McKinsey Global Institute.

Homer, Sydney and Richard Sylla (2005): *A History of Interest Rates*, fourth edition, New Jersey: John Wiley & Sons.

Kalecki, M. (1943–71): 'Political Aspects of Full Employment,' *Selected Essays on the Dynamics of a Capitalist Economy*, Cambridge: Cambridge University Press, pp 138–45.

Karaian, Jason (2016): 'A Third of Government Debt Now Has Negative Interest Rates,' Quartz, 7 July, https://qz.com/725005/a-third-of-all- government- bonds-are-guaranteed-money-losers/.

Kothari, S.P., Jonathan Lewellen and Jerold B. Warner (2015), 'The Behaviour of Aggregate Corporate Investment,' http://www.lehigh.edu/~jms408/kothari_2015.pdf.

Kuntz, Phil (2016): 'Negative-yielding Bonds Jump to Almost $12 Trillion,' Bloomberg, 3 October, https://www.bloomberg.com/news/articles/2016-10-02/negative-yielding-bonds-jump-toalmost-12-trillion-after-ebbing.

———— (2016a): 'Negative-Yielding Bonds Plummet to $8.7 Trillion After Trump Win,' Bloomberg, 15 November, https://www.bloomberg.com/news/articles/2016-11-15/negative-yielding-bondsplummet-to-8-7-trillion-after-trump-win.

OECD (2015): *OECD Economic Outlook*, 2015, Issue 1, Organization for Economic Cooperation and Development, Paris: OECD Publishing.

———— (2016): *OECD Economic Surveys: United States June 2016*, Organization for Economic Cooperation and Development, Paris: OECD Publishing.

Patnaik, Prabhat (2010): 'The Theory of the Global "Savings Glut",' MR online, 10 March, https://mronline.org/2010/03/01/the-theory-of-theglobal-savings-glut/.

Pozen, Robert (2016): 'Negative Rates Are a Counterproductive Reach Beyond the Limits of Rate Stimulus,' *Real Clear Markets*, 7 September, http://www.realclearmarkets.com/articles/ 2016/09/07/negative_rates_are_a_counter-productive_reach_beyond_the_limits_of_rate_ stimulus_102341.html.

Reuters (2016): 'Share of Euro Zone Sovereign Debt with Negative Yields Falls to 41 pct – Tradeweb,' Reuters, 18 November, http://www.reuters.com/article/eurozone-bonds- yieldsidUSL8N1DJ21Q.

Rogoff, Kenneth (2016): *The Curse of Cash*, Princeton: Princeton University Press.

Samson, Adam (2016): 'Rout Shrinks Universe of Negative Yielding Bonds by $2.5 Trillion,' *Financial Times*, 6 December, https://www.ft.com/content/ 9253b220-bb03-11e6-8b45- b8b81dd5d080.

Schneider, Howard and Lindsay Dunsmuir (2016): 'Fed Lifts Rates, Sees Faster Pace of Hikes in Trump's First Year,' Reuters, 15 December, http://www. reuters.com/article/us-usa-fedidUSKBN1430G4.

Smialek, Jeanna (2016): 'Yellen Doesn't Rule Out Negative Rates in Letter to Congressman,' Bloomberg, 13 May, https://www.bloomberg.com/ news/articles/2016-05-12/yellen-doesn-t-rule-out-negative-rates-in-letter-to-congressman.

18

The New Moral Economy

Demonetisation, Digitalisation and India's Core Economic Problems

Atul Sood and Ashapurna Baruah

Convincing billions of Indian citizens that demonetisation and digitalisation is a panacea for the country's growth challenges and a solution to its core economic problems requires constructing a new moral economy, and a 'different' imaging of India in the minds of the people. Incorrect economic arithmetic and the illusion of digitalisation are not the only problems to be negotiated. The moral political project overtly and covertly being attempted is of far greater significance.

The arguments advanced in support of demonetisation are that it will help (i) eradicate black money, (ii) remove counterfeit currency, (iii) curtail terrorism, and (iv) facilitate a movement towards a cashless economy. There is a silent and an implicit message behind these claims. It is being suggested that India's current development challenge is merely of slackening growth, and by bringing investments, all development challenges will be addressed. Demonetisation is then presented as a panacea, and it is claimed that the likely increase in bank deposits will foster investment and growth. In addition, streamlining transactions through digitalisation will address all problems of unequal exchange.

Both these propositions are rooted in the dominant view in economic thinking that the primacy of production can be replaced by a central focus on money markets, together with exchange and transaction processes. The moral political dimension of the demonetisation discourse and the imagining of India promoted in the idea of digitalisation, therefore, as we argue in this chapter, help create this disconnect between appearance and reality and act as powerful channels to foreclose imaginative and critical thinking about India's real development problems and their solutions.

I: Moral Political Project

The Prime Minister's announcement of the withdrawal of Rs 1,000 and Rs 500 notes ranks amongst the most significant measures taken by his government. The audacious move has given birth to wild hopes of a decisive blow to the black economy and counterfeit currency. It is also being lauded for its potential to convert India into a cashless economy. The economic arithmetic and digitalisation are not the only problems with the 8 November 2016 demonetisation announcement. The moral political project overtly and covertly being achieved through this is of far more significance.

Through this announcement, the State has been unleashed on us in the name of protecting our own virtue. There is a new kind of politics in it that is redefining the relationship between the citizen and the State. The government does not want to be answerable to the citizen. It has gambled without reasonably establishing the costs and benefits and producing a policy document. It does not feel the need to do so. This policy measure entails total mobilisation of society on a scale, where literally every citizen is being enlisted in a policy cause, without being told how it is guaranteed to work, and if it works what problems do they resolve. Even the goalposts of evaluating the success or failure of this programme are not clearly articulated. People are being convinced on a premise, as limited as saying, since something tastes terrible it must be good for one's health.

The moral and the political are in one leap intertwined, when standing in line to withdraw our own money is a way to honour our country. We are told by the government that it will do the best for its citizens and the citizens need not understand the rationale or reasoning. Questions are not to be asked, only sound bites are to be repeated—so runs the new moral political argument of the government.

The new moral political is also about newer ways of personification of policy and ensuring participation in nation building, all individually, with no associations or solidarities. Questions of distributive consequences and transparency are to be effaced. Every citizen appears either as a patriot or a criminal, and the State tells us that the honest have nothing to fear. The Pradhan Mantri Jan Dhan Yojana (PMJDY) and Vijay Mallya are put at par in terms of financial fraud. The State epitomises virtue and stands above us.

There is one more moral aspect to this project: black money as a by-product of individual unethical behaviour, where nothing is institutional about the process that has generated so much 'black money' in the last many years in India.

Not only has the process of money-making been individualised, the government has tried to turn the entire narrative about demonetisation into an individual one about the leader's ethics or his political career. The rhetoric suggests that the one who truly deserves sympathy in the present scenario is not daily wagers, street vendors, and farmers—whose already precarious livelihoods have been disrupted—but the government or the Prime Minister. In one stroke, it rendered all criticism suspect.

The real moral and political dimension of demonetisation is this new imagining behind the move, from morality to statism, from systemic to individual, from exploitation to corruption, from questioning to complete loyalty. One could debate the merits and demerits of demonetisation as the best strategy to curb the black economy. One could also debate the merits and demerits of a 'fast' demonetisation versus 'slow' or gradual demonetisation, and the manner of execution. One could debate the impact of this elimination of 86 per cent of the currency in circulation on ordinary people's lives. But none of this was done, and is not needed now.

The new version of virtuous, moral, participative, and individualised politics is bringing the poor and lower middle classes back to the centrestage of politics in a new *avatar*. The 1990s policies of 'economic liberalisation' were made in the name of the poor, for the rich and the big corporates. In the last 7–8 years, an attempt was made to make the same policies in the name of the rich for the rich. Now, a new attempt is being made where the poor participate in supporting the policies, on individual moral and ethical grounds, that will benefit the corporates, the investors and the speculators even more than in the past. The debate on the economy has been reduced to one around exchange, so that no structural or production issues are discussed.

II: Digitalisation of Transactions

Formal transactions, informal production relations

The State's imagery of financial inclusion is entwined with the digitalisation of transactions. It dwells upon the idea that digital money will formalise transactions, which in turn would curb black money. However, formalising transactions through digital money in an informal economy does not tantamount to eradicating the black economy. This is because, first, corruption and tax evasion will still be possible unless cash is totally banned, which does not seem realistic; and second, the growth of a formal economy does not come about with mere formalisation of exchange but with intrinsic change in production relations within the economy.

Financial inclusion, again, has a much deeper connotation. It is seen not only as a process of ensuring universal access to financial services but also timely and adequate credit to vulnerable sections at a reasonable and affordable cost. Mere provisioning of banking infrastructure by itself will not inculcate formalised banking habits, unless the real economic problems of production and employment are addressed.

In reality, the predominance of the informal sector is a characteristic feature of the Indian economy, and the demand for cash as a preferred mode of transaction, is rooted in this informality. Informal employment constitutes a significant share of the labour market. As per the National Sample Survey Office estimates, informal employment accounted for 91.9 per cent of the total employment in 2011–12, which is only a marginal fall from 92.7 per cent share registered in 2004–05. This informal employment is characterised by the presence of a huge share of self-employed and casual workers in the workforce. Of the informally employed workforce, self-employment and casual work constituted 56 per cent and 33 per cent respectively in 2011–12. The very nature of casual and irregular employment makes earnings infrequent and irregular. This sustains a cash-based economy.

According to the World Bank Global Findex Data, in India a meagre 4 per cent of the total wage recipients (aged 15 years and above) reported using a bank account to receive wages in 2014. The share was even lower for rural areas at 2.96 per cent. Among the poorest 40 per cent of the households, only 1.7 per cent of the adults reported use of an account to receive wages in the past year. These figures clearly suggest that cashless payment constitute only a minuscule share of the total transactions in the Indian economy.

Thus, the power ascribed to digitalisation by the government not only creates a false imagining about financial access, but also attempts to disengage the citizens from the official macroeconomic policy discourse that promotes informality as a competitive tool in the global economy. It is being suggested that formalisation of transactions is good enough to overcome the informalisation of the production structure and the exploitative informal labour relations. In truth, this formalisation does not alter the precarious economic conditions of those who are engaged informally in the formal and informal sector. As far as production conditions and labour relations are concerned, it can be business as usual. Since so much is being hyped about the cash-less economy and digital transactions, discussing the details of this proposal may be in order.

From Digital Money to Money

'Digital money in effect curbs black money' is the nature of message that the government has claimed in its advertisement campaigns. These propaganda campaigns promote the use of prepaid digital instruments, wherein daily wage earners such as a cobbler and an auto-rickshaw driver are being educated on the usage and merits of what are proclaimed as convenient modes of transaction.

There are primarily five modes of digital payments that the government is increasingly promoting. These are unified payment interface (UPI), mobile wallets, unstructured supplementary service data (USSD), debit card and Aadhaar Enabled Payment System (AEPS). Amongst these, UPI, USSD and AEPS are introduced and implemented exclusively by the government.

The UPI launched by the National Payments Corporation of India (NPCI) earlier in 2017 uses the immediate payment service (IMPS) platform to transfer money between two bank accounts. Mobile wallet constitutes a virtual wallet, wherein the information of physical plastic cards can be carried in a digital form in a mobile device to make digital transactions. While the UPI and mobile wallets require a smartphone with Internet connection, the USSD method works on the voice network that can be operated on a feature phone even without an Internet connection. The AEPS mode can be used by Aadhaar cardholders by linking their unique identification numbers to their respective bank accounts, thus transforming an Aadhaar card to a virtual debit card. Access to a bank account is a mandate for operating each of these digital payment modes. The additional mandates and specific procedures to be followed are given in Table 18.1.

Digital money innately requires access to a bank account and a mobile phone, together with availability of bandwidth. All these mandates involve substantial amounts of real and opportunity costs to be borne by the user. In Table 18.1, although basic details and processes are presented with respect to the customers, the necessary conditions are to be met by sellers/ merchants as well. In addition, the merchants have to meet other requirements and incur other costs as well. For instance, to use AEPS and debit card, bandwidth availability is not mandatory for customers to make purchases, but it is a must for merchants. To accept payments, merchants should have a running Internet connection and point of sale (POS) system.

TABLE 18.1   Mandates and Basic Details of the Five Digital Methods

Methods/ Mandate	Bank account	Mobile phone	Smart phone	Internet	User cost	Process
UPI	Yes	Yes	–	Yes	IMPS fee of Rs 5+ service tax	Download the bank's UPI app. Create a virtual payment address as per availability. Generate a Mobile Money Identifier (MMID), a seven-digit number issued by bank on registration.
Mobile wallet	Yes	Yes	–	Yes	1%– 4%	Download wallet app. Fill customer details like mobile phone number and email address. Load money through plastic cards or net banking.

(*Cont'd*)

TABLE 18.1   *(Cont'd)*

Methods/ Mandate	Bank account	Mobile phone	Smart phone	Internet	User cost	Process
USSD	Yes	No	Yes	No	–	Register mobile number with one or multiple bank accounts. Dial *99# from the phone keypad. Respond to USSD message that asks for the first three letters of the bank or its short name, or the first four letters of the IFSC (Indian Financial System Code). Check balance akin to checking balance of prepaid phone but transactions require a MMID like the UPI.
AEPS	Yes	No	No	No	–	Link Aadhaar card to bank accounts. Can be used in point of sale (POS) by giving Aadhaar number and one of the two biometrics: finger-print, or iris scan.
Debit card	Yes	No	No	No	–	Can be used at POS terminals by entering the PIN (personal identification number) code. Can be used at ATM for transfer of money.

Under the AEPS, the merchants also need to invest in a smartphone and a fingerprint scanner. While the POS machine can be acquired free of cost from the concerned bank where the merchant has an account, she is required to pay the merchant discount rate (MDR). The MDR on debit card payments, as capped by the RBI, is 0.75 per cent of the transaction for amounts up to Rs 2,000 and 1 per cent for the transaction amount for values above Rs 2,000, except for the government-introduced RuPay cards, where MDR reduces to 0.45 per cent and 0.65 per cent for the respective amounts. Along with the bearing of costs, the merchants should also be well aware of a large number of technical and management issues, including concepts such as self-declaration and KYC (know your customer) norms.

So, as we can see from the details above, India is now at an interesting cusp, where even if you have legal tender with you and the seller is willing to sell you some commodity, that is not going to be enough for you to complete the transaction. We now need all kinds of intermediate 'processes' to complete the loop for the transaction to happen. And these middle processes will require active and in-depth participation (and therefore gains) of the banking and the telecom sectors, and Internet service providers. The huge scope for increasing the size of the market and higher profits for private sector banks and telecom operators implicit in the proposal of digitalisation is a dimension that immediately pops out, given the absence of any concrete gains for an ordinary Indian citizen in this proposal of digitalisation. Digitalisation hardly appears to be a public good for which the sovereign Indian state should be batting with such enthusiasm.

III: Access, Exclusion and Inequality

Let alone use, even fewer Indians are aware of the concept of digital money. The Financial Inclusion Insights Survey (FII 2016) reports that only 10 per cent of the total adults in the population were aware of the concept of mobile money in 2015, and usage was low at 0.5 per cent. According to the Census of India, 26 per cent of the population in India was illiterate in 2011. It is to be mentioned that improvement in basic literacy and mere awareness about mobile money may fail to ensure widespread usage. There are issues of acquiring digital knowledge. Language constitutes another major hurdle, as English is the operational language for most of these digital instruments. For an illiterate person, the cumbersomeness of creating a virtual payment address, generating an MMID (mobile money identifier) number, and finally making transactions, has the effect of limiting her access to digital mode of payments.

The Census of India of 2011 estimates that 58.7 per cent of the total households in the country had access to banking services. This was 67.7 per cent in the urban areas and much lower at 54.5 per cent in the rural areas. This not only reveals the low degree of financial inclusion but also shows how the digitalisation drive eschews a significant share of the population. In an attempt to facilitate access to banking, the Government of India launched the PMJDY in August 2014. With the aim of opening an account for every household in the country, the yojana was made lucrative by allowing for zero balances, overdraft facilities, issue of RuPay debit cards and free life insurance.

There was a marked rise in the number of account holders under the scheme. Until January 2016, a total of 258 million accounts were opened under this scheme. According to the FII survey (2016), a share of 47 per cent of the total adult population had registered bank accounts in 2013. This share rose to 63 per cent in 2015. Despite the unprecedented rise in account penetration, 23 per cent of these accounts under PMJDY remained as zero balance accounts.

This suggests that opening of accounts does not ensure the use of accounts to receive salaries/wages or undergo any form of transaction. The accounts have remained dormant as these were not set up for an explicit purpose, such as to receive wages or government transfer payments (Demirguc-Kunt *et al.* 2015). Although, financial inclusion as seen in terms of the number of account holders has increased over the years, the actual penetration of banking habits among the masses, especially in rural areas, is doubtful.

The RBI (2015) shows that there has been a significant progress in the use of pre-paid instruments (PPI) such as mobile wallets and PPI cards in 2013–14 and 2014–15. The report states that the value of PPIs increased from 79.2 billion in 2012–13 to 213.4 billion in 2014–15, and it is the non-bank PPI, that is, mobile wallets that contributed to a major part of the growth. However, the growth of such electronic modes of payment remains confined to a small section of the society.

Clearly, even as the access to electronic modes of payment is low, there is variation in the extent of usage among different sections of the population in the country. For instance, in the past one year, a share of only 3.25 per cent of females aged 15 and above is reported to have used debit card as compared to nearly 18 per cent of adult males. The digital divide in gender is found in the case of the other two modes of payment as well.

It follows that access to banking, mobiles, bandwidth availability, the burden of transaction costs and fees, and language are some issues that will decide if digital money is the way forward for India. It is also clear that a significant share of the population is not going to be part of this digital world. Once we map the challenges of digitalisation with the formal and informal nature of economic activity in India, the implications of digitalisation and the bias implicit in it becomes even clearer.

Downplaying Reality

The question that ought to be asked is whether the Indian economy has the necessary wherewithal transit to a digitalised cashless economy, irrespective of the supposed gains for the 'white' economy. The RBI's report card on acceptance infrastructure (RBI 2016) lays bare the context in which the government is claiming digitalisation as a way towards financial inclusion. The report clearly documents both the supply and demand side impediments to digitalisation in the Indian economy. There are also issues of costs related to payment of merchant fees, capital cost of equipment and maintenance integration with merchant system, transparency and taxation, KYC documentation, certification process related to safety and security of transactions/systems, annual fees for cards, levy of convenience charges/surcharge on use of cards, feel of convenience generally associated with cash payments, etc. There are also impediments pertaining to provisioning of adequate infrastructure. Within the purview of infrastructure, there are interrelated issues of providing for growth of the acceptance infrastructure, widening geographical coverage, and ensuring risk-free and secured systems for digital transactions which further affect usage and access.

The report also acknowledges that the supply of the acceptance infrastructure has not kept pace with the growth in debit cards. It states that growth of the acceptance infrastructure has not been uniform, and such infrastructure is concentrated in urban areas and larger towns, and with larger merchants. Thus, the usage of cards has been constrained by the lack of accessible acceptance infrastructure, especially in rural areas, where growth in card issuance has been high in recent times. The predominance of debit card usage at automated teller machines (ATMs) (90 per cent of all debit card transactions) relative to POS or other digital transactions raises the issues of costs and risks associated with cash management of ATMs, and the risk of fraudulence and phishing, among other reasons, make digital transactions less preferable.

Most interestingly, apart from the rich technical details of challenges to move towards digitalisation, the RBI report is clear and upfront in identifying those that digitalisation caters to, and the population it excludes. For example, it points to the unviability of digital transactions for small merchants, and in rural areas, where low card footfalls and low transaction values, besides other costs associated with merchant acquiring, ultimately forced acquiring banks to withdraw the POS terminal. Lack of adequate and low-cost telecommunication infrastructure makes it difficult for merchants to access networks which are required to accept electronic payments and process transactions. Poor connectivity in many areas leads to fewer transactions, and consequently, affects the revenue of acquirers. Lack of incentive for merchants to accept card payments is another inhibiting factor. Further, transparency and audit trails associated with card payments often act as a deterrent for accepting card payments by merchants.

Given that the government is well informed about the constraints to the usage of digital money, the question that arises is: what is the government's agenda behind the present thrust towards digitalisation? With the demonetisation–digitalisation exercise, there is little ambiguity that the motive is to expand the formal sector or formalise economic activity in India. If we see this policy initiative in the larger macroeconomic framework of this regime (Sood 2016), the aim of the current initiative is clearly intended to promote the growth of the corporate formal sector at the expense of the informal sector, and not go through the slow and painful route of transforming the prevalent informal sectors of the economy into formal ones.

The move to a cashless economy through use of digital money will formalise transactions even in the informal economy. It is said without contention that the informal economy in India comprises largely of small producers and traders, who are mostly own account workers. These small commodity producers make earnings at the margin and are susceptible to shocks and risks. With meagre earnings, they cannot be competitive if they have to pay the same taxes as big corporates. The union budget of 2015 had proposed to reduce the basic rate of corporate tax from 30 per cent to 20 per cent for the next four years, stating that the aim of the policy was to ensure higher investments, higher revenues, and to make domestic industries globally competitive. With the purpose of broadening the tax base, the same rate will be applicable to small commodity producers.

The increase in cost as a result of moving to digital money, together with the additional burden of taxation will gravely affect earnings in the informal sector and is likely to make informal production uncompetitive, forcing the poor to buy goods from the formal sector at much higher prices. The policy of tax rate reduction on profit will strengthen corporate houses in the formal sector, and create conditions for the formal sector to thrive at the cost of the informal sector.

References

Bhardwaj, Krishna (1986): *Classical Political Economy and Rise to Dominance of Supply and Demand Theories*, Second Revised Edition, India: Universities Press.

Demirguc-Kunt, A., L. Klapper, D. Singer and P.V. Oudheusden (2015): 'The Global Findex Database 2014: Measuring Financial Inclusion around the World,' *Policy Research Working Paper 7255*, World Bank Group, http://documents.worldbank.org/curated/en/187761468179367706/pdf/WPS7255.pdf.

FII (2016): 'India: FII Tracker Survey,' Financial Inclusion Insights, Intermedia, http://finclusion.org/uploads/file/reports/2015%20Inter-Media%20FII%20INDIA%20QuickSights%20 Summary%20Report.pdf.

RBI (2015): 'Report on Trends and Progress of Banking in India, 2014–15,' Reserve Bank of India.

——— (2016): 'Concept Paper on Card Acceptance Infrastructure,' Reserve Bank of India.

Rogoff, Kenneth (2016): 'India's Currency Exchange Gamble and the Curse of Cash,' Wire, http:// thewire.in/81410/indias-currency-exchange-curse-cash/.

Sood, A. (2016): 'Politics of Growth: Script and Postscript,' *Economic & Political Weekly*, Vol 51, No 29, pp 56–60.

IV (b) Theoretical Perspectives

Chapters in this section offer perspectives on demonetisation from the standpoint of economic theory. In his invited contribution to this volume, Prabhat Patnaik uses a simple Kaleckian framework to explain the slowdown in the Indian economy over the 3rd and 4th quarters of 2016–17. Parag Waknis analyses demonetisation from a segmented markets perspective.

19

The Legacy of Demonetisation

Prabhat Patnaik

It is perfectly possible that when 'real' GDP at market prices shows an increase, the real condition of the workers as a whole can deteriorate in absolute terms, even when there is no adverse shift in income distribution from wages to profits and even when the economy is demand-constrained. The GDP at market prices, in short, is simply the wrong thing to look at, if we are concerned with the condition of the working people.

I suppose that by now it will be generally agreed that demonetisation has failed singularly to achieve its purported objective of making a dent on the black economy. Whether the tax raids being conducted occasionally of late, and the other measures that the government has been talking about, will have that effect is irrelevant here. Demonetisation itself has nothing to do with these measures, and cannot be credited for whatever impact these other measures, if sustained, may have in future.

The government's argument in this regard was that demonetisation would damage the black economy because the black money operators would not dare to approach banks to exchange or deposit their demonetised currency notes; such notes therefore would simply get extinguished which would inflict crippling losses on the black economy. This expectation has been belied: about 99 per cent of the total value of demonetised currency have been deposited back into the banks. The inescapable conclusion is that demonetisation has been an utter fiasco in the matter of tackling the black economy.

Two other objectives had also been mentioned in the Prime Minister's speech on 8 November 2016, but they had carried little conviction even then. One such objective, namely disabling counterfeit currency, was too insignificant to warrant demonetisation (since the estimate of the value of such currency was a mere Rs 400 crore); besides, it could also have been achieved if demonetisation had occurred over a longer period than the four hours given by the government. The other objective, namely making people move to a cashless economy, was not just impractical given the state of connectivity and digital literacy in the country; it was also unacceptable in a democracy, since cashless transactions involve a cost while cash transactions are costless, and no democratic government should coerce citizens into paying for the profits of companies that manage cashless transactions. These objectives therefore could not be taken seriously. The only one that could possibly be, has eluded demonetisation.

Essentially, what demonetisation has achieved is to transfer a huge amount of currency from the possession of the public to the vaults of the banks. And this has been doubly harmful. On the one hand it has had a demand-contractionary impact on the real economy, especially on the informal sector which relies mainly on cash transactions and which accounts for as much as 45 per cent of the gross aalue added (GVA) and 82 per cent of total employment. On the other hand, banks, holding all this idle cash that has been deposited with them, have to pay an interest to the depositors, which damages their profitability; and shoring up their profitability entails a drain on the government's budget.

I: Falling Growth Rates

Some doubt had been thrown on the veracity of the first of these claims when the Central Statistics Office (CSO) had released advance estimates of the gross domestic product (GDP) for the third (October–December) quarter of 2016–17, within which demonetisation had occurred. Indeed the fact that the economy had still shown a 7 per cent growth rate had been an occasion for much celebration in government circles. It had been used by the government to argue that, contrary to the claims of the critics, demonetisation had not hurt the economy.

This claim however had been contested even then (Ghosh, J. 2017; Nagaraj 2017; Ghosh, S.K. 2017). It had been clear that a major reason for this 7 per cent growth figure was a downward revision of the third quarter GDP estimate for 2015–16, the base on which the third quarter growth for 2016–17 was calculated. A retrospective revision of the base in short had artificially boosted the growth rate figure. Besides, the full impact of demonetisation, it was pointed out, would take time to manifest itself.

The fourth quarter (January–March) GDP estimates released by the CSO on 31 May 2017 indeed show a significant slowing down of growth, to 6.1 per cent for this quarter. Even this statistic, however, does not fully capture the slowing down of the economy. The GDP figure is compiled at market prices and, hence, includes net indirect taxes levied by the government; it does not accurately reflect production trends. To capture the latter we have to look at figures of GAV. And these show a 5.6 per cent growth over the fourth quarter of 2015–16, down from 6.7 per cent in the third quarter. The corresponding growth figures for the third and fourth quarters of 2015–16 were 7.3 per cent and 8.7 per cent respectively, which means a whopping 3.1 per cent drop in the growth rate figure in the fourth quarter compared to a year ago.

Even this drop however does not adequately capture the jolt to the economy because of demonetisation. Quite apart from the fact that *none of these figures* properly cover the petty production sector, where the impact of demonetisation has been most severe, there is an additional factor to consider. After two successive drought years, 2016–17 was a year of recovery for agriculture. While demonetisation would have had an adverse impact on agricultural *prices*, the favourable weather conditions generally kept up agricultural *output* during this year. In the fourth quarter, for instance, agricultural output grew by 5.2 per cent over the previous year, compared to 1.5 per cent in the corresponding quarter of 2015–16. Now, if agriculture is taken out of the reckoning altogether, then we find that the fourth quarter growth for the non-agricultural sector, where the impact of demonetisation would have been felt most pronouncedly, slipped from 10.5 per cent in 2015–16 to 5.7 per cent in 2016–17, which is a dramatic collapse.

The GAV figures for individual sectors also bear this out. Construction, which is highly employment-intensive, actually shrank by 3.7 per cent, and manufacturing grew by only 5.3 per cent in the fourth quarter. (The manufacturing growth rate figure, according to the new method of calculation, is likely to be an overestimate for all quarters, but we are talking here of comparisons across years). All these fourth quarter growth rate figures for 2016–17 are much lower than the figures for earlier quarters, and also for the fourth quarter of 2015–16.

Taking the annual figure, we find that GAV increased in 2016–17 by 6.6 per cent, which was a drop from the 7.9 per cent recorded for 2015–16. This is quite remarkable because agriculture which had recorded a growth rate of 0.7 per cent in 2015–16 grew by 4.9 per cent in 2016–17. Again if we take agriculture out of the reckoning, then we find that the rate of growth of the non-agricultural sector was 9.7 per cent in 2015–16 and fell to 7 per cent in 2016–17, which is a pretty sharp drop. There can be little doubt therefore that demonetisation had a significant adverse impact on the economy, exactly as the critics had anticipated when it was announced.

At the same time however it would be a serious error to see the *entire* slowdown of growth in the Indian economy in 2016–17 as a consequence of only demonetisation, as some neo-liberal economists are suggesting. The slowdown began long before demonetisation, but demonetisation has greatly accentuated it, whence it follows that even if remonetisation is completed, if ever, the growth rate will never again bounce back to the levels reached earlier *for this reason* (apart from the legacy of demonetisation itself, on which more later).

This reason, to recapitulate, consists in the fact that the neo-liberal order has reached a dead end, where stagnation, interrupted only occasionally and transiently by asset-price bubbles, will be the new 'normal;' and countries like India, unless they break out of the neo-liberal regime, which must mean a degree of delinking from globalisation, will also be caught in this stagnation.

The revised estimates of GDP growth for the four quarters of 2016–17 (over the corresponding quarters of the previous year), were: 7.9 per cent, 7.5 per cent, 7.0 per cent and 6.1 per cent. While one has to be careful comparing growth rates across quarters (since each is calculated over the GDP figure one year ago, and those base year figures may have moved in all sorts of ways), it is clear nonetheless that there is a distinct slowing down of growth through the year. In fact, many see the economy as slowing down from the second quarter of 2016–17, which is striking as it has occurred despite a remarkable increase in agricultural growth. And demonetisation has compounded this slowdown.

II: Value Added and the Workers

Our focusing above on GAV has a deeper theoretical justification. It is often not appreciated that movements in the GDP at market prices, even assuming for argument's sake that it is deflated by an 'appropriate' price index, *is simply incapable conceptually of capturing the distress of the working people even when there are no shifts in 'factor shares.'* Put differently, it is perfectly possible that when 'real' GDP at market prices shows an increase, the real condition of the workers as a whole can deteriorate in absolute terms, even when there is no adverse shift in income distribution from wages to profits and even when the economy is demand-constrained (with both unemployment and unutilised capacity coexisting). The GDP at market prices in short, quite apart from estimation problems, is simply *the wrong thing to look at*, if we are concerned with the condition of the working people.

This is true both as a general theoretical point and also in the context of the current demonetisation, as can be demonstrated with the help of a very simple illustrative Kaleckian model. Consider an economy, which has two vertically-integrated sectors, one producing consumption goods and the other investment goods. With the system being demand-constrained, we have a profit mark-up on the unit prime cost and an indirect tax mark-up on top of that. With both mark-ups fixed, the price has a fixed ratio to unit prime cost, which, with a given money wage rate, is assumed to be invariant with respect to output. Let us assume both profit and tax mark-ups to be the same for both the sectors. Let us also assume, to start with, that the government spends entirely on investment goods and its budget is balanced, that all wages are consumed, and that the capitalists consume a fixed absolute amount of the consumption goods. Since money prices in the two sectors are assumed not to change, we can choose our units in such a manner that each sector's price is equal to 1.

Demonetisation is assumed here, for simplicity, only to affect the consumption demand of the workers (this is changed in a later model presented in this chapter), and cause a primary fall in their total consumption by S_w (which let us suppose is the amount of cash they are forced to deposit with banks). Denoting total investment by I, capitalists' investment by I_p, capitalists' consumption by A, their profits by P, and the shares of wages, profits and indirect taxes in the value of output by λ, π and τ (which together add up to one), we have the following total output before demonetisation:

$$Y = I + C = (I_p + A)/\pi \ldots \tag{i}$$

After demonetisation the total output is given by:

$$Y' = I + C' = (I_p + A - S_w)/\pi \ldots \tag{ii}$$

where C' is the new consumption good output which is obviously lower. The entire drop in output has occurred *ex hypothesi* in the consumption goods sector; and since the capitalists' absolute consumption has not fallen, the workers' consumption has.

It may be thought, however, that while the workers are worse off in terms of consumption, the fall in their consumption is because of their bank deposits which increase their wealth, so that they may not be worse off overall, i.e. taking their consumption and addition to wealth together. But such is not the case. It can be seen from (ii) that the drop in workers' consumption, which is nothing else but the drop in consumption good output, is S_w/π, while the increase in their wealth is just S_w. The drop in their consumption is greater than the increase in their wealth (since $\pi<1$), which is simply a result of the working of the 'multiplier.' It follows that demonetisation leaves the workers absolutely worse off.

At the same time however indirect tax collection may go up, despite the tax rates remaining unchanged and despite the output actually falling, as a way of capitalists' getting rid of demonetised notes in the form of advance tax payment. If the rise in tax collection is sufficiently large and this additional revenue is not immediately spent, then even as GAV falls, and the condition of workers becomes worse, the GDP at market prices may actually increase. Hence, an increase in GDP at market prices need not capture the change in the condition of the working people. This proposition, discussed as a special case here in the context of demonetization, has a general validity, which is of interest and which I explain in a footnote.[1]

---

[1] Consider the same Kaleckian model as above and suppose in the initial situation there is zero taxation and zero government expenditure. Now the government decides to impose an indirect tax only on the consumption good so that its price rises to $(1 + \alpha)$ times what it was; and the proceeds of such taxation are spent entirely on buying investment goods (so that the budget remains balanced). The price of the investment good remains unchanged since there is no indirect tax on it. In this case too there will be a fall in the consumption good output in the new situation; and since the condition of the workers is given by the excess of consumption good output over the fixed amount of capitalists' consumption, there will be a deterioration in their condition (taking both employment and real wage effects together). If C' denotes consumption good output in the new situation and C in the initial situation, then it can be shown that

$$C'/C = [1 + \alpha.A/C(1 - \mu)] / [1 + \alpha] \dots \tag{iii}$$

There is a line of argument which the RBI has advanced of late, which states that even though demonetisation *did* have an adverse impact on the level of activity, that phase of adverse effect is now over; that with remonetisation the recessionary impulse, which was necessarily only a transitional phenomenon, is now over. As an RBI document (2017) puts it, '..the impact of the liquidity shock was assessed to largely dissipate by mid–February ...'

The same RBI document however which makes this claim also shows that by mid–February, the value of cash with the public was still no more than 60 per cent of what it had been on the eve of demonetisation, and that bank deposits were higher by Rs 5,549 billion on 17 February 2017 than on 28 October 2016. It is intriguing how the recessionary impact of a cash shortage can be deemed to be over when the cash with the public is just 60 per cent of what it had been before the shortage began. And what is more, *even by mid–June it turns out that the extent of remonetisation had not exceeded 86 per cent!*

III: Demonetisation and Banks

If demand contraction in the real economy is one of the costs exacted by demonetisation, the other is the cost exacted by the unwanted cash that

---

where A is capitalists' real consumption and μ the share of wages in value added at factor cost (without taking indirect taxes into account), which is assumed to be identical for both sectors. Since A must be less than $C(1 - \mu)$ which is the entire surplus of consumption goods in the initial situation (that also has to support the investment good workers), C'/C is necessarily less than 1, i.e. there is a fall in consumption good output in the new situation. It can be seen that the greater is α, the rate of indirect taxation, the greater is this fall.

The 'real' GDP at market prices however, or GDP at market prices deflated by a Laspeyre's price index, will be higher than in the initial situation if the r.h.s. of (iii) exceeds $(1 + \alpha)/ (1 + 2\alpha)$; that is, if

$$[1 + \alpha.A/C(1 - \mu)] /[1 + \alpha] > [1 + \alpha]/[1 + 2\alpha].... \qquad \text{(iv)}$$

For a whole range of plausible parameter values, condition (iv) is easily satisfied. For instance if $\alpha = 0.1$ (i.e., 10 per cent tax rate), and the share of consumption of both sectors' capitalists in the total physical surplus of the consumption good in the initial situation $(A/C(1 - \mu))$ is 0.4 (i.e. 40 percent), then condition (iv) is satisfied. It follows therefore that *even when there is an increase in 'real' GDP at market prices, the condition of the working people can well deteriorate even without any reduction in their 'factor share'.*

has accumulated with the banks. Since credit demand from 'worthwhile' borrowers has no reason to increase (indeed the above-mentioned RBI document says that during the period when bank deposits went up by Rs 5,549 billion, bank credit increased only by Rs 1,008 billion), the cash which has been deposited with banks and on which they have to pay an interest, threatens their profitability.

To shore up their profitability, two methods are being adopted. One is the reverse repo operation by the RBI which means that income-yielding government securities in the possession of the RBI are now being put into the portfolios of banks, against the cash they currently hold, in order to increase their incomes. But this only means that the income that would have otherwise accrued to the RBI is now going to accrue to banks. Shoring up banks' profitability in this manner entails therefore a transfer of profits from the RBI to the banks, and since the RBI's profits constitute an income term in the government budget, such shoring up means the use of budgetary resources.

The second way of shoring up banks' profitability is by the government selling special bonds to banks under the market stabilisation scheme (MSS), as it had done when foreign exchange was flooding into the Indian economy and the banks' profitability had been similarly threatened through a surge in deposits, and it had run out of government bonds to sell to banks under reverse repo operations. The rupees obtained by the government through the sale of such special bonds under the MSS are not spent by it but are simply deposited with the RBI, so that the fiscal deficit does not increase; but the government nonetheless pays an interest to the banks on these bonds in their possession. This amounts to a transfer of budgetary resources to banks for no reason whatsoever, other than just to shore up their profits (since the bond-sale proceeds are not spent). It is nothing else but a 'dole' given to banks out of the budget, and that too ironically by a government that is manifestly opposed to 'doles' being given to the poor!

Since the economy, even before demonetisation, had been demand-constrained anyway, and since demonetisation has made it even more severely demand-constrained, if the government spent the proceeds of such bond sales to banks, then that would have no adverse consequences for the economy. (On the contrary, it would negate some of the adverse consequences of demonetisation especially if it stimulates demand for the informal economy.) What is more, government expenditure, while generating larger aggregate demand and employment, would also be a way of putting cash back into the economy, which would thereby provide a further boost to aggregate demand and employment (since the value of the Keynesian multiplier depends also on cash availability). Put differently, if cash is to be injected back into the economy, then instead of its happening through people withdrawing new currency from banks in lieu of the deposits they have been forced to make because of demonetisation, a better way *could be* for new currency to flow in through government expenditure of *certain kinds* from such bond sale.

If the cash needs of the economy are met at least in part in this manner, rather than by people just withdrawing the deposits they had made, then not only would demand be higher than even before demonetisation, but people would also end up holding larger deposits than before when output touches its pre-demonetisation level, which would also aid the movement towards cashless habits that the government desires. But the reason this is not happening, and instead the banks are just being given a 'dole' out of the budget, is because any increase in fiscal deficit (which such spending from bond sales would be counted as) is anathema for globalised finance. The government which has no compunction about imposing a draconian demonetisation on the people that has indubitably caused great distress to them, is by contrast remarkably sensitive to the feelings of finance. This is an inevitable outcome of the economy's remaining stuck within the vortex of globalised finance. But let us leave this aside. The point here, to recapitulate, is that demonetisation is also extracting a cost in the form of budgetary resources having to be 'doled' out to banks that are saddled with unwanted cash.

IV: Persistent Cash Shortage

The presumption underlying the RBI document that things will be back to normal in due course is questionable; and this is so for at least three reasons. First, as the government has made clear, it has no intention of restoring to the economy the full value of the demonetised currency, since it wants to push people into cashless transactions. Attorney-General Mukul Rohatgi told the Supreme Court that Rs 1.5 lakh crore–2 lakh crore less of new currency would be supplied to the economy than what has been demonetised. The finance minister too has reiterated this position subsequently. And the fact that by mid-June only 86 per cent of remonetisation has occurred lends credence to such a scenario. In such a case, the cash shortage will not just be a transient phenomenon but an enduring one; and consequently the cash-shortage-induced output fall in the informal sector will also be an enduring one.

Second, even if the full value of the demonetised currency is restored to the economy, that is, even if the cash shortage turns out to be only a transitional one, the transitional strain on the informal sector caused by demonetisation, would itself leave behind an enduring impact. This is because petty entrepreneurs who go out of business because of absence of demand, will find it difficult to restart business. Once the cash flow gets interrupted and a business gets liquidated, or gets into debt at exorbitant interest rates, its revival becomes that much more difficult. There is in short an asymmetry, whereby it is easier for a business to close down than to restart. Hence, if particular circumstances cause it to close down then the reversal of those circumstances will not necessarily lead to its restarting. A degree of what Karl Marx had called 'centralisation of capital' is inevitable as a result of demonetisation.

The third reason is of importance and deserves to be examined in some detail. One can think of two different kinds of expenditure in an economy: one kind which depends upon current income, of which non-durable consumption is the most obvious example; and the other kind where confidence regarding *the growth of income is crucial*, of which investment is the obvious example. It is not just investment by producers adding to their productive capacity that is dependent upon the expectation of market growth and hence of income growth; even additions to the stock of durable consumption goods by households depend upon whether an income flow is expected by the household in the future, and in a growing economy there would be greater confidence on this score.

Once this growth of incomes comes to a stop for whatever reason (in the present case because of cash shortage), this second type of expenditure falls, so that, even if the cash shortage is subsequently fully overcome, the level of activity does not bounce back to what it might have otherwise been in the absence of the cash shortage, but remains lower owing to the lower level of demand. Even a transient cash shortage therefore, despite being fully reversed after a time lag, leaves behind an enduring effect on the time profile of aggregate income and employment. (This argument, being analogous to, though not exactly identical with, what underlies the standard multiplier-accelerator models of business cycles, should be a familiar one.)

A simple example will make the point clear. Let us denote the part of aggregate expenditure that depends on the current income in period t by $c.Y(t)$. The other part $E(t)$, consisting of investment (including construction), expenditure on durable consumption goods, and such like, can simply be designated by $[E(t-1)^* (1 + g(t-1))]$, where $E(t-1)$ is the previous period's such expenditure and $g(t-1)$ is the previous period's growth rate, i.e. $[Y(t-1) - Y(t-2)]/Y(t-2)$. A heuristic reason for this can be given as follows. Since $E(t-1)$ denotes last period's expenditure of this kind, economic agents plan to spend, and do spend, an amount in the current period that simply grows at the same rate as last period's actual income growth (which they had expected to continue into the present period). We thus have, since income depends upon expenditure in this demand-constrained system,

$$Y(t) = E(t-1)(1 + g(t-1)) + c. Y(t) .. \qquad \text{(v)}$$

Given $Y(0)$ and $g(0)$, the time-profile of income gets determined in this model, and the initial growth rate continues. (This system, as is obvious, does not have any unique equilibrium growth rate and just carries forward the initial growth rate into the future.)

Now, suppose in some particular period t, a cash-shortage is created because of demonetisation, whose impact is felt equi-proportionately (for simplicity) on both kinds of expenditure, and which ensures that the level of income does not increase over what it was in period $t-1$. (This obviously can be relaxed to allow simply for a slower growth owing to cash shortage than would have otherwise occurred.) In this case, $g(t)$ becomes zero, so that the economy settles down at zero growth in all subsequent periods, despite the cash shortage being reversed in all subsequent periods, i.e. despite people being given complete freedom to convert their deposits (which they had been forced to make in lieu of cash) back into cash.

Those who argue that cash supply with the public can simply be turned off and on without having any non-transient effect on the level of activity in the economy, are thus mistaken. Demonetisation will leave behind a legacy that will last even after complete remonetisation is permitted, if at all it is.

[The author thanks Pronab Sen, without incriminating him for the errors that remain in this chapter, for commenting on an earlier draft.]

References

Ghosh Jayati (2017) 'Quarterly GDP Estimates: Curiouser and Curiouser', March 2, www.macroscan.com

Ghosh S.K. (2017) 'Deciphering the GDP Numbers', Ecowrap, State Bank of India, Issue Number 82, March 1, Mumbai.

Nagaraj, R. (2017) 'Quarterly GDP Estimation: Can It Pick Up Demonetisation Impact?', *Economic & Political Weekly*, March 11.

Reserve Bank of India (2017) 'Macroeconomic Impact of Demonetisation: A Preliminary Assessment', March 10, Mumbai.

20

Demonetisation through Segmented Markets

Some Theoretical Perspectives

Parag Waknis

The decision to demonetise 86 per cent of India's currency has been widely and substantially debated by notable scholars of political science and economics. This chapter wishes to add to that debate, by focusing on macroeconomic theory and how the policy decision affects the organised and unorganised sectors of the Indian economy—provided certain assumptions remain in place. The following analysis is based on the money-multiplier theory and the segmented markets model of economic and monetary policy analysis.

There have been a number of commentaries on the impacts of the recent demonetisation policy in the formal as well as informal media (like the blogosphere) as people try to make sense of this huge deliberate monetary shock to the Indian economy. There have also been articles based on detailed analysis as well as opinion pieces by economists like Basu (2016), Chanda (2016), Chandrashekhar (2016), Dasgupta (2016), Rai (2016) among others. In what follows, I contribute some theoretical perspectives based on the essentiality of money and the segmented markets model, to this literature. For the purpose of this chapter, demonetisation is understood as: deeming either some or all of the currency denominations ineligible to be used in transactions.

Money supply is understood as M2—which is the sum of currency in circulation, demand deposits with commercial and cooperative banks, interbank deposits, and post office savings deposits.

Money and the Possible Set of Allocations

It is generally accepted that money facilitates more trades and improves welfare, than what is possible without it. Monetary theorists would call this as money being 'essential'—because the total set of transactions achievable with money is much larger, than the ones achievable without money (Wallace 2001; Nosal and Rocheteau 2011: 47). From this perspective, the demonetisation decision of 8 November 2016 definitely reduced the economic well-being of the Indian people overnight. The overall effect also may not just be this one-time reduction in the achievable set of transactions/allocations, but also a reduction in the ones taking place in the immediate future. While current markets in goods and services facilitate current consumption and investment, credit markets allow economic agents to smooth production and consumption over time. A pervasive reduction in liquidity therefore, however, in the short-term, is bound to adversely affect both current and future consumption and investment decisions. This effect could be pronounced, as in the case of the Indian economy where a huge proportion of transactions is in cash—including, cash used for lending through informal channels like moneylenders as well as microfinance institutions.

There would be some benefits, as the set of allocations that are implemented by cash include ones that use counterfeit currency and those that finance terrorism. Once these transactions cease, they will have a positive impact on the economy. We do have to note that draining cash is not the long-term solution for preventing counterfeiting or curtailing terrorism.

Currency Deposit Ratio and the Money Multiplier

Some people have argued that, based on the money-multiplier model, the money supply would increase because of demonetisation. Because as currency in circulation would go down and deposits would go up, for a given reserve ratio, the banks will have more money to lend. If the money-multiplier model is taken literally, then this analysis is correct.

However, the real question is how far can we trust this model? Some research suggests that there are significant reasons to suspect it

(Carpenter and Demiralp 2012). The reason is pretty simple: if reserve requirements are not binding, that is, if banks are already holding excess reserves, then a further increase in deposits would not lead to an increase in money supply. Second, the money-multiplier model may not accurately describe how banks create money. For example, when describing banking in England, McLeay *et al.* (2014) argued that banks in the modern economy created money through loans, and that their ability to do so depended on the competitiveness of the entire banking industry, the availability of profitable investment opportunities, and not necessarily on the availability of deposits.

Any shortfall, in terms of maintaining reserves with the central bank, is met through active borrowing and lending in the call money markets or through borrowing from the central bank using something like the liquidity adjustment facility (LAF). This does not mean that banks can create unlimited loan deposits—the Reserve Bank of India (RBI) can and does control it by changing the repo/reverse repo rate through the LAF. If the money creation process described by McLeay *et al.* (2014) is applicable to the Indian banking sector, then the money-multiplier model is not the correct means by which we understand how banks contribute to the money supply. Also, the increase in deposits because of demonetisation is deemed to be temporary. This combined with a 100 per cent incremental cash reserve ratio (CRR) on new deposits and no change in the menu of profitable investment opportunities, means that it is highly unlikely that banks would create new loans through the new deposits and therefore, increase the money supply.

Segmented Markets and Demonetisation

So far, we have looked at an analysis using just aggregates, without worrying about how the response of people to demonetisation, would affect those aggregates. Which model could we use to conduct such analysis?

Clearly, through the use of cash and electronic means to settle payments and debt, we have two sets of firms and consumers in the Indian economy—one, which predominantly uses cash and the second, that depends on electronic payments and formal credit markets. Therefore, to understand the effects of demonetisation on the Indian economy from this point of view, the best suited model is that of the segmented markets model—based on the work by Grossman and Weiss (1983), Rotemberg (1984) and Lucas (1990).

This chapter works with a simpler textbook version of it as presented in Chapter 12 of Williamson (2011). The segmented markets model is a flexible, prices and wages model which displays monetary non-neutralities during the short run. It is a micro-founded model, where agents in the economy base their decisions on constrained optimisation. The decisions and assumptions are as follows:

Consumers optimise on two dimensions:

- current consumption and leisure given the wage rate and goods prices. This gives rise to the standard upward sloping labour supply curve (N^s).
- current and future consumption given the real interest rate, r. This gives rise to the savings curve in the market for financial capital and changes in the real interest rate affect ($N^s(r)$).

• Firms optimise to choose two variables:
  - current demand for labour taking wages as given. This gives rise to labour demand curve (N^d) for a given capital stock and total factor productivity.
  - current demand for capital given the interest rate and its marginal productivity.
• Output demand (Y^d) comes from equilibrium demand for current consumption, investment goods and government expenditure respectively and is affected by changes in real interest rate through consumption and investment expenditure.
• Output supply (Y^s) determined by total employment for a given real interest rate and the production function.
• Money demand (M^d) is a function of price level and output. Money supply (M^s) is fixed by the central bank.
• Government balances the budget.
• Competitive equilibrium: All markets clear.

In the standard version of the segmented markets model, it is assumed that only firms and some consumers have access to formal financial markets. If the central bank conducts an open market operation to increase money supply, the interest rate declines and makes it attractive for firms to hold on to money. Since firms are the first ones to get access to money, they decide to hire more labour, after which, all the real effects follow. Segmented market models are characterised by a short-term liquidity effect as the real interest declines because of an increase in the money supply.

Here, I adapt the model to suit the current economic situation in India. Demonetisation means that a decrease in the money supply is not associated with open market operations by the RBI. Let us say there are two sets of consumers and firms as argued above.[1] One set is of firms and consumers that are connected with the formal financial markets, and settle payments and debt through electronic transfers. This will represent firms and workers in the organised formal sector. The second set, of consumers and firms are unconnected and do not transact through formal credit markets or through an electronic payment systems, but they settle their payments and debt through cash. This group represents firms and workers from the unorganised or informal sector. For simplicity, we assume that there is not much spillover between the connected and unconnected economic agents. So market segmentation works through the goods markets and access to formal financial markets.

What would be the effect of demonetisation in such a setting that closely represents the structure of the Indian economy? Let us work with graphs to figure it out. We will start with the set of unconnected consumers and firms. Assume that the economy is in equilibrium to begin with. Figure 20.1 shows the effect.

In Figure 20.1, panel (a) shows the labour market; (b) the goods and services market and (c) the money markets:

- Demonetisation shows up as reduction in money supply in the economy. So the money supply curve shifts left (panel-c). Because the unconnected consumers and firms have less cash now, output demand will go down (Y_1^d to Y_2^d). This is because consumption falls and any investment plans are stalled. Note that this shift could be dampened by credit arrangements that consumers have with their neighbourhood grocery stores.
- The left shift in the output demand curve (panel b) leads to a reduction in the real interest rate. In panel-a, this affects the labour supply curve ($N^S(r_1)$ to $N^S(r_2)$)—reduction in real interest rate reduces the opportunity cost of current labour. Or simply put, people have to skip work to stand in line to exchange/deposit their old notes.
- The second effect is on the labour demand side. The unconnected firms do not have enough cash to pay wages and therefore, they reduce their labour demand or shut down. In all, employment declines and

---

[1] The terminology of 'connected' and 'unconnected' consumers is from Williamson 2009.

the output supply curve also moves to the left (Y_1^S to Y_2^S) reinforcing the decline caused by falling aggregate demand in panel-b (Y_1^d to Y_2^d). Because output falls, eventually there will be a decline in the demand for money, arresting some decline in the aggregate price level caused by demonetisation. To summarise, the unconnected economy experiences a significant decline in employment, output, real interest rate and aggregate price levels.

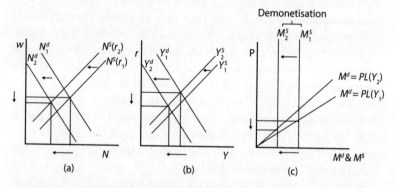

FIGURE 20.1 Demonetisation in Segmented Markets Model: Unconnected Firms and Consumers

What about the connected economy? Figure 20.2 shows the effect on the connected consumers and firms:

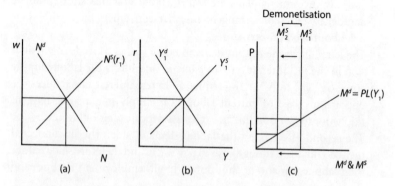

FIGURE 20.2 Demonetisation in Segmented Markets Model: Connected Firms and Consumers

As you can see in the diagram, for the connected consumers and firms, not much happens. Demonetisation shows up as a decline in money supply but this decline is primarily in cash. These consumers and firms have access to electronic payment systems and the credit markets, which allows them to ride the shortage of cash with minor inconveniences. They also experience a decline in the price level, which means that there *could* be an increase in output demand, in the near future. As there is no change in real interest rate or because organised firms do not have any issues paying wages—wages and salaries get credited to employee bank accounts—there is not much change in the formal labour market either.

What is the total effect on the economy according to this model? It depends on the relative contribution to the gross domestic product (GDP) of the connected and unconnected sectors, respectively. The unconnected sector, representing the informal sector here, employs about 75–80 per cent of the total labour employed in the economy (Ghani *et al.* 2013), but it contributes roughly only 20 per cent to the GDP (Enste and Schneider 2000). As has been shown and argued by literature on informality (LaPorta and Shleifer 2008, 2014), informal firms are significantly less productive than their formal counterparts. Therefore, the model seems to suggest that the impact on output or real GDP (GDP adjusted for inflation) might not be as dramatic as suggested by the diagram on unconnected firms.

However, there are several factors that would revise the estimated damage, upwards, compared to the benchmark scenario. One, the human impact in terms of reduced consumption, employment and wages would be experienced by a larger section of the population. Second, some firms in the unconnected or informal sector that shut down may not actually revive after the money supply with the new currency is restored (Shah 2016). Third, in the simple model above, we assumed that there is no relationship between the connected and unconnected economy, which is obviously not true. A lot of raw material suppliers to the formally connected firms are from the informal sector. If the latter suffers, because of drained-out cash, then there would be an effect on the total output supply for the overall economy. Some of this effect could be permanent, as not all the firms that shut down would ever be revived. Fourth, some of the output from the informal sector (agricultural produce, textiles, and some fast moving consumer goods) is consumed by the connected consumers as well. If they cannot buy these goods and services because of a temporary shortage in cash, there will be a fall in their consumption demand.

Thus, despite the mitigating factors contributed by the connected or formal economy, the above analysis suggests that the Indian economy will be depressed for at least a few quarters. As the money supply is restored, the economy will not bounce back until all the adjustments, following the surprise demonetisation decision forced on to consumers and firms, pans out. I doubt anything would change in terms of future flows to the black economy as they depend on factors like the complexity of the tax system, labour market regulations, and trust in the ability of the government to provide public goods among others.[2]

References

Basu K. (2016): 'In India, Black Money Makes for Bad Policy,' 27 November, New York Times.

Carpenter, S. and S. Demiralp (2012): 'Money, Reserves, and the Transmission of Monetary Policy: Does the Money Multiplier Exist?,' *Journal of Macroeconomics*, Vol. 34, No. 1, pp 59–75.

Chanda, A. (2016): *Notes (and Anecdotes) on Demonetisation*, http://sites01. lsu.edu/faculty/achanda/wp-content/uploads/sites/136/2016/12/Notes-on-Demonetisati on.pdf.

Chandrashekhar, C.P. (2016): 'The Budget after Demonetisation,' 21 December, *International Development Economics Associates (IDEAs)*, http://www.net-workideas.org/whats-new/2016/12/the-budget-after-demonetisation/.

Dasgupta, D. (2016): 'Theoretical Analysis of 'Demonetisation,' *Economic & Political Weekly*, Vol 51, No 51, pp. 67–71.

Enste, D.H. and Schneider, F. (2000): 'Shadow Economies: Size, Causes, and Consequences,' *Journal of Economic Literature*, American Economic Association, Vol 38, No 1, pp 77–114.

Ghani, E., W.R Kerr and S.D. O'Connell (2013): 'The Exceptional Persistence of India's Unorganized Sector,' *Policy Research Working Paper Series*, No 6454, World Bank.

Grossman, S. and L. Weiss (1983): 'A Transactions-based Model of the Monetary Transmission Mechanism,' *American Economic Review*, American Economic Association, Vol 73, No 5, pp 871–80.

La Porta, R. and A. Shleifer (2014): 'Informality and Development,' *Journal of Economic Perspectives*, American Economic Association, Vol 28, No 3, pp 109–26.

———— (2008): 'The Unofficial Economy and Economic Development,' National Bureau of Economic Research, Working Paper, No 14520.

[2] *See* Enste and Scheider 2000 and LaPorta and Schleifer 2014 on causes and determinants of informality.

Lucas, R. (1990): 'Liquidity and Interest Rates,' *Journal of Economic Theory*, Elsevier, Vol 50, No 2, pp 237–64.

McLeay M., A. Radia and R.Thomas (2014): 'Money Creation in the Modern Economy,' Bank of England, *Quarterly Bulletin Q1*.

Nosal, E. and G. Rocheteau (2011): *Money, Payments, and Liquidity*, MIT Press, Ed 1, Vol 1, MIT Press Books.

Rai, S. (2016): 'The Demonetisation Decision: Event, Impact, Narrative and Meaning,' 2 December, https://ajayshahblog.blogspot.ca/2016/12/the-demonetisation-decision-event.html.

Rotemberg, J.J. (1984): 'A Monetary Equilibrium Model with Transactions Costs,' *Journal of Political Economy*, University of Chicago Press, Vol 92, No 1, pp 40–58

Shah A. (2016): 'A Monetary Economics View of the De-monetisation,' 13 November, *Business Standard*.

Wallace, N. (2001): 'Whither Monetary Economics?,' *International Economic Review*, Vol 42, pp 847–69.

Williamson, S. (2009): 'Transactions, Credit, and Central Banking in a Model of Segmented Markets,' *Review of Economic Dynamics*, Elsevier for the Society for Economic Dynamics, Vol 12(2), pp 344–62.

———— (2011): *Macroeconomics*, fourth edition, Pearson, Boston, MA.

IV (c) Impact on the Economy

Demonetisation had a crippling impact on the Indian economy. It also led to an acute crisis of livelihoods for a range of working people. Chapters in this section are comments on the impacts of demonetisation on multiple sectors and spheres of the economy.

Ashok K. Lahiri made two important points in his article published in December 2016: one, that the full impacts of demonetisation would be felt only in Q4 and not in Q3; and two, the cash shortage would be overcome fully only after July 2017.

Writing in November 2016, Ashok K. Nag predicted a shrinkage of the GDP and loss of informal sector jobs. R. Nagaraj's chapter, which was published soon after the Q3 estimates of the GDP were published in February 2017, is a short but precise account of the problems with India's GDP estimation methodology. The article by Ritika Mankar and Sumit Shekhar is an interesting critique of the Q3 estimates of the GDP. R. Mohan's article is a review of a study report commissioned by the Kerala State Planning Board on the impact of demonetisation on Kerala's regional economy.

P. Sainath and Rahul M. offer two interesting field insights from rural India on demonetisation. Sainath documents the impacts among farmers, landless labourers and petty traders in Chikalthana village in Maharashtra, while Rahul documents the case of Varda Balayya, who killed himself and tried to poison his entire family by mixing pesticide in their chicken curry in Dharmaram village in Telangana.

21

Demonetisation and Cash Shortage

Ashok K. Lahiri

Demonetisation of Rs 500 and Rs 1,000 notes has resulted in a cash shortage. Non-cash medium of payments may be encouraged by this shortage, but, with supplies only from the domestic currency presses, the shortage is unlikely to disappear by the end of 2016. Import of currency printed abroad may provide a solution for ending it sooner. The impact of the shortage, if it continues, will be fully felt in the last quarter of 2016–17. Its growth impact in 2016–17 could be 0.7–1.3 per cent depending on how much shortage continues, and for how long.

The aim of this chapter is to analyse two questions. First, when is the cash shortage likely to disappear? Second, what is likely to be the impact of the cash shortage on growth in the economy?

I: How Long Will the Cash Shortage Persist

Initial popular sentiments appeared to endorse the government's announced crusade against corruption and black money with demonetisation. Problems have arisen with the resulting cash shortage, disrupting people's lives and economic activity. A temporary cash shortage may have been ignored, but the persistence of the problem has raised questions about how long this shortage is likely to persist.

The government has claimed that the shortage will disappear by the end of the current calendar year. Some commentators (Chaudhuri 2016) have said that it will take much longer, perhaps as long as up to May 2017. So, how long will it take? The answer depends on how much of the demonetised currency notes will have to be substituted with valid notes of equivalent value, and how soon they can be printed and distributed.

How much of the demonetised notes will have to be substituted with valid notes in turn depends on two factors. First, how much was presented for over-the-counter conversion, and how much will be deposited in bank and post office accounts. In 1946, when currency notes of the value of Rs 500, Rs 1,000 and Rs 10,000 were demonetised by an ordinance, such notes in circulation were of Rs 143.97 crore. By the end of 1947, Rs 134.9 crore, or 93.7 per cent were exchanged. In 1978, when currency notes of denominations Rs 1,000, Rs 5,000 and Rs 10,000 were demonetised, the total amount in circulation was Rs 145.42 crore. Of this, 89 per cent or Rs 129.4 crore came back for exchange.

It is reasonable to assume that, for the fear of detection, some 'black money' circulating in the form of currency will have a tendency not to come back for exchange. Given the decrease in the proportion surrendered for conversion between 1946 and 1978, and the increased efficiency of tax administration and banking industry in 2016 in monitoring such conversion, 85 per cent can be taken as a conservative estimate of such conversion in the current round. An optimistic estimate can be 80 per cent.

Second, even when the demonetised notes are deposited in bank or post office accounts, these may be kept as deposits, without necessarily being withdrawn in the form of currency. It is likely that the current cash shortage may have given a stimulus to the banking habits and cashless transactions among the population. Compelled by the cash shortage, many may have realised the potential of the debit and credit cards, online transfers, and other digital payment facilities such as mobile payments. Furthermore, the preference for cash in transactions is partly motivated by the objective of avoiding detection for tax purposes. If avoiding detection becomes more difficult, tax compliance may improve and also exert a downward pressure on the transaction demand for cash relative to that for deposit.

It is important to note, however, that the demand for currency relative to deposit money also depends on the confidence that people have in the banking system and its ability to convert deposits into cash at sight. During the Great Depression in the United States, that began in November 1930 and persisted for two and a half years, the nominal gross national product (GNP) fell by 38 per cent, deposits fell by 33 per cent, and currency with the public rose by 55 per cent, resulting in a rise in the currency–deposit (CD) ratio (Boughton and Wicker 1979: 405). Will the recent demonetisation exercise, by shaking up public confidence in the banks' unrestricted ability to convert deposits into cash, also work the same way in enhancing the CD ratio? Given that people seem to have accepted the demonetisation as a one-off exercise for tackling black money, this stimulation of the demand for currency relative to deposits is likely to be negligible.

As Figure 21.1 demonstrates, the CD ratio in India has been on a declining trend. But this ratio is still almost 50 per cent higher than that in the Organization for Economic Cooperation and Development (OECD) countries, and is likely to go down further. The recent demonetisation may give a fillip to the process, at least temporarily. What happened in Europe during the euro cash changeover in 2002 is likely to happen in India as well following the recent demonetisation, namely, a sharp reduction in the CD ratio followed by slow recovery (ECB 2003). A reduction in interest rates because of excess cash in banks is likely to reduce the opportunity cost of holding currency relative to deposits in banks, and help the equilibration of the CD ratio.

Of the Rs 16.6 trillion currency in circulation on 31 March 2016, a total of 85.2 per cent (Rs 14.2 trillion) was in Rs 500 and Rs 1,000

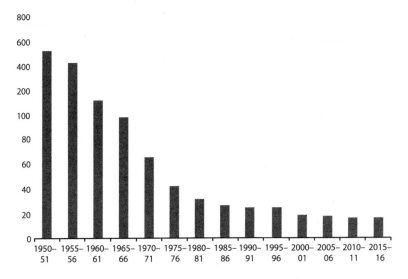

Figure 21.1 Currency-Deposit Ratio

notes. Of this Rs 14.2 trillion, 3.98 per cent (Rs 0.7 trillion) were held by banks. Assuming the same proportion of Rs 500 and Rs 1,000 notes held by banks on 8 November, the value of Rs 500 and Rs 1,000 notes held by the public are obtained as Rs 7.5 trillion and Rs 6.1 trillion, respectively.

Note that on the eve of demonetisation on 8 November 2016, the money stock must have been higher than the stock on 31 March 2016. Between 31 March 2015 and 31 March 2016, Rs 500 and Rs 1,000 notes in circulation grew by 19.7 per cent and 12.7 per cent, respectively. So it is reasonable to assume that Rs 500 and Rs 1,000 notes held by the public on 8 November could have been around 8.3 trillion and 6.5 trillion, respectively, that is about 10 per cent and 6.5 per cent higher than the corresponding figures on 31 March 2016. Based on these assumptions, number of Rs 500 and Rs 1,000 notes with the public on 8 November 2016 is obtained as 16.6 billion and 6.5 billion, respectively (Table 21.1). Though all the old Rs 500 and Rs 1,000 notes held by banks will also have to be substituted by other notes, it need not be done immediately as long as the exchange of such notes held by the public goes on smoothly and total deposits do not dip below the level on 8 November.

TABLE 21.1 Post-Demonetisation Conversion of Rs 500 and Rs 1,000 Notes into Currency

	Number in billion		
	Rs 500	Rs 1,000	Rs 2,000
On 8th November 2016			
i) In circulation	17.28	6.74	–
ii) With the public (96 per cent of circulation)	16.59	6.47	–
Post demonetisation iii) Conservative estimate: 85 per cent deposited or converted a) converted or deposited in accounts	14.10	5.50	–
b)With the public in currency	12.98	–	2.53
iv) Aggressive estimate: 80 per cent deposited or converted a) converted or deposited in accounts	13.27	5.17	–
b) with the public in currency	12.15	–	2.37

If a uniform 15 per cent of such notes do not come back because of the measures against black money, then only 14.1 billion Rs 500 notes and 5.5 billion Rs 1,000 notes will be deposited into accounts or presented for conversion into other notes. A more aggressive assumption of 20 per cent of such notes not coming back yields 13.3 billion Rs 500 notes and 5.2 billion of Rs 1,000 notes for conversion or deposits (Table 21.1).

How much of these deposits of old demonetised notes will be withdrawn in the form of currency is the next important question. Between 28 October and 11 November 2016, currency with the public went down from Rs 17.0 trillion to Rs 15.3 trillion, while currency with banks rose from Rs 759 billion to Rs 2.6 trillion, time deposits from Rs 96.5 trillion to Rs 97.5 trillion, and credit to the commercial sector declined from Rs 79.6 trillion to Rs 79.0 trillion. The CD ratio, as a result, went down from 15.9 per cent on October 28 to 14.1 per cent on 11 November 11, but not because people wanted less currency, but because they could not withdraw cash even if they wanted to.

While some of the 'de-hoarding' of high-denomination notes is likely to be reversed over time, the CD ratio is unlikely to go back to its 28 October value. If the CD ratio does not go back up beyond 15 per cent, which is likely for the reasons already adduced and the reduction in currency with the public is entirely in terms of Rs 500 and higher denomination notes, the holding of such notes may go down by a further total of Rs 1 trillion which is the rise in the time deposits with banks between 28 October and 11 November. This is over and above the amount that does not come back as deposit at banks or for conversion into valid notes under the two scenarios.

Distributing this Rs 1 trillion reduction in the same ratio as Rs 500 and Rs 1,000 notes circulating on 28 October, that is, 56.2 per cent and 43.1 per cent, the number of Rs 500 notes that will be demanded in the form of cash is obtained as 12.98 billion under the conservative scenario and 12.15 billion under the aggressive scenario. Since what is being supplied in terms of currency notes in denomination higher than Rs 500 is Rs 2,000, under the simplifying and somewhat heroic assumption that the public will willingly accept the substitution of Rs 1,000 old notes by the new Rs 2,000 notes, the corresponding numbers for Rs 2,000 notes are 2.53 billion and 2.37 billion.

The payments system in India indeed is in 'the cusp of a revolution' (Joseph *et al.* 2013). The Indian payments revolution of the future may be as fast as the revolution in mobile telephony in the recent past. But India still is a cash-intensive country. Though it may be moving towards being less cash-intensive, the ongoing payments revolution by itself is unlikely to solve the post-demonetisation cash shortage in the immediate future.

Bank notes are printed at four note presses: at Currency Note Press, Nashik and Bank Note Press, Dewas, both owned by Security Printing and Minting Corporation of India Ltd (SPMCIL), and at Mysuru and Salboni, owned by Bharatiya Reserve Bank Note Mudran Private Limited (BRBNML), a wholly-owned subsidiary of the RBI. SPMCIL is wholly owned by the Government of India. The printing capacities of these four units are not readily available in the public domain. But, the RBI's *Annual Report 2016* provides the indents for and supply of currency notes by the four units during the three years (Table 21.2).

Table 21.2 does not paint a rosy prospect for the rapid amelioration of the cash shortage. The total number of pieces of currency supplied was 20.9 billion in 2013–14, 23.6 billion in 2014–15 and 21.2 billion in 2015–16. Supply fell short of indent by 17.5 per cent, 2.3 per cent and 11.3 per cent in these three years in sequence. The maximum Rs 500 and Rs 1,000 notes supplied in the last three years were in 2014–15, and at 5.0 billion and 1.0 billion, respectively.

The required number of Rs 500 notes in the two scenarios to wipe out the cash shortage is 12–13 billion pieces, which is more than twice the maximum produced in 2014–15. Similarly, even if the old Rs 1,000 notes are replaced by Rs 2,000 notes, the corresponding requirement of

TABLE 21.2   Indent and Supply of Bank Notes by BRBNMPL and SPMCIL (in Million Pieces)

Denominations	2013–14		2014–15		2015–16		2016–17
	Indent	Supply	Indent	Supply	Indent	Supply	Indent
5	–	–	–	–	–	–	–
10	12164	9467	6000	9417	4000	5857	3000
20	1203	935	4000	1086	5000	3252	6000
50	994	1174	2100	1615	2050	1908	2125
100	5187	5131	5200	5464	5350	4910	5500
500	4839	3393	5400	5018	5600	4291	5725
1000	975	818	1500	1052	1900	977	2200
Total	25362	20918	24200	23652	23900	21195	24550

Source: RBI Annual Report, 2016, p 90.

Rs 2,000 notes at 2.4–2.5 billion pieces exceeds the maximum annual production of Rs 1,000 notes achieved in 2014–15 by a factor of more than two.

The maximum number of pieces of currency notes, irrespective of denominations, produced by all the four currency presses together was 23.7 billion. The total requirement of Rs 500 and Rs 2,000 notes for removing the cash shortage is between 14.5 and 15.5 billion, or between 32 and 34 weeks of the rate of production achieved in 2014–15. Thus, even if the currency presses were to produce only Rs 500 and Rs 2,000 notes with the same level of efficiency as in 2014–15, the shortage would disappear only by mid-June or the first week of July 2017.

A little more than a fortnight before the demonetisation, it was reported that '[The RBI] has very nearly completed preparations for introducing this new high-value currency … The notes have already been printed, and their despatch from the currency printing press in Mysuru has commenced' (Sridhar and Vageesh 2016). While no figures are available about how many Rs 2,000 notes were printed before 8 November, it is assumed that such production was negligible at around a couple of million at most.

Meeting the demand for Rs 500 and Rs 2,000 denomination notes in 50 days would require a daily production of 290 million to 310 million pieces, which is 106 billion–109 billion pieces per year. Meeting the 50-day deadline thus, requires the currency printing presses to ramp up their production at least four-fold. Operating three shifts instead of two will increase production by no more than 50 per cent. A four fold enhancement of output of the four currency printing presses within a short time may be a mission impossible.

A quick way to relieve the shortage would be to consider the strategy that the government under Prime Minister Atal Bihari Vajpayee adopted in 1998. Among other things, it decided to import 3,600 million pieces of printed notes adding up to a face value of Rs 1 trillion to rapidly wipe out the cash shortage (Vikraman 2016).

II: How the Cash Shortage Will Affect Inflation and Growth

Currency and deposit money or credit cards are not perfect substitutes as medium of exchange in many transactions. For example, the daily wage of an unskilled or semi-skilled worker, retail purchases from a street vendor, or even vegetables in the mandis or wholesale markets in many places cannot be paid for in anything but cash. The cash shortage has affected trading and production in many segments of the informal economy. An additional cost is the mandays lost queuing up at banks for conversion or deposit of old currency.

The cash shortage may have already affected the prices of perishable goods and services. Prices of vegetables in wholesale markets, according to newspaper reports, have fallen significantly. Vegetable prices go down around this time of the year because of seasonality, but cash shortage reportedly was an additional factor. Overall inflation may come down because people have less of one common medium of exchange, namely cash, to transact, but this decline in inflation will be tempered by how much output also falls because of the lack of cash as working capital.

Money is the lubricant that keeps the wheel of economic activity moving. A standard, albeit simplistic, approach to analysing the impact of the cash shortage is to fall back on the Cambridge equation of the quantity theory of money. Three scenarios are considered.

In scenario I, both currency with the public and the demand deposits at the end of March 2017 are 10 per cent higher than the corresponding figures a year ago. Effectively, in scenario I, at the end of 2016–17, currency with the public gets more than restored to what it was before demonetisation. Although the year-on-year (Y-o-Y) growth of both currencies with the public and demand deposits is the same 10 per cent, post-demonetisation, growth of currency is over Rs 2.3 trillion compared to only Rs 84 billion growths in demand deposits.

Under scenario II, Y-o-Y growth of currency and demand deposits is 6.5 per cent and 5 per cent, respectively. While the Y-o-Y growth in demand deposits is 5 per cent, such deposits decline by Rs 419 billion after demonetisation signifying a shift from demand deposits to currency. At the end of 2016–17, while currency with the public exceeds the pre-demonetisation level by Rs 556 billion in scenario I, the pre-demonetisation level is just about restored under scenario II.

Scenario III considers the case where the authorities fail to make up for the cash shortage by the end of March 2017, and currency with the public, with Y-o-Y growth of only 4 per cent, falls short of the pre-demonetisation level by Rs 402 billion. Demand deposits grow, Y-o-Y, only by 4 per cent, and like under scenario II, is Rs 670 billion lower than what it was on 11 November 2016 post-demonetisation.

In all the three scenarios, the growth of M1 from 11 November 2016—the first reporting Friday for banks after demonetisation—to 31

March 2017 has been assumed to follow a straight line path of equal absolute change every fortnight. Gross domestic product (GDP) at current prices for the third and fourth quarters of 2016–17 is projected by assuming the income velocity values.

Needless to say, Table 21.3 is for illustrative purposes. It shows that the impact of the cash crunch, if it persists, is going to be the most severe in the fourth quarter. Almost half the third quarter had passed before the cash crunch set in. If the cash shortage persists, nominal growth could be as low as 4–7 per cent in the fourth quarter, depending on how severe the shortage is.

TABLE 21.3 GDP and Narrow Money: Three Scenarios with Demonetisation (Growth in %)

	GDP at Current Prices		M1 (average)		GDP/M1 (average)
	in Rs billion	Growth Year-on-Year	in Rs billion	Growth Year-on-Year	
2015–16					
Q1	31,746	8.85	23,576	10.34	1.35
Q2	32,486	6.41	23,425	10.26	1.39
Q3	34,760	9.07	24,102	11.56	1.44
Q4	36,768	10.36	25,200	12.62	1.46
2016–17					
Q1	35,055	10.42	26,784	13.61	1.31
Q2	36,420	12.14	27,131	15.82	1.34
Scenario I (cash shortage more than made up by 31 March 2017)					
Q3	39,126	12.56	26,983	11.96	1.45
Q4	40,924	11.30	28,030	11.23	1.46
Scenario II (cash shortage just made up by 31 March 2017)					
Q3	38,637	11.15	26,831	11.33	1.44
Q4	39,489	7.40	27,234	8.07	1.45
Scenario III (cash shortage is reduced but not made up by 31 March 2017)					
Q3	38,236	10.00	26,739	10.94	1.43
Q4	38,247	4.02	26,746	6.13	1.43

Source: Weekly Statistical Table No. 6, RBI and Press Releases of Central Statistics Office, Ministry of Statistics and Programme Implementation, Government of India dated 3 May 2016 and 30 November 2016.

The GDP for 2016–17 is obtained by adding up the quarterly GDP figures. Growth declines from 11.6 per cent in scenario I to 10.2 per cent in scenario II and 9 per cent in scenario III. Under the heroic assumption that nominal growth will be coming equally from real growth and inflation, the growth impact of the cash shortage is 0.7–1.3 per cent depending on how much of the cash shortage continues to persist and for how long. Of course, over the long run, how the economy will be affected will depend on how far the demonetisation is followed up by suitable and effective measures to control the shadow economy.

III: Conclusions

Demonetisation of Rs 500 and Rs 1,000 notes on 8 November 2016 has become a matter of intense debate. Production of high-value notes have been discontinued by many countries because these are often used for money laundering and organised crime. The Indian demonetisation is considerably different from such scrapping of high-value notes. Such scrapping typically involves stopping the production of high-value notes and asking the banks to return such notes for destruction by the central bank. But the high-value notes continue to be legal tender. In India, the old Rs 500 and Rs 1,000 notes have ceased to be legal tender, and not only does the production of new Rs 500 notes continue, but a new Rs 2,000 note has been introduced as well.

The post-demonetisation situation has been complicated by a cash shortage disrupting people's lives and economic activity. Sentiments of a large section of the people appear to endorse the government's announced crusade against corruption and black money with demonetisation. But the persistence of cash shortage may not only erode such support but also affect the economy, particularly in the fourth quarter of 2016–17. It is imperative that the cash shortage be rapidly removed by suitable action, if necessary through import of currency printed abroad.

High-value notes have been demonetised three times so far in India— in 1946, 1978 and 2016. On all the three occasions, the objective was to contain black money. The outcome after the two previous exercises in 1946 and 1978 has not been very inspiring. This time, there appears to be a concerted plan of action, including changes in tax laws and legal treatment of benami transactions. Only time will tell whether 2016 is different from 1946 and 1978. In 1946 and 1978, 6.3 per cent and 11 per cent, respectively of the demonetised currency did not return to the banking system. If 15 per cent or more, that is, at least Rs 2.3 trillion worth of old Rs 500 and Rs 1,000 notes, does not come back for exchange, it will give an early indication that this time may be different from the past. But even after clearing the muck of currency that was mediating illegal or unaccounted transactions in the recent past, what will remain is the larger job of preventing its accumulation in the future.

References

Boughton, James M. and Elmus R. Wicker (1979): 'The Behavior of the Currency–Deposit Ratio during the Great Depression,' *Journal of Money, Credit and Banking*, Vol 11, No 4, pp 405–418.

Chaudhuri, Saumitra (2016): 'Even as world changes under Trump, India's Currency Shortages Will Stay for Months,' The Economic Times Blogs, November 15, http://blogs.economictimes.indiatimes.com/et-commentary/even-as-world-ch....

ECB (2003): 'The Demand for Currency in the Euro Area and the Impact of the Euro Cash Changeover,' *Monthly Bulletin*, European Central Bank, January, pp 39–51.

Sridhar, G. Naga and N.S. Vageesh (2016): 'Coming soon to your wallet: Rs 2,000 notes,' *The Hindu Business Line*, October 21.

Joseph, Nikhil, Ruben Korenke, Benjamin D Mazzotta and Bhaskar Chakravorti (2013): 'Cash Outlook—India,' Working Paper 13–01, Institute for Business in the Global Context, Fletcher School, Tufts University.

Lahiri, Amartya (2016): 'The Demonetisation Boondoggle,' *Business Standard*, 4 December.

Varma, Subodh (2016): 'Veggie Wholesale Rates Crash, Retail Prices Only Dip In Cities,' *The Economic Times*, 2 December, http://economictimes.indiatimes.com/news/economy/agriculture/veggie-whol....

Vikraman, Shaji (2016): 'In fact: How NDA under Atal Bihari Vajpayee Saw High Value Notes,' *The Indian Express*, November 16.

22

Lost Due to Demonetisation

Ashok K. Nag

Sudden demonetisation of Rs 500 and Rs 1,000 notes, an elimination of existing money stock that enables economic transactions, is bound to have an economic impact, apart from penalising those who hold this money as the store of their tax-evaded illegal wealth. Considering various possible scenarios, a loss of gross domestic product (GDP) will be inevitable.

On 8 November 2016, Prime Minister Narendra Modi met three defence services chiefs and the national security adviser. Speculations were rife on social media that India was embarking upon another punishing move against our recalcitrant neighbour. But the bolt from the blue came from elsewhere. The Prime Minister came on national television to announce what has been called a 'surgical strike' against the black economy.

The stated objective of this demonetisation of high-value notes of denominations Rs 500 and Rs 1,000 as per the Gazette notification (Ministry of Finance 2016) are:

i) to curb the menace of fake currencies;
ii) to wipe out unaccounted and tax evaded money stored in such high-value notes; and
iii) to prevent use of high-denomination notes for terror financing.

To begin with, let us look at how the denomination-wise distribution of currency held by the public has evolved over the years. The share of

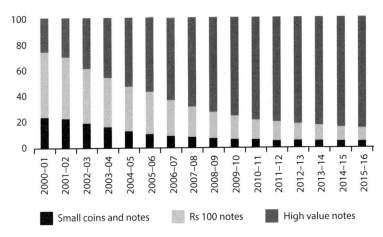

FIGURE 22.1 Denomination-wise Composition of Currency in Value Terms

high-value notes (notes of Rs 500 and Rs 1,000) in value terms went up from 26 per cent in 2000–01 to 85.2 per cent by the end of March 2016 (Figure 22.1). In volume terms, the growth was from 3.1 per cent to 24.4 per cent. To provide another perspective, let us consider M1 (narrow money) comprising demand deposits, currency in circulation and a small component called 'other deposits with the RBI.' For all practical purposes, M1 represents transactional demand of the economy. The share of high-value notes in M1 has gone up from 14.8 per cent in 2000–01 to 54.5 per cent by the end of March 2016. In other words, high-value notes are increasingly supporting the transaction demand for money, rather than its 'store of value' demand.

Economic Impact

In economics, currency used to carry out a sudden injection of money uniformly to all economic agents is known as 'helicopter money.' Nobel laureate Milton Friedman first used this metaphor in his 1969 paper titled 'The Optimal Quantity of Money.' If a central bank drops currency to all citizens of a country from a helicopter for their keep forever, the result, in Friedman's monetarist formulation of the thought experiment, would be inflation. Economists have pointed out that this experiment is nothing but a fiscal stimulation whereby the government gives a cheque to all its citizens drawn on the central bank. The immediate effect of this experiment is that the currency liability of the central bank increases with proportionate increase in loans to the government on the asset side of the central bank.

Demonetisation can be thought of as opposite to 'helicopter money,' to the extent that a part of the money supply gets extinguished because of the reluctance of holders of such unaccounted and tax-evaded money to exchange it for new legal tender. We may call it a 'vacuum-cleaning' of some part of the money supply. What would be the outcome of this experiment?

Before we look at the various possible outcomes of this experiment, it would be instructive to consider some scenarios which are neither apocryphal nor mere canards spread by opponents of this move. Let us consider a large company which routinely engages labour contractors for their infrastructure projects like highway construction. The contractor in turn engages casual labourers who are paid in cash on a daily basis. Once the demonetisation process sets in, the cash flow dries up because of non-availability of required or even lower denomination notes. The project is stalled, albeit temporarily. But it results in loss of wage of labourers, reduction in profit of contractors and the process rolls up to the large conglomerate at the top. Even if there is disruption for 2–3 days, its monetary impact for an organisation of this magnitude would be at least a few millions of rupees.

My second example is typical of any small to medium-sized town of India. A liquor trader with a chain of retail shops is saddled with a stash of around Rs 50 million in cash. S/he is looking for Jan Dhan accounts that can be used for this purpose. Ironically, the process of vacuum-cleaning unaccounted money itself is generating such money again. The trader does his business only in cash; buying in cash from wholesaler and selling in cash to the retail customers. It is impossible for him to give credit to his customers in a trade like this. Most probably, s/he has to scale down his business drastically for the next couple of months.

Loss of Business and GDP

As we have already explained, a large part of high-value notes are used for transactional purpose, that is, as a medium of exchange and not as a store of value. In the cash economy, high-value notes are the principal form of working capital. For the consumers, the propensity to consume leisure, hospitality and luxury goods is also very high for income in unaccounted cash. It would be possible to work out monetary value of the gross domestic product (GDP) generated by use of such cash in a purely monetarist framework of money. We are using this framework only as a way of illustration. In 2015–16, the ratio of GDP at market price to M1 was around 5.2. We may reasonably assume that velocity of money in a purely cash economy would be less, as compared to that of a formal economy which is digitally connected. We can now create the following scenarios presented in Table 22.1.

TABLE 22.1 Scenarios of GDP Loss

Assumed Velocity of Transactional Cash in Pure Cash Economy	Assumed Part of High Value Money That Supports Exclusively Cash Economy	GDP Generated by the High Value Notes in the Cash Economy (in Rs billion)	Reduction in GDP (percentage in parenthesis (assuming 10% of cash will not be exchanged)
2.5	0.25	8862	886 (1)
2	0.2	5672	567 (0.4)
1.5	0.15	3190	319 (0.2)
1	0.1	1418	142 (0.1)

The benchmark velocity of 5.2 is computed using GDP at current market prices for 2015–16 and M1 as at the end of 2015–16. Column 2 represents the percentage of high-value notes at the end of March 2015–16 (Rs 14,179.43 billion) that will be taken a measure of money and which is used for transactions that generate and support tax-evaded and unaccounted economic activities. Using this percentage we get the stock of high value money that supports the pure cash economy. We get GDP generated by this money by multiplying it by assumed velocity. Thus computed value of (0.25*14,179.43*2.5) is Rs 8,862 billion. Now if 90 per cent of cash is exchanged with new notes and continue to support the corresponding economic activities, there is no impact on GDP. So we get Rs 886.2 as the GDP lost because it goes out of circulation and cannot be used for any economic activity.

Informal Credit Disruption

According to a study undertaken by Timberg and Aiyar (1984), informal credit markets account for as much as 20 per cent of total credit outstanding in many Indian markets they studied. Based on their survey, they observed that creditworthiness in such informal markets are assessed based on the 'cash flow' of the borrowers and not their assets. This is quite logical, as in India the prospect of any recovery by way of attachment of properties is almost nil. In a private conversation two general managers of two of the largest public sector banks confided that in their career of more than 30 years they had never recovered a single rupee from any court-ordered attachment, although they routinely obtained such attachments as a matter of office procedure.

It would not be wrong to assume that a large part of the unaccounted cash economy would not have access to formal credit market. Vacuum-cleaning of cash from a cash economy would deal a severe blow to the creditworthiness of the borrowers and would surely dent their economic activities. Furthermore, many borrowers would resort to repaying their borrowings using denotified cash leading to further disruption in this market. The extent of impact may be difficult to assess but it cannot be insignificant.

In such a relationship-driven credit market, cascading effect of default by any one borrower would be severe, as social, political and economic interrelationship between borrowers and lenders are much more extensive and deeper for this market.

Penalising Evaders

Demonetisation affects the stock of unaccounted and tax-evaded cash, but not necessarily any flow or generation process of such cash. It is possible that bureaucrats and politicians are primarily responsible for generation of unaccounted cash. But officials of the private sector are also not immune. The only difference is that the private sector, particularly large companies, generally avoids publicity and criminal prosecution of culprits. But all these people represent only the demand side of the corruption. The supply side of the corruption is represented by businesses, including the corporate sector.

Demonetisation affects more severely the people who operate on the demand side of corruption. This is so because the money received by them is most likely to be used either for consumption or for purchase of assets like gold, real estate, etc. These people are not entrepreneurs who would use such tax-evaded money for business purposes. As such, unaccounted money in the form of cash is received over a long period; the likelihood of such people being caught with a huge stash of money at any point of time is much more than businessmen who keep unaccounted cash to meet the current demand of such cash. Even those businessmen who operate exclusively in the cash economy, particularly traders, would keep cash only as a part of working capital and not as a store of value. Thus, any demonetisation is always targeted against those who hoard cash as a store of value.

Liquidity Impact on the Banks

The immediate reverse flow of cash from the purely cash economy to the formal banking sector would cause a huge surge in liquidity of regulated banking sector. The figures are staggering. The total value of high-value notes outstanding as at end of March 2016 was Rs 14,179.43 billion. The corresponding 'total cash in hand' of scheduled commercial bank stood at Rs 574.38 billion as against the total cash with the banking sector being at Rs 653.68 billion. Applying this share of scheduled commercial banks to total outstanding value of high-value notes, these banks are looking forward to an inward flow of Rs 12,459.28 billion. The actual flow would be lesser by the amount that would get 'vacuum-cleaned.' Furthermore, a significant proportion would get exchanged with new notes and not remain as deposits. Even if actual flow that adds to the stock of cash in hand of the banks happens to be 50 per cent of the outstanding amount, the liquidity of the scheduled commercial bank would increase by a factor of 10.8 times. A significant part of this new-found liquidity would flow to the bond market and result in an increase in bond prices and concomitant reduction in yield. The resulting gain in a bank's bond portfolio may help many banks to clean up the balance sheet which would have been badly damaged due to a rise in non-performing assets. Concomitantly, the banks would be compelled to seek an enhanced credit offtake by reducing their lending rates.

However, the surge in liquidity will have an adverse impact too. Let us assume that this liquidity injection remains for a couple of days in the savings bank account of banks. A 4 per cent interest for one day on Rs 1 billion would be around Rs 1 lakh. Even if Rs 1 trillion attract interest for five days the interest cost to the banks would be Rs 500 million. If the market takes time to return to its normal state, this cost would increase significantly.

Government Tax Receipts

Even if 10 per cent of the new cash flow to the regulated sector attracts penal provisions of taxation, the government coffers would be richer by at least Rs 10 billion to Rs 20 billion. We may recall that around Rs 650 billion were declared by the recent voluntary disclosure scheme. A little above Rs 29 billion was received by the central government by way of penal tax. Out of Rs 1.5 trillion deposited so far, if the government can levy tax to the tune of 100 per cent on even 10 per cent of this amount of money, it would be richer by another Rs 150 billion as against the expected receipt of Rs 3.5 trillion.

RBI's Balance Sheet

Currency notes with the public are a liability for the RBI. Once a part of outstanding high-value notes get 'vacuum-cleaned' they cease to be a liability to the RBI. According to the latest balance sheet, its total liabilities stood at Rs 32.4 trillion. The liabilities on account of issuance of currency stood at 52.65 per cent of the total liability. As we have already noted, around 85 per cent of currency liabilities would be on account of high-value notes which now stand denotified. A 10 per cent 'vacuum-cleaning' would amount to reduction of RBI currency liabilities to the tune of Rs 1.4 trillion. If the RBI writes it back and treats as its income, the RBI would reap benefits. Let it be noted that the RBI transferred only Rs 658 billion to the Government of India last year while the budget deficit for the financial year 2015–16 was around Rs 5.32 trillion.

As the budgeted fiscal deficit for 2016–17 remains the same in absolute amount, this could mean the deficit would come down at least by one percentage point. Thus, if the central government does not use the extra transfer from the RBI for additional capital expenditure and thereby offset the contracting effect of 'vacuum-cleaning' of high-value notes, the country on balance is a net loser on account of this move of the central government.

Only a Minor Bump

Finally, the most important point that needs an answer from the policy-makers is whether this demonetisation initiative would be followed with policy measures that would stop or at least curb the generation of black money. Elimination of the current stock of unaccounted and tax-evaded money does not imply that generation of such money is being stopped. It would only mean that a new set of players would replace the older ones, but the game would continue. To give one example, the RBI has repeatedly warned against misuse of participatory notes (P-Notes) in capital market transactions. Nothing has been done so far. In many countries government spending at transactional level has been released under an open data licence. This has been a very effective anti-corruption move. Many similar measures can be suggested which will strike at the root of corruption. Demonetisation can at best be a temporary road bump, but it would not stop the onward journey of the chariot of corruption.

References

Ministry of Finance (2016): 'The Gazette Notification No 2652, November 8,' New Delhi, Controller of Publications.

RBI (2005): *History of the Reserve Bank of India (1967-81)*, Vol III, viewed on 17 November 2016, https://rbidocs.rbi.org.in/rdocs/content/ PDFs/90077. pdf.

Timberg, Thomas A. and C.V. Aiyar (1984): 'Informal Credit Markets in India,' *Economic Development and Cultural Change*, Vol 33, No 1, pp 43–59.

23

The Cashless Economy of Chikalthana

P. Sainath

The government's demonestisation has devastated farmers, landless labourers, pensioners, petty traders and many others across Maharashtra. In Chikalthana village, the prime minister's dream of a cashless economy seems to have been realised. Nobody has any cash.

In Chikalthana village, on the edge of and merging with Aurangabad town in Maharashtra, Prime Minister Narendra Modi's dream of a cashless economy seems to have been realised. Nobody has any cash. Not the banks, nor the ATMs and certainly not the people queuing up in and around them in despair. Even the policemen sitting in the vans outside bank branches haven't any. But cheer up. They'll soon have ink marks on their fingers.

In the State Bank of Hyderabad (SBH) at Shahganj within the walled city of Aurangabad, you can see equally desperate bank staff struggling to help their impoverished clients. There and in other branches of every single bank in the town, soiled notes worth crores of rupees in denominations of Rs 50 and Rs 100—meant to be sent to the Reserve Bank of India (RBI) for final destruction—are being reintroduced into circulation. The RBI knows of this but condones it through silence.

'What option do we have?' ask people working in these banks. 'The public really needs small notes now. All their work and transactions have come to a halt.' As we speak to the staff inside, Javeed Hayat Khan, a small vendor, comes up to us from a queue that runs close to a kilometre outside the bank, on a Sunday. He hands us an invitation to his daughter Rasheda Khatoon's wedding.

'All I have in my account is Rs 27,000,' he says. 'All I ask for is Rs 10,000 of that for my daughter's wedding coming up in three weeks. And I'm not allowed to withdraw it.' The bank held back since he had withdrawn Rs 10,000 the previous day, though he is entitled to take out the same sum today. Because they feel there isn't enough cash to go around the serpentine queues. And they hope to give some small amount to each person in those lines. A couple of them are now trying to help Khan. They point out that such money as he has in his account came from breaking a fixed deposit he had set up for his daughter's marriage.

As several writers, analysts and official reports have already pointed out, the bulk of India's 'black' economy is held in bullion, benami land deals, and foreign currency. Not in stacks of notes in grandma's old oak chest. The chairman of the Central Board of Direct Taxes said so in a 2012 report on Measures to tackle black money in India and abroad. The report also said (page 14, Part II, 9.1) demonetisation 'miserably failed' on two past occasions in 1946 and 1978. Yet, this action is what the Bharatiya Janata Party government has repeated. The 'Modi masterstroke', a term contrived by assorted anchors and other clowns on television to hail an unbelievably stupid action, is spreading agony and misery in its wake across the countryside. If there's been any stroke, it's the one the heart of the rural economy has suffered.

The recovery time from the stroke was first dismissed by the finance minister and his party colleagues as 2–3 days of discomfort. 'Doctor' Arun Jaitley then modified that to 2–3 weeks. Soon after, his senior surgeon, Narendra Modi, said he needed 50 days to restore the patient to health. So we're already into 2017 with this course of treatment. Meanwhile, we do not know how many people across the country have died waiting in queues, but their number mounts daily.

'In Lasalgaon in Nashik district, farmers driven by the cash crunch closed down the onion markets,' says Nishikant Bhalerao, editor of the weekly *Adhunik Kisan*. 'In Vidarbha and Marathwada, cotton prices have plummeted by 40 per cent per quintal.' Barring a few transactions, sales have come to a halt. 'No one has any cash. Commission agents, producers and buyers alike are in serious trouble,' says Jaideep Hardikar, a reporter with the *Telegraph* in Nagpur. 'Depositing cheques in the rural branches was always a tedious process and right now, withdrawal is a nightmare.'

So, very few farmers will accept cheques. How can their households function while waiting for those to be realised? Many others simply do not have active bank accounts.

One important public sector bank in this state has a total of 975 ATMs across the country. Of these, 549 were serving up no denomination other than despair. Most of those non-functioning ATMs are in rural areas. A particularly cynical rationalisation of the impact is the claim that 'rural areas function on credit. Cash means nothing.' Really? It means everything.

Transactions at the lowest levels are overwhelmingly in cash. Bank employees in small rural branches foresee a law and order crisis if small denomination cash doesn't arrive in a week. Others say the crisis is already here and will not abate even if some cash arrives in that time.

At another queue in Aurangabad, Pervez Paithan, a construction supervisor, fears his labourers will soon turn violent. 'They need to be paid for work already done,' he says. 'But I cannot lay my hands on cash.' In Chikalthana village, Rais Akhtar Khan says she and other young mothers like her are finding it increasingly difficult to feed their children. When they do, 'it is after great delays because we are spending so much of our day in these queues. The children go hungry for hours after their normal eating time.'

Most women in the queues say they have 2–4 days of provisions left. They're terrified to think the cash flow problem might not be resolved in that time. Alas, it will not be.

Farmers, landless labourers, domestic servants, pensioners, petty traders, all these and many other groups have taken a terrible hit. Several including those employing workers will go into debt, borrowing money to pay off wages. With some others, it's to buy food. 'Our queues are growing, not diminishing, with each passing day,' says a staffer at the Station Road branch of SBH in Aurangabad. Here a few employees are trying to cope with huge and increasingly angry queues of people. One staffer points out a flaw in the software sent out for the authentication of ID and other details.

People are allowed to exchange a maximum of eight notes of Rs 500 or four of Rs 1,000 for two of Rs 2,000 in value. This is a one-time transaction. 'Yes, it does trip you up if you try duplicating your act the next day. But you can get around that. Just use a different ID. If today you use your Aadhaar card, tomorrow bring your passport and the day after that, your PAN (permanent account number) card, you can repeat the transaction without detection.'

Now, very few people have actually done this. Most are unaware of it. But the government's response borders on the insane. They have decided to start marking the fingers of the people in the queues (post-exchange) with indelible ink as they do in voting. On a right-hand finger so there is no confusion when people vote in by-elections coming up in some states.

'Never mind what orders or instructions government might issue,' says R. Patil, a small contractor, in the Station Road queue. 'The fact is most of the hospitals and pharmacies do not entertain the Rs 500 or Rs 1,000 rupee notes.' Standing beside him is Syed Modak, a carpenter who had run from clinic to clinic to save a seriously ill relative. 'We were turned down everywhere,' he says. 'Either they don't accept the couple of Rs 2,000 notes or say they have no change to give us.'

Meanwhile, all eyes are on Nashik from where the newly-printed currency will go out across India. No one's got it yet in the rural regions, but all pin their hopes on its happening.

[This chapter was prepared as part of the project on 'People's Archive of Rural India', or PARI.]

24

Curry Mixed with Demonetisation and a Pinch of Pesticide

Rahul M.

When the government outlawed 86 per cent of India's currency, bury-
ing his hope of selling land to pay off growing debts, Varda Balayya of
Dharmaram village in Telangana killed himself and tried to poison his
entire family by mixing pesticide in their chicken curry.

A week before Prime Minister Narendra Modi announced demonetisation on 8 November, Varda Balayya, a 42-year-old farmer from
Dharmaram village of Siddipet district in Telangana, was about to sell
an acre of his farmland. The plot is located next to the highway con-
necting Siddipet and Ramayampet. His corn crop was destroyed due
to unseasonal rains in October. The interest on the loans he had taken
from moneylenders and from Andhra Bank—a total of around Rs 8–10
lakhs—was rising. He didn't want to face his lenders without money, so
he began looking for potential buyers for the most profitable one-acre
portion of his four-acre plot.

'Someone has come forward to buy the land,' he told his elder daughter Sireesha before the demonetisation.

In 2012, Balayya came under great financial strain when he borrowed
Rs 4 lakh for Sireesha's wedding. He was further burdened by the loan
he took of Rs 2 lakh to dig four borewells, of which three had failed. All
this had contributed to his growing debt.

A few months ago, Balayya's younger daughter, Akhila, 17, reached the intermediate level or Class 12 at college; her sister too was married at the same age. Balayya was anxious about Akhila's marriage. He also wanted to repay all his accumulated debts.

The land Balayya wanted to sell is right next to the highway and would have easily fetched him around 15 lakh rupees for one acre, say people in Dharmaram village. That would have solved many of his problems: the debts due to the failed corn crop, the moneylenders who were hounding him for the interest, and the anxiety about Akhila's wedding.

But Balayya's plans turned upside down after the government demonetised currency notes of Rs 500 and Rs 1,000. His potential buyer backed off. 'My father was okay at first. Then, looking at what was happening to the notes, he realised that no one would give him money [for the land]. He became very sad,' Akhila recollects.

Still, Balayya didn't give up and continued searching for buyers. But in the eyes of many, their savings had become useless overnight. Many people here don't even have active bank accounts.

By November 16, a week after the demonetisation, Balayya realised no one would be able to buy his land for a while. He went to his farm that morning and sprayed pesticide over the soya bean he had planted after his corn crop failed. In the evening, he cut a hen in his field as an offering to goddess Maisamma, and returned home with it for dinner.

At Balayya's home, chicken was cooked only during festivals, or when Sireesha came home from her husband's village. Balayya himself always cooked the meat. Last Wednesday, perhaps he wanted his last meal to be festive, a dinner to forget the week that had turned one of his best assets into one of his worst nightmares. Balayya mixed pesticide pellets in the chicken curry. No one in his family knew he had done this. 'He didn't want to leave his family with a huge [financial] burden. So he decided to take them all along,' a relative of Balayya says.

At dinner, Balayya didn't speak a word except when Prashant, his 19-year-old son, asked him about the strange smell in the curry. 'I sprayed [pesticide] from morning till evening. That's the smell'—Akhila remembers her father's words from their last meal together.

Of the six family members, four ate the chicken curry—Balayya, his wife Balalakshmi, Prashant, who is studying for a B.Tech degree, and Balayya's 70-year old father, Gaalayya. Because Akhila and her grandmother do not eat meat, they survived the fatal dinner.

'After dinner, Grandfather started feeling dizzy and he lay down. Then saliva was dripping from his mouth,' Akhila remembers. 'We thought it was an attack of paralysis and rubbed his feet and hands.' Moments later, Gaalayya died.

Balayya also started vomiting and lay down. Suspicious and scared, Akhila and Prashant brought in their neighbours for help. Once they realised that pesticide was mixed in the chicken curry, they called an ambulance to take Balayya, Balalakshmi and Prashant to a hospital. Akhila stayed home with her grandmother, looking after her grandfather's body.

On the way to the hospital, Balayya died. His wife and son are being treated at a private hospital in Siddipet town, around 20 kilometres from their village. Sireesha and her husband Ramesh are at the hospital trying to pay the bills and taking care of the mother and son. 'Prashant was admitted to the emergency ward, so he is being treated under Arogyasri [a health scheme]. But we are paying for his mother with the money loaned to us [by people in the village] and using our own savings,' Ramesh says. He is saving all the hospital bills carefully because the state government has announced help for the family after Balayya's death.

Back home, Akhila has taken care of her father's and grandfather's funeral rites with money borrowed from neighbours, and Rs 15,000 reportedly given by district officials.

She is stoic, but gloomy about her future: 'I am very interested in studies. I love mathematics. And I wanted to write EAMCET [the qualifying exam for engineering and medical students],' she says. 'But now, I don't know...'

[This chapter was prepared as part of the project on 'People's Archive of Rural India,' or PARI.]

25

Impact of Demonetisation in Kerala

R. Mohan

The report by a committee constituted by the Kerala State Planning Board to study the impact of demonetisation clearly delineates its effects on state revenues, capacity of the government to intervene in the social sector, and the hardship faced by the cooperatives and the traditional and service sectors.

The report of the Committee to Study Demonetisation on the State Economy of Kerala (GoK 2017) prepared by an expert group headed by the eminent economist, C.P. Chandrasekhar, on behalf of the Kerala State Planning Board, is a comprehensive document covering every aspect of the impact of demonetisation of Rs 500 and Rs 1,000 notes announced on 8 November 2016. The Left Democratic Front (LDF) in Kerala was in the forefront of mobilising people across the state in a human chain to express resentment against this decision. Apart from organising protests, the LDF government also made a serious attempt to analyse the impact of this decision.

The committee was to study the short-run and the long-run impact of the demonetisation on (i) employment, income, and economic activity in the major sectors of the state; (ii) economy and livelihoods of different sections of the labour force; (iii) cooperative sector in Kerala, and the banking sector and credit provision in general; (iv) government revenues; and (v) gross state domestic product (GSDP) (in general and sector-wise).

Strained Fiscal Space

The report also discusses in good detail, the lesser highlighted impacts of demonetisation. It demolishes the myth that a bulk increase of cheap funds in the form of current and savings accounts (CASA) with the banks would lead to lower lending rates, which would catalyse private investment. The report points out how excess liquidity with the banks resulted in a rush to invest in government securities leading to the decision of the Reserve Bank of India (RBI) to impound the entire incremental deposits as cash reserve ratio (CRR). After this temporary measure, the RBI and the Government of India decided to absorb these in government securities under the Market Stabilisation Scheme (MSS).

MSS was originally brought in as a measure to mop up excess money supply in the system arising from burgeoning foreign exchange reserves. As part of the agreement between the government and the RBI, the former could not utilise it for expenditure, and the same would also not form part of the fiscal deficit of the government. The interest payable on these would be the revenue expenditure of the government. The limit for MSS was raised from Rs 30,000 crore to Rs 6 lakh crore after demonetisation.

As rightly pointed out by the report, the straining of fiscal space subsequent to rising interest expenditure would lead to contraction of expenditure in social and economic sectors, as deficit targets seem to be held as sacrosanct under all circumstances. This does not augur well for an economy exhibiting signs of a slowdown for quite some time (through falling investment GSDP ratio from 34 per cent to 29 per cent) and hit by knee-jerk contractionary effect of withdrawal of 86 per cent of value of currency in circulation. In short, the situation is one of a coerced fall in private final consumption expenditure (PFCE), and a fiscal stance with contractionary elements dominating. A fall in economic growth is a necessary consequence of this.

Eroding Share in Taxes

Despite claims of the central government, the overall tax revenue is set to grow at 12 per cent during 2017–18 as against 17 per cent for 2016–17. The states' share in union taxes, which is based on the 'pain or gain principle,' is set to suffer an erosion in the coming year. For a state like Kerala, where consumption expenditure is a major determinant of economic growth, it is a double whammy.

Kerala's own tax revenue, which is based on consumption expenditure will decelerate and the central tax share would also decline. With a higher level of commitment on social and economic services, the state would be compelled to run higher revenue deficits and would have little to spend for capital expenditure from budgetary sources.

The report discusses alternative scenarios of revenue deceleration for Kerala. Now that the budget documents are published, the revised estimates for 2016–17 are available. The own tax revenue has fallen short of the budget estimates by Rs 3,066 crore for 2016–17. The targeted growth rate was 19.89 per cent against which the revised estimate is at 14.23 per cent, with the tax to gross domestic product (GDP) ratio remaining at 6.71 per cent as against 6.85 per cent expected in the budget estimate. After a robust period of revenue growth from 2006–07 to 2011–12, Kerala's own tax revenue started experiencing a state of sclerosis by falling to 10 per cent growth rate from 2013–14 to 2015–16.

The efforts to raise the rate of growth of revenue to almost 20 per cent would have succeeded as a part of revenue-led fiscal consolidation had not the demonetisation decision of 8 November 2016 come as a bolt from the blue. As expected by the report, the revenue-led fiscal consolidation process has been derailed at least till 2018–19. This is a serious setback, but the Kerala budget of 2017 chalks out a path towards fiscal consolidation for Kerala, albeit a delayed one.

Focus on Cooperatives

The report next focuses on the cooperative sector, which has not only been an integral part of the rural and urban economy, but also of the social and cultural ethos of Kerala. With the illustrative example of Kasargode district, the report succinctly points out how the cooperative movement has moved into areas unbanked by scheduled commercial banks, even after five decades of bank nationalisation. By prohibiting exchange of demonetised notes, the cooperative sector was virtually shut down, putting a large number of people to hardship.

The report points out that the findings of the task force of the RBI on cooperative banks and societies should have addressed state- and region-specific sensitivities and peculiarities instead of making one-size-fits-all comments. The cooperative movement in Kerala has several pro-people interventions in educational, health, and consumer protection areas. The report also addresses the campaign against the cooperative sector as a haven of unaccounted money and parallel economy. It makes positive suggestions such as improving computerisation, permanent account number (PAN) card registration, tax deduction at source (TDS) and know your customer (KYC) norms as prerequisites for improving the cooperative credit structure. The report prepared after interacting with a wide range of people having domain knowledge in this area, is worth a detailed reading. Temporary measures to overcome the crisis by the primary agricultural credit societies (PACS) by opening mirror accounts with the district cooperative banks has been discussed in the report. It is suggested that government agencies should bank with the PACS in this hour of crisis.

Hardships Multiply

As far as the Kerala economy is concerned, the report examines the hardship faced by traditional sectors like coir and handloom, and agricultural and related sectors. Currency shortage has brought their activities to a standstill for the time being. The committee has examined the plight of the construction sector, where substantial segment of the labour force are migrants from other states. Due to the stalemate of activities, the migrant labourers were returning in large numbers to their native states. The agriculture and allied sectors in Kerala have been exhibiting negative growth rates in real terms in 2013–14 and 2014–15. Undoubtedly, these cash dependent sectors would suffer a setback in meeting the payment requirements of labour and other inputs, and in effecting sale of output. The report reveals the gravity of the situation in the traditional and informal sectors in the immediate future after demonetisation.

It has become clear that, given the multiple levels and varying values of the transactions involved in the informal sector, not all transactions can be made cashless, and definitely not in the short run. The result has been an inability to make payments, even for wages. Moreover, in sectors trading perishables such as vegetables and fruits, pressure to sell the product results in falling prices. Despite the decrease in prices, off-take remains low because of the cash crunch, leading to loss of produce because of spoilage. In the dairy industry, farmers are not being paid in time for milk supplied and are unable to buy adequate cattle feed because of the cash deficit. The fisheries sector has been particularly hard hit because, starting with payments for fish auctioned at the point of landing, most transactions, including payments of wages by boat owners, supply to wholesalers and retailers, etc, are in cash. As business has declined, workers get less work and lower earnings, and have had to get into debt to meet their daily expenses (GoK 2017: 9).

The workers and small producers in the informal sector in Kerala are facing yet another issue. Due to the lackadaisical approach in operationalising the Central Food Security Act by the previous government, there is a huge shortfall in allocation of food grains under the public distribution system and rise in the price of different varieties of rice in the open market. The sharp decline in incomes along with jump in price of food grains is adding to the woes of the poorer sections in the traditional and informal sectors. Intervention by the state government, which it is doing on an emergency basis, is putting additional stress on state finances, especially in the face of demonetisation that has induced slowdown of the own tax revenues such as commodity taxes, stamp duty, and registration fees.

Tourism Adversely Affected

Kerala is one of the acclaimed tourist destinations and the 'trade, hotel and restaurants' sub-sector of the GSDP is substantially dependent on tourist arrivals. The report points out that the arrival of domestic and foreign tourists declined by 17.7 per cent and 8.7 per cent respectively, during November 2016 over that of corresponding month in 2015. During October 2016, the month immediately prior to demonetisation, there was a positive growth of 5.2 per cent and 6 per cent of domestic and foreign tourist arrivals respectively.

The share of trade, hotels and restaurants (which is highly dependent on tourist arrivals) is 15.82 per cent of GSDP, and is the single largest contributor to the services sector. An adverse impact on the growth of this sector will lead to an economic downturn, and the palpable indication of decline in domestic and foreign tourist arrivals is a clear pointer to an economic slowdown in the short-run.

This comes on top of other grey spots like return migration from Gulf countries and falling commodity prices (which has started rallying again recently). The nominal GSDP growth projected is 13 per cent in the *Macro Economic Vision Statement* of Government of Kerala, 2016 (GoK 2016). If this falls to the all-India average of 10 per cent, there would be serious adverse consequences on the revenue as well as expenditure side of the state budget, as genuinely apprehended in the report.

Slowdown in Growth

The concerns expressed by the report turn out to be substantial with the estimates of gross value added (GVA) at the national level showing a slowdown of 1 percentage point for 2016–17 at 6.7 per cent, as against 7.7 per cent for 2015–16. At the national level, growth rate of many sectors like manufacturing, construction, finance, real estate, and other professional services has fallen in the third quarter of 2016–17, while growth in agriculture is due to a low base effect. But one has to wait for the revised estimates of GVA at national level, which is more reliable than the quarterly estimates, to see whether a further downturn from 6.7 per cent would result or not. Nevertheless, the stark reality is that there is at least 1 percentage point downturn in GVA (at constant basic prices) growth during 2016–17, when compared to 2015–16. Signs of slowdown in the immediate run are clear.

The report makes the suggestion of relief grants to be disbursed by the centre to the states to overcome the economic fallout of demonetisation by constituting a National Demonetisation Impact Relief Fund. The suggestion is worth considering as the measure of demonetisation has placed a heavy economic and social cost on the states. With the prevailing view of fiscal orthodoxy at the centre, which has stymied even a modest increase in fiscal deficit to 3.5 per cent as suggested by the committee on Fiscal Responsibility and Budget Management Act (FRBMA), the centre is unlikely to give it the serious look it deserves.

But Kerala's budget, presented on 3 March 2017, after the report came out, has taken a cue from this and has proceeded to deviate from the beaten track of fiscal conservatism by increasing spending for 2017–18, even in the face of rising revenue deficits, while retaining the hope that increased revenues later would ameliorate the situation.

The report is a rare initiative to address the issues involved seriously and flag the same in public domain. The content is rich both in substance and data and is devoid of rhetoric of any sort. The report has a positive approach towards digitalisation but raises the pertinent questions of right to privacy of a citizen and where a line has to be drawn. The forced prevention of use of cash is not considered a desirable method. Use of cash has strong linkage with the culture of the people, states the report, citing cross-country examples. Our cash–GDP ratio at 12 per cent does not seem abnormally high when compared to 18 per cent in Japan and 6.5 per cent–7 per cent for the United States, given the level of currency substitutes available in comparison with these countries.

Concluding Remarks

The impact of demonetisation is now clearly emerging. At the national and state levels, the economy has been exhibiting signs of slowdown, even prior to demonetisation. Along with a deficit target centric fiscal policy, the abnormal contraction of cash availability (which has come to be called monetary vacuum cleaning) has hamstrung the levers of growth. In a federal set-up, states are more or less followers of imposed priorities and recipients of adverse impacts of policies like demonetisation. Under these constraints, Kerala has taken a lead to analyse the issues arising out of the sudden announcement of demonetisation and has taken some bold steps in the state's fiscal policy. At a time when high decibel slogans drown the scope for any serious discussion on the impact of demonetisation, the report is a sound voice. This is a useful addition to the debate along with the Economic Survey and the RBI's study 'Macroeconomic Impact of Demonetisation' (RBI 2017). The report of the Kerala State Planning Board is more extensive in its coverage, as it benefits from the consultative approach with as many stakeholders as possible, unlike the other two.

References

GoK (2016): 'Macro Economic Vision Statement,' Budget 2016–17, Government of Kerala.

———— (2017): 'Committee to Study Demonetisation on the State Economy of Kerala,' Kerala State Planning Board, Government of Kerala, February.

RBI (2017): 'Macroeconomic Impact of Demonetisation—A Preliminary Investigation,' Reserve Bank of India, 10 March.

26

Quarterly GDP Estimation

Can It Pick Up Demonetisation Impact?

R. Nagaraj

The latest quarterly estimates of gross domestic product (GDP) by the new National Accounts Statistics (NAS) methodology are once again in the news for the wrong reasons. With inadequate accurate information available on a quarterly basis, the estimates hardly represent the state of the economy and reflect the effects of demonetisation over the October–December 2016 period.

In principle, demonetisation—which in the recent case meant sucking out 86 per cent of the value of cash in circulation, leading to a sharp contraction in money supply—would reduce economic activity in the short run. As critics of demonetisation have argued, it has led to a massive retrenchment of workers and reduction in production, particularly in the unorganised (or informal) sector accounting for over 90 per cent of employment and over half of domestic output and which is also a sector in which transactions are almost entirely based on cash. Demonetisation's proponents, however, have contended that it would cleanse the economy of black money, make transactions more formal and digital; hence improve tax collection, and enhance long-term growth prospects.

Since the demonetisation on 8 November 2016, numerous news reports and some quick surveys have demonstrated its widespread adverse impact most of all on daily wage workers. Many large consumer goods firms (such as Nestlé) and industry associations (such as the one of cement producers) have also reported a steep decline in quarterly sales. Financial brokerages and credit rating agencies have variously forecast a 1–2 per cent fall in domestic output in the third quarter (Q3), that is October–December 2016, as a result of the policy shock. Dismissing such claims as anecdotal, the government took credit for speedy replenishment of the new currency notes, reportedly restricting economic loss and hardship for the poor.

According to the Central Statistics Office's (CSO) 28 February 2017 press release, in Q3, in real terms, the GDP grew at 7 per cent along with a 11.2 per cent rise in private final consumption expenditure (PFCE, or consumption for short) over corresponding estimates in the previous year. The Q3 growth rate is only marginally lower than that in Q2, but consumption expenditure witnessed a huge jump. These numbers surprised (or baffled) many with predictable responses: the government claiming vindication of its policy stance with critics questioning the official estimates. Many now predict that the true effect of the demonetisation will be evident in the next quarter's (Q4) estimates. The chief statistician of India has said results of one quarter are inadequate to judge the effect of the policy.

Undoubtedly, demonetisation was a severe macroeconomic shock that occurred at a time when growth in bank credit had decelerated sharply, turning negative for some sectors such as manufacturing. Demonetisation's impact was only marginally cushioned by a spike in card-based and digital transactions, mostly in urban areas. So the puzzle is: in Q3, how could a cash and credit-starved economy clock a growth rate of 7 per cent and consumption growth of an incredible 11 per cent? Is the methodology underlying the quarterly estimation appropriate to pick up the ground reality?

National income is estimated by three different methods—output (value added), expenditure, and income—all of which, in principle, should yield identical values of domestic output. Ideally (or, simplistically speaking), if all enterprises followed a double entry bookkeeping method, and periodic households income and consumption survey results are available, then estimating domestic output would be pretty straight-forward.

But the real world is messy, especially a developing country, with households engaged both in production and consumption in self-employed enterprises; with a large informal sector where enterprises do not (or cannot) maintain audited books of account, and where workers are under-employed or disguisedly-unemployed. In the national accounts, the output of this sector is estimated indirectly, as balance sheet data are unavailable for a direct estimation of output. The indirect method of estimation is, in simple terms, the product of benchmark estimates of value added per worker (based often on dated sample surveys) and an estimate of the number of workers employed in a year (or a quarter). The recent revision of the NAS, which has sought to improve upon this method, still remains an indirect method.

Similarly, there is no direct estimation of household consumption in NAS. Therefore, production is taken as a proxy for consumption (after netting out consumption by other sectors), by what is known as the 'commodity flow approach.' This is evident from *NAS—Sources and Methods 2012*, a book of methodologies underlying the various estimation procedures, which clearly states the following:

> 1.91 Private Final Consumption Expenditure (PFCE): The basic data on output and prices utilised in the estimation of private final consumption expenditure are mostly the same as those used in the preparation of GDP estimates and as such the improvements/changes in data sources and coverage etc in GDP estimates are included in the estimates of PFCE. (CSO 2012: 14)

Matters get worse for the quarterly estimates as there are no quarterly primary data that go into such estimation; these are mostly derived from the annual estimates, based on some advance information and assumptions. The press note released on 28 February 2017 clearly states this:

> The approach for compiling the advance estimates is based on benchmark-indicator method. The sector-wise estimates are obtained by extrapolation of indicators like index of industrial production of first 9 months of the financial year, (ii) financial performance of listed companies in the private corporate sector available up to quarter ending December, 2016, (iii) second advance estimates of crop production, (iv) accounts of central and state governments, information on indicators like sales tax, deposits & credits, passenger and freight earnings of railways, passengers and cargo handled by civil aviation, cargo handled at major sea ports, sales of commercial vehicles, etc, available for first 9/10 months of the financial year. (CSO 2017)

NAS—Sources and Methods 2012 also offers the following details on the 'benchmark indicator approach,' mentioned above:

The production approach is used for compiling the QGDP estimates, in terms of gross value added (GVA) and is broadly based on the benchmark-indicator method. In this method, for each of the industry-groups ... a key indicator or a set of key indicators for which data in volume or quantity terms is available on quarterly basis, are used to extrapolate the value of output/value added estimates of the previous year ... In general terms, quarterly estimates of GDP are extrapolations of annual series of GDP. The estimates of GVA by industry are compiled by extrapolating value of output or value added with relevant indicators. (CSO 2012: 298)

From the foregoing, it is abundantly clear that quarterly GDP estimates really lack suitable primary data, and hence may not truly reflect the ground reality. This could be a possible reason for the recent Q3 growth estimates failing to pick up the potential effect of demonetisation.

There are apparently more reasons for the scepticism. Some of the 'fresh' data that go into Q3 GDP estimation could have other shortcomings as well. For instance, in the new NAS series with 2011–12 as the base year, (i) index of industrial production (IIP) figures are used for the non-corporate manufacturing sector and quasi-corporations in the non-financial private corporate sector, and (ii) the ministry of corporate affairs' (MCA) quarterly corporate financial results are used for estimating corporate sector GDP.

As the IIP is based on production data of relatively large factories, can it be deemed appropriate for quasi-corporate enterprises, which are not registered under the Companies Act, but are said to maintain books of account? Whether the IIP data is a suitable proxy output of tiny proprietary and partnership firms is worth questioning.

Similarly, the quality and veracity of the MCA database has been too widely debated to bear repetition here (*see*, for instance, Nagaraj 2015). It suffices here to raise a simple empirical query. As the press release shows, the GDP grew at 12 per cent in real terms during Q3, which seems way too high compared to what most corporate quarterly results show. To illustrate, ICRA, the credit rating agency, has reported Q3 sales growth of a mere 4.4 per cent in nominal terms for about 1,100 (relatively large) companies, implying very meagre output expansion in real terms. How credible are the GDP estimates which are based on seemingly shaky numbers obtained from the MCA database? Perhaps it is worth pondering.

Conclusions

Domestic output (GDP) in Q3 of 2016–17 was 7 per cent and PFCE was 11.2 per cent, over the same quarter, the previous year. These estimates are expected to show the impact of demonetisation announced on 8 November 2016. The rosy growth rates for Q3 have elated the ruling dispensation, but left the critics and financial firms (which anticipated a fall in the growth rate) wringing their hands. Both the expressions are perhaps unwarranted (or misplaced) for the simple reason that the quarterly GDP estimates are not based on quarterly primary data on output, and consumption (as widely assumed); hence, the Q3 growth estimates may in fact not reflect the ground reality. The reasons for it are the following.

In the NAS, for lack of primary data, no direct estimates of production and consumption are available on a quarterly basis. The only significant 'moving parts' in the quarterly estimates are (i) the IIP used for estimating output of quasi-corporations and household manufacturing, and (ii) the quarterly (unaudited) corporate results, as aggregated in the MCA database, and hence can (and do) undergo serious revisions subsequently. Therefore, the much-debated Q3 estimates for assessing the impact of demonetisation remain hypothetical since the methodology underlying the estimation of quarterly data is seriously flawed and may not pick up the underlying reality of production and consumption.

References

CSO (2012): *NAS—Sources and Methods 2012*, Central Statistics Office, Government of India.

———— (2017): 'Press Note on Second Advance Estimates of National Income 2016–17 and Quarterly Estimates of Gross Domestic Product for the Third Quarter (Q3) of 2016–17,' Central Statistics Office, Ministry of Statistics and Programme Implementation, Government of India, http://mospi.nic.in/sites/default/fi les/press_re-lease/nad_pr_28feb17r.pdf.

Nagaraj, R (2015): 'Seeds of Doubt on New GDP Numbers: Private Corporate Sector Overestimated?' *Economic & Political Weekly*, Vol 50, No 13, pp 14–17.

27

Demonetisation and the Delusion of GDP Growth

Ritika Mankar and Sumit Shekhar

The Narendra Modi-led National Democratic Alliance (NDA) decided to demonetise 500 and 1,000 rupee currency notes on 8 November 2016 thereby destroying the value of 86 per cent of the currency in circulation in one stroke. This was unprecedented in every sense. No other country had ever experimented with such a policy measure to curb the size of the black economy. No other country had ever imposed on itself such a massive economic shock endogenously.

Whilst this move (combined with other measures aimed at crunching the size of the black economy) will yield benefits in the long term, we highlight the fact that the move undeniably affected the gross domestic product (GDP) growth rate adversely in the short term. Even as the negative impact appears obvious, the need to explain and quantify the same is necessitated by the fact that the country's apex statistical body has declared that the GDP growth in 3QFY17 was recorded at 7.1 per cent Y-o-Y in real terms which is just 10bps slower than the GDP growth rate of 7.2 per cent Y-o-Y recorded in 1HFY17.

The subsequent part of this chapter is divided into four distinct segments. The first segment highlights why it is almost impossible that India's GDP growth was unaffected by demonetisation given its large informal sector and given its high dependency on cash transactions. The second segment attempts to query the official GDP statistics by showing how either the formal GDP growth data or the bank credit data provided by the RBI can be true. In the third section we show using high-frequency indicators provided by industrial bodies that economic momentum slowed decisively in 3QFY17, recovered in 4QFY17 but not to the same levels seen pre-demonetisation. Finally, we conclude with our view regarding India's GDP growth prospects in FY18. We highlight that even as cash comes back into the system, we expect the informal sector to deliver a lower GDP growth in FY18 than it would have been the case if the government had not aggressively enforced an increase in tax compliance as it has been pursuing over 2HFY17.

Why Is It Hard to Imagine that India's GDP Growth Was Unaffected by Demonetisation in 3QFY17

Unlike more developed economies, India's informal sector is large and more importantly it is labour intensive. The informal sector accounts for ~40 per cent of India's GDP and employs close to ~75 per cent of the Indian labour force according to the National Sample Survey Organisation (NSSO). In absolute terms, this means that the informal economy generates GDP roughly worth $950 billion and provides employment to 398 million of India's total labour force of 530 milllion (historical growth rates are applied to NSSO's FY12 estimates to arrive at workforce number for FY18).

Given that the informal sector relies on cash heavily (from making payments to employees, acquiring raw material from suppliers to collecting revenue from customers) and given that this sector accounts for a large chunk of the Indian economy, *prima facie* it appears unlikely that a move aimed at destroying the value of 86 per cent of the cash in the system had no impact on the economic activity levels of this segment of the Indian economy. Besides, it is worth noting that India is a heavily cash-reliant country where more than 80 per cent of all transactions take place in cash, according to RBI data.

Now the plot thickens in the Indian context because despite the size of the informal sector being material, there is a serious inadequacy of data in capturing the health of this sector on a contemporaneous basis. The main source of pan-India informal sector data is provided by the NSSO. To complicate matters: (i) this data is published with a lag of a year; and (ii) this data is captured at a frequency ranging from 2–5 years! For instance, for the noughties, this data is available for FY00, FY05, FY10 and FY12. Therefore, to independently gauge the short-to-medium term impact of demonetisation on the informal sector, we relied on a combination of qualitative and quantitative tools.

We first conducted a survey spanning 88 small and medium-sized enterprises (SMEs) across India. The responses were collected over the post-demonetisation period spanning 22 November 2016 to 2 December 2016. Even as the sample size is very small, the extreme nature of the findings suggests that the SME sector was undeniably under duress in the post-demonetisation weeks. The survey yielded four key takeaways, namely: (i) SMEs in India remain highly dependent on cash with more than 50 per cent of the costs and receivables being transacted in cash; (ii) sales growth for SMEs was likely to come under meaningful pressure in the short term with almost 50 per cent of SME promoters believing that their sales would collapse by 40–80 per cent; (iii) 59 per cent of the SMEs expected competition from the organised sector players to pick up in the medium term; and (iv) non-performing loans in the SME segment seemed likely to increase for lenders as many SMEs said they will not be able to collect dues from their customers and could see a prolonged adverse impact on their sales. In specific, 32 per cent of surveyed SMEs felt that they will not be able collect more than 50 per cent of their dues from their customers.

Apart from the survey, we travelled extensively over the course of December 2016 and January 2017 into the interiors of India focusing mainly on the SMEs in the informal sector. The first and most important takeaway from these travels was that businesses in the unorganised/informal sector that sold products mainly in cash and also covered their costs in cash were affected most severely. For instance, Panipat in Haryana is the textiles hub of North India. It is a Rs 310 billion industry with Rs 60 billion worth of goods being exported. It employs around 350,000 labourers. Whilst our interviews suggested that that the export-focused units were largely unaffected, the domestic component of the industry saw business activity fall by 40–80 per cent as this component of the business was more reliant on cash. As a result, almost half of the 350,000 labourers employed in the region had been temporarily laid off as demand collapsed in the domestic market and there was no cash to pay the wages.

Similarly, we visited Tiruppur in Tamil Nadu which is a textiles hub of South India. However, it is much larger than Panipat. The textiles industry in Tiruppur is roughly Rs 500 billion–600 billion in size and employs around a million workers. Here too, the export-focused units and the units operating in the organised segment did not experience major disruption due to demonetisation. However, the domestic segment, of which 40–50 per cent of the market is unorganised, was facing problems that were similar to those in Panipat. The units were running only three days a week (compared to seven days before demonetisation) owing to the lack of demand. A bank official with a local private sector bank in Tiruppur made the point that prior to 8 November 2016 their branch used to disburse Rs 40 million weekly to their clients as they needed to pay their labourers. This amount had dropped to Rs 6 million due to the shortage of cash.

Despite the overwhelming evidence suggesting that India was dealing with an unprecedented economic shock and the fact that the informal sector was crippled by the shortage of currency following demonetisation, the Central Statistics Office's (CSO) quarterly GDP estimates for 3QFY17 failed to capture the same. This, to be clear, is likely to be an error of omission and stems from two technical reasons. First, the quarterly estimates published by the CSO by definition are a result of an extrapolation exercise based on partial data from the organised sector. This is likely to be problematic as 3QFY17 marked an inflexion point and such a point cannot be captured by the formal estimates if they rely on extrapolation. Second, the quarterly numbers published by the CSO estimates growth in the informal economy using formal economy-related data. This can be problematic especially because the informal sector of India is where the GDP growth slowdown is likely to be concentrated. In fact, the Economic Survey for FY17 admitted that the CSO's GDP statistics will underestimate the impact of demonetisation, noting, '*The national income accounts estimate informal activity on the basis of formal sector indicators, which have not suffered to the same extent. But the costs have nonetheless been real and significant.*' However, even the authors of this fine document for an inexplicable reason refused to admit that the adverse impact on GDP growth was meaningful. In their assessment, the demonetisation move would only shave off 30-50 basis points (BPS) from India's steady state GDP growth rate.

Does the GDP Growth Data and the Monetary Data Provided by the RBI Add Up?

As per the CSO, the GDP growth in 3QFY17 was recorded at 7.1 per cent in real terms and at 10.6 per cent in nominal terms. Separately, the RBI reported that the bank credit growth in 3QFY17 collapsed to a multi-year low of 6 per cent Y-o-Y. Reading these two data points about the same economy makes it difficult to imagine how a bank-funded economy like India (where ~60 per cent of corporate funding comes from the banking sector) managed to grow at the pace that it did when bank credit growth was languishing at a multi-year low.

In fact, history suggests that under the new GDP series, the delta between nominal GDP growth and nominal bank credit growth reached an all-time high in 3QFY17 (Figure 27.1). In other words, never before has the GDP growth data been so out of sync with the bank credit data provided by the RBI. Even as the CSO does offer technical reasons to explain this anomaly, for an investor looking to know where economic momentum in the country is headed, it is clear that the CSO data is underestimating the GDP growth slowdown which materialised in India in 2HFY17. It is worth noting that even after adding non-bank borrowing to the bank credit data, credit growth trends remain weak (*see* Figure 27.2).

Besides the bank credit growth angle, another way of triangulating the validity of the GDP growth data is through the 'velocity' route. In a very simplified sense, the nominal GDP can be thought of as the product of 'currency in circulation' (hence referred to as CIC) and the 'velocity' with which this money circulates (hence referred to as v). The CIC is a variable that the RBI/Central Government controls whilst the v tends

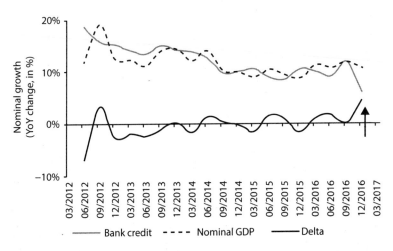

FIGURE 27.1 The Gap between Nominal GDP Growth and Bank Credit Hit a Multi-year High in 3QFY17
Source: CEIC, Ambit Capital research

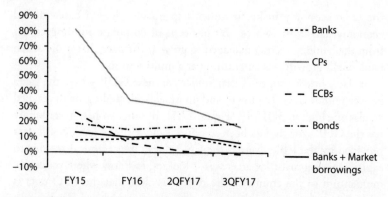

FIGURE 27.2   Credit Growth Including Market Borrowings is Also Decreasing (Y-o-Y)

Source: SEBI, RBI, Bloomberg, Ambit Capital research; Data for ECB is not available post Jun'16 hence we have kept the number constant

to be determined by the levels of business confidence in an economy as well as the underlying structure of the economy. Consequently, v tends to be extremely stable and is known to be very sticky. For instance, under the new GDP series, the implied v in India (i.e. derived by dividing the CSO's estimate of quarterly nominal GDP by the CIC) has been rangebound between 2.0x to 2.3x. However, if the nominal GDP data provided by the CSO for 3QFY17 is correct, then that would suggest that India's v miraculously shot up to 4x times in this quarter (*see* Figure 27.3). Again, it appears highly unlikely that at a time when business confidence plummeted to historic lows is when the velocity of CIC shot up to a multi-year high.

Finally, it is worth noting that as at the end of 3QFY17, the currency in circulation stood at Rs 9.4 trillion or 6 per cent of GDP in relative terms. This is exactly half of the CIC that was maintained in the economy before 8 November 2016 at 12 per cent of the GDP. Even if we were to make the generous assumption that v remained unscathed by the record economic uncertainty that businesses experienced in 2HFY17, it is difficult to imagine how GDP growth too remain unscathed even as the remonetisation process has been far from complete (*see* Figure 27.4). For instance, the latest data from the RBI suggests that CIC stood at Rs 13.6 trillion or 9 per cent of the GDP as of 7 April 2017.

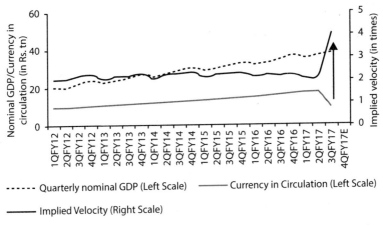

FIGURE 27.3 If the CSO's 3QFY17 GDP data is indeed accurate then it implies that the velocity of circulation of money shot up to a multi-year high in the quarter
Source: CEIC, Ambit Capital research

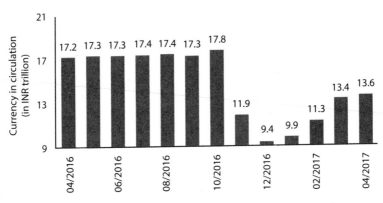

FIGURE 27.4 The Re-monetisation Exercise Is Far from Being Complete
Source: CEIC, Ambit Capital research

What do High-frequency Macro Indicators Tell Us?

Even as the official GDP data continues to be far removed from the economic realities on the ground, high-frequency indicators (referred to as HFIs hereon) continue to tell a different story. We look at 13 such

TABLE 27.1   Gauges Related to Consumption Nosedived after Demonetisation

Indicator	Y-o-Y change in 2QFY17	Y-o-Y change in 3QFY17	Y-o-Y change in 4QFY17	Sequential Change 3Q vs 2Q	Sequential Change 4Q vs 3Q
Two-wheeler sales (units)	15%	–4%	–1%	–20%	3%
Passenger vehicle (PV) sales (units)	18%	6%	11%	–12%	6%
Non-oil bank credit (Rs)	11%	4%	3%	–7%	–1%
Retail credit (Rs)	20%	14%	12%	–6%	–2%
Cement production (Tonnes)	3%	0%	–16%	–3%	–16%
Petroleum Products Consumption (Tonnes)	9%	6%	–1%	–3%	–8%
Rural wages (Rs)	5%	6%	7%	1%	0%
Coal production (Tonnes)	–3%	–1%	1%	2%	2%
Bank Deposits (Rs)	10%	13%	12%	3%	–1%
Electricity generation (GWh)	1%	5%	3%	4%	–2%
Non-oil exports (US$)	1%	6%	13%	5%	7%
Bitumen Production (Tonnes)	–4%	5%	–17%	9%	–22%
Commercial vehicle (CV) sales (units)	–10%	2%	5%	12%	3%

Source: CEIC, RBI, Ambit Capital research.

HFIs (*see* Table 27.1) in order to get a sense of the real health of the economy in an environment where the official GDP data in India is losing credibility.

As is evident from the table above, 3QFY17 saw gauges relating to consumption in the economy such as two-wheeler sales, passenger vehicles sales and retail credit growth nosedive. It is worth noting that for the same period, the CSO reported that the private final consumption expenditure growth in India grew at 10 per cent Y-o-Y in real terms. It is worth noting that consumption expenditure on transport equipment accounts for 14 per cent of the total spends. Thus, it is difficult to imagine consumption growth rising to a multi-year high even if the monsoons were good at a time when this chunk of consumption expenditure was under visible pressure.

As regards 4QFY17, on expected lines, gauges related to consumption have started recovering from the lows of 3QFY17 but are nowhere near the levels seen in 2QFY17 (*see* Table 27.1).

Will GDP Growth in FY18 Recover Fully to the Levels that Were Expected Before Demonetisation?

As the economy recovers from the shock of demonetisation and as remonetisation takes place, a recovery from the painful lows seen in 3QFY17 is but obvious. However, what is critical to note is that the informal economy will shrink rapidly as the government's crackdown on black money will make it difficult for businesses to operate in the informal sector without paying taxes.

Even as the effects of demonetisation are fading as the pace of remonetisation improves, the government has launched a host of regulations which will affect the functioning of the informal sector in the short term. On 8 February 2017, the Parliament passed the Wages Act mandating business units to pay workers through the banking system and not in cash. The Act seeks to enable employers to pay wages to workers through cheques or directly crediting to their accounts. The new legislation will help to keep in check the exploitation of workers engaged in the unorganised sectors and they will get exact salaries in their bank accounts. If the businesses continue to pay the wages in cash, then the law mandates that they will not be able to offset the wages as costs. This will increase the wages costs for the firms operating in the informal sector as the businesses in this sector kept their wages cost low when they paid in cash by avoiding a host of other benefits which should accrue to a worker by law. Moreover, increased tax compliance and the advent of the goods and services tax (GST) could make a host of informal sector businesses unviable. The government has also empowered the junior-most officials in the income tax department to conduct raids.

Finally, it is worth noting that under the Finance Act, 2017, cash transactions above Rs 3 lakh will not be permitted: (i) to a single person in one day; (ii) for a single transaction (irrespective of number of payments); and (iii) for any transactions relating to a single event. Amendments to the Finance Bill, 2017 propose to lower this limit from Rs 3 lakh rupees to Rs 2 lakh. Therefore, even as the informal sector will be in a much better state in 4QFY17 as compared to 3QFY17, it seems highly unlikely that this segment of the economy will find itself undertaking the same activity levels that it would have if all these measures had not been launched over the course of 2HFY17. In other words, even as the ephemeral impacts associated with demonetisation abate, we expect the informal sector to deliver a lower GDP growth in FY18 than it would have been the case if the government had not aggressively enforced an increase in tax compliance.

Whilst analysts and economists can differ on the extent of the impact the demonetisation had on GDP growth in 2HFY17 and FY18, the fact that it was material and the fact that it was adverse is undeniable.

Index

About the Editor and Contributors

Editor

R. Ramakumar is professor and dean at the School of Development Studies, Tata Institute of Social Sciences, Mumbai, India. He holds a PhD in quantitative economics from the Indian Statistical Institute, Kolkata, India, and was earlier with the El Colegio de Mexico, Mexico City, and the Centre for Development Studies, Thiruvananthapuram, Kerala, India. His areas of interest include agrarian studies, agricultural economics, rural banking and national identity schemes. From September 2016, he has also been a non-ministerial member with the Kerala State Planning Board, India.

Contributors

Shankar Acharya was chief economic advisor to the Government of India (1993–2001). He also served as a member of Securities and Exchange Board of India (1997–2000), Prime Minister's Economic Advisory Council (2001–03), Twelfth Finance Commission (2002–04), and National Security Advisory Board (2009–13). Earlier he served with the World Bank and led the World Development Report team in 1979. He has been honorary professor at Indian Council for Research on International Economic Relations (ICRIER), New Delhi, since 2002 and chairman of Kotak Mahindra Bank since 2006.

Amitava Bandyopadhyay is in the faculty of the Statistical Quality Control and Operations Research (SQC & OR) Division of the Indian Statistical Institute, Kolkata, India. He is involved in teaching, research and consultancy in the areas of quality management, operations research, development of quality systems and quality improvement using statistical and operations research methodologies for over 30 years, and has served many organisations in the private and public sector. He is currently working with the Government of Tamil Nadu towards the development of a cleanliness index for the Swachh Bharat mission and with the Indian Ordnance factories to improve the defence production system. Apart from the works with the government, he has worked with many private sector organisations.

Ashapurna Baruah is a research scholar at the Centre for the Study of Regional Development, Jawaharlal Nehru University, New Delhi, India.

C.P. Chandrasekhar is a professor of economics at the Centre for Economics Studies and Planning, Jawaharlal Nehru University, New Delhi, India. He obtained his PhD from the same university in 1980. His areas of interest include the role of finance and industry in development and fiscal, financial, and industrial policy reform in developing countries. He is also a columnist for leading Indian magazines and newspapers.

Jagdeep S. Chhokar was a professor of Management and Organisational Behaviour at the Indian Institute of Management, Ahmedabad, India, from 1985 till November 2006. He is a citizen-activist for improving democracy and governance in India; a bird watcher and conservationist; and a trained lawyer. He is one of the founding members of Association for Democratic Reforms (ADR), New Delhi, India.

O.P. Chopra is an economist, and has worked extensively on questions of black economy in India.

I.S. Gulati obtained his PhD from the London School of Economics and Political Science in 1955, where he also served as tutor during 1954–55. In August 1956, he joined M.S. University, Baroda, India, as reader in economics where he worked till 1968. He became a fellow of Centre for Development Studies, Thiruvananthapuram, India, in 1972. He was a member of the Sixth Finance Commission (1972–73) and twice the vice-chairman of Kerala State Planning Board. On 27 May 2002, he passed away in Thiruvananthapuram at the age of 78.

Poonam Gupta is a country program manager at the World Bank. Prior to joining the bank, she was the Reserve Bank of India Chair Professor at National Institute of Public Finance and Policy (NIPFP), a professor of macroeconomics at Indian Council for Research on International Economic Relations (ICRIER), associate professor at the Delhi School of Economics and an economist at the International Monetary Fund, Washington, DC, where she served in the Asia and Pacific Department, European Department, and the Research Department.

Sanjeev Gupta is the deputy director in the Fiscal Affairs Department of the International Monetary Fund (IMF). He has also worked in the IMF's African and European Departments. Gupta has authored and coauthored over 150 papers on macroeconomic and fiscal issues covering advanced, emerging and low-income countries, many published in well-known academic journals. He has also authored, coauthored, and co-edited twelve books.

Shinzani Jain is an independent researcher and has also co-authored two books: *The Black Hole* with Ajit Abhyankar and a forthcoming book with Paranjoy Guha Thakurta.

D. Ravi Kanth is a journalist based in Geneva, Switzerland. He writes for *Washington Trade Daily*, *Third World Network*, *Mint* (India), *Indepth News* (Berlin), *Economic & Political Weekly*, and *Business Times* (Singapore). Earlier, he worked for *Indian Post*, *Independent*, the *Economic Times*, *Business Standard*, *Asia Times* (Bangkok), and *Deccan Herald*.

Dev Kar is the chief economist emeritus at Global Financial Integrity (GFI), Washington, DC. Prior to joining GFI, Kar was a senior economist at the International Monetary Fund (IMF), Washington, DC. During a career spanning nearly 32 years at the IMF, he worked on a wide variety of macroeconomic and statistical issues and participated in different types of IMF missions to member countries. Kar is a fellow at Yale University, has a PhD and an MPhil in economics from the George Washington University, and an MS (Computer Science) from Howard University, Washington, DC.

Vineet Kohli obtained his PhD in economics from the Jawaharlal Nehru University, New Delhi, India. Currently, he is assistant professor at the School of Development Studies, Tata Institute of Social Sciences, Mumbai, India. His areas of research interest are macroeconomics, financial economics and economic history.

S.S.S. Kumar holds a PhD from IIT Dhanbad, Jharkhand, India. He is currently a professor in the area of finance, accounting and control at Indian Institute of Management Kozhikode, Kerala, India. He simultaneously holds the position of a distinguished adjunct professor at School of Management, Asian Institute of Technology, Bangkok, Thailand. His research focuses on analysis of foreign institutional investments in emerging markets, IPOs, and volatility studies in capital markets.

Ashok K. Lahiri retired as executive director at the Asian Development Bank (ADB), Manila, in 2013. Before ADB, he served as chief economic advisor, Government of India; director, National Institute of Public Finance and Policy; senior economist, International Monetary Fund; and reader, Delhi School of Economics (DSE). A graduate in economics from Presidency College, Kolkata, he did his MA and PhD from DSE.

Rahul M. is an independent journalist and a 2017 People's Archive of Rural India fellow from Anantapur, Andhra Pradesh, India. He completed his masters in Modern Indian History from Jawaharlal Nehru University, New Delhi, India, before pursuing a career in journalism.

Ritika Mankar is Senior Economist (Vice President) at Ambit Capital, Mumbai, India. She completed her studies from the Gokhale Institute of Politics and Economics, Pune and the CFA Institute, Charlottesville, Virginia.

Dipak K. Manna is in the faculty of the Statistical Quality Control and Operations Research (SQC & OR) Division of the Indian Statistical Institute, Kolkata, India. He is involved in teaching, research and consultancy in the areas of quality management, operations research, development of quality systems and quality improvement using statistical and operations research methodologies for over 30 years and served many organisations in the private and public sector. He is currently working with the government of Tamil Nadu towards the development of a cleanliness index for the Swachh Bharat mission and with the Indian Ordnance factories to improve the defence production system. Apart from the works with the government, he has worked with many private sector organisations.

R. Mohan was an officer with the Reserve Bank of India and later with the Indian Revenue Service. He voluntarily retired when serving as a Commissioner of Income Tax (Appeals). He has an MPhil degree in applied economics from Centre for Development Studies, Jawaharlal Nehru University, New Delhi, India.

Sacchidananda Mukherjee is an associate professor at National Institute of Public Finance and Policy (NIPFP), New Delhi, India. His research interests include public finance, environmental economics and water resources management. His recent co-edited books include *Environmental Scenario in India: Successes and Predicaments* and *Environmental Challenges and Governance: Diverse Perspectives from Asia.*

Ashok K. Nag, a former senior executive of the Reserve Bank of India, is an alumnus of the Indian Statistical Institute, Kolkata, India. He has more than 30 published articles in national and international refereed journal in the areas of application of statistical techniques to financial and monetary data.

R. Nagaraj is a professor at Indira Gandhi Institute of Development Research, Mumbai, India. He has a PhD in economics from the Centre for Development Studies, Thiruvananthapuram, Kerala, India. His areas of research include aspects of India's industrialisation, applied macroeconomic issues, public sector performance, industrial labour market in India, and macroeconomic statistics.

Advait Rao Palepu studied comparative politics at the London School of Economics and Political Science, and is an independent researcher.

Prabhat Patnaik is a distinguished political economist. He obtained his DPhil from the University of Oxford in 1973. He moved to the University of Cambridge, England, in 1969 to join the Faculty of Economics and Politics. Between 1974 and 2010, he was a faculty member at the Centre for Economic Studies and Planning at the Jawaharlal

Nehru University, New Delhi, India, where he is currently professor emeritus. Between 2006 and 2011, he was vice-chairman of the Kerala State Planning Board, India.

Gopinath Pradhan holds a PhD in economics and has been a post-doctoral visiting scholar at the Centre for Asian Development studies in Boston University (1989–90), Concordia University (1994), and University of Victoria, Canada (2003), and a visiting fellow at the National Institute of Finance and Policy, New Delhi, India (2003–04). In 2012, he was appointed the vice-chancellor of the Indira Gandhi National Open University, New Delhi, India.

J. Dennis Rajakumar is the director of Economic & Political Weekly Research Foundation, Mumbai, India. He received his PhD (Economics) and MPhil (Applied Economics) from the Jawaharlal Nehru University, New Delhi, India, through Centre for Development Studies, Thiruvananthapuram, India.

M. Govinda Rao was a distinguished member of the Fourteenth Finance Commission. He previously served as the director of National Institute of Public Finance and Policy (NIPFP) in New Delhi, India, and as the Director of Institute for Social and Economic Change (ISEC) in Bangalore, India. He was also previously a member of the Economic Advisory Council to the Prime Minister.

R. Kavita Rao is a professor at the National Institute of Public Finance and Policy (NIPFP), New Delhi, India. Her research interest includes design and implementation of goods and services tax (GST), value added tax (VAT), tax reforms, tax exemptions, and revenue mobilisation.

P. Sainath is founder-editor of the People's Archive of Rural India. He is a Ramon Magsaysay award-winning journalist and reporter for 37 years, has covered rural India full-time for 25 of those, and was the rural affairs editor of the *Hindu* for a decade from 2004.

J.C. Sandesara obtained his PhD from Mumbai University, India, in 1959. During his 34 years since then, he was a post-doctoral fellow, Princeton, New Jersey, and a professor at MS University, Baroda, Mumbai University, India, and Indian Institute of Management, Ahmedabad, India. He has authored and edited several books.